ELEMENTARY PRINCIPLES
OF THE
ROMAN PRIVATE LAW

ELEMENTARY PRINCIPLES
OF THE
ROMAN PRIVATE LAW

BY

W. W. BUCKLAND, M.A.,
FELLOW AND TUTOR OF GONVILLE AND CAIUS COLLEGE, CAMBRIDGE

Cambridge:
at the University Press
1912

CAMBRIDGE
UNIVERSITY PRESS

University Printing House, Cambridge CB2 8BS, United Kingdom

Published in the United States of America by Cambridge University Press, New York

Cambridge University Press is part of the University of Cambridge.

It furthers the University's mission by disseminating knowledge in the pursuit of education, learning and research at the highest international levels of excellence.

www.cambridge.org
Information on this title: www.cambridge.org/9781107634329

First published 1912
First paperback edition 2014

A catalogue record for this publication is available from the British Library

ISBN 978-1-107-63432-9 Paperback

PREFACE

THE following pages form a running commentary on the Institutes of Gaius and those of Justinian, designed especially for students who have read their Institutes but little more. The aim of the writer has been throughout to discuss institutions rather than to state rules, to suggest and stimulate rather than to inform. Considerations of space have made selection necessary, and a few topics which give students special difficulty (e.g. *Bonorum Possessio*) have been allowed to occupy a disproportionate amount of space. But an attempt has been made to bring home to the student a fact which, at least in his earliest stages, he is apt to forget, the fact that the Roman Law is not merely a set of rules on paper, a literary product, but a group of institutions under which the Romans actually lived. The hope may be permitted that the student will learn more than the book tells him, and more than was present to the mind of the writer. Our knowledge of the Roman Law is but the knowledge of a track in the wilderness. Around every rule that the student sees there lie innumerable questions. Most of these are, in our state of knowledge, unanswerable, but the student who has learnt even to formulate some of them has made a great step towards the understanding of what he has read.

The true spirit of an ancient institution is hard to capture. In studying the Roman Law it is difficult to rid our minds of experiences and preconceptions acquired in the course of many centuries. It is not rendered less difficult by the fact that the great line of German scholars to whom we owe most of our knowledge have of necessity been concerned till recently not only, indeed not mainly, with the exposition of Roman Law, but with the development of it. It is not without change that a rule laid down by Julian is made to serve modern needs. We look at the Roman Law through a medium of which we know that it distorts, while for the estimation of the nature and degree of distortion we have but a very imperfect apparatus. These pages attempt to look at legal principle, so far as possible, in the Roman way.

The indebtedness of the book to many writers will be obvious, but in a book which does not aim at stating new doctrine it has not seemed needful to attempt to trace the paternity of each idea mentioned: references to modern literature are given not so much to confirm statements in the text as to direct the reader to sources of fuller information. Accordingly the books cited are in the main those to be found in the libraries of most English law schools. Few references are given to the Institutes: the student ought to be able to find these for himself. References to the Digest are more frequent. Few things are more useful to a student than the tracing of doctrines to their source: the citations are therefore so limited in number that reference to the original texts should be no intolerable burden.

I am much indebted to Dr Henry Bond of Trinity Hall, who has been so kind as to read all the sheets, every one of which is the better for his valuable suggestions.

W. W. B.

CAMBRIDGE, *August* 1912.

TABLE OF CONTENTS

CHAPTER I

INTRODUCTION. THE SCHEME OF THE INSTITUTES

1. THE book to which we owe most of our direct knowledge of the Classical Law is the Institutes of Gaius. Few books have had a more remarkable destiny. Written, as it seems, as a course of elementary lectures, by a professor of no marked distinction, it appears to have grown steadily in reputation. It is thought that Ulpian and Paul used it, and made its method the basis of their own. It is certain that after three centuries, or thereabouts, Theodosius gave its writer posthumous rank as a privileged jurist, and that, a century later still, Justinian directed Tribonian to adopt it as the basis of the new institutional book which was to supersede all others. At this point its influence died away. The Barbarian legislators were preparing their systems of law for those of their subjects who "lived Roman law" before Justinian's reforms. They do not seem to have set much store by Gaius. All that any of them has of his Institutes is an amazingly bad abridgement. They appear to rely mainly on later writers, especially on Paul, chiefly, no doubt, precisely because they are later, but also because they are easier and more practical. For Gaius is not really easy, and he is given to historical and discursive treatment of his subject. In the efforts at the reconstruction of the classical Roman law, from the fifteenth to the end of the eighteenth century, Gaius was little used, since his original text had disappeared. Then, about a century ago, there came the dramatic discovery of his text in a palimpsest manuscript, hidden under theological writings. The effect was that the history of the Roman Private Law had to be rewritten. Some of it still remains to be rewritten, for there can be little doubt that many opinions are still current which were formed before we possessed the text of Gaius, and still retain a certain following, by reason of a secular tradition in their favour, though they never would have seen the light if the great humanist lawyers had possessed the text of Gaius.

The other surviving texts of the classical age, though together they make up a considerable volume, are much less enlightening than Gaius. Paul's *Sententiae* are from a somewhat corrupt and abridged text in the *Breviarium Alaricianum*, and Ulpian's *Regulae* we have also only in abridged form, the omitted parts being those which were obsolete, as to which Gaius is so valuable. Next to Gaius in importance stands Justinian's Digest, in which work nearly forty of the great jurists speak, at length, in their own names. Much caution, however, is necessary in using this source of information. Tribonian and his colleagues have amended the texts, as they were instructed to do, so as to eliminate differences of opinion and also doubts, and so as to make the texts express the law of the sixth century and not that of the much earlier centuries in one or other of which they were written. It is not easy to tell in any given case whether it is Tribonian or the old jurist who is speaking. Much learning and acumen have been bestowed on the interesting subject of these "Interpolations" as they are called. Much remains to be done, and as the signs of interpolation are often obscure and uncertain, some of what has been done is of questionable soundness. Hardly less interesting than the enquiry into the cases in which Tribonian has altered the texts so as to make them express the later law is the converse enquiry into the cases in which he has allowed texts to stand which express rules which are no longer law. Such cases are not uncommon, and some of the omissions or oversights, whether due to hasty work or to some other cause, at any rate emphasise the necessity of treating the whole *Corpus Iuris* as one work. Thus we are told in the Institutes of a great change in the law of theft from a *Commodatarius*, and we can see in the Code the enactment of 530 by which the change was made[1]. Yet, in the Digest, of A.D. 533, the old law is stated[2] and no reference is made to any change. These cases of imperfect correction have been very helpful in the discovery of interpolations: perhaps the most striking instance of this is the fact that recent researches into the history of pledge in Rome have had as their starting-point a text of Pomponius in which Tribonian, by carelessly allowing *eam* to stand where grammar requires *id*, has betrayed the fact that the text has been altered and was originally written of *Fiducia* and not of *Pignus*[3]. But in dealing with both these cases, that of interpolation and of insufficient correction, there remains a further uncertainty: it is possible that the words may be neither from Tribonian nor from the jurist: they may represent only a debased fifth century tradition. Books handed down in manuscript may alter a good deal in three or four centuries. From all this it will be evident that the Digest must be used with caution as evidence of the classical law.

It is sometimes said that the Institutes of Justinian are merely those of Gaius brought up to date. This statement has some truth in it: the order and method of Justinian's book are those of Gaius, as the compilers understand him. But their grasp of the method of Gaius is not perfect, and they occasionally introduce topics in such a way and in such a context as greatly to obscure the plan of the book. Of the actual matter of the Institutes, however, a great part is not taken from those of Gaius. Justinian's preface tells us that besides the Institutes of Gaius, the *Res Cotidianae* of the same author and other institutional works were used. But there are also passages taken from less elementary works, from the practitioners' treatises which are the chief source of the Digest. A question of some little importance is this: did the lawyers who drew up the Institutes copy from the original works, or did they use the Digest, which must have been substantially complete when

[1] C. 6. 2. 22. [2] *e.g.*, D. 47. 2. 14. 15.

[3] D. 13. 7. 8. 3. See also *h. t.* 34. For this and similar cases see Gradenwitz, Interpolationen, 37 *sq.*

they were preparing the Institutes? If they went to the original books then, though no doubt they maltreated the texts, still the Institutes would be an authority independent of the Digest, as to the content of some of the lost classical books. The most probable view seems to be that, for institutional books, the compilers used the original works themselves. We can see that they did so for the Institutes of Gaius, and we know, from Justinian's preface, that they were told to do so for the others. As to the less elementary books they seem to have gone to the Digest, though there are one or two books which they are said, on rather doubtful evidence, to have copied directly.

2. The arrangement of the Institutes is expressed in the famous text: *Omne ius quo utimur vel ad personas pertinet vel ad res vel ad actiones.* What is the origin of this classification? It is stated in the above words in the Institutes of Gaius, from which it is copied into the Institutes of Justinian, and it occurs again in the Digest[1] where it is expressly referred to the Institutes of Gaius. This state of the texts has naturally led to the view that the proposition and the classification which it expresses are both due to Gaius. Natural, however, as this inference looks, it is far from inevitable, and there are some circumstances which tend to discredit it. The "Institutes of Gaius" is the only elementary treatise of the classical age which has come down to us in a form which clearly shews the plan on which it was designed, and the fact that Justinian cites the text from Gaius does not prove, in view of the respect in which Gaius was held by Justinian, that he was the first inventor of the arrangement. There are other elementary books of which we have a considerable part, and there are yet others of which the general order can be made out from the passages preserved in the Digest, owing to the fact that in that book each fragment is referred to the section or *liber* in which it occurred in the work from which it is taken. Lenel, in his

[1] D. 1. 5. 1.

Palingenesia, has set before us all these surviving passages, in order, according to their rubric, so that we can see at once what was dealt with in each *liber* of each work, though of the order within the *liber* we cannot be sure. When we find the same order of treatment recurring in treatise after treatise, it is reasonable to infer that a common classification underlies it, and if the order is that of the Institutes of Gaius it is at least highly probable that the system of classification is the same. We know of five other books called *Institutiones*. Callistratus adopts the same order. So do Marcian and Ulpian, but they do not seem to go beyond succession on intestacy. Florentinus puts manumission and inheritance after obligations, and does not deal with actions, but in other respects the order is similar. Of Paul's Institutes so little is left that the order cannot be told. Of works called *Regulae*, four have the same order, two have not, and three are uncertain. The so-called *Fragmentum Dositheanum* is evidently the beginning of some writer's *Regulae*, and it discusses slavery. The *Res Cotidianae* of Gaius are in the same order except that *hereditas* is placed after *obligatio*. Thus the majority of the elementary writers known to us adopt this order and presumably this plan. Most of them lived with or after Gaius and may possibly have copied him. The case of Neratius is however interesting. Of his *Regulae* very little is left, too little to enable us to say with any confidence what was his order. But the remains such as they are do in fact strongly suggest that the order is that of Gaius. Neratius must have died at the latest when Gaius was a child, so that if there was any copying it must have been the other way. On the whole the most acceptable view, in a very uncertain matter, is that Gaius did no more than adopt a traditional order[1]. He may indeed have popularised it, though even this is hardly probable, since it is used by some of his contemporaries who, so far as is known, never refer to him. He seems to have been of little importance in his own time. There is no certain reference to him till at least two hundred years after his

[1] See Girard, Textes (3) 201 *sqq*.

death, though there is an increasing acceptance of the opinion that his writings were known to and utilised by Ulpian and Paul.

3. We are told by Sir Henry Maine[1] that there is no reason to suppose that the Romans set much store by this classification: it is confined to institutional books, and has not much legal importance. It is true that it is so confined, so far as is known, though titles v, vi and vii of Book I of the Digest, and the rubric *de obligationibus et actionibus* in the Digest and Code, seem to be suggested by it. But this is a circumstance which rather adds to than detracts from its importance from every point of view except that of the pure practitioner. Scientific arrangements of the law usually make their first appearance in books of this sort, and the criticism is a reflection rather on Tribonian than on Gaius. If we seek an orderly arrangement of the English law, we do not go to the Statute Book or to the Law Reports, or even to the treatises designed for practitioners: we go to books written primarily for instruction. The modern Codes which have adopted a scientific order have derived it from books written in the main by teachers of the law. It may also be worthy of note that the real question for us is not of the value of this order to the Romans, but of its value to us. Nothing is more helpful to the understanding of a system of law than expositions of it arranged from different points of view. This is precisely what we have in the Institutes as contrasted with the Digest and the Code.

4. The question remains: what do the terms of this classification mean? They are so general as to be ambiguous, and examination of the various topics discussed under the different heads has left room for wide difference of opinion as to the real nature of the distinctions intended. The difficulty of the question is increased by the obvious consideration that the loose logic usual with the Roman lawyers in matter of

[1] Early Law and Custom, p. 367.

classification makes it not unlikely that, whatever the scheme was, some part of the resulting disposition of matters will be inconsistent with it. Of the various interpretations which this threefold scheme has received, there are two of which each has been so widely accepted that it is desirable to state them with some fulness, and to give some of the reasons which have been urged in favour of them.

According to one, and certainly the most obvious view, it is the object of the arrangement to divide the law into three branches, the Law of Persons, the Law of *Res*, and the Law of Actions. This way of looking at the matter is strongly supported by the occurrence of such expressions as *Ius quod ad personas pertinet*, and gives a neat result, acceptable to modern readers. But acceptance of this explanation still leaves open the question: what is intended to come under each head? There is not much difficulty about the law of actions: in the main it is the law of procedure—the law descriptive of the steps to be taken in enforcing rights. But the relation of the *Ius quod ad res pertinet* and the *Ius quod ad personas pertinet* is a more difficult matter. There are all sorts of opinion as to what is really intended to be discussed in the law of persons. According to some, but they are nowadays few, it is the law of the rights and duties of persons in exceptional positions. Of this view it is enough for the moment to say that in point of fact the rights and duties of such persons are not discussed in that book, though they find their place in the notes and commentary of modern editors. According to others, it is the Family law, but this is open to the same objection. Other explanations starting from the same main hypothesis are to be found discussed by Dr Moyle[1], but they all fail to take account of what seems the most striking characteristic of the Book I of Gaius, *i.e.*, that it contains scarcely a word about rights and duties, except as concerning changes of status.

According to another view, Gaius does not contemplate a division of the law into three branches. His proposition is

[1] Moyle, Inst. of Justinian, Introd. to Bk I.

held to mean that every rule of law has three aspects: it may be regarded from the point of view of the persons it affects, or from that of the rights and duties it creates, or from that of the remedies[1]. This is in fact the view of the text taken by the sixth century commentator, Theophilus, who understands it to mean that every rule of law has three objects. It has been objected to this view that it is too abstract, but it is not too abstract for Theophilus, and it may be that some misconception underlies this criticism. The matter is too controversial to be entered on here, but it may be said that the conception of a right as it is used in modern law, so familiar to us as to seem obvious, represents a feat of abstraction which the Romans never thoroughly mastered, and as the usually accepted explanation really makes distinctions of right and duty the basis of the classification, it would have seemed to the Romans more abstract than that now under discussion.

It is particularly in connexion with persons that this view is enlightening. The matter will be more fully considered under that head: here it is enough to say that the topics which one would expect to find in the law of persons are scattered all over the Institutes, while Book I is concerned with a description only of the principal among those different classes of persons whose distinctive characteristics are legally important. It has been said, further, that if Gaius had intended to divide the law into three distinct masses, he would have said, not *vel* but *aut*. It appears however to be the better opinion that the practice of Latin writers in the second century is not such as to justify us in attaching any considerable weight to this consideration. It may be remarked finally that Justinian follows up our text with the remark that all the law is made for persons, and we must therefore know what these are. Gaius has somewhat similar words. This kind of language suggests that they are setting out to discuss not the law of persons, but persons. And though the expressions *ius personarum* and *ius rerum* do occur, the word *ius* is never used in the passages which serve to make

[1] Girard, Manuel (4) 7.

the transition from one topic to another. The expressions used are *videamus de rebus, superest ut de actionibus loquamur,* not *de iure rerum* or *de iure actionum.*

5. Both Gaius and Justinian begin their books with some observations on the origin of the rules of which the law is made up. It is not within the present purpose to enter into detail as to the speculative questions connected with the ideas of *Ius Gentium, Ius Naturale* and *Ius Civile,* but it may be worth while to compare the accounts of the two writers. For Gaius, the law is made up of two elements: one, the *Ius Civile,* conceived of as peculiar to Rome; the other, the *Ius Gentium,* conceived of as common to all nations. This universality Gaius contemplates as due to the fact that these rules are implanted in us by nature, and he speaks of them as established by *naturalis ratio.* He does not here use the expression *ius naturale.* Justinian adopts this language of Gaius, prefixing however some phrases in which, on the authority of Ulpian, he declares the law to be of threefold origin, based, that is to say, on natural rules, on those of the *ius gentium,* and on those of the *ius civile.* He follows this with a short discussion of the *ius naturale,* in which, on the same authority, he describes this *ius naturale* as consisting in the animal instincts, adding that the lower animals must be considered as acquainted with this law. Ulpian[1] indeed goes on to give, as the essential difference between *ius gentium* and *ius naturale,* the fact that the former is peculiar to man while the latter is not. This kind of *ius naturale,* based on a confusion between animal instincts and moral intuitions, is peculiar to Ulpian: it is quite distinct from the *naturalis ratio* of Gaius, and is of no value for legal or other purposes. In any case the conception of *ius naturale* seems of little immediate use, for it has been shewn that there is no single specific rule of Roman law known to us which can be assigned to the *ius naturale* as opposed to the *ius gentium.* It is at the most an ideal to which it is desirable that the law

[1] D. 1. 1. 1. 3, 4.

should conform: it is never made by the Romans themselves a test of the validity of any rule.

In these texts the expression *ius civile* is used to mean the specially Roman part of the law, in whatever way created. But this meaning is relatively late to develope. In earlier law it is used in a narrower sense. It means the rules of law evolved by the jurists, in what Pomponius calls the *disputatio fori*, as opposed to that which is the result of express enactment. This law, *a prudentibus compositum*, he describes as having no special name, but adds, *communi nomine appellatur ius civile*[1], language which shews acquaintance with both meanings. Modern writers are divided in opinion as to the date at which the wider and more familiar meaning appears. An extreme view places it as late as the latter part of the second century after Christ, while, on the other hand, Girard finds it in a text of Cicero[2].

6. Upon the more practical question of the different forms which legislation may take, Justinian follows Gaius, except that while Gaius confines himself to *ius scriptum*, Justinian divides the law into two branches, the *ius scriptum* and the *ius non scriptum*, describing the latter as custom which has acquired by long usage the same validity as enacted law. Though the validity of this customary law is repeatedly insisted on by Justinian, it is difficult to see much importance in it for his day, so far as the general law of the Empire is concerned. Perhaps the main application of the idea is in connexion with those local variations of law and usage, of which modern research is giving us an increasing knowledge, and thereby considerably modifying the notion, hitherto widely prevalent, that Roman domination tended to mean iron uniformity.

The order in which Gaius states the sources of the *ius scriptum* may conceivably be based only on relative importance, but it seems more probable that it is historical. The writer, having in mind the consolidation of the Edict under Hadrian,

[1] D. 1. 2. 2. 5. [2] Manuel (4) 42.

places the *Edicta Magistratuum* after *Principum Placita*, which were by this time already recognised as sources of law. The case of *Responsa Prudentium* calls for a brief examination. For Gaius, writing after the legislation of Hadrian, to which he specifically refers, they form a part of the *ius scriptum*, and the somewhat loose expressions, *sententiae et opiniones* are not enough to justify us in attributing the whole passage, as is sometimes done, to some later hand. For Pomponius, writing before this legislation, but after that of Augustus, which he sets forth in his Enchiridion, they are a part of the *ius non scriptum*[1]. Indeed it is plain that at least in his view, Augustus had not materially altered the legal character of *Responsa*. He says nothing of any binding force. For him they are still the *ius civile quod sine scripto in sola prudentium interpretatione consistit*. They are not, for him, essentially distinct from custom. This fact, coupled with the form of his citation of the enactment[2] (*maior auctoritas* hardly suggests so great a power) and the omission by Gaius of any reference to Augustus in this connexion, suggests that Augustus did no more than confer a certain honorific distinction on one or two chosen lawyers, their *responsa* remaining without binding force until the legislation of Hadrian. And it is not easy to see by what authority Augustus could have done what he is sometimes supposed to have done. He could not himself have lawfully compelled a certain judgment: how should his nominees have had the power?

Justinian's language in speaking of the *responsa* differs from that of Gaius, though not so much as might have been expected. There had been legislation as early as Constantine, perhaps earlier, culminating in the well-known Law of Citations[3] (a convenient but quite unauthorised name), in which authority was given by Theodosius the Great, not merely to *Responsa*, but generally to the writings of various lawyers. Of this legislation his language does not expressly take account. His reason may be that it is all rendered obsolete by the enactment

[1] D. 1. 2. 2. 5. [2] D. 1. 2. 2. 49. [3] C. Th. 1. 4. 3.

of the Digest. It is possible however that the words in Gaius are not in their original form, but that the allusion to *sententiae* and *opiniones* is the work of some later hand, in view of this legislation. It must be noted that the whole classification has little but historical interest in Justinian's age and book. Except the Emperor's enactments, not one of these sources of law still exists. For *leges, plebiscita, senatusconsulta, edicta magistratuum* and *responsa,* the Digest is now the sole authority, and as all these sources, and particularly the last, have undergone much editing at the hands of Justinian's compilers, we are carefully warned by Justinian that the form which appears in the Digest is to be regarded as the authentic text, and that no attention is to be paid to any other versions which may happen to have survived.

CHAPTER II

THE LAW OF PERSONS

7. THE subject of Book I of the Institutes of Gaius is not the Law of Persons in any reasonable sense of that expression. The text tells us little or nothing about the differences of Right, Duty and Capacity, which result from differences of Status. If we desire to learn the effect of an acquisition of property, or of a contract or of a delict, by a *filiusfamilias*, we must look for it elsewhere. It will be found under the Law of Property or Contract or Actions. What we really get in Book I is an account of the more important variations in position which are of legal significance: we get a definition of the status and an account of the ways in which it may be acquired or lost, and, practically, we get no more. In very few passages does Gaius depart from this standpoint. In his discussion of the *tutela* of women he adverts to the marked difference which exists between the powers of the *tutor* of a woman, and those of the *tutor* of an *impubes*. This is merely an interjected remark, which in a modern book would have been put into a footnote. Justinian, by introducing a separate title on the *auctoritas* of *tutores*, a title plainly suggested by the remark of Gaius, has in fact obscured the whole plan of the book. There are some similar remarks to distinguish the two classes of Latins, and *dediticii*, and there is a phrase or two on the position of slaves. But that seems to be the whole contribution by Gaius, in Book I, to the "Law of Persons" in this sense. His subject does not in the least resemble the Law of Persons as conceived by Austin, or Bentham's Special Codes. Dr Moyle has shewn

that Savigny's conception of it as the Law of the Family is quite inadmissible. It is in fact hardly possible to mark it off as a branch of the law, having as its subject-matter any set of rights and duties. That is not the writer's point of view: he is merely giving an account of the principal differences of Status which the student will meet.

It is plain that not every difference of Status which is legally material is considered by Gaius. We get no discussion of Vestal Virgins, *Auctorati*, *Decuriones* and others who nevertheless have many and important special capacities and incapacities. What then was the principle of selection intended by Gaius? What "Persons" did he mean to include? Gaius himself gives us no information on the matter. We are dealing with an elementary book, and we shall therefore find only the most important. We know of course that he is concerned only with those differences which have legal effects, but we have to remember that in inferring his method from the classes discussed we have to face the fact that his plan may not have been carried out with absolute correctness. The fact that a class is not mentioned may mean that it is not within the scheme, but it may equally well mean that it was omitted by oversight.

As a matter of fact very few persons are considered: the Slave, the *Libertinus*, the *Filiusfamilias*, the person *in Manu* or *in Mancipio*, the *Paterfamilias*, under guardianship or of full powers, the *Tutor* and the *Curator*. Wife and husband are considered not as part of the subject-matter of the book, but only incidentally, as being material to the description of one of the classes directly discussed. So-called Fictitious Persons, *Collegia*, *Hereditates Iacentes*, and the like, are not discussed at all: the writer is concerned only with what Ulpian calls *Personae Singulares*[1]. *Peregrini* are not discussed at all, perhaps, as Dr Moyle says, because there is nothing to say. But in fact Gaius is concerned only with the everyday *civis*: he starts from the proposition, implied but not expressed, that

[1] D. 50. 16. 195. 1.

Status can best be considered from the three points of view of Liberty, Citizenship and Family. He is not concerned with *peregrini* as such, and all that we hear of them is in connexion with access to citizenship. Slaves and Latins are discussed, partly because of their importance in everyday life, but also because they are sources from which in the time of Gaius the class of *Cives* is largely and continually recruited. Manumission is one of the most important investitive facts of Citizenship: it is therefore necessary to consider when it does and when it does not confer that status. This it is which leads to the curious result that in discussing the grades of freemen who are not *cives*, Gaius appears to confine himself to those who are *libertini*. The only topic in connexion with Latins in which Gaius shews interest is that of the means of access to *Civitas* which are open to them, and these he treats in considerable detail. Of *Dediticii* he has little to say except that they cannot attain Citizenship. In support of this view of the scheme of Gaius it may be worth observing that in the *Regulae* of Ulpian, a work of which the general plan is unmistakably the same as that of Gaius, there is a title which in its present form bears the rubric *de Latinis*[1], but which deals exclusively with the ways in which a Latin can acquire *Civitas*.

8. What is a *Persona*? The question may be put in the form: is a slave a Person? The most generally accepted view is that he was not so regarded by the Romans. But, as a slave can be looked at from two points of view, either as a chattel, a subject of property, or as a man capable of conscious action, and as, though he is a nullity at civil and praetorian law, he is, *iure naturali*, a man like other men, it would not be surprising if there was some divergence of view in the texts. But the fact is that while there are many texts in the *Corpus Iuris Civilis*, and in earlier juristic literature in which personality is ascribed to slaves, there is no text, in the *Corpus Iuris* or in the classical texts, to the contrary, and the very few legal

[1] Ulp. *Reg.* 3.

texts in which a denial can be traced are late, and of only secondary authority at the best. It is clear therefore that the Roman lawyers did call a slave a person[1].

The truth is that this word *Persona*, like many other legal terms, has a history. It has not always meant the same thing. At first signifying a mask, it came, by a natural transference, to bear the significance of the part played in life by a man, and, hence, the man who plays it. It is in this untechnical sense that the Romans use it when they call a slave a person or speak of his *persona*. The first sign of a more technical meaning appears in texts which speak of a more or less complete *persona*: slaves and young persons, incapable of taking part in legal proceedings, are regarded as having only an imperfect *persona*. Very late in Roman development, only in the Byzantine age, and not, as it seems, represented in the *Corpus Iuris* at all, there appears a definite technical sense for the word, in which it has come to mean a being capable of legal rights and duties. It is in this sense that personality may perhaps be denied to a slave, but, so far as has been shewn, this is not done by the Roman lawyers themselves[2].

But units other than individual men can be thought of as capable of acts, or of rights and liabilities: such are Corporations and even *Hereditates Iacentes*. Accordingly the way is clear to apply the name of person to these also. The mediaeval lawyers did so, but as they regarded Corporations as endowed with personality by a sort of creative act of the State, and received from the Roman lawyers the conception of the *hereditas iacens* as representing the *persona* of the deceased rather than as itself being a person, they called these things *Personae Fictae*, an expression not used by the Romans. Gradually the idea emerges that as the essentials of personality are merely capacities for rights and duties, the personality of a corporation may be as real as that of a man, its collective will a real will and the notion of Fiction unnecessary. Modern legal thought goes further: German lawyers have evolved the idea of a pure

[1] Buckland, Roman Law of Slavery, 3 *sq*.

[2] Windscheid, Lehrbuch, 1. § 49 n. 6.

"Stiftung" or Foundation, a fund destined to specific permanent applications, of which the various assets are regarded as vested in the Fund itself and not in its administrators. Thus the Stiftung is itself a person, and as it is capable of obligations, its personality, at least for some thinkers, is in no way fictitious—it is a real personality[1]. But all these developments are of a much later age than that with which we are concerned.

9. Roman legal definitions are not usually very good. Thus, in the Institutes, Liberty is defined as the power of doing what you will so far as you are not prevented by law or force. It is difficult on such a definition to find a person who is not free—certainly slaves come within its terms. Nevertheless, their definitions are usually so framed as to bring out, at least roughly, what is for them the chief characteristic of the institution they are defining. Slavery is defined as a condition in which one man is subject to the ownership of another. This definition finds little favour with moderns. It is pointed out that there were slaves, *servi poenae* and others, who were not owned by anyone, and the definition usually adopted is that slavery is a condition of rightlessness, an absolute status not dependent on relation to any other person. The objections on which this criticism and substitution are based are sound. There were slaves without owners. Slaves were practically rightless. Slavery was an absolute status. Nevertheless it seems better to adhere to the Roman definition, taken from Florentinus by Justinian[2], regarding it as fundamentally sound, but inaccurately expressed. From the Antonine age onwards the slave was not absolutely rightless: there were cases in which, where he was ill-used, he could himself set the law in motion for his own protection. And alien enemies under arms were, as it seems, equally rightless. A more serious objection to the proposed definition is the fact that it does not bring out a characteristic of slavery which is at least as important as

[1] Schuster, Principles of German Civil Law, 41; Maitland, Collected Papers, 3, 356.

[2] D. 1. 5. 4. 1.

rightlessness and is in the same plane of thought, *i.e.* the fact that over a very large field of law the slave was dutiless. *In personam servilem nulla cadit obligatio*[1]. A judgment against a slave is a nullity: it binds neither the man nor his master. In the same spirit we are told that slavery is akin to death[2]. If a man is enslaved his debts cease, and they do not revive on manumission[3]. The definition of Florentinus seems a better expression of these ideas than the modern substitute. That slavery means subjection to ownership does not require that every slave shall be at every moment owned. A slave, like any other chattel, may be at the moment a *res nullius*. What Florentinus means is that a slave is the one human being who can be owned—the one human chattel. There is nothing relative about the status thus defined. The Roman definition seems better and more likely to be useful than the modern one, taken from a different, abstract and un-Roman, point of view.

10. Though slaves were *pro nullis* at civil and praetorian law, we know that in practice they were far from nullities. We find them carrying on great businesses with a perfectly free hand, dealing even with their own masters, borrowing and lending money, and renting lands, from them and others. We find them partners in firms, and we learn that if a slave in such a firm was sold the partnership was not necessarily ended, though the firm would be technically a new one[4]. The institute which rendered possible the almost complete absorption of the world of private trade by slaves was the *Peculium*. Such funds, though dating from much further back, owe their importance to the growth of wealth and luxury in the Augustan age. How was the rich Roman to reconcile his desire to invest his money in commerce with his dislike himself to engage in trade? The Limited Liability Company did not yet exist. Large partnerships, *e.g.* for contracts with the State, did exist, and it is quite clear that many partners in such concerns contributed nothing but capital. But these covered only part

[1] D. 50. 17. 22. *pr.*
[2] D. 50. 17. 209.
[3] D. 44. 7. 30.
[4] D. 2. 13. 4. 3; D. 17. 2. 58. 3.

of the ground. The free *procurator* was a later development. Agency was hardly developed at all, and there were dangers in the unlimited liability involved in the appointment of an *Institor*, and even in becoming a sleeping partner in an ordinary firm. The fact that acquisitions by slaves went to their masters was a beginning for practical agency by slaves. On the other hand, the traditional untrustworthiness of slaves (*quot servi, tot hostes*) made it impossible to enable them to bind their masters. The Roman poets are full of allusions to the rascalities of slaves. The institution of the *peculium* and the *actio de peculio* exactly met the need. It was agency with limited liability, since the master would not be liable beyond the *peculium*, even though he knew of the trading. The liability could be cut short at any moment by a mere expression of intent, subject only to the rights of existing creditors, and alienation of *res peculiares* needed authorisation.

11. We are accustomed to regard the legislation of the Empire as having ameliorated the position of slaves, but it is important to distinguish between the legislation of the first century of the Empire, punishing and penalising various forms of cruelty to slaves, and that of the Antonine period. The former only shews that slaves were worse treated than they had been, and that protection had become necessary. The latter shews a great advance: the slave himself can appeal to the magistrate. There is, however, one respect in which the slave was worse off in the Byzantine age than in earlier days. The minor public offices, clerical posts, had usually been held by slaves. But in the later Empire slaves are definitely excluded from all administrative posts[1]. The *servus publicus* of Gaius (of the state or of a municipality), to whom security is given for a variety of purposes, is replaced in later law by a *publica persona* who is not a slave. A change of this sort, important as it is, leaves little mark on the private law, but the increasing utilisation of the free *procurator* is only another illustration of the same tendency.

[1] C. 10. 71. 3; *cf.* C. 11. 37. 1.

In law slaves were incapable of marriage, but they habitually contracted permanent unions which were marriage in all but legal recognition, and the evidence of countless funereal inscriptions shews that the family tie was as sacred among slaves as among freemen. Even in law, blood connexion among them was not unimportant. Documents of sale and legacies were construed so far as possible so as not to involve the separation of relatives. Servile relationships and affinities were a bar to marriage after freedom, and in like case children could not bring proceedings against their parents (*vocare in ius*). In A.D. 334 it was enacted that in dividing an inheritance slaves related were to be kept together. If several slaves, brothers, were sold, one could not be "redhibited" without the others. If a freedman by his will made *filius meus* his *heres*, and he had no son but one born in slavery, the inheritance went to him[1]. Justinian went further and provided that if a *servus* had children by an *ancilla*, or an *ancilla* had children by a slave or a freeman, such children, if the parties became free, were allowed to succeed to, and be succeeded by, the parents or by other such children, or by freeborn children of the parents.

12. In the Rome of the time of Gaius, and later, a slave was usually such by birth. Subject to some well-known exceptions, the child of a slave woman was a slave and that of a freewoman was free, whatever the status of the father. This is a simple application of the general rule, to which the rule applied to children of *iustae nuptiae* is only an exception, though a very important one, that a child takes the status of its mother. Of the cases in which a freewoman's child is a slave, the only important one is that under the *Sc.* Claudianum, a case which Hadrian abolished for *inelegantia*. The cases in which a slave woman's child is free are more numerous. None of them, with one possible exception, seems to be older than Hadrian. The most important cases are those of the woman who, though she be a slave when the child is born, was free at any time during her pregnancy, and that of a woman to whom

[1] C. 3. 38. 11; D. 21. 1. 35; D. 28. 8. 11.

liberty is due under a *fideicommissum*, but has been wrongfully delayed, though she has demanded it[1].

A freeman may however be enslaved. The cases in which this might occur at different epochs are many, but few can have produced many slaves. The case of Captivity is classed with birth, as a *iure gentium* ground of slavery, and doubtless in the late Republic, and early in the Empire, captives were a great source of supply to the slave market. The law as to the captured Roman citizen has some points of interest. If he returns to Roman territory the rule of *postliminium* restores him to his original position in most respects, and he is again an *ingenuus*. He again becomes owner of his property, but he does not possess, until he regains actual control. His marriage is not reintegrated. If he is ransomed, his *postliminium* is deferred till he has paid off the ransomer, whose right over him is sometimes called a lien, and sometimes ownership, the matter being governed by a *constitutio* only obscurely known. If he dies a captive, his will operates, by virtue of some provision in a *lex* Cornelia, the nature of which is obscure, though it might have been expected that, as he died a slave, his will would be void. These peculiarities have led to the view that in strictness the *captivus* is not a slave at all[2], but it is difficult to hold this view, in face of the very explicit language of the texts[3].

The case of penal slavery also presents some peculiarities. The *servus poenae* belongs to no one and has thus no derivative capacity. A transfer of property to him is void, and the exact effect of a payment made to him it might be difficult to state. No one is noxally liable for him, so that for any delict of his which is not also a crime, there seems to be no remedy at all. There could be no question of manumission and any release must be an administrative act. Pardon might be such a complete restitution as quite to wipe out the enslavement. It might be less than complete restitution, but it does not appear that a pardoned *servus poenae* who had been a freeman before condemnation was in any case a *libertinus*[4].

[1] D. 40. 5. 26. 7.
[2] Mitteis, Röm. Privatrecht, 1. 128.
[3] *e.g.*, G. 1. 129; D. 49. 15. 19. 2.
[4] Buckland, Slavery, 410.

The *libertinus* condemned, for ingratitude, to re-enslavement, does not appear to have been common. There were lesser punishments for various degrees of *iactantia*, and there is very little evidence indeed for the infliction of the extreme penalty. It may be worth noting, as evidence of the fact that the taint of slavery was extended to some extent to the son of a freedman, that in later law even the child of a freedman could conceivably be re-enslaved for ingratitude[1]. The case of the adult freeman who is sold with his own connivance as a slave is of some interest. We are told that he is forbidden *proclamare in libertatem*, *i.e.*, to claim his liberty. This might mean that he is not really enslaved, but is merely "estopped" from claiming his liberty. It is clear, however, that at least in later law it was true enslavement, and a *capitis deminutio maxima*, and the view that it was merely a procedural bar[2] till after the time of Gaius has little support in the texts. The origin of the rule is obscure and it is uncertain to what cases it originally applied. But it may be said with some certainty that while in Justinian's law it was essential that he should have intended to share the price, so that it is merely a case of common fraud, there were in earlier times other cases. Thus if the pretence were made in order that the man might be eligible to a class of work open only to slaves this was at one time enough to make the sale create a bar in the same way. And it is clear, on the evidence of Paul, that sale was not the only form in which the pretence could occur with the same result[3].

13. A slave may become free in some cases without the consent of his master, but the occurrence of this is rare, and in general, if a slave becomes free it is by manumission. Of this transaction it is not easy to determine the essential feature. It has obvious affinities with transfers of property, and it has itself been sometimes considered as an act of conveyance. But it is not in fact a conveyance: the man does not become owner of himself. A freeman's personal independence is

[1] C. Th. 4. 10. 3.
[2] Karlowa, Röm. Rechtsgesch. 2. 1116.
[3] D. 40. 12. 23. 1.

not ownership, which is the reason why a man has no Aquilian action for injury to a member. Nor can it be considered as an alienation of liberty: the right given to the man is not the same as that which the master held. It is clear also that a manumission by will is not a legacy. The release is not an abandonment or *derelictio*. It leaves many rights in the former master, and the freedman is certainly not a *res nullius*: he has in fact ceased to be a *res* at all. The ways in which it is effected have no close relation to modes of conveyance. The fact is that it is a twofold transaction, of which the name does not fully express the character. It is more than a release from *manus* or ownership. It is on the one hand a release from the capacity of being owned, and on the other it is the creation of a *civis*. *Datio civitatis* is regarded as the normal result of manumission, and Ulpian tells us that the rights of the patron are a return for having made the man a *civis*[1]. Hence the public control.

Of the three formal modes of manumission the character is familiar. All of them express the public control which is essential in view of the fact that manumission is the making of a *civis*. The intervention of the Censor and the Praetor probably implies, at least for early law, a power to refuse their cooperation, and the fact that wills were made before the *Comitia* gave a similar guarantee in the case of manumission *testamento*. But by the close of the Republic all these safeguards have become unreal, and restrictive legislation has become necessary. The details of these restrictions are given in a confusing and occasionally inconsistent way by the institutional writers. Thus Gaius seems to speak of rules as laid down by the *lex* Aelia Sentia, which Ulpian puts down to the *lex* Iunia[2], and it is still far from clear which of these *leges* was the earlier. On the whole it seems more probable that the *lex* Iunia was the earlier—at any rate this assumption makes it easier to state the history of the matter coherently. The use of the name Norbana, which in association with the name Iunia seems to require the date A.D. 19, is not found earlier than Justinian,

[1] D. 38. 2. 1. *pr*.

[2] Ulp. *Reg*. 3. 3.

and may well be an error. It is not worth while to stay over these details, but it may be worth noting that some general statements, readily made, go beyond the warrant of the texts. Thus it may be said that a slave freed under thirty becomes a Latin, by the *lex* Aelia Sentia, unless cause of manumission is shewn. But this can be shewn only for manumission by Will: no text anywhere speaks of a slave freed *Vindicta* as becoming in any case a Latin. And there is no text which speaks of *Iteratio* as applicable to a slave so freed. It was this fact which led Vangerow to the opinion that manumission was essentially an act of Conveyance[1].

Manumission was as a matter of course most frequently effected by Will. It is for this reason that the *lex* Fufia Caninia sets limits on the numbers which may be so freed: there is no serious danger of a man's going to too generous extremes at his own expense. Manumission by *Fideicommissum* presents curious characteristics. It is set going, so to speak, by a Will, but it is a manumission *inter vivos* which ordinarily completes it. This ambiguous character led to difficulties. Thus it was only express legislation which made it clear that such gifts came under the restrictions of the *lex* Fufia Caninia. It was for some time doubtful whether slaves so freed, simply or conditionally, were *statuliberi*. There were doubts as to the extent of the patronal rights enjoyed by the person who freed under the trust. And there were difficulties settled only by drastic legislation, where the fiduciary failed to carry out the trust. It was ultimately provided that, on proof of such facts, the Praetor would declare the man free[2]. Somewhat similar provisions were made, a little later, in cases in which a slave had been transferred *inter vivos* with a direction to free[3], where a slave had been bought with a view to manumission expressed, the money having been provided on his behalf, and, finally, where an owner had received money on the understanding that he would free a certain slave[4]. The provisions differ in detail,

[1] Vangerow, Latini Iuniani, 148.

[2] D. 40. 5. 26. 7.

[3] C. 4. 57. 4.

[4] D. 40. 1. 4. *pr.*; D. 40. 12. 38. 1.

but they all rest on the fact that even in those cases in which the neglect to free was a breach of an enforceable obligation, no action for damages could be brought by the slave or would benefit him if brought by anyone else.

Formal manumission is a very ancient institution. Informal manumission is on a different footing. It gave no liberty at all till the Empire, and it did not give citizenship till the time of Justinian. The only thing that need be said of it is that it is not clear that any declaration sufficed to secure praetorian protection for the man in the later Republic, and Latinity after the *lex* Iunia. Classical law admitted probably only of two modes: declaration before witnesses (frequently called *amici* in other connexions) and letter of enfranchisement. Even the mode *in coena* is not known till later times.

14. There must have been a considerable number of Latins in the third and later centuries, though the extreme facility of access to citizenship no doubt tended to keep down the numbers. Besides the familiar cases of Latinity under the *leges* Iunia and Aelia Sentia, there were at least a dozen others introduced by later legislation. In general a Junian Latin is a slave stopped, so to speak, midway on the road to citizenship. But just as colonies were given Latin right, to save, as it were, the trouble of elaborating a new class, and irregularly freed slaves were given Latin status for similar reasons, so in later law we find cases of persons classed with Junian Latins who in fact had never been slaves at all. Thus, by an enactment of A.D. 326, it was provided that the child of a freewoman who cohabited with a slave of the Fiscus should be a Latin, the mother's status being unaffected. And under an enactment of Constantine, and perhaps earlier, a *civis libertus* might be put back into the position of a Latin for certain forms of ingratitude[1]. In the texts of this time the word Junianus is rarely or never used. There are in fact no other Latins. But in some of the cases it is difficult to see a patron, and in truth there is great obscurity as to the position of some of these various kinds of Latins, and

[1] C. Th. 2. 22. 1.

especially of their children, in the centuries immediately before Justinian.

It is somewhat odd to modern, or at least to British, eyes, that vast numbers of free subjects of the Roman State were not citizens, were excluded not merely from political rights, but also from the more important rights under private law. One of the most striking characteristics of the Roman community is the continued existence in the same city of numbers of persons, often identical in race, language and education, with widely different civil rights. The absence of any perceptible difference led, naturally, to mistakes, and at one time the project was mooted of making all slaves wear a distinctive dress[1]. It was abandoned for the reason, it is said, that if slaves found out how numerous they were, the tables might be turned. The difficulties of distinguishing led to an extraordinary prominence, in Roman law, of rules providing remedies for cases in which such mistakes had occurred. The principle is neatly put in the rule that if a freeman is by mistake sold as a slave, the transaction is to be valid as a contract, *quia difficile dignosci potest liber homo a servo*[2]. There are many other very familiar instances, *e.g.*, the rules as to fraudulent sale of a freeman, as to *erroris causae probatio*, as to attestation of a Will by a slave supposed to be free, as to acquisition through a *liber homo bona fide serviens*, as to institution of a slave as a freeman (the case of Parthenius), as to the position of the child of an *ancilla* supposed to be free, as to persons *de statu suo incerti*, and many others. Some less familiar cases give rise to very striking rules. A slave could not of course be appointed arbitrator, but if one who was supposed to be free was so appointed, and gave his decision, and was afterwards shewn to be a slave, we are told that his decision was valid[3]. Where a fugitive slave succeeded in getting himself appointed Praetor, and acted in that capacity, Ulpian declares that his official acts were valid[4]. A different rule is applied where there was no mistake. In the troubled times of the fourth century, it

[1] Lampridius, Alexander, 27. 1.
[2] D. 18. 1. 5.
[3] C. 7. 45. 2.
[4] D. 1. 14. 3.

was not unusual for pretenders to assume high office, and to force their authority on the people. The acts of such persons were in general declared void, though they were in some cases confirmed by express legislation[1]. Our English law has no general principle which meets these cases of error. A state of things closely analogous with that described by Ulpian arises where a layman passes himself off as a clergyman, and in that capacity solemnises marriages. Such marriages are void at law, and it has been repeatedly found necessary to pass Acts of Parliament to validate them. The procedure was regularised by a Statute of 1905, but it still remains true that every validation requires a legislative act.

The ways in which a Latin could acquire citizenship form a long and not very instructive list. It may however be observed that most of them give rise to a status which is in essence intermediate. If the patron of a Junian Latin has not assented to the steps by which the Latin acquires citizenship, his rights are in general unaffected, so that the man is a *civis* for most ordinary purposes, but a Latin for the purpose of the law of succession to him. This it was which rendered necessary the rule of Hadrian that a man who had acquired citizenship in this way was not debarred from proceeding under the rule of the *lex* Aelia Sentia as to *anniculi probatio*, though the *lex* in terms applies only to those who are still Latins. The right it confers is much better, since it gives, both to him and to his family, *civitas* for all purposes.

15. The well-known rules of *Anniculi probatio* have a bearing also on the Family law, since they give *potestas* over the children, as well as conferring *civitas* in ordinary cases on all parties. But their chief importance is certainly in connexion with *civitas*. It must be remembered that the rule as at first introduced was designed merely as providing a back way to citizenship for a certain narrow class of Latins, namely those who were so because they were freed under 30, a class who would have been *cives* in any case if the restrictive *lex*

[1] See, *e.g.*, C. Th. 15. 14. *passim*.

Aelia Sentia had never been passed. In the more comprehensive form which it ultimately assumed it gave citizenship and *potestas* to a much wider class, and may be regarded as having had for its aim the facilitation of access to *civitas* to Junian Latins in general.

The confusing and imperfectly known rules of *erroris causae probatio* were discussed at such length by Gaius as to shew that they were practically important. They seem to have been laid down from time to time as cases occurred, so that it is hardly possible to state them in a general form. But some general rules can be made out. The chief seem to be these. The primary matter in view is citizenship, and thus, while the rules are never applied except where the effect is to give someone citizenship, their benefits are not extended to any party to the marriage, who, being himself a *dediticius*, is incapable of *civitas*. It is not necessary to shew that both parties were in error, but it is only the party in error who can avail himself of the rules. On the other hand the party in error can always do so, if it is the male, but the female only if she is the superior, *i.e.*, a *civis*, or else a *latina* who has married a *peregrinus*. But a *peregrinus* who shews cause under these rules does not acquire *patria potestas* except by special imperial decree.

16. The topic of *Familia* occupies the greater part of Book I of the Institutes, and Gaius adheres almost exactly to his plan, *i.e.*, of expounding the investitive and divestitive facts of each status, and saying nothing of their results. He has to consider *Potestas*, *Manus*, Civil Bondage and Guardianship, of which only the first and the last are of great importance in his day.

In discussing any status from the point of view of *Familia* the law of Marriage has to be considered. But it has on its own account no place in the law of Book I. It is considered as one of the steps in the most important of the ways of acquiring the status of a *filiusfamilias*, *i.e.*, by birth *ex iustis nuptiis*. Of course, as, apart from *manus*, the wife does not change her status, in any way, there is not much to be said about the matter in connexion with status, but very little is said of it anywhere in the Institutes. The reason is plain: so soon as we begin to consider the effect of the marriage on the parties as opposed to their issue, we discover that, broadly speaking, the law knew of none. This is a result of the Roman conception of *liberum matrimonium.* Whether two persons were married or not was important if there were children, and, accordingly, full rules are laid down as to what is essential to the contracting of a valid marriage. But that is its chief interest: between the parties it produced no legal effects to speak of. If a marriage was contracted under an error of status, with the result that expected rights over issue did not arise, there were rules under which, in certain cases, and under certain conditions, the effects of the error were set aside, if there were any issue. But, till the birth of issue, there was no relief. The parties could end the relation without aid of law, and there was no need of special rules. The title in the Digest on Marriage is called *de Ritu Nuptiarum,* and says nothing of the effects of marriage. Nor does the title *de Nuptiis* in the Code. The definition of *Nuptiae* in the Digest as *consortium omnis vitae, divini et humani iuris communicatio*[1], as applied to the later marriage does not look like that of an institution of which the legal aspect was the most important. It would, of course, be incorrect to say that marriage produced no legal effect at all between the parties. Adultery was a crime, but this is public law. There could be no ordinary gifts between the parties[2], a rule introduced as it seems for reasons similar to those which caused the introduction into our law of restraints on alienation, in gifts to married women. In any action between the parties there was what commentators have called the *beneficium competentiae.* The wife was associated with her husband's cult, a rule which may be a survival from the system of *Manus,* or may be due, as has been said, to the usual though legally superfluous religious ceremony. She must live with her husband, and she owes him *reverentia.* No action involving *infamia* lies between them[3]. The whole law of *Dos*

[1] D. 23. 2. 1. [2] D. 24. 1. 5. 5. [3] D. 25. 2. 1.

and *Donatio ante (propter) nuptias* depends on the existence of a marriage. *Dos* no doubt originally arose out of *manus*, but its importance in later law is due to the independence of the parties to a marriage, and it gives a means of repressing by forfeiture certain forms of misconduct for which there was no other remedy. But all these rules do not amount to much: they are no more than an irreducible minimum.

Upon this view of the attitude of the law towards marriage, the old controversy as to whether marriage ought to be considered as analogous to conveyance, or whether it is not more in the nature of a contract, seems rather empty. These are conceptions appropriate to the law of things, concerned with the creation and transfer of rights having a money value. They are essentially and ordinarily legal transactions. None of this is true of marriage. Whether two persons are married or not is a question essentially of fact, in which the law is concerned in the same way as it is in the question whether a person is over 14. It is not as a transaction that the law is concerned with marriage. Its freedom from legal regulation is attested by many texts, and by many collateral rules, notably by the rule that agreements to marry or not to divorce are absolutely void[1]. If we treat marriage as a contract, an agreement creating rights and duties between the parties, we have the difficulty that we can find no remedies. If a husband did not maintain his wife or if the wife left her husband, or did not shew him *reverentia*, it is not easy to see in the time of Gaius any direct means by which observance of these duties could be enforced. Divorce can hardly be treated as the remedy, for in the classical law this was quite free to either party whether there had been misconduct or not. Even in later times such restrictions as appear on causeless divorce are penalties, not prohibitions[2]. And in any case annulment alone can hardly be called a remedy for breach of contract. No doubt forfeitures of part of the *Dos* for misconduct formed an indirect check. Even in the time of Gaius the domestic authority of the wife's father was a real resource.

[1] D. 45. 1. 134; C. 8. 38. 2.

[2] See Girard, Manuel (4) 161.

But the need to appeal to these institutions shews how far we are from the conception of contract.

If, on the other hand, we treat marriage as a conveyance, creating rights and duties against third persons, we have to face still greater difficulties. Each must be regarded, since equality is the mark of the Roman marriage, as divesting himself or herself of some right in favour of the other. It is difficult to see of what right either has been divested, as against third parties. But even apart from this, and considering the transaction as a transfer from the wife to the husband, we have still to ask: what are these rights, and what the remedies? It does not appear that the husband had the *actio utilis* Aquilia if the wife was injured. There was no civil remedy for adultery. A man had indeed an *actio iniuriarum* for an insult to his wife, but only because it was of necessity an insult to himself. The only serious exception to this absence of remedy is a rule, which seems to belong to the later law, that if her father or any other person detained a married woman, her husband was entitled to an interdict to have her produced so that she could come back if she wished[1]. It is a conveyance of nothing. These considerations seem to shew that the whole discussion as to whether marriage is analogous rather to a contract or to a conveyance, rests on a mistaken view of the classical conception of marriage. It has no useful affinities with the *ius rerum*.

17. *Nuptiae iustae* and *nuptiae non iustae, matrimonium iuris civilis* and *matrimonium iuris gentium*, are sometimes regarded as distinct institutions. But it seems more correct to consider the difference as existing between the parties to the marriage rather than between the modes of marriage. Persons who have *connubium*, if they intermarry, contract *iustae nuptiae*—they have not a choice. Persons who have not *connubium* with each other contract, if they marry, *matrimonium non iustum*. A marriage between persons who have not *connubium* becomes *iustae nuptiae*, if at any time during the marriage they acquire

[1] D. 43. 30. 2.

connubium. A recorded case carries the principle even further. Where two slaves cohabited, and one was allowed by the *dominus* to give the other a sum, by way of *dos*, out of the *peculium*, and he afterwards freed them both *inter vivos*, without taking away the *peculium*, the union automatically became *iustae nuptiae*[1], and the fund a *dos*. A similar rule would, it is clear, apply if two peregrines married and afterwards acquired citizenship. Marriage consists in living together with the intent of being married, having the necessary qualifications, and the nature of the marriage depends only on the qualifications of the parties. It seems true to say that if two persons, both of whom have *connubium*, are united, their union must be either *iustae nuptiae*, or no marriage at all. If two persons too nearly related live together, their union is not marriage at all, but merely incest. This was to be expected, but what is less inevitable is the fact that exactly the same is said of unions between dignitaries and abject persons, *praesides* and women of their province, *tutores* and their wards, Jews and Christians. In all these cases the texts make it clear that there is no marriage at all, the union being forbidden[2]. So also we are told that if persons otherwise capable of *iustae nuptiae* with each other marry without any necessary consent of another person, their relation is no marriage at all until the necessary consent is given, the need for this consent being based by Justinian, not merely on the *ius civile*, but on *naturalis ratio*.

Marriage with *manus* is on a very different footing from the marriage of later law. Here there is a clear transfer of a right, and in two of the three modes in which *manus* could be created, the case of transfer of property is directly imitated. No doubt there was a time when *manus* was an accompaniment of all recognised marriage, but in the time of Gaius and long before, it had become a mere occasional accessory transaction, of increasing rarity. The language of Gaius shews that it had become unusual. He tells us that *Usus* was obsolete. As to marriage *farreo*, he tells us that it still existed, but merely because only the issue of such a marriage was eligible for

[1] D. 23. 3. 39. [2] *e.g.*, D. 23. 2. 16; D. *h. t.* 66; C. 1. 9. 6.

certain priesthoods, and Tiberius had provided that where the process was gone through in view of this, it did not create *manus* for ordinary purposes. It appears that *coemptio* for ordinary marriage still existed. Ulpian does not mention it, though he does speak of *confarreatio.* Paul seems to know nothing of *manus.*

18. Towards the end of the Republic the process of *coemptio* had come to be applied to purposes which had nothing to do with marriage, as a part of a rather complicated process called *Coemptio fiduciae causa.* The three purposes were change of tutors, destruction of *sacra* and acquisition of the power of testation. From the language of our two authorities, Gaius and Cicero[1], it seems that change of tutors was the earliest application of the method, and acquisition of the power of testation the last to appear and the first to disappear. The form, as described by Gaius, was a *coemptio,* followed by *mancipatio,* which in turn was followed by a manumission. It is not clear why the agnates assented to a step which removed the woman from their control, and destroyed their chance of succession, but it is possible that they were compellable to consent from an early time. It is also not clear why the *ingenua* could not make a will with their consent as she could under Hadrian's legislation. It is true that the *tutela* of agnates over adult women had been abolished by his time, and it may be that the reason of the earlier rule was that agnates might, by consenting, be barring the claim of others than themselves, since the nearest agnates at the woman's death might well be not themselves, but persons in an entirely different line. In the course of the lengthy process the woman suffers *capitis deminutio,* and is for the moment reduced to a semi-servile condition, and it may be that, as has been suggested, the need for this underlay the whole process. It is clear, in any case, that the desired result could not have been produced by her being merely freed from the coemptive tie by the *coemptionator*: he would have been her *legitimus tutor,* and would

[1] *Pro* Murena 12. 27.

have had the powers it was desired to put an end to. Nor does it appear that it was possible for a citizen, male or female, to sell himself or herself into civil bondage directly. Complicated as the process seems it is not easy to see how it could have been shortened.

Of the two accounts which we possess that of Gaius is fairly full, while that of Cicero is a mere allusion. It is however full enough for us to see that there has been a considerable change in the process by the time of Gaius. In Cicero's day the *coemptio* was to some old dependent, sometimes, as it seems, an old slave bought and freed for the purpose (though this rests only on a very unsafe inference from some words of Plautus, which quite probably have no bearing on the matter), who may or may not have acquired any rights by the process, but at any rate dared not exercise them[1]. Nothing is said of any legal means of compelling him to carry out the next step, and it is possible that there were no such means: they were not necessary. By the time of Gaius, the *coemptio* was recognised as merely formal, *dicis gratia*, conveying no rights at all, and thus it was no longer necessary to have an old dependent. It might be gone through with anyone, except, indeed, the actual husband: if the wife coempted herself to him, even with this purpose, the *coemptio* produced its normal effect, and she was *in loco filiae*. Moreover, she could compel (*cogere*) the *coemptionator* to remancipate her, though we have no details of the mode of compulsion. It is a result of the *manus* arising from such a *coemptio* with her husband, that as there was difficulty in bringing any peremptory process against a husband, she must, if she had gone through the *coemptio* with her husband, divorce him before she could compel him to remancipate her.

The connexion of the *fiducia* with the *coemptio* is not very clear. It is sometimes said that the *coemptio* was itself accompanied by a *fiducia*. There is no evidence for this in the time of Cicero, and it is improbable for the time of Gaius. There are circumstances which strongly suggest that the *fiducia*,

[1] See Roby, Roman Private Law, 1. 71 *sq*.

which certainly played a part, was not in connexion with the *coemptio* but with the *remancipatio*. Nowhere is the transaction called *coemptio cum fiducia*. Occasionally it is called *coemptio fiduciaria*, but its usual name is *coemptio fiduciae causa*. This form suggests that it led to a *fiducia*, *i.e.*, that the *remancipatio* was subject to a *fiducia*. If indeed there was a *fiducia* in the *coemptio*, it must have been imposed by the woman herself, for it is clear that she is the party to the *coemptio*—she sells herself, her father or tutor, as the case may be, merely authorising the transaction. If so, it must have been before the *coemptio*, for after it she was *in manu*, and could hardly have imposed a *fiducia* on the *vir*, while it is certain that the *fiducia* was never an integral part of the form of conveyance. But there seems to be no other case of a *fiducia* preceding the conveyance. This point is however not very conclusive, since we know that in the time of Gaius the *manus* was merely *dicis gratia* and ineffective. The absence of any *fiducia* in the *coemptio* would explain why in Cicero's time the process was gone through with an old dependent who dared not be guilty of any encroachment. As time went on the *manus* came to be regarded as conferring no right at all; hence followed disuse of the precaution, and the development of means of compelling the *coemptionator* to go through the rest of his part. This compulsion Gaius calls *cogere*, an expression which does not suggest an *actio fiduciae*. On the other hand, *fiducia* in connexion with *mancipatio* is a familiar idea, and a comparison of three texts shews that this case of *tutela* resulting from *coemptio fiduciae causa* was regarded by Gaius as an ordinary case of *tutela fiduciaria*[1], in which it is generally held that the *mancipatio* was subject to a tacit or express *fiducia*.

It should be mentioned that according to some critics the process of *coemptio* and *remancipatio* did not apply, in the time of Cicero, to the process for destroying the *sacra*. They hold that in this case there was merely an actual marriage, with *manus*, to an aged dependent. Such a marriage transferred the woman's property to the *vir*, but destroyed her *sacra*. Before

[1] G. 1. 115 a, 118 a, 166 a.

long he would die, and she would inherit her property again. In the account given by Gaius this case is not mentioned[1].

19. The circumstances under which *potestas* could be obtained over issue not born *ex iustis nuptiis* have already been incidentally mentioned. The chief cases are *Anniculi Probatio* and *Erroris causae probatio.* The process in these cases may be called loosely legitimation, but it must be remembered that all children affected by them were in a sense legitimate already: they were all born *ex nuptiis,* though not *ex iustis nuptiis.* In later law the principle was indeed carried further, under the influence of Christianity. It was possible to bring under *potestas* issue not born in marriage, but even here they must have been issue of the recognised connexion called *concubinatus,* not mere issue of illicit intercourse. For these last adrogation was the only method. Of legitimation it is enough to say that in reading the considerable amount of legislation on the matter belonging to the later centuries, it is important to note that the gift of rights of succession does not in all cases imply *potestas* in the father, and that legitimation for all purposes as between parent and child does not in all cases imply legitimation as against other relatives. It is in connexion especially with legitimation by *Oblatio Curiae* that this is material.

20. *Adoptio* and *Adrogatio* are primarily, as stated in the Institutes, methods of bringing under *potestas* persons other than issue. But at least as far as *Adrogatio* is concerned, it could be applied equally well to issue not born in wedlock, and there is abundant evidence that it was so utilised, in particular by *libertini,* who procured the manumission of children they had had in slavery, and then adopted them.

The rules of *Adoptio* and *Adrogatio* are in the main simple. It may be worth while, however, to remark that, while the form of *Adoptio* in the time of Gaius was very different from that introduced by Justinian, both Gaius and Justinian speak

[1] See Roby, Rom. Priv. Law, 1. 71.

of it as effected *imperio magistratus,* an expression which appears at first sight much more descriptive of the later than of the earlier form. The truth is, however, that what is called the form of *Adoptio* consists of two elements, a process of triple sale and a *cessio in iure.* Of these the first is not, properly speaking, a part of the adoption: it is a preliminary, necessary as being the only way of destroying the existing *patria potestas.* The *adoptio* is the *cessio in iure* which follows. It is this alone which Gaius has in mind when he speaks of *Imperium magistratus,* and Justinian's method is merely a simplification of this.

It does not seem to have been found necessary to subject *Adoptio* to any but obvious restrictions, but the case is very different with the more ancient institution of *Adrogatio. Adoptio* cannot directly injure any but the parties immediately concerned. But with *Adrogatio* the case is different: it is of considerable public importance, it destroys a family, and it may interfere with *sacra.* It is allowed therefore only with the intervention of the *comitia,* and only to provide a *heres.* Even so, it interferes with rights of succession in the agnates, at least on one side, and probably in most cases on both. From these considerations spring nearly all the special rules to which it is subject, though the prohibition of adrogation of *impuberes* may rest on other obvious considerations.

21. Besides the ordinary types of adoption mentioned in the Institutes, there are traces of others which should be mentioned.

(*a*) Adoption by Will. If we consider the form of Adrogation and that of the Will made before the *Comitia,* and remember that the notion of legacy as opposed to *hereditas* is not very early, we shall see that it is not easy to distinguish one institution from the other. But long after Adrogation has become undoubtedly a distinct institution we find traces of adoption by will. Julius Caesar adopted Octavius in this way, and though such a case is not strong as a precedent, there are several other recorded cases among less autocratic people[1]. This is in effect

[1] See Girard, Manuel (4) 173.

an *adrogatio post mortem*, and it appears to have followed in the main rules of *Adrogatio*. It needed confirmation by a *lex curiata*, and it was applied only to persons *sui iuris*. There seems no trace of it left in the time of Gaius.

(*b*) Adoption of a Slave. Justinian records a dictum of Cato, that owners could adopt their slaves. We do not know how this was done. It may have been by a collusive conveyance, followed by the ordinary *cessio in iure* of *Adoptio*, but we have no evidence of this, and it would be rather the adoption of another person's slave. It is more generally thought that it was by *Adrogatio*. To this it has been objected that as a slave could not appear before the *Comitia*, he could not be adrogated any more than a woman could. There is however the difference, whatever it may be worth, that the *adrogatio* would have the effect of making him *capax*, which was not the case where a woman was concerned. The institution seems to leave no trace in the classical law: that to which Justinian also refers in the same text, and regulates elsewhere[1], is merely a rule that if a master declares formally that he regards a certain slave as his son, this, though as an adoption it is void, is a good manumission.

It appears from a remark of Aulus Gellius[2] that in ancient times it had been lawful for owners to give their slaves in adoption. There is no trace of this in later times, but Gellius says that it was declared to be lawful by many ancient lawyers. As he speaks of it as having been done *apud Praetorem*, it must have been simple adoption. There would be the *Cessio in iure*, but no triple sale: this, as we have seen, was no part of the *adoptio*, but an accidental feature necessary for the destruction of the *patria potestas* where that existed. As it did not exist here, the *cessio in iure* would be all that was required. The legal sources say nothing of this institution. In later law the desired effect was produced by manumission followed by adrogation. This led to the establishment of a rule that a *libertinus* did not by adrogation enter the class of *ingenui*, a rule reasonable in itself, if rather illogical. (It may be remembered that in earlier

[1] C. 7. 6. 1. 10. [2] *Noct. Att.* 5. 19. 13.

law it was possible for a patrician to become a plebeian, and thus eligible to the Tribunate, by being adrogated by a plebeian, but there is no evidence that the converse step could be taken.) In classical law the rule went further: it was forbidden for any one but his patron to adrogate a *libertinus*. The rule seems to have been directory rather than imperative. The effect of the texts on the matter appears to be that if the fact that he was a *libertinus* came to light in the preliminary investigation, the adrogation would not be permitted, but that if it was carried through in ignorance the adrogation was valid; the man however remained a *libertinus*, and his patron's rights were not affected. *Non debet fieri, sed factum valet*[1].

(*c*) Adoption under Justinian of a person *alieni iuris* but not a *suus heres*. *Adoptio minus plena* was introduced by Justinian to avoid the risk of loss of rights by capricious emancipation after capricious adoption. Accordingly, if the adoptor was a natural ascendant, as it was thought that in such a case there was no real risk, the new rule was not to apply, and the *adoptio* was to be still *plena*. Carrying out the same idea in a curiously technical way, Justinian further provided, but did not insert the rule in the Institutes, that if the person given in adoption was not a *suus heres, i.e.*, was a grandchild whose father was in the family, then, even though the adoptor was an *extraneus*, the *adoptio* was to be *plena*. The idea was that as the person adopted had, in strictness, no rights in the inheritance of his grandfather, he did not lose any rights by the adoption. It is clear however that he would have rights if his natural father died before the grandfather, and Justinian provided for this case by the further rule[2] that, if, in the event, the father did so die, so that, but for the *adoptio*, the child would have been a *suus heres* of the grandfather, the *adoptio* at once became *minus plena*, and he was at once restored to his rights as a *suus heres*.

It is said by Justinian that he makes the change in the law of adoption to avoid the risk of injury resulting from capricious emancipation of an adopted child, a step which put him in the

[1] D. 1. 7. 15. 3; D. 2. 4. 10. 2; D. 38. 2. 49.

[2] C. 8. 47. 10. 4.

position of an emancipated child of his own father. But there was a great difference between the effects of emancipation in early law and those in Justinian's time. In early law the emancipated child lost all share in the *sacra* of the family, all right to maintenance, all right to a provision in his father's will, all claim on intestacy, all claim to the *tutela* of his brothers and sisters: he passed out of the family altogether and was without means, unless, as was commonly the case, where the emancipation was not a punishment, some provision for him accompanied it. But in the time of Justinian hardly anything of this is left. The *sacra* have long gone with the old faiths. He has claims to maintenance, to succession, and to *tutela*. His right of succession is somewhat lessened in certain cases, and that is all. And most of these changes are of long standing. What then was the risk of loss which Justinian guarded against by his introduction of *adoptio minus plena*? He explains it[1] as occurring in certain exceptional, but always possible, cases. Such facts as the following might arise. *A* gives his son *B* in adoption, and dies. His estate is distributed, and *B* has of course no claim. Some years later the adoptor emancipates him. He now falls back into the position of an *emancipatus* of his natural father, but it seems that there is no retroactive effect in this, so that he cannot claim a share as an *emancipatus*. And even if he were entitled to claim, the estate having long since been distributed, it would be difficult for him to make his right effective: the estate might indeed have been all dissipated, and the *heredes* be insolvent.

22. The institution of civil bondage, the condition described as *in mancipio esse*, suggests two or three legal problems, the materials for the solution of which are rather scanty, since the institution, almost obsolete in the time of Gaius, has disappeared altogether under Justinian. The duration of an individual case of bondage has been much disputed. The opinion that it lasted for the life of the person subjected to it is hard to reconcile with the law of the XII Tables[2], which made three sales into

[1] C. 8. 47. 10. *pr.*

[2] Bruns, Fontes, 1. 22.

this position put an end to the *potestas,* and the same rule negatives the view that it was for the life of the *paterfamilias,* an opinion which would otherwise have been plausible. That it was not for the life of the holder is made certain by the fact that one of the modes of release from it was manumission by Will. Gaius tells us that in any case except that of noxal surrender, and that of the sales in connexion with the process of emancipation or adoption, in which the sale was merely formal, the bondsman could release himself *censu* at the next *lustrum, i.e.,* he could have himself entered on the census roll in his proper family position, so that the bondage would be ended, without the consent of the holder. The effect would be that it would not last more than five years. If this is to be understood as an ancient rule it settles the question, and it has an ancient and formal look. There is however the possibility that it is a rule introduced only when the institution was in decay, and we must remember that, at the time when Gaius wrote, the Census was obsolete, and the only cases in which the institution of bondage survived, in practice, were just those two to which he says the rule did not apply.

It may be noted that Gaius says he could free himself *censu*: he did not become free, *ipso facto,* by the arrival of the next census. If he took no steps, he would remain in the same position for another *lustrum,* and it is quite likely that this was a not uncommon course: it provided the man with a maintenance which he might not be able to gain from his own father or in any other way. The Jewish law had a very similar institution: it was possible for a Jew to be in a position of quasi-slavery, an Ebed, to another Jew. This was temporary in much the Roman way, *i.e.,* it lasted till the next Jubilee year, which could not be more than seven years, at which time it was possible for the Ebed to become free by declaring his wish to do so. This rule is too ancient to be coloured by Roman notions, but it is surprisingly similar. He did not become free *ipso facto* by the arrival of the Jubilee, but only by an act of his own. There is however the difference that if he did not claim his liberty at the first Jubilee he could not do so at any later one: there was a formal ceremony and he was an Ebed for life.

This limitation to five years for the duration of rights is found in many branches of the Roman law. It was the ordinary term for tenancies of land and for tax-farming contracts[1]. A man who had been manumitted might not, after five years, in ordinary cases, set up a claim to *ingenuitas*[2]. There is in late law a curious revival or survival of a rule at least analogous to the one we are now considering: a citizen captive redeemed by purchase had to serve his redeemer for five years[3].

23. The case discussed in the sources is always that of sale by the *paterfamilias*. The question suggests itself whether a man could of his own free will sell himself into bondage. It is clear that he could not in classical or earlier law sell himself into actual slavery in Rome. But bondage, though it may at one time have been the same thing, is a very different matter in historical times. There is nothing inherently improbable in the idea that he could. We have seen that it was possible in Jewish law; it was allowed in Anglo-Saxon law, in a slightly disguised form in the England of the thirteenth century, in other Germanic law[4], and, as it seems, in the older law of different parts of the extreme East. In fact if Roman law never admitted it, it stands in an exceptional position. But there is no direct evidence of any such thing, and it is most probable that no such right existed. There is indeed some slight evidence in the other direction. *Coemptio* is said to be a modification of *Mancipatio,* and it is perfectly clear that in *coemptio* the woman sold herself. Whether she was *sui* or *alieni iuris* she was the actual contracting party, *auctore tutore vel patre,* as the case might be. It may however be answered to this that it may well have been because the form was modified, so as not to treat the woman as a chattel, that this self sale was possible. And it is unsafe to argue from an artificial construction of this kind to a normal application

[1] D. 19. 2. 9. 1. *etc.* [2] D. 40. 14. 2. 1. [3] C. Th. 5. 7. 2.

[4] Pollock and Maitland, Hist. of Engl. Law, i. 12, 408.

behind it: the law is not perfectly logical. It might also be contended that, if she could have sold herself into bondage, the process actually done by a lengthy process in *coemptio fiduciae causa* might have been done at one step. But this ignores the need of a third person to create and enforce the *fiducia*, so that her manumitter would be a fiduciary tutor.

There is the further fact in favour of the possibility that in the form of mancipation, as recorded by Gaius, nothing is said by the transferor or the subject. All is done by the receiver. But elsewhere there are indications that more was said than Gaius mentions[1].

There is a still more important piece of evidence if we can accept the view, formerly dominant, and recently revived with strong argument, that what is called the contract of *Nexum* was essentially at its origin nothing but a mancipation of the man, by himself, as security for his debt[2]. The position of a *nexus* is of course very different from that of a man *in mancipio*, but the recorded cases on which the opinion just stated rests seem to leave no doubt but that it was possible for a man to go through the form of *mancipatio*, with himself as subject-matter. We cannot however infer self-sale into bondage from such cases as these: it cannot be assumed that every logically possible development actually occurred.

A further question may be raised: was a person in bondage assignable? Could the holder transfer his right to another person? There is one well-known case which suggests that he could, *i.e.*, the practice, in emancipation, for the alienee to sell the son back to his father, in order that he might free, and have the rights of a patron or quasi-patron. How could this be done if a person *in mancipio* was not assignable? But here, as in some of the other cases discussed, there is the difficulty that we cannot safely infer a general rule from provisions designed in formal transactions to get over difficulties.

24. We are told in several texts that a person sold into

[1] Festus, sub v. *Rodus*. Bruns, Fontes, 2. 32.

[2] See the reff. in Girard, Manuel (4) 476.

civil bondage underwent *capitis deminutio.* It was of course *minima,* but it was peculiar from certain points of view. It is well known that upon a release he reverted, if it were not a third occasion, to his old position, not to a new position similar to the old, but to the same position: the *capitis deminutio* and all its effects were wiped out. This makes it, so to speak, a revocable or provisional *capitis deminutio,* a thing as it seems unique in the law. This has been ingeniously explained by the hypothesis that *deminutio* was essentially an alteration in the entry on the census roll, and that in this case the entry was not struck out. He was still in his father's family, but a note was made on the roll that he was *in mancipio* to a third person. This was struck out when he reverted, which as Gaius tells us was another *capitis deminutio*[1]. However this may be, the effects of the transaction, regarded as a *capitis deminutio,* are remarkable. His children born during the bondage were it is clear still in the *potestas* of the original *paterfamilias.* But we learn from Gaius that all *capitis deminutio* destroys the agnatic tie. It follows, therefore, either that this statement is not correct for the *capitis deminutio* produced by sale into bondage, which however is the very case in connexion with which Gaius lays down the proposition, or that a child may be born into an agnatic group to which his father did not belong at any time between the conception and the birth of the child. But Gaius also tells us that persons thus once or twice sold are still *sui heredes.* We know from Gaius that the three sales which destroyed the *patria potestas* were a *capitis deminutio,* which seems an unnecessary piece of information, since he has already told us that each one of the sales was itself a *capitis deminutio.* If the holder freed the bondsman after the third sale we know from the Epitome of Gaius (the original text is illegible) that the manumitter succeeded as patron to the exclusion of the true father. What was the result if after the first sale the father died, and manumission by the holder then followed? Gaius tells us that the person so freed could succeed as a *postumus* to his own father. It

[1] See Cuq, Inst. Jurid. des Romains, 1. 202.

would seem to follow that the manumitter could not succeed to him. On the whole it must be said that the single *mancipatio* produced a very imperfect *capitis deminutio.* It is true that the difficulty has been avoided by supposing (1) that the statement that each *mancipatio* in the process is a separate *capitis deminutio,* is a later addition not due to Gaius, (2) that in the words which precede this statement[1] it is meant that the *mancipatio* and the manumission from it together form a *capitis deminutio,* and (3) that at least, in the case of a son, Gaius does not mean each such transaction but only the third one. It seems far more probable that the scheme of *capitis deminutio* given by Gaius was a modern one not consistently worked out.

The truth is that the conception of *capitis deminutio* is full of difficulties, owing to the imperfection of our information as to its course of development. As we see it in the Institutes of Gaius and of Justinian, it is a kind of civil death, more or less complete, accompanied in some cases by re-birth as a new man. This notion that the reappearance of the *capite minutus* on the legal scene is, as it were, a new avatar, is allowed to produce the most surprising results. A person enslaved and afterwards freed is, apart from express restitution, another person, who is for example entirely free from liability for old debts and unrelated to his old agnates[2]. The civil death may be more or less complete. *Capitis deminutio maxima* results from enslavement, *media* from loss of *civitas* without enslavement, *minima* from any such change in family position as destroys existing agnatic ties. Hence, it is said, it may be suffered in respect of *Libertas, Civitas* or *Familia,* loss of the first necessarily involving that of the others, loss of the second necessarily involving that of the third. This provides a convenient scheme, and it is the basis adopted by Gaius and other classical jurists, for their whole discussion of the law of persons. It has been pointed out however that it is not so symmetrical as it seems. *Familia* is a conception linked to *civitas,* and having for Romans no signification beyond it. Every *Civis* has *Familia.* Every

[1] Gai. 1. 162. [2] C. 9. 51. 5, 9.

one who has *Familia* has *Civitas*. But though every *civis* has liberty, not every freeman has *civitas*. Moreover a glance at any statement of the effects of *capitis deminutio* will shew that in the classical law some of these effects had no application to *C. D. Minima*, and as to most of the others they were, in effect, evaded by various interventions of the Praetor.

Capitis deminutio is only civil death. It does not affect *ius gentium* or *ius naturale*. Subject to the restrictions which have just been mentioned it is civil death in the case of *minima* as much as in the other cases. But these restrictions began in very early times, and call for a little more detailed treatment. A *capite minutus* was still liable for his delicts[1]. This is due to the fact that such liability is in the nature of a ransom, for revenge on the body of the offender. The injured person is bought off by payment. As the body of the offender still remains the same, this liability still exists. Another exception is of a less obvious kind. Ordinary contractual debts ceased to exist at strict law, though this unfair rule very early underwent modification where there were assets which had gone to someone. But debts which the *minutus* owed not on his own account, but by reason of inheritance, debts, that is to say, of a person whose *heres* he was, remained still due at civil law. They could be recovered from a person into whose *potestas* he has passed, by simple direct action, with none of the devices by which liability for other debts was ultimately, but only to the extent of the assets, brought home to him. For the rule as to hereditary debts Gaius assigns the reason that the adrogator has now become *heres*, and the man himself has ceased to be *heres*. The adrogator is *heres* to the man to whom the *adrogatus* had been *heres*, not to the *adrogatus* himself. This is said to rest on the notion that as a son acquires everything to his father he is considered to have so acquired this *hereditas*, and thus as the adrogating father is *heres*, he is liable to the creditors. This is not inevitable logic. The *hereditas* as such ceased to exist at the moment when the future *adrogatus* entered on it, and its debts then became personal debts of the *heres*. It may

[1] *Post*, § 139.

be that originally some religious idea entered into this: in the classical law it rests on a principle we shall have to consider later[1].

25. It is fairly certain that the elaborate scheme of *capitis deminutiones* presented to us by the classical lawyers is not primitive. It is held by many modern writers that early law knew of only one degree or kind of *capitis deminutio*, though there is much disagreement as to the fundamental character of the change of position denoted by this name. According to one view, based mainly on the meaning of the name itself, *capitis deminutio* is essentially not a destruction of the personality, but a mere diminution of civil right. It has been pointed out that this view, *a priori* extremely probable, owes some of the discredit into which it has fallen to the attempt of Savigny, its chief supporter, to explain by means of it all the applications of *capitis deminutio* in the classical law, ignoring the fact that the whole conception had undergone great changes. It is of course a consequence of the adoption of this view that we must hold that the name *capitis deminutio* was not applied, in very early law, to any cases in which the man concerned passed out of the civic society altogether. There is however much room for doubt as to the exact cases to which the conception did on this view actually apply. According to another view *capitis deminutio* was essentially a destruction of the personality, irrespective of the question whether a new personality was created by the change or not[2]. Whatever may be the truth of this matter it is perfectly clear that in the time of Cicero there were only two degrees of *capitis deminutio*: *maxima*, incurred by one who passed completely out of the civic circle; *minima*, incurred by one who remained a citizen, but had undergone some change in respect of his rights and liabilities dependent on agnation[3]. Logically this scheme might have sufficed for the classical lawyers, for, so far as can be seen, the effects of *capitis deminutio* are precisely the same for the man enslaved as for the *deportatus*. But it is obvious that there is in practice

[1] *Post*, § 57. [2] See Eisele, Beiträge, VIII.
[3] Cicero, *Pro* Caecina, 33. 96.

a wide difference between these cases. The slave is extinct for legal purposes: the *deportatus* is not, and he may, immediately after his deportation, be engaging in transactions with Roman citizens on his own account, to the extent to which his new position allowed of these. The same would be still more obviously true of a *civis* who had entered a Latin colony. It is easy to see that this difference would soon reflect itself in the language of lawyers, and accordingly there appears a new degree of *capitis deminutio*, midway between the existing ones, *capitis deminutio media*.

It is by no means certain that the original conception of *capitis deminutio minima*, as distinguished from the greater forms, is that presented to us by Gaius. Many of the cases in which his *capitis deminutio* occurred are creations of relatively late law, and only one, *Adrogatio*, can be regarded as extremely ancient. It has accordingly been suggested that this *deminutio* needed originally more than passing from the family group, that it resulted only from passing outside the gentile circle, a change which in view of the religious ideas of early Rome was of a more momentous character. However this may be, it seems clear that, in the classical law, the essential of *capitis deminutio* was such a change in family position as ruptured old agnatic ties, or created new ones or did both. Savigny's attempt to explain them as all involving either a definite change for the worse, or reduction to a semi-servile position in the process, is in conflict with uncontradicted texts in the case of the woman *alieni iuris* who goes into *manus*, and in that of the children of an *adrogatus*[1]. But it must be remembered that to say that this is not correct for classical law does not negative its truth for the original conception of the institution.

Even if we assume the history of the matter to be somewhat as is suggested above, it does not follow that it was logically treated by the jurists. We have just seen that the account given by Gaius is not consistent in its details, and there are questions into which he does not enter which are difficult to answer. It must suffice to mention one or two of them. Could

[1] See Poste, Gaius, 98, for a statement of the cases.

a Latin suffer *capitis deminutio* of any kind? If he could, did he suffer it by becoming a citizen? Was *Transitio in plebem* ever regarded as a *capitis deminutio*, other than *minima*, which it would of course be if carried out by *Adrogatio*[1]? Did a son, noxally surrendered, suffer *capitis deminutio*? Yes, if this involved transfer by *mancipatio*, and if the text of Gaius just discussed[2] is to be accepted. But both these points are controverted, and the actual case is not mentioned.

26. The rules of *tutela* are for the most part straightforward. The complete change in the conceptions underlying *tutela* which occurred in the course of the development of Roman law, so that an institution which was originally designed for the protection of the property in the interest of the successors, became Guardianship in the modern sense, never found expression in the fundamental rules of the institution. Instead of abolishing the rule that *tutela* of boys ended at 14, a rule quite out of harmony with the new view of *tutela*, the Romans preferred to retain the rule, but to supplement it with devices like *Restitutio in integrum* and *Curatio*, which gave a similar but less effective protection. The perpetual *tutela* of women was not abolished when its absurdity became clear, but a class of *tutores* was invented who could not refuse their assent. This sort of conservatism is to be found in every branch of the law.

Upon the classification of *Tutelae* the texts tell us a very confused story. Gaius, having enumerated *Legitimae, Testamentariae, Fiduciariae, Dativae, Cessiciae* and temporary Praetorian *Tutelae*, remarks that these are all the *species*, but that on the question under how many *genera* they should be distributed, the ancient jurists were hopelessly divided. Ulpian classifies tutors under the odd heads *Legitimi, ex Senatusconsulto* and *Moribus*. The Institutes of Justinian roughly follow Gaius, omitting his last two cases as obsolete. The Digest has no rubric for Fiduciary tutors. Perhaps not much turns on these

[1] As to other possibilities, Girard, Manuel (4) 169.

[2] *Ante* § 24.

classifications, but the fact that the class of *Fiduciarii* is rather hazily conceived is not unimportant.

The *paterfamilias* and the *paterfamilias* alone has the right to appoint a testamentary tutor, but we are told of cases in which a father appoints, for example, to an emancipated son, and the Praetor confirms the appointment without enquiry, an institution which has been called *tutela testamentaria imperfecta*. There were further cases in which the appointment might be confirmed after enquiry, for instance, where an *extraneus impubes*, without other means, was made *heres*[1]. But this is not properly speaking *tutela testamentaria* at all: it means only that the Praetor, in appointing, will choose this man if he sees no reason to the contrary. A tutor could be appointed by Will or by confirmed Codicil, and the usual form seems to have been *Titium tutorem do*. It does not seem that appointment by a praetorian will could have been valid, though no doubt such an appointment would usually be confirmed.

The name *tutor legitimus* seems to have been used with a stricter and with a wider signification. In its strict and most usual sense it means a tutor whose *tutela* is due to his civil law right of succession under the XII Tables. But Ulpian speaks of the name as covering any tutor who owes his appointment to any *lex*[2], though it does not seem that he would have extended it to one who was appointed by a magistrate under the *lex* Atilia or the *lex* Iulia Titia. Gaius speaks in uncertain tones as to the *parens manumissor*, whose title, though it is based remotely on the XII Tables, is in fact a later development. Ulpian may perhaps mean to treat *Fiduciarii* as a subhead of *legitimi*[3], a scheme which has been supposed to be that of Servius Sulpicius, mentioned by Gaius.

27. The conception of *Tutela Fiduciaria* is one presenting some difficulties. What is the exact meaning of this expression? There are two kinds of case which do not seem to have much in common. There are on the one hand the *extraneus manu-*

[1] D. 26. 3. 4. [2] Ulp. *Reg.* 11. 3. [3] *Ib.* 11. 5.

missor and the tutor obtained by a woman by *coemptio fiduciae causa*. We have seen that these are at bottom much the same institution. The *fiducia* is expressly mentioned in the latter case, and it is reasonable to infer that it existed, either express or tacit, in the case of the *extraneus manumissor*. The form of *mancipatio* provides a ready means for the *fiducia*, though in fact Gaius and Ulpian, who alone discuss it, say nothing of the *fiducia*. This may mean that the *fiducia* was merely tacit, but it is more probable that as the case can hardly have been common it was very shortly treated. It seems a very natural assumption that *tutela fiduciaria* was so called because it rested in some way on a *fiducia*. On the other hand there is the case of the children of the *parens manumissor*, where there can be no question, so far as the children are concerned, of any *fiducia*. It is not possible to put it down to some change in the meaning of *tutela fiduciaria* between the times of Gaius and Justinian, since, although it was the only such *tutela* that survived to Justinian, it already existed in the time of Gaius. Why was the *tutela* of the *liberi parentis manumissoris* fiduciary? Why was it not, like that of the *filius patroni*, *legitima*? Gaius indicates the fact without comment. Justinian makes an attempt at an explanation, which is sometimes thought to be derived from Modestinus. He remarks that the cases of the patron and *parens manumissor* (quasi-patron) are alike in the fact that if the manumission or emancipation had not occurred, the slave, or son, would have been under their control. Therefore their *tutelae* are alike *legitimae*. The same is true of the *filius patroni*: if there had been no manumission he would have had control of the slave, and thus his *tutela* of the freedman is *legitima*. But if the son had not been emancipated, the brothers would have had no *potestas* over him, and thus their *tutela* is not *legitima* but fiduciary. This plausible reasoning is, however, very defective. It proves too much, for by it the *tutela* of the *extraneus manumissor* ought to have been *legitima*. It does not cover all cases, since if a grandfather emancipated, the father would in course of time be fiduciary tutor as child of the *parens manumissor*. Yet he should have been *legitimus*, since, had the emancipation not occurred, he would have had *potestas*. And the children of the patron were *legitimi* even though they had been disinherited, and thus could never have had control. The argument rests *legitima tutela* on control, but its right basis is right of succession under the XII Tables. Agnates were *legitimi tutores* though they could never have had control. And the argument does not in the least shew why the *tutela* was *fiduciaria*. There is no suggestion of a *fiducia*, and the *liberi* do not take the *tutela* voluntarily, as Gaius says fiduciary tutors do.

If it could be shewn that the *tutela* of the *parens manumissor* was itself fiduciary in classical law, this would explain the matter. There is indeed some evidence that this was the case. His right of succession at civil law is exactly the same as that of the *extraneus manumissor*, and he takes the *tutela* voluntarily, exactly as the *extraneus* does. Probably they were both *legitimi tutores* in early law, and the conception of fiduciary *tutela* dates at first from a time later than the introduction of the edict postponing the *extraneus* to the *decem personae*. It is clear that the *parens* was a *legitimus tutor* in the later law. Gaius gives the reason: he is very like a patron and similar honour is to be paid to him. But the texts shew a somewhat uncertain state of doctrine as to the exact limits of *legitima tutela* and of its relation to fiduciary *tutela*, and a case can be made out on the texts for the view that for the classical lawyers the *parens* was in strictness a fiduciary tutor. Gaius incidentally calls him a *legitimus tutor*, but does not mention him as such in his classification of tutors. The longish passage in which he appears to do so is an insertion of modern editors, who insert the words with no authority because they think they ought to be there. In one passage (G. 1. 172) he plainly calls him a fiduciary tutor, but adds that as he is like a patron *et legitimus habeatur*, where the *et* and the *habeatur* are both significant. Ulpian makes the same omission and remarks further that an *extraneus* who is admittedly fiduciary is tutor *per similitudinem patroni*. The similarity of this language to that of Gaius, if the passage is read as it is in the manuscript, strongly suggests that the course of thought of Ulpian and Gaius was the same. Even in the Digest, Ulpian appears as suggesting that there is something exceptional in the *tutela legitima* of the *parens*: *vicem legitimi tutoris sustinet*[1]. Ulpian also tells us that the *lex* Claudia abolished the *legitima tutela* of women, except that of the patron. It certainly did not destroy the *tutela* of the *parens*. Gaius speaks of it as having destroyed the *tutela* of the agnates. It seems to follow that when that law was enacted, either the *parens* was not distinguished from the patron, or he was not regarded as a *legitimus tutor*. Either view makes the proposed insertion in Gaius very doubtful. But all this can be suggested only as a possible solution of the difficulty.

The appointment of *tutores* by the magistrates was the subject of repeated legislation, much of the constitutional significance of which is lost. It is an ancient institution, since the *lex* Atilia dates from, at the latest, about 200 B.C. The appointment of *tutores* was regarded as a very important duty, and it was then probably a rare one, since it was to be exercised by the Urban Praetor and the majority of the Tribunes. It is stated not to be included in either *Imperium* or *Iurisdictio*, but to depend in every instance on a statutory provision[2]. In the classical law it was possible for the tutor appointed to object to the appointment, and to shew that there was another person better qualified for the post—*potioris nominatio*. And Paul tells us that this better qualification might consist either in more near connexion or in greater resources[3].

28. The tutor's control over the fortunes of the ward is complete, since, while the latter can engage in transactions which cannot impose any obligation on him, unilateral transactions, such as stipulation, in which he is the creditor, he cannot bind himself without the *auctoritas* of the tutor, while the tutor, on the other hand, by his power of administration—*negotiorum gestio*—can act on behalf of the *pupillus* in most cases. There were some acts however which could not be done by representative, and as

[1] D. 26. 4. 3. 10. [2] D. 26. 1. 6. 2. [3] Paul, *Sent.* 2. 28. 2.

to these it seems that some difficulty must have arisen in early law. Of these *Actus Legitimi*, the most important from this point of view were *Cessio in iure* and *Cretio*. It would appear that so long as the *pupillus* was *infans*, or *infantiae proximus*, these acts could not be done at all, since the child was too young to be prompted through them. An *infans* has no *intellectus*. In the classical law there were informal methods which might usually be employed, so that the *tutor* could act, but it seems that in earlier law there must have been some way out, some way, for instance, with which we are not acquainted, by means of which an infant *pupillus* could make formal *cretio* on an inheritance.

No doubt bilateral transactions with a *pupillus* without the cooperation of his tutor would not be common, but it must be noted that the result of them would not be quite so onesided as might appear from the bare statement of the rules. If, for example, the child agreed to sell or to buy, the other party could not be compelled to fulfil his part unless the *pupillus* was prepared to do his part also. Such a transaction would be in effect one which the child might enforce or avoid, but which could not be enforced against him, a state of things which exists in English law with regard to many contracts made by a person under age. The case is more complex if the ward is entitled to performance without any render, immediately, on his part, if, *e.g.*, the vendor has agreed to give credit without security. It is easy to see that the vendor's position is bad. He is presumably bound to deliver, and he cannot require payment. When the agreed term of credit has expired, he has, not exactly his action for the price, but only for so much of it as is represented by the actual enrichment of the *pupillus*. How this enrichment is calculated we are not clearly told.

The perpetual *tutela* of women, like the guardianship in chivalry of our law, has in view quite other interests than those of the woman herself. Gaius observes that the notion that women are too lightminded to look after themselves affords merely a specious pretext. The maintenance of the power of *legitimi tutores*, and the nature of the transactions to which their consent could not be compelled, shews clearly enough that it was the retention of the property in the family which was the governing idea. It is worth while to notice, however, that although Gaius speaks of the institution as still existing, it has long since ceased to be very oppressive. In the case of an ordinary *ingenua*, after the abolition of the perpetual *tutela* of agnates, the *legitima tutela* could arise only in the case of emancipated women, and in their case only in the father, and so long as he lived. There is nothing very oppressive in a control by a father during his life over property of which perhaps the greater part, if not all, was wealth to which in the ordinary way the woman would not have succeeded till after his death.

The term *curatio* covers institutions so different as to have very little in common. Two cases of *Curatio*, that over *Furiosi* and that over *Prodigi* are ancient institutions of the civil law, and resemble *tutela* far more than they do the two other cases of *Curatio*, one of which, that over minors above 14, is as a general institution almost post-classical, while the other, *Cura pupillorum*, is certainly not very ancient. The question may be asked why the ancient forms were not classed as *tutelae*. The answer seems to be that the power involved in *tutela* is conceived of as an extension of the *patria potestas*, and essentially continuous with it, but the power of the curator may supervene at a later time in life, after the lunatic or spendthrift has been in full enjoyment of his rights as an adult *civis sui iuris*.

Curatio of minors over 14 is an outcome of the Praetor's practice of refusing *Restitutio in integrum*, even where the minor's interests have clearly suffered, if the transaction had been gone through with independent advice. As a general institution of the law it is a novelty in the time of Gaius, and, owing to the defective state of his manuscript, we do not know what he had to say about it. Apparently in the classical law a minor who had received a *curator* on his application (for in general no one was bound to have a *curator*) could still act without him if he preferred to rely on the older system, though it is likely that *Restitutio in integrum* was less readily granted.

But under Diocletian a change was made: the acts of a minor who had a *curator* did not bind him unless the *curator* had assented, so that he was very like a person under *tutela.*

29. We have seen that the law of Persons as stated in the Institutes does not contemplate what are called Moral or Juristic Persons: the term Person is not used in a technical sense. Nor do the Roman jurists of any age speak anywhere of what are now called "juristic persons," by that name. But it must not be forgotten that they did recognise groups of persons as capable in their collective capacity of rights and duties, which were regarded as vesting in the body itself and not in its members[1]. They had what we call Corporations, and they called *Universitates,* of various kinds. The State, or *Populus,* itself according to Roman theory the necessary creator of all Corporations, is nevertheless a Corporation. It is, however, a Corporation, the importance of which lessens as the Emperor's ascendancy grows. On the other hand, there is nothing corporate about the Emperor's property, whether the *Privata Res Caesaris* or the *Patrimonium.* As to the *Fiscus,* the dominant opinion is that what are called fiscal rights are really the property of the Emperor, and have nothing corporate about them. But we cannot here enter on the question whether the *Fiscus* had or had not a juristic personality. If it had, the persistent usage of attributing the ownership of *res fiscales* to the Emperor may be explained as due to the fact that, as they were clearly not the property of the Roman people, there was no other way of finding any human being or beings who could be regarded as their owner. Lawyers of that age were certainly not able to take the step, of considering the property as belonging to the abstract fund itself, which is taken by modern German law.

Another important type of Corporation or *universitas* were the municipalities, the townships and colonies of various kinds, of which Roman legal theory required that the State should be the creator. It has, however, been observed that they must

[1] As to these cases, see Mitteis, Röm. Privatrecht, 1. 339 *sqq.*

have existed before the State itself, inasmuch as the Roman State was nothing but an expanded municipality.

In addition to these there were the various forms of *Collegium,* the religious *Sodalicia,* the craftsmen's Guilds, the burial clubs and friendly societies, and perhaps the *Societates Publicanorum.* But the questions to which of these, and when, and under what conditions, and to what extent, juristic personality was extended are much too controversial to be here considered.

It is perhaps hardly necessary to say that there is no warrant in the Roman texts for the view expressed by Austin that juristic personality was attributed to the *Praedium dominans* to which a praedial servitude was attached.

CHAPTER III

THE LAW OF THINGS. PROPERTY

30. THE *Ius quod ad Res pertinet* resembles Austin's Law of Things in that it contains the greater part of the law, but this is almost all their resemblance. The two schemes start from different points of view. The special effects of contracts by persons in exceptional positions, such as *filiifamilias*, are considered under this branch of law, while for Austin they are certainly matter for the Law of Persons[1]. The *Ius Rerum* is not that general part of the law which cannot be more conveniently treated in detached provisions. It is the law of *Patrimonium*, the discussion of all those rights known to the law, which are looked on as having a value capable of estimation in money—anything, as Dr Moyle says, by which one is actually or prospectively "better off," all these expressions being substantially equivalent. The rights which are incidentally mentioned under the Law of Persons do not constitute a difficulty, since they do not in general admit of estimation in money. A man may bring an action asserting or denying liberty, a father may "vindicate" a son, but there can be no question of damages in either case. The rights which owners and other persons can have in a slave are *dominium*, servitudes and the like, and are therefore part of the *Ius Rerum*. There is indeed somewhat more difficulty with respect to those rights which are incidentally discussed in connexion with the *Ius quod ad Actiones pertinet*. Besides pure procedure, this branch of the law contains discussion of some cases of obligation, of rights

[1] Austin, Jurisprudence, 2. 706.

of action as well as procedure in actions. Some of these, indeed most of them, are introduced merely incidentally as illustrating the form of action at the moment under discussion. This is plainly the case with those which are mentioned in the course of the explanation given by Gaius of *Actiones Fictitiae.* The same is evidently true of the *Actiones Adiectitiae Qualitatis* available against his master on a slave's contracts, as to which Gaius expressly says that he is compelled to discuss them because he has just had occasion to mention the *actio de peculio.* The reference which he mentions does not indeed survive, but it was doubtless in the course of the two now illegible pages, which occur a little earlier. The discussion of this first class of accessory actions brings with it, of course, that of the others, the various noxal actions. But all these accessory actions are discussed very fully, and not merely allusively, and the question arises why it appeared more convenient to discuss them here, rather than in connexion with the law of Obligations. This point will have to be considered later: here it is enough to say that the obvious affinity between the conception of an Obligation and that of an Action, especially where the obligation is a right of action, is one which has left many traces in the Sources, and renders transfers of this kind very intelligible.

31. A *Res* is hardly easier to define than is a Thing. Without attempting absolute precision, a task from which the Roman lawyers themselves would probably have shrunk, it may be said that, for the purposes of the *ius rerum*, a *Res* was an element in wealth, an asset, something which would appear on the credit side in a man's statement of affairs. Essentially it appears to be an economic conception. That is to say it is not only a different notion from the Austinian Thing, but it belongs to a wholly different range of ideas. For Austin a thing is apparently a purely physical conception. A thing, he says, is a permanent external object perceptible to the senses[1]. It is a material object, and it may be supposed that he is really thinking of objects over which there may be ownership. This

[1] Austin, Jurisprudence, 1. 368.

conception may have some utility in legal analysis, but it is of no help in the study of the Roman Law.

It would perhaps be more exact to say that this definition of a *Res* as an element of wealth is a definition of those *res* which the law was concerned with: the air and the sea are *res*, but they could hardly be assets. The important point is that it is economic, or legally guaranteeable, value which is present to the author of this classification.

32. Gaius and Justinian both begin their discussion with certain classifications of things, obviously not in any way confined to physical objects. The main classification is according to the rights which exist over them, the distinctions turning on the questions, how far, and by what manner of owner, they are owned. The writer is no doubt thinking primarily of physical objects, the rights over which depend somewhat on their actual nature. But rights of all kinds have their place in this scheme: an obligation or a servitude may be a *res universitatis*, as well as a piece of land. The other important classification is into *res corporales* and *res incorporales*, and here, subject to a certain confusion, it may be said that the classification is according to physical nature. Rights are *res incorporales*. Physical objects are *res corporales*. All rights are necessarily incorporeal: they cannot be made perceptible to the senses. But one right, and that the most important, is consistently treated as if it were corporeal. The writers do not indeed definitely say that ownership, or rather *dominium*, is a *res corporalis*, but they do not in terms distinguish between a physical object and the right of ownership of it. Thus what in the texts are called the modes of acquisition of *res corporales* are really modes of acquisition of *dominium*. In refusing to class *dominium* as a *res incorporalis*, they are merely adopting an inveterate habit of everyday speech which any one may observe for himself. In English law an Estate in Possession in a piece of land is called a corporeal hereditament. It may be added that, in Roman law, the usage is more or less justified by the fact that the word *habere* has a technical sense in which it means "to hold with title[1]," so that *fundum habere* and *dominium fundi habere* mean the same thing. Another aspect of this verbal confusion is seen in the Roman treatment of Possession, where the person who holds the object has a right less than *dominium, e.g.* usufruct. They say that *res incorporales* cannot be possessed, and the *usufructus* is a *res incorporalis.* Hence it follows, though the texts are not too clear on the matter, that a usufruct cannot be possessed, but is the subject only of *quasi possessio* or *possessio iuris*[2]. Yet what is possessed is clearly the physical thing. It may be that, as has been said, this is a device for reconciling independent possession, by the owner and the fructuary, with the principle that two persons cannot independently possess the thing *in solidum.* The question may be asked whether the inferior modes of ownership, bonitary ownership and the like were considered as *res corporales.* The answer seems to be that these different types of right are not considered in the Institutes as independent institutions at all. It will be remembered that the sources provide no name for them. They are protected by *actiones fictitiae,* and may best be described as states of fact which are treated by the help of fictions as if they amounted to *dominium.*

In describing *iura* as *res,* the lawyers do not distinguish between rights *in rem* and rights *in personam*: the right of usufruct and the rights resulting from a contract are alike *res.* It may, however, be well to note that the word *Ius,* standing alone, and used to mean right, not law, ordinarily means what we call *Ius in rem,* and especially *ius in rem* less than ownership, *e.g.* a servitude, or differing from ownership, *e.g. ius potestatis.* If a Roman lawyer speaks of a *ius* over property he practically never means ownership. If a man brings an action to recover property, his *formula* claims that the thing is his. If he is claiming a servitude he claims that he has such or such a *ius* over the land. It is not often that a right *in personam* is called a *ius*: we do indeed occasionally see such

[1] D. 45. 1. 38. 9.

[2] Gai. 4. 139; D. 4. 6. 23. 2; D. 41. 2. 12. *pr.*; D. 7. 6. 3.

an expression as *ius obligationis,* but never in the *formula* of an action, or in any context in which it is necessary to use exact language. This limitation of the conception of a *ius* as what we should call a *ius in rem* is well illustrated in certain rules as to the capacity of slaves. A slave could stipulate for his master, *i.e.*, for money or any other thing to be given to him for his master, but if he stipulated for a *ius* of any kind to be given to him, using the word *mihi,* this was literally impossible, since he could not have a *ius.* Accordingly the stipulation was invalid, unless the words were such that an untechnical sense could be put on them[1]. Justinian tells us in the Institutes that where a slave stipulates that he shall be allowed to cross a field, this is quite valid, but the words used say nothing about a *ius.* There is no servitude, but a mere contractual right. Such right as the contract creates vests, as all rights must, in his master. But what was contracted for was that the slave should be allowed to cross the field, so that the right which the master acquires is that the slave shall be allowed to cross the field: the master himself has no such power.

33. The *ius rerum* is treated under two main heads, the discussion of what moderns call *iura in rem,* including *universitates iuris,* being followed by that of *iura in personam,* called by the Romans *Obligatio.* Any exact logical arrangement of this kind is likely to be difficult of application to any actual legal system. The complexity of facts and resulting legal relations is so great that there will inevitably be found to exist rules which cannot conveniently be placed under either rubric. Austin found it necessary to make two other classes of rights, which he called less and more complex combinations of *iura in rem* and *iura in personam,* the former being such things as mortgage, the latter being *Universitates Iuris,* of which the *hereditas* may be taken as the type. He shews the insufficiency of the Roman arrangement, but the point of his criticism is somewhat blunted by the fact that he is compelled

[1] D. 45. 1. 38. 6–9.

to admit, in the same context, that it is impossible even on his own arrangement of the *Corpus Iuris* to observe with strictness the various distinctions on which it is based[1]. As to the Roman scheme, it must be admitted that the conception of *hereditas* as a unit—a *ius in rem* acquired by the act of entry, though it was evidently convenient—was a bold fiction without logical justification. It is, however, to be borne in mind that what is always present to those who speak of the *hereditas* as a unit is the *iura in rem* it contains. This fact is brought out in the rules of the *hereditatis petitio.* This was the action for the recovery of the *hereditas* or part of it, as such, and it lay in general only against persons who held it claiming to be *heredes*, or alleging no title at all, and only where what they held consisted of *iura in rem*, bits of property belonging to the estate. It is true that there was one exception to each of these limitations[2], but, without going into them in detail, it may be said that they are merely extensions on grounds of obvious convenience. The *hereditatis petitio* did not ordinarily lie for the recovery of debts, and there was no corresponding collective action for these. Separate actions must be brought for each of them.

Of what Austin calls the less complex combinations the only one which needs mention is Pledge. It is the practice of modern commentators to treat this as a *ius in rem,* since the possessory right is valid against third persons, and to give it a place with *emphyteusis* and *superficies,* as a *ius in rem* other than servitudes. Neither Gaius nor Justinian so deals with it. The reason seems to be that the pledge possessor can take no economic advantage from the thing. His wealth is not increased by it, though his security is. His right is nothing more than the right to retain or regain possession: this right is secured by the machinery of the Interdict, the *actio* Serviana, etc. and is rather matter for the law of actions. It may be added that the institution of pledge of a debt, recognised by the later

[1] Austin, Jurisprudence, 1. 44 *sqq.*

[2] D. 5. 3. 13. 4. *Utilis actio* against buyer of the whole *hereditas.* See also *h. l.* 13–15.

classical law, cannot well be brought under the rubric of *iura in rem*[1]. Modern English law has seen a considerable development of the doctrine that a *ius in personam* can generate a *ius in rem*. Thus a contract creates essentially a *ius in personam*, but there is a right against every one that he shall not induce the other party to break his contract. This idea is not prominent in Roman law, but there are signs of it. If A destroys a thing which B is bound by contract to give to C, so that B is released by *casus*, A is liable to an *actio doli*[2]. Altogether it is fairly clear that an exact division of the law under these two rubrics cannot be looked for.

34. *Dominium* is a conception which needs careful examination. The name is sometimes conveniently employed as a collective term, to cover all *iura in rem*, but this usage has little or no warranty in the texts. The sense in which we are here considering it, that in which the Romans ordinarily used it, is one of which Ownership is a rough translation. *Dominium* is commonly defined, by an expression which though not Roman is of respectable antiquity, as "*ius utendi, fruendi, abutendi*," the right of using, enjoying and destroying. Except that these words say nothing expressly about rights of alienation, they are a fair description of the rights of an unencumbered owner in possession, but a few obvious illustrations will shew that they do not in the least represent the Roman notion of *Dominium*. In the classical law, a man who had received a *res mancipi* by *Traditio* from the *dominus* had all the rights enumerated in the definition, but he was not *dominus*: he held the thing *in bonis*, but he had not *dominium*. In the same case the old owner had none of these rights, but he still had *dominium*. The underlying idea of *dominium* is akin to that of feudal lordship. It is that right over a thing, vested in a person who has *commercium*, which has no right behind it. However much of the material content of the right be cut away and transferred to other persons, so long as the *dominus* has not divested himself, or been in some way deprived of, the *nudum ius*

[1] D. 20. 1. 20.
[2] D. 4. 3. 18. 5.

Quiritium, he is still *dominus* of the thing. Even where someone else holds the thing in perpetual *emphyteusis*, so that the right of the owner is reduced to almost nothing, he is still *dominus*. The same idea may be expressed roughly, though perhaps not quite accurately in another way. To determine whether a person in actual enjoyment of a thing is its *dominus*, assume that he abandons it. If no one then has any claim on it, against a person without title who seizes it, the person who abandoned it, if a *civis*, was the *dominus*. In general the term *dominus* is not applied by the jurists to any person but the holder of the *dominium ex iure Quiritium*, the ultimate right. There are of course exceptions: the term is not always used in the strict sense. Gaius, in one or two texts, speaking of different kinds of owners, uses the word *dominos* to include them all. The holder *in bonis* is one of them. But he does not call the holder *in bonis*, *dominus*, or his holding *dominium*, though he has to use circuitous expressions to avoid doing so, and his sentences would run much more smoothly if he did. A good deal later there are enactments of Diocletian in which the name *dominus* is applied to the holder of provincial lands[1]. So, too, Justinian in abolishing the inferior varieties of ownership, speaks of the various cases as *differentiae inter dominos*[2]. But these texts are very few, and shew a laxity of usage corresponding to the decline in importance of civil law conceptions: they throw no doubt on the real classical usage of the word.

Short of this *Dominium* there were of course many inferior kinds of holding which were practically ownership, and were protected in their various ways. Such were the cases of ownership of *solum provinciale*, and of *ager vectigalis*, of ownership by peregrines, and, of far greater importance for the study of Gaius, the case of ownership of a *Res Mancipi*, acquired by *Traditio*. It may be worth noticing that so far as names go, we shall find no indication in the texts that these are cases of ownership: there is no substantive that expresses the right. Early commentators have indeed invented the name *Dominium Bonitarium*, which seems in strictness to be meant to apply

[1] *Frag. Vat.* 315, 316. [2] C. 7. 25. 1.

only to the last named but is sometimes extended to others: it is, however, obvious that there is nothing Roman about this expression. So far as names go, persons holding these rights are no more than possessors. In fact of course they are very different from possessors without title, since their rights have all the practical stability of ownership. But there is nothing but circumlocution and actual description of the rights to express the various differences.

35. Much the most important of these cases of inferior ownership is that of the person who has received a *res mancipi* from the owner by *traditio* merely, without the formal *mancipatio* which was necessary to the transfer of *dominium*. He is said *rem habere in bonis,* and it is a commonplace that he is as well protected as if he were the *dominus*. It is also a commonplace that a main part of his protection is the *Actio* Publiciana. Yet we are nowhere told in the Sources that this action was available to him. The case being obsolete in the time of Justinian, owing to the abolition both of formal conveyances and of all the distinctions between different kinds of ownership, we could not learn it from him, and we are not expressly told it by Gaius or in any other surviving classical text. There are, however, many texts from which this application of the *actio* Publiciana may be more or less safely inferred. Without discussing the various arguments which have been used in favour of one or the other opinion, we may say that there is now almost complete unanimity in favour of the view that the holder *in bonis* could use this action, though there are still many differences of opinion on the question whether the *formula* was the same in this case as in the case, to which we know that the action applied, of the *bona fide possessor*, *i.e.*, one who has received the thing in good faith, either with or without formal conveyance, from one who was not in fact its owner.

The working of the protection of the bonitary owner is in some of its details imperfectly known, but it is possible to give a general account of it. So long as the holder is in actual possession, it is plain that he cannot be effectively attacked by anyone but the *dominus* or someone claiming under him, assuming, that is, that the *dominus* had been at the time of the transfer in a position to give him a good title. If indeed there were an outstanding usufruct, or the property had been pledged by the *dominus*, the holder of the right could of course claim the thing from the bonitary owner, but he could have done so equally if there had been a formal conveyance, so that we need not consider that case. Apart from this, if anyone else claims the property from the bonitary owner, the claim must necessarily fail, since no other person can prove any title to the thing, and a claimant must prove his title. It follows that so long as he is in possession the bonitary owner needs no special protection against third persons. But the old owner, not having formally divested himself of *dominium* is still *dominus*, and is thus in a position to prove what the plaintiff in a real action has to prove, *i.e.*, that the thing is his *ex iure Quiritium*. This would be conclusive at civil law, but the Praetor's Edict comes to the relief of the bonitary owner. It gives him what is called the *Exceptio rei venditae et traditae*[1]. That is to say, he is allowed to plead that the plaintiff, or someone from whom the plaintiff derives his claim, has sold the thing to him and delivered it, and proof of this would amount to a complete defence. The exact wording of the *exceptio* is not known, though its name probably follows it fairly closely. It will be noticed that it speaks of sale, and no doubt at first it applied only to the case of sale, but in classical law it applied, *mutatis mutandis*, to gift as well, indeed to any case of transfer *ex iusta causa*. It is plain that this is complete defensive protection, at least where no claim but that of ownership is set up. But, as we have seen, the case is different if there is an outstanding *ius in rem*, *e.g.* usufruct. If it was created prior to the sale the holder will have no defence against a claimant who sets it up. The *exceptio* must be ineffective against one who does not claim under the vendor, or whose right was prior[2]. What is the position if the usufruct was created, as it might have been (since the transfer left the

[1] Lenel, Ed. Perp., 491. [2] D. 21. 3. 3.

vendor *dominus*), after the sale and delivery to the buyer? The case is not discussed, but it appears that the *exceptio* must have applied in this case, though no doubt with some change of form.

It might, however, happen that from some cause the holder lost actual possession. It might happen, for example, that during his absence some other person entered on the property, in good or bad faith, and refuses to give up possession. How is the bonitary owner to get it back? In some cases the interdict *Uti Possidetis* would serve his turn, but there are many cases of adverse possession which are not within the terms of that interdict. The bonitary owner is not *dominus*, and thus he cannot bring a *vindicatio*: he cannot allege, as a plaintiff in this action must, that the property is his *ex iure Quiritium*. Here too the Praetor comes to his relief by providing in his Edict an action called the *Actio* Publiciana, which serves his purpose equally well. This action is based on the fact that the bonitary owner whom we are considering will, in the ordinary course of things, become *dominus*, by lapse of time, by *Usucapio*, of which he satisfies all the requirements, since he holds the property *bona fide ex iusta causa*. The *actio* Publiciana is a *vindicatio*, so far modified in form that it directs the *iudex* to give judgment in favour of the plaintiff, if he would have been the owner had he held the property in question for the period of usucapion. It is presumed in his favour that the time of usucapion has run. This is all that is presumed: it is still for him to prove that he is *in via usucapiendi*. This he can readily do if, as will normally be the case, the thing is *habilis* and free from any *vitium*. It is an *actio fictitia* in which the claimant *fingitur anno possedisse*. This is not the same thing as saying that he is presumed to have acquired it by *usucapio*. Gaius does indeed once use unguarded language of this kind: he says, *fingitur usucepisse*, but usually he is more exact. It is obvious that such a fiction would leave the *iudex* nothing to try, for if, in a real action, we begin by presuming that the thing belongs to the plaintiff, there is nothing left to do but to give judgment in his favour. All that is presumed in the present case is lapse of time, which is conclusively presumed, and *bona fides*, which is always presumed, though of course the presumption may be rebutted. In our case, however, there can be no question of this, since on the facts there is obviously good faith. All the other requirements of *usucapio* the plaintiff has to prove. It is clear that with this action and the beforementioned *exceptio* the bonitary owner is sufficiently protected.

The *actio* Publiciana is also available, perhaps even primarily available, to a *bona fide possessor*, *i.e.*, one who has received the property in good faith from one whom he supposed to be capable of transferring the ownership to him, but who in fact was not so capable. It is clear, however, that his protection must be less complete. It is not the object of the Praetor to destroy the law of usucapion, or to prevent an owner from recovering his property. The *bona fide possessor* is not protected against the true owner, but only against third persons. Thus the *exceptio rei venditae et traditae,* which is useful only against the vendor or those claiming under him, has no application to this case. The mere *bona fide possessor* has the *actio* Publiciana against all but the true owner. Indeed he has it in a sense even against the owner, but the latter is allowed to plead in defence the *exceptio iusti dominii,* an allegation that he is the true owner of the property[1]. When we say that a *bona fide possessor* could bring this action we must remember that a *bona fide possessor* does not know that he is not the owner. As he thinks he is owner he will ordinarily bring *vindicatio.* It is only when this fails him, as he is shewn to have no title, that he will bring the *actio* Publiciana. For our purpose therefore, a *bona fide possessor* is one who is *in via usucapiendi,* as his possession began in good faith: it is immaterial that he has now discovered his mistake.

There is another point which must be made clear before the working of these proceedings can be understood. We must understand that when the parties come into court the Praetor, who has, in all probability, never heard of any of them before, cannot know, though he has to issue the *formula,* whether the claimant is a *bona fide possessor*, or a bonitary owner, or whether

[1] D. 6. 2. 16, 17.

the defendant is the *dominus* or not. He cannot without trying the whole case determine these points, and that is not his business. He cannot take their words for it, and, indeed, cases can be readily supposed in which the parties themselves do not know the true situation of affairs until the matter is thrashed out. Some of the facts might be known or admitted. Thus it might be admitted that the plaintiff was only a *bona fide possessor*, in the above sense, but the defendant's allegation that he was the *dominus* might be challenged. In such a case the formula would be easily drawn. It would run somewhat as follows, "If it appears that A.A. would be *dominus* if he had possessed for a year, then, unless it appears that N.N. is the *dominus*, condemn N.N.; if it does not appear, absolve N.N." This is of course an abbreviated form, but it gives the essential parts. We are told that the *exceptio iusti dominii* was given only "*causa cognita*[1]," *i.e.*, only after enquiry, and thus the Praetor would refuse it if he was satisfied that the defendant had sold and delivered the property to the plaintiff. There were other more complicated cases of which we shall have to make some mention, in which the Praetor would have to make some enquiry into the facts before issuing or refusing this *exceptio*. If all the material facts were disputed, as they well might be, the *formula* would run somewhat as follows: "Let T be *iudex*. If Aulus Agerius would be owner of the *Fundus* Cornelianus if he had held it for two years, then, unless it appears that Numerius Negidius is the *dominus*, and even then if it appears that Numerius Negidius or someone under whom he derives title sold and delivered the land to Aulus Agerius, condemn Numerius Negidius to pay the value, unless he restores the land at your discretion. If it does not so appear absolve Numerius Negidius." It will be seen that this *formula* submits the whole issue to the *iudex*, and if he decides the matter in accordance with these instructions, the result will be what has been laid down in the foregoing paragraphs as to the protection of the bonitary owner and the *bona fide possessor*. Some details are doubtful: it is not clear, for instance, that all

[1] D. 17. 1. 57.

the texts dealing with the *exceptio iusti dominii* are in accord —it may be that there were different views as to formulation[1].

36. Of the many complications which might occur, and the controversies to which they have given rise, we can indicate only a few, but some account of them is necessary to an understanding of the part played in legal life in Rome by this system of remedies.

It might happen that a bonitary owner or a *bona fide possessor* lost possession and the new possessor acquired the thing by usucapion. Was it still possible to bring the *Actio* Publiciana? It is clear that on the *formula* as we stated it, this might still be possible, for it might still be true that if the bonitary owner had possessed the property for a year, he would now be owner. But it is equally clear that to allow it would be to defeat justice and the general purpose of the action. As to what really happened there is little authority and much diversity of opinion. According to one view, the action is refused, or fails, because even though he had possessed for the necessary time he would not now be owner because there has been a transfer of *dominium* to another person. According to another view[2], the action is available in principle, but is rebutted by the *exceptio iusti dominii.* According to a third, the rule is as last stated, but only where the alienation has been involuntary. But there is no real difference of opinion as to the practical outcome.

One of the points which it is necessary to decide before forming an opinion in these questions is whether the possession which is pretended for the purpose of this action is to be dated forward from the *traditio,* or backward from the time when the action is brought. This point is material also in relation to another point. If a bonitary owner has once brought the *Actio* Publiciana successfully, and afterwards chances to lose the possession again, before he has completed his usucapion, there is of course nothing to prevent his bringing the action again, and as often as he needs it. But how does the matter stand in

[1] Appleton, Propriété Prétorienne, Ch. XVI.

[2] See D. 17. 1. 57.

the case of a *bona fide possessor?* If he has once brought the action and contemplates bringing it against a new disturber of his possession, and the possession which is feigned is dated back from the time of the action, then it is his new possession. But that did not begin *bona fide*, for when he acquired it he knew that he was not owner, or at any rate may have known it, for it is possible he may still have thought himself bonitary owner. But, apart from that case, he is not *in via usucapiendi*, for the texts are clear that a second possession begun in bad faith cannot be added to the first for the purpose of usucapion. On that reasoning he cannot again bring the *Actio* Publiciana. But there is a good deal of controversy as to these questions[1].

It may well be that two persons are each entitled to the *Actio* Publiciana. It may happen, for instance, that a bonitary owner has lent the thing to the *dominus*, who dies, and whose *heres* sells and delivers the thing to a third person. Difficult questions may arise as to which of these is entitled to the action against the other. If one is a bonitary owner, and the other a mere *bona fide* possessor, the law is clear: the former will win both as plaintiff and defendant, though in the last case the form of his defence is not known. If both are *bona fide* possessors the texts are not clear, but it seems that if they had both received the thing from the same non-owning vendor, the first to receive *traditio* would prevail, but if they had received it from different non-owners, then the actual possessor. In the case given above to illustrate the possibility of a double claim, both were bonitary owners, for the *heres* being *dominus* could make a good conveyance. Here it was held that the first vendee could recover it from the other[2].

There is some reason to think that this bonitary ownership became very common in the Empire, and that *traditio* practically superseded *mancipatio*, at least in the transfer of moveable *res mancipi*, long before Justinian. There are records of sales of slaves about A.D. 150, and again about A.D. 350. The former are nearly all by *mancipatio*; the case in which it was by *traditio*

[1] See Appleton, *op. cit.*, Ch. XV. *in fin.*

[2] See Appleton, *op. cit.*, Ch. XVII.; D. 6. 2. 9. 4; D. 19. 1. 31. 2.

occurred in Asia Minor. The case at the later date was by *traditio*, but it is possible the parties were not *cives*[1]. It appears, however, that in case of land, the fact that in *mancipatio* it was not necessary to go to the spot, as it was in the case of *traditio*, led to the retention of the more formal mode of conveyance, at least till the fifth century.

It has been observed that there is nothing in the *formula* of the *Actio* Publiciana to confine it to the bonitary owner and the *bona fide* possessor, and there is some evidence of its extension in a modified form to the holders of provincial land[2]. But there is nothing to prevent its use by one who is in fact *dominus*, and the view has been suggested that in the later Empire it practically superseded the ordinary *vindicatio*. But the evidence is all against this opinion. In all the texts in which its use is noted the time of usucapion has not yet run, and the absence of reference to it in the Code, together with the prominence of *vindicatio*, and the language of some of the texts, has led to the more general acceptance of the opinion that it was used in practice only where the period of usucapion had not yet run, and therefore only in a very small percentage of the cases of litigation. Its chief advantage over *vindicatio* on the same set of facts would be that there was no need to prove that time had run, and further, that, though, as in *vindicatio*, the plaintiff would have to prove conveyance to him, still, evidence that the conveyance was not by the true owner would not of itself be necessarily fatal, as it would, apart from usucapion, in a *vindicatio*. It is only in a very small percentage of cases that these points would be material, and this it is which accounts for the fact that the practitioners have little to say about this action.

37. It has hitherto been assumed that the case in which the *Actio* Publiciana lay was one of *traditio* of a *res mancipi*, specifically. But there are many other cases in which a holder under a praetorian title will become *dominus* by usucapion, so that his remedy in the meantime may be the *Actio* Publiciana. Such are the cases of the *Bonorum Emptor*, in bankruptcy, of

[1] Bruns, Fontes Iuris, 1. 329, 366. [2] D. 6. 2. 12. 2.

the *Bonorum Possessor*, and of the person to whom an inheritance has been handed over under a *fideicommissum*. In the first of these cases it is not unlikely that he actually had the *Actio* Publiciana, if the thing had actually been handed over to him so that he was *in via usucapiendi*, but it is not anywhere so said. In the case of the other two it is clear that they had other special remedies, so that they did not need it. On the other hand, some writers have found ground for applying the *Actio* Publiciana to cases other than ownership, for instance to cases of rustic praedial servitudes, but there is little or no real evidence upon this point.

The holding of provincial land is not *dominium*, but it is a form of ownership. Apparently the action available to the holders of such land, to recover it from persons who have entered on it, is a modified form of *vindicatio*, in which the words *eius esse ex iure Quiritium* are replaced by *habere possidere frui licere* or the like. And of course as such persons are at least possessors, they will have in appropriate cases the possessory interdicts. It is also said, in one text, that an *actio* Publiciana is available under the principles of *longi temporis praescriptio*, but there is some reason to suspect this text of having been tampered with by Tribonian[1].

Ownership by *peregrini* may be regarded as another instance of ownership short of *dominium*. It is clear that *peregrini* too had a modified form of *vindicatio*, but it is impossible to say in what the modification consisted, though, as they had not *commercium*, they certainly could not allege *dominium ex iure Quiritium*. It is plain that their ownership of *res nec mancipi* was not in any practical way inferior. In relation to *res mancipi*, there are several questions of some interest to which the texts give us no answer. If a *peregrinus* has received a *res mancipi* from the *dominus* by mere *traditio*, the fact that it is a *res mancipi* is, so far as the *peregrinus* is concerned, quite immaterial. It is impossible for him to become owner of it by usucapion, since he is not capable of civil ownership. If, after having held the thing for three years, he now sells and delivers

[1] D. 6. 2. 12. 2. See Girard, Manuel (4) 352.

it to a *civis* the question arises, who is now the *dominus?* If we may apply the rules of *accessio temporis*, and allow the citizen buyer to add his vendor's time to his own, the *dominium* will, on the facts we have supposed, pass instantly from the old *dominus* to the acquirer from the peregrine, and if the peregrine has held it for less than the necessary time, the period of *usucapio* for the buyer from him will be shortened. In any case the buyer will usucapt in the ordinary way. It is obvious that inconveniences would result from the fact that the purchaser of a *res mancipi* from a peregrine would never be at once *dominus ex iure Quiritium*. He might want to buy and free a certain slave, but he could not do so, at least so as to make the man a *civis* (even on the assumption that he could add the two possessions together), without knowing the past history of the man. There is indeed another possible way out of the difficulty. It is at least possible that a *res mancipi* loses its special character when it gets into the ownership of a peregrine. It has been pointed out that there are two texts[1], which strongly suggest that this was so, that is to say, that as between *cives* and *peregrini* the distinction between *res mancipi* and *res nec mancipi* disappeared. The two texts are not however conclusive, and if they are so regarded, they give the unlikely result that the forms of *mancipatio* could be evaded, for example, in a remote place where *cives* were few, by using a peregrine as an *interposita persona*. The *civis*, wishing to convey Quiritarian ownership to another *civis*, could convey the thing to a peregrine, who would in turn convey it to the other *civis*. It would be easy, by appropriate agreements, to avoid the difficulties which would result as to liabilities for defect of title, and so forth. But all this is little more than guesswork.

38. No topic in the Roman law has been the subject of so much controversy as that of possession. It is easy enough to give a rough description of the conception. A man "possesses" if he is in actual control of the thing, if he "has"

[1] Ulp. *Reg.* 1. 16; *Frag. Vat.* 47 a.

it, whether he has any title to it or not. If I am walking along the street with my watch in my pocket, I possess it. If, now, I drop it, and some person sees it in the road, picks it up, and keeps it, I no longer possess it, though of course I am still owner: it still belongs to me. It is my watch, but it is in the finder's possession. From rough description of this sort to exact definition is, however, a long step, and before attempting to indicate some of the ways in which that step has been made, or attempted, it seems best to consider the legal importance which attaches to the position of a "possessor." Its chief legal importance is that a person who has possession, whether he has any legal title or not, and subject to some reservations for the case of one whose possession is tainted by certain forms of wrongdoing, has the protection of what are called the possessory interdicts.

Leaving out of account for the present some distinctions and difficulties in the working of the system, we may say that the general principle of these remedies is that a man who has actual possession has a right not to be disturbed in his possession, whether he has a title or not, except by legal process. Even the owner may not take away the thing from the possessor, though there is nothing to prevent his bringing a *vindicatio* for his property and recovering it by that means. If I am in occupation of a house, which in fact belongs to you, and you eject me by force, I shall be able by means of a possessory interdict to compel you to give it back to me, and you will not be allowed to plead, in reply to my claim, that you are the real owner. But it will now be open to you to do what you ought to have done in the first instance, that is, to bring a *vindicatio*, as a result of which, if you succeed in proving your title, I shall be finally compelled to give the house back to you.

The question why the owner was not allowed to plead and prove his title in reply to the interdict itself will be more conveniently considered later: of the question why mere possession was protected at all, it is enough to say[1] that

[1] Girard, Manuel (4) 267.

according to one view the object is the protection of a person with no title against others who have no better, while according to another the real principle is that a peaceful possessor usually is entitled, and that, by enabling him to recover by merely proving the fact of possession, the law is, or assumes that it is, in the majority of cases enabling an owner to recover his property from an aggressor without putting him to the trouble and expense of proving his title. From this point of view, possession has been called an outwork of property. If in some cases the effect is to give protection to a wrongful possessor against the owner, this is an accidental result, and can be adjusted by later proceedings. Whether it is in fact true that a peaceful possessor is more likely to be in the right than his disturber is a question too speculative for us to consider[1], and a negative answer would shew, not that this is not the Roman theory, but only that they agreed on a false theory.

Not everyone whose position agrees with the rough description of possession above set forth has possession for the purposes of the protection here set forth. We have no difficulty in seeing that my guest at my table has not possession of the cutlery he is using, or that my servants have not possession of the implements they are using. The possession, in such cases, of course remains with me. But the Roman law goes much further. A *commodatarius*, a depositee, a tradesman to whom an article has been sent for repair—none of these has possession. And there is the further difficulty already adverted to that where the holder has a civil law *ius in rem* less than ownership, he is held not to have possession, but only quasi-possession or *possessio iuris*. The confusion of thought which seems to underlie this has already been adverted to: it is more curious than important, for the usufructuary was protected in his holding[2], without proof of title, exactly like a possessor.

Those persons who, though they hold the thing, have not possession for the present purpose, are said to have *possessio naturalis* (*detentio*, though a convenient expression, has little

[1] Holmes, The Common Law, 208. [2] *Frag. Vat.* 90.

textual authority), the proper name for such possession as gives interdictal protection being *possessio civilis*, though the word *possessio* standing alone is commonly used to denote this, which may be called interdict possession. A slight confusion is caused by the fact that the expression *possessio civilis* is also sometimes, but rarely, used to denote such possession as will ripen by usucapion to ownership[1], which may be called usucapion possession, that is to say, possession with *iusta causa*, *bona fides*, and so forth. But for our present purpose this sense of the expression may be safely disregarded.

39. The question what is the exact definition of possession to give the results here very briefly outlined is one of extreme difficulty. It may be, indeed, that no answer is possible. Among the classical jurists, in whose writings if anywhere the solution is to be found, it is plain that there were differences of opinion on a great many fundamental points, and there is none on which difference of opinion is more easily conceivable than on this delicate question of the exact definition of possession. Examination of the texts on some points of detail suggests that the same jurist does not always speak in the same voice on this matter, a thing readily conceivable when we remember that the lawyers do not in every case go back to first principles, and that it is very much more important to have a good practical set of rules than to have one which is logically impeccable. Many attempts however have been made to answer the question[2], and of these two have received so much more attention than any of the others that a very short account of them must be given.

Of these opinions that associated with the name of Savigny[3] was the earlier, and may be said to have been accepted almost universally till recently, and perhaps to be still the more widely held. According to this view, which rests mainly on words of Paul, in which he alludes to, and argues from *animus possidentis*[4], possession consists of physical control, together with the

[1] D. 43. 16. 1. 9. *Cf. h. l.* 10.
[2] See Windscheid, Lehrbuch, § 148, n. *.
[3] Savigny, Recht des Besitzes.
[4] D. 13. 7. 37; D. 41. 2. 1. 20.

intention to hold as one's own: *detentio* with *animus habendi*, or *animus domini*. This is plainly lacking in the cases of *detentio* which we have mentioned, and in the cases of usufruct and the like which gave only quasi-possession. If we find nevertheless that possession is attributed to *emphyteuta* and to pledgee, who clearly do not claim to hold the thing as their own, but recognise an ownership in another person, this, says Savigny, is a case of derivative possession. Later writers have avoided the difficulty thus created by adhering to the expression *animus possidendi*, and speaking of intention to hold the thing to the exclusion of anyone else, a way of putting the matter which still enables them to retain Savigny's theory. The fact that a depositee does not possess even though he has made up his mind to keep the thing is explained from this point of view, on textual authority, as resting on the principle: *nemo potest causam possessionis mutare*[1]. The initial *animus* is decisive.

This view of the matter was strongly attacked by Ihering. It is impossible to go into detail on his criticism, but it must suffice to say that, while he draws attention to the fact that the theory does not explain certain concrete cases, such as that of the continued possession of a fugitive slave, his chief attack is directed on the conception of the *animus domini*. He observes that it rests entirely on certain texts of Paul, in which he expresses and argues from the idea that for possession an *animus possidendi* is needed. He maintains that this is an opinion peculiar to Paul. No other jurist, he holds, gives any support to this "subjective" theory, which makes the answer to the question, possession or no possession, depend on the state of intention on the part of the holder. He shews the unpractical nature of the idea, and the impossibility of proof. He points out that this impossibility, coupled with the rule that a man cannot change his *causa possessionis*, has driven later supporters of the subjective theory to look at the *causa* for proof of the intention, in such a way as to give a practical result which does not greatly differ from that arrived at by

[1] See, *e.g.*, 41. 2. 3. 19.

those who look for their test in external circumstances alone. But their false theory leads them, according to him, to self-contradictory conclusions on points of detail.

Ihering's own theory[1] defines possession as the externals of ownership. A man possesses who is, in relation to the thing, in that position in which an owner of such a thing ordinarily is, the *animus possidendi* being practically an intelligent cognisance of the fact. This is, in effect, an external fact, for this sort of *animus* practically proves itself. He shews that the physical relation is not absolutely decisive. Whether, in given circumstances, a man possesses a certain thing or not, may depend on the nature of the thing concerned. Thus, I possess my carriage if it is standing at the side of the road by my house, but I should not be in possession of my watch if it was lying in the gutter at the same point. All the cases of *possessio naturalis* Ihering treats as states of fact in which the law has, for reasons which differ widely in the different cases, definitely taken away possession from persons who satisfy the requirements of the theory.

40. Besides the controversies as to the reasons why possession as such was protected, and as to the exact nature of the possession which was protected, there has been much discussion of another question, *i.e.*, whether possession is a mere fact or a right. The texts are not very helpful; at any rate they do not speak clearly in either sense. While there are many texts which speak of possession as a mere *res facti*[2], there are at least as many which speak of it as a right[3]. Perhaps the true solution is that the two propositions are not really in conflict. It is plain that, on Savigny's theory, the question whether possession exists or not is one of pure fact, and this is equally true of Ihering's. It is only to rebut inferences drawn from the fact of possession that questions of law are material. On the other hand, it is equally plain that possession is a right, a provisional right indeed, but, so far as

[1] Ihering, Grund des Besitzesschutzes; Besitzwille.

[2] *e.g.*, D. 41. 2. 1. 3, 4.

[3] *e.g.*, D. 41. 2. 49. *pr.*

it goes, a right, a right *in rem*, the right to protection by the possessory interdicts. The elements that go to make up possession are a set of facts: the resulting position is a right in the possessor.

This matter is bound up with a somewhat more difficult and important question. In almost all modern treatises the topic of possession is dealt with in close connexion with that of ownership, and, at least from some points of view, the connexion is obvious. Possession, regarded as a right, is certainly a *ius in rem*. It is therefore reasonable to discuss it in close connexion with other *iura in rem*, and since many of the inferior modes of ownership are called *possessio*, so far as they are given a substantive name at all, it seems the most natural course to discuss *possessio* in connexion with ownership. In fact, though nothing can be clearer than the distinction between *dominium* and *possessio*, yet if we examine the different kinds of protected holding, we can make a sort of descending scale, with *dominium* at civil law at one end, and *possessio ad interdicta* at the other, and find it very difficult indeed to say where there is a distinct break. The truth is that the line must come either immediately above interdict possession or immediately below civil law *dominium*, and the latter is really the right point. For *dominium* differs in character from all these other rights: it is the ultimate right, and it is a *res corporalis*, which none of the others really is. Nevertheless it is necessary also to draw a line immediately above interdict possession. For the right here is purely provisional, and if there are cases in which the decision under a possessory interdict is in effect final, *e.g.* where the winner happens to be owner, or a *bonorum possessor cum re* succeeds in *Quorum Bonorum*, this is not due to the possessory remedy itself, but to extraneous circumstances.

When we turn to the Roman institutional writers we shall find that they do not deal with possession, as such, anywhere in connexion with *dominium*. They deal with it wholly in connexion with interdictal procedure. Thus Gaius, in Book II, discusses *dominium* and some inferior modes of ownership, but says nothing about *possessio* except allusively, in the sections dealing with persons through whom we can acquire. Even *bona fide possessio*, which is sometimes regarded as a form of relative ownership, is only mentioned as a mode of acquisition of *dominium* over fruits, and in the same region possession comes in as one of the elements of usucapion. At first sight the method of the Digest seems in sharp contrast. The title which deals with modes of acquisition of ownership is immediately followed by a title which deals with the modes of acquisition and loss of possession[1]. But, as the immediately following titles shew, this is due to the fact that possession is a most important factor in the law of usucapion, and in this title it is considered as an introduction to the discussion of that subject, with which the titles that follow are concerned.

41. The truth seems to be that though the jurists do occasionally speak of *ius pignoris*, and the like, they do not in general regard possession as a *ius in re aliena*, a *ius* in the sense in which servitudes were *iura*. The reason for this is presumably, that if one does begin to discuss possession as a *ius*, the first discovery made is that there is nothing to be said. It is a *ius* with none but a procedural content. All the rights regarded as *iura* give some kind or other of rights of enjoyment. The holder of them can in some way or other draw profit out of the thing. But a mere possessor as such cannot: all he has is a remedy if he loses possession, and a defence if his possession is attacked in certain ways. Thus it is not surprising, in view of their conception of an action, that the jurists held this to be a topic for the *ius quod ad actiones pertinet*, and say all that they have to say there, in connexion with interdicts. Thus *possessio* is not mentioned in any of the lists of *res incorporales*. It does not appear ever to be called a *res*, and it may be doubted if the classical lawyers would have thought it one. This way of looking at the matter finds some support from the treatment of pledge in the institutional

[1] D. 41. 1; 41. 2.

books. We know that pledge gives possession, even more than possession, for the pledge creditor will defeat the owner even if the latter vindicates the property. The pledgee has even an action *in rem* of his own. Accordingly it is commonly treated, in modern books, as one of the *iura in re aliena* other than servitudes, along with *emphyteusis* and *superficies*. But neither Gaius nor Justinian so deals with it. Pledge as a contract is treated in Book III: the possessory right is discussed in the treatment of interdicts. Pledge gives no right to profit and has no place in the scheme of *Res*. We hear nothing of loss of rights by pledgee by non-use. In a text dealing with another matter the remark is made, *nullum enim est pignus cuius persecutio denegatur*, while the same text remarks that a usufruct, the claim for which is barred by the same facts, still exists till it has been lost by non-use[1]. This sharp distinction seems to turn wholly on the fact that a *pignus* has no content except its enforceability: it is a matter for the law of actions. This is not to say that possession has no value. It is of the utmost importance from a procedural point of view, and there are many texts which shew it to have a value estimable in money[2], though the estimation must have been difficult. All that is meant is that, notwithstanding its economic value, the considerations above mentioned prevented the jurists from contemplating *possessio*, in general, as a *res*.

42. All the modes of acquisition of Ownership enumerated by Gaius, and by Justinian (with the possible exception of Donatio), contain, not necessarily delivery, but some act or circumstance shewing actual control of the thing acquired. This is obviously true of the cases of transfer—the so-called Derivative modes of acquisition. But it is not less true of *Occupatio*, or of *Accessio* and *Specificatio* which are closely akin thereto. The modes are classified by Gaius as being based on

[1] D. 9. 4. 27.

[2] D. 4. 2. 21. 2; D. 43. 17. 3. 11. See Ihering, Grund des Besitzesschutzes, § VI.

either the *ius civile* or the *ius naturale.* By this distinction he appears to mean that some modes are conceived of as peculiar to Rome, while the others are regarded as universal. If, however, we look at the concrete cases we can see what at least look like inconsistencies. Usucapion and *Thesauri Inventio* are alike in that the principle of each of them is universal, while the details are in each case governed by Roman Statutes. Yet Usucapion is treated as *iuris civilis,* and *Thesauri Inventio* as *iuris naturalis.* The point is that Usucapion is treated in the XII Tables, and no doubt all the civil law methods of Gaius are so classed because they belong to the old formal law. Justinian, in the Institutes, adopts the same classification, and in a text in the Digest, which is attributed to another work of Gaius, the *iure naturali* methods are alternatively described as *iure gentium*[1]. It is probable that this identification is not due to Gaius, but to Justinian, borrowing perhaps from some late classical jurist. The text goes on to attribute to Gaius views which are certainly not his. He is made to say that, as the *ius gentium* is older than the *ius civile,* it is right to begin with the older forms. Upon this matter, it must suffice, without discussing the truth of the proposition, as to relative antiquity, with all the controversies connected with the expression *ius gentium,* to remark that the order here indicated is precisely that which Gaius does not adopt and Justinian does.

With the exception of *Traditio,* none of the *iure naturali* methods of acquisition is of much practical importance in everyday life. *Occupatio,* not being derivative, but original, is treated as the primary mode, and the others have, or most of them have, a close affinity with it. Thus, in *Specificatio*—the acquisition by creation of a *nova species* out of the materials of another person—the Proculians attribute ownership to the maker precisely because he has created and "occupied" the new thing in question. In *Thesauri inventio,* there being no trace of earlier ownership, the case is essentially one of regulated *occupatio,* and in *fructuum separatio* and *perceptio* the

[1] D. 41. 1. 1. *pr.*

idea of *occupatio* of a new thing is not far off, though it would hardly be correct to speak of the case as one of *occupatio*. *Alluvio*, and the arising of an island in a river, are mere applications of the rule that what is attached essentially to my soil vests in or accrues to it, assisted by the circumstance that on the facts there is no previous ownership to be considered. The same rule is also illustrated by the principle applied in the case of a measurable piece of land deposited by the force of a stream on my land. This becomes mine when by the rooting of trees it has become essentially one with it. It is also negatively illustrated by the rule that an island arising in the sea (*quod raro accidit*) belongs to no one, and vests in an "occupier." The riparian owner owns the soil of the river to the middle, and an island on his side is part of his land. But no one owns the soil under the sea. The cases of *accessio* in the case of buildings are applications of the same notion, and their apparent complication is due in part to the fact that questions of compensation are discussed in connexion with the question of ownership, and in part to the somewhat metaphysical distinction between ownership of the house and latent ownership of the materials of which it is made, capable of becoming effective if they are separated. As to *accessio* of moveables to moveables, since it is in general excluded whether the things united are readily separable or not, it can occur only where the one thing is accessory or subordinate to the other, and the only question in any case is the not very important or interesting question of fact whether in the given case it is an accessory or not.

The texts in the Institutes which deal with these various modes of acquisition confine themselves in general to the bare question: who is owner? They do not discuss the important question of compensation: that is matter for the law of obligation, and treatment of it would be out of place in the law of ownership. It must not be forgotten that compensation was in general obtainable. The reason why it is discussed in connexion with certain cases of *accessio* in which buildings are concerned seems to be that in most of these the compensation may have, as an alternative, or as an accompaniment, a restitution of the thing itself. Space is lacking for a full statement of these rules, but two points may be mentioned. Where *A* builds on his own land with *B*'s materials, *B*'s right to double damages is inaccurately stated in the Institutes: it arises only where the materials have been actually stolen by some one, not necessarily the person who used them: it must be a *tignum furtivum*[1]. Where *A* builds on *B*'s land with his own materials, and is still in possession, the texts distinguish according as he was in good or bad faith. The point of time considered is that at which he built, not that at which he acquired possession of the land.

43. The rules of *Traditio* are fairly simple. The various forms which it may take, actual or approximate delivery, and *Traditio brevi manu, longa manu,* all have the common quality which is the only essential external characteristic of *Traditio*: they are the actual giving of control over the thing to the acquirer. They are more than expressions of intent. They are realisations of the intent, and thus it is important to note that in approximate delivery there is nothing symbolic. The key, for instance, of the warehouse in which the goods are stored, handed over on the spot, is not a symbol of control: it is the actual means of control. It may be worth while to point out that *Traditio brevi manu* and what has been called *Constitutum possessorium* are converse expressions of the same idea. In the first case the holder of a thing acquires possession of it and therewith ownership, by the assent of the owner, who was, till this assent was given, in technical possession of the thing. In the second case, the vendor of a thing, who is by agreement to retain it as hirer, ceases, by the agreement, to possess, and becomes a mere *detentor*[2]. In each case the form of delivery and redelivery is dispensed with on obvious grounds, and they are not to be regarded as inroads on the principle that *Traditio* needs delivery. It may also be worth while to add that the essential of *Traditio* is transfer of control, rather than transfer

[1] D. 47. 3. 1. [2] D. 41. 2. 18. *pr.*

of *possessio*, and that cases may be conceived in which there has been a valid *Traditio*, though technically *possessio* has not yet passed. Thus where property has been conveyed to a slave by *traditio*, the master becomes owner at once, though it is well known that he does not technically "possess" what has been put into the hands of his slave unless and until he knows of it, leaving out of account the case of previous authorisation[1].

The rules that *Traditio* requires mutual intent directed to the transfer of ownership, and that there must be a *iusta causa*, are not really distinct, and do not appear to be so stated in the sources. *Justa causa* is not a requirement independent of intent: it is the external circumstance from which this intent will be inferred. No other evidence of it is required or is in any ordinary case likely to be forthcoming. It is this character of *iusta causa* which explains two of the most striking rules. Putative *causa* was sufficient, for, if there was supposed to be a legacy or sale, and thereupon the delivery took place, the evidence of intent would be clear enough, though in fact there was no such legacy or sale as was supposed. Again, we are told that if the parties have different *causae* in view, the deliverer, for instance, thinking it is a *mutuum*, and the receiver taking the thing as a gift, or *vice versa*, there is a valid *Traditio*, since on the facts the intent to transfer is clear[2]. We must note that there is no difficulty in adjusting the matter. The only immediate point is that there is a valid transfer. If the transferor thought that he was handing over the thing under a binding contract of sale, he has a *condictio indebiti* to recover it. If the error was the other way, there is no injustice to set right. On the other hand, if the circumstances shewed an error which negatived the intention to transfer, the *Traditio* was void, as, *e.g.*, if the transferor did not know that he was owner, and was acting as agent for another, or if he was mistaken as to the identity of what he was

[1] *Post*, § 56.

[2] D. 41. 1. 36. Julian. Ulpian, however, is inclined to think there is no transfer of ownership. D. 12. 1. 18. *pr*.

transferring[1]. But discussion of this last rule would lead us into difficulties.

Traditio might be conditional, and ownership would not pass till the condition was satisfied, and in case of sale there was the further tacit condition, based on the XII Tables, that the ownership could not pass, in the absence of special agreement, till the price was paid. Resolutive conditions, *i.e.* that the conveyance was to operate at once, but was to be void if a certain event happened, were not possible till the time of Justinian. Till then, any such agreement would not operate to devest the property *ipso facto* on the occurrence of the event, but would only give a right of action for reconveyance, useless against third parties[2]. Similarly, apart from certain special rules in the case of slaves[3], any undertaking as to what was to be done with the thing had in general only contractual force. And it must be remembered that the *Fiducia* of which we shall have to say something in connexion with *Mancipatio* could not be used in a case of *Traditio*.

44. Usucapion is the Civil law form of acquisition through long possession. Its principle is perfectly simple, but its applications bristle with difficulties. It must first be observed that the rules of usucapion are quite independent of the law as to limitation of actions by lapse of time. It is a definite "mode of acquisition." When a man has acquired property by usucapion he is *dominus* of it, and though his usucapion may in some cases be undone, there is never any question of his having become owner as against Titius, but not as against Balbus. The periods in which ownership can be acquired in this way are surprisingly short, one year for moveables, two for immoveables. This is intelligible in a small and primitive community, but the retention of these periods after Rome had become a State with wide territories is remarkable. No doubt the requirements of initial good faith and *iusta causa* were juristic inventions to prevent the injustice which must frequently have resulted from the earlier state of the law,

[1] D. 41. 2. 34. *pr.* [2] C. 8. 54. 3. [3] *Post*, § 52.

and these, coupled with the power of rescission in certain cases of absence, made the rule a workable one. But that it was not wholly satisfactory is shewn by the fact that all the later ancillary systems of *praescriptio* provided for considerably longer terms.

The general rule was that *bona fides* was necessary at the time when the possession began. We know from Gaius that there were several cases in which, for various reasons, good faith was not required. The case of *usucapio pro herede* is too familiar to need discussion, and that of the acquirer from an adult woman is simple. But the other cases, those of *usureceptio ex fiducia* and *ex praediatura* are remarkable. Why did the old rule survive in these cases, for that is, no doubt, what happened? We must not think of a special concession. The one case is that of *fiducia*, either to a creditor, the debt being still unpaid, and the creditor not assenting, or to a friend: the other is that of property pledged to the State by a *Praes* or surety for a contractor with the State, and sold by the State. In the last case the ordinary periods are necessary, while in the case of *fiducia* one year suffices even for land. Nothing is known about the matter and it is useless to guess, but the last-mentioned difference suggests that in the case of *fiducia* the origin is pontifical and wholly different from that of the other.

But Gaius does not tell us what it is worth while to point out, that there were certain cases in which the requirements as to good faith were considerably extended. We know that besides good faith there had also to be *iusta causa* or *iustus titulus*, that is to say, the possession must have originated in some external fact which is ordinarily a basis of acquisition. These various *causae*, sale, legacy, gift and the like, had their own detailed rules and differences. In the case of usucapion resting on sale, as it is technically called, *usucapio pro emptore*, we are told that good faith was needed, not only at the time of the delivery as in all other cases, but also at the time when the contract of sale was made[1]. The reason is not certainly known,

[1] D. 41. 4. 2. *pr.*

but what seems the most probable view is that the rule dates from a time when in the ordinary way the two events would occur simultaneously. This view finds some confirmation in the fact that the words in the Publician Edict are *qui bona fide emit*[1], a form which brings out the same point, since it ignores the moment of *traditio*. In fact the frequent use of the word *emere* to signify "acquire" indicates the same thing. But many views are held on the matter.

In the case of *usucapio pro donato*, and indeed in all lucrative usucapion, that is, where the acquisition is pure profit, there is some reason to think that, before Justinian, the requirement was even more severe. He lays it down in one passage that even in *usucapio lucrativa* supervening bad faith is not for the future to be a bar to usucapion, and he uses somewhat similar language elsewhere[2]. Again, the *Basilica*[3] contain this text last mentioned, indicating that there is a difference in the rules applied in the case of gift and in that of purchase, since a donee must have good faith throughout the period of usucapion. The rule is there stated in reference to a particular case, but there seems to be no reason to doubt that it is intended to be general, though in the *Basilica*, compiled long after Justinian's changes, it is a complete anachronism. It must, however, be admitted that many modern writers doubt the inference which these texts so plainly suggest.

45. There is another rule in the law of usucapion which has given rise to much discussion. It is the rule that there must be a real *iusta causa*—a putative *iusta causa* does not suffice. If I seek to acquire *pro soluto*, there must have been an actual debt: it is not enough that I thought at the time of the delivery that there was one. If a thing was lost and I found it, and kept it, thinking it had been abandoned, I could not acquire it by *usucapio pro derelicto*[4]. If, on the other hand, Titius, thinking a thing to be his own, while it in fact belonged to Balbus, threw it away, and I picked it up, it is not mine

[1] D. 6. 2. 7. 11.
[2] C. 7. 31. 1. 3; D. 6. 2. 11. 3.
[3] Bas. 15. 2. 11.
[4] D. 41. 7. 6.

because it has not been abandoned by the owner, but I can acquire it *pro derelicto*[1]. But the rule that a putative *causa* does not suffice is not without exceptions, and it is in connexion with these that it has been found difficult to get at a principle. The texts which refer to it are very few, and leave room for much speculation. Perhaps the most probable view is that the earlier lawyers were in disagreement on the question whether a real *causa* was necessary or not, as indeed is easily proved by the texts, and that Julian caused the adoption of a middle view, according to which putative *causa* sufficed where, though there was no real *causa*, the circumstances were such as would have led a reasonable man to suppose a real *causa* to exist, and the acquirer did in fact so suppose. But even if this be adopted (and very different and more elaborate explanations have been given[2]) it will still be uncertain whether the relaxation was absolutely general, or whether it was not in effect confined to acquisition under sale, *usucapio pro emptore*, and perhaps even here only when the transaction or supposed transaction was through a slave or other agent. But the whole matter is extremely controversial.

It will be observed that though *traditio* and *usucapio* both need a *iusta causa*, these *iustae causae* are not the same thing. Thus if I hand over to you a thing of mine, believing I owe it to you under a contract of sale, and there has been in fact no sale, the *traditio* will transfer the ownership. I can, no doubt, bring an action claiming reconveyance, a *condictio indebiti*, but in the meantime the thing is yours. If however the thing had not been mine, then, although we both thought it was, you will not acquire it by usucapion. There was only a putative *causa*. The *iusta causa traditionis* is no more than any circumstance evidencing intention to transfer. The *iusta causa* or *iustus titulus* of usucapion was, at least in the settled doctrine of the later classics, some actual juristic fact which is ordinarily a basis of transfer.

As has been said above, usucapion is Acquisitive or Positive: the possessor becomes owner. The system of *longi temporis*

[1] D. *h. t.* 4. [2] See, *e.g.*, Esmein, Mélanges, 202 *sqq*.

praescriptio as formulated by the Edict was not acquisitive: it was extinctive or negative. All that lapse of time did was to bar the claim of the old owner. If he brought an action claiming the property as his, by the modified *vindicatio* which we have seen to be available to the owner of provincial land, the plea of lapse of time would bar his action. But the person who has held the property for ten years is not owner. What then is his position if from any cause he happens to lose possession? It would seem that at first he was, so far as proprietary remedies are concerned, unprotected by the law. But this gives a very false view of his position. He was of course a possessor, and thus the provisional protection of the interdicts was at his service. Again there is a text which definitely states that a modified form of the *actio* Publiciana was available to him, even before the time had expired, though this text is not free from suspicion[1]. In any case it is clear that, before Justinian, some form of modified *vindicatio* had been extended to holders of provincial lands[2]. It is likely that this applied to one who claimed by long possession as well as to one who had received a grant of it. Of course in his day the distinctions are gone, and usucapion and prescription are one system.

Usucapion has been spoken of as creative of ownership, but it must be remembered that until the passing of a certain *lex* Scribonia servitudes could be acquired thereby. After the passing of this statute, of which the date is uncertain, they could be acquired by Praetorian prescription by quasi-possession for ten or twenty years[3].

46. The process of *Mancipatio*, as recorded, has a strange look to modern eyes. Gaius gives us the typical form, but it is clear that the actual words used—the *nuncupatio*—differed in the different cases. Thus Gaius gives us a very different form for the *mancipatio familiae* in the mancipatory will, and the words must have been different again in the sale of a son into bondage. We are told expressly that *coemptio* was a

[1] D. 6. 2. 12. 2. See Girard, Manuel (4) 352.

[2] *Frag. Vat.* 314, 315.

[3] Moyle, Instit., ad Inst. 2. 3. 4.

modified form of *mancipatio*. The first thing that strikes us is that very little is done by the transferor. So far as we can learn from Gaius, the words are all spoken by the acquirer: the alienator does nothing but receive the *aes* which represents the price. Much the same thing is found in *Cessio in Iure*. It is odd to find the binding act proceeding not from the party who transfers, but from the acquirer. It has, however, been pointed out that this is in keeping with the general attitude of Roman law, which makes the initiative always fall to the acquirer. A still more striking case is that of release *per aes et libram*, in which the words of release are said by the debtor. He releases himself from the obligation. It may be noted, however, that in the *mancipatio familiae*, the form is different: in that case the transferor, the testator, also speaks. Indeed it has been contended that in the ordinary *mancipatio* the transferor did in fact say something, but there is little real evidence for this.

Still more remarkable, at least at first sight, is the apparent illogicality in the formula pronounced. There is an opening statement that the thing belongs to the acquirer: "I declare this thing to be mine by Quiritarian right." This statement is not true at the time at which it is made, and the inaccuracy is brought out by the words which follow, which speak of the acquisition as an effect now to be produced. It is quite conceivable that the property may never pass at all, for, as we know, it is essential, apart from express agreement, that the price should be paid. The apparent contradiction can be got rid of by treating the whole formula as parts of an individual whole, but even so, it seems somewhat remarkable that the assertion of ownership did not come last. The actual position of the assertion has been explained as being due to the fact that the assertion of ownership was originally the whole formula, the statement of sale and payment being a later accretion. This view it is difficult, though perhaps not impossible, to conciliate with the fact that there is at least one case, *mancipatio familiae*, in which this assertion of ownership does not occur at all. It should be added that the difficulty in treating the matter as one transaction is lessened, if we read, in Gaius, *emptus est* instead of *emptus esto*. A passage in the Vatican Fragments (which also gives only this member) and one in Boethius, quoting Gaius, do so give it[1]. But Gaius, the earliest and best authority, gives us *esto* twice, and so describes the course of the proceeding as to make this the only admissible form, if his account is otherwise correct.

It will be observed that the words of the assertion of ownership are identical with those of *cessio in iure*. There they are correct, for the essence of the transaction is a fiction that the thing belongs to the claimant. There is nothing to suggest any fiction as designed here, and there are cases of *mancipatio* in which this assertion does not occur at all. Thus in the Vatican Fragments we have parts of both forms, and in *mancipatio* the writer inserts only the second member, while, what is still more surprising, he puts in that part the clause of *deductio* where the vendor is reserving a usufruct. One would have thought that this would have occurred in the assertion of the extent of his right if this assertion occurred in the form. Again, in the form in which Gaius gives us the *mancipatio familiae* in the mancipatory will, the assertion of ownership does not occur, though editors shew inclination to insert it[2]. The truth is that it would serve no purpose here, but its absence is rather against the idea that the first member is the essential part of the mancipation. It seems to be now most generally held that this solemn assertion of ownership served a specific purpose which would not always be in view, an opinion not inconsistent with either view as to the original constitution of the formula. The XII Tables shew that an acquirer of property had a remedy in early law, if, through some defect in title, the thing which he received was taken from him before he could acquire it by usucapion. The vendor, or *auctor*, was bound to pay him compensation in such an event, to the extent of double the price, the obligation being enforced by an action supposed to have been called the *actio auctoritatis*. It is thought

[1] *Frag. Vat.* 50; Boethius, *In Top.* Ciceronis, 5. 28 (*lib.* 3).

[2] See the note to G. 2. 104 in Krueger's text.

that this declaration was essential to place the vendor under this obligation, a view which would account for the fact that it did not occur in *mancipatio familiae*, where there could be no question of a guaranty, or, as we know it, of a transfer of *dominium*. In course of time the obligation became dissociated from the form: it became usual to make an express stipulation, and as a further development this stipulation came to be taken for granted. But many traces of the old *actio auctoritatis* have been found in the Digest, and the association with *mancipatio* is still evidenced by some of the recorded *mancipationes* which we possess[1]. Where the *dominium* did pass, but with no real price, and thus no real guaranty, as in cases of gift or *fiducia*, the price was usually declared as *nummus unus*. It may be presumed that an ordinary *mancipatio*, in its second member, actually stated the price, though Gaius does not say so.

The other details of the form have but little legal interest, though there is no doubt history behind them. The *antestator*, who is mentioned in some allusions has been explained in many ways, but seems now to be clearly identified so far as mancipatory wills are concerned with the first or chief of the five witnesses. It has, however, been remarked that while this is no doubt true of the *antestator* in the mancipatory will there are extant documents in which there is an *antestator* who is not one of the five witnesses. The suggestion is made that he is in fact a figure added in later law to make up the number of seven witnesses, which figures so frequently and increasingly in the classical and later period[2]. These witnesses no doubt represent the Roman people, but though the number of them has been commonly explained as due to a representation of the five Servian classes, this is no more than a mere guess. It has been objected to on various grounds, but it must be confessed that the arguments against the hypothesis are little stronger than those in favour of it[3].

It may be worth while to point out that delivery forms no

[1] Bruns, Fontes Iuris, 1. 329.

[2] Kniep, Gai Institutionum, I. 207 *sqq*.

[3] See Girard, Manuel (4) 285.

part of *mancipatio*: the transaction is complete even though the thing remains in the possession of the mancipator. He has ceased to own, though he still possesses. Accordingly, *mancipatio*, when it is applied to a *res nec mancipi*, is probably a mere nullity. If the thing is in fact handed over the *traditio* is the conveyance, the *mancipatio* being mere surplusage. There are, however, differences of opinion on this matter. The point that delivery is not essential to conveyance by *mancipatio* is well illustrated by the rules applied under the *lex* Cincia. We know that a promise to give is not binding if it exceeds a certain amount, but that if the gift has been carried out, it cannot be recalled. If a man has promised a gift of land in excess of the legal limit, and has actually mancipated it, but still retains the possession of it, the ownership of it has passed, but if the donee brings a *vindicatio* for it he can be met by the *exceptio legis* Cinciae. If the actual delivery had also been made there would have been no means of getting it back[1].

In the process of mancipation the acquirer, during the declaration, has his hand on the thing. Thus the element of control is present, but it is clear that by the time of the classical lawyers this has become, at least in the case of land, no more than symbolic, if even that. It need not be done on the land. It is for this reason that *mancipatio* remained in use for the alienation of land after it had been superseded by *traditio* in practice for moveables. Perhaps a turf was present, though even that is not certain.

47. *Mancipatio* with a trust appended, *mancipatio cum fiducia*, must at one time have played a very important part in everyday life, far more important than would appear from the present state of the texts. We can see it indeed in operation in connexion with *coemptio fiduciae causa*, in adoption and emancipation, and in *tutela fiduciaria*. These were living institutions in the time of Gaius, but most of its applications in the law of things were then obsolete or obsolescent. The

[1] *Frag. Vat.* 293.

transactions which we know as the contracts of *commodatum* and deposit were unquestionably effected originally by a *mancipatio cum fiducia*, a transfer of ownership with a trust for reconveyance. There is evidence that the same is true for *donatio mortis causa*, and there are other possible applications of *mancipatio cum fiducia, cum amico. Mancipatio cum fiducia, cum creditore*, a conveyance to the creditor on trust for reconveyance when the debt is paid, is a very well-known institution: it is only gradually superseded by the informal *pignus*, and it appears to have been in full vigour up to the time of the later classical jurists[1].

There are a number of highly controversial questions in connexion with this institution, but they cannot be considered here. It must suffice to indicate one or two main principles. The first point to observe is that this so-called trust has no force against third persons: it is a purely contractual matter. If the friend or creditor transfers the ownership to a third person in breach of his trust, the old owner has no remedy at all against the third person: his remedy is solely against his faithless trustee. This remedy is, at least in those cases which are concerned with the *ius rerum*, an *actio fiduciae*, but there are some indications which have led to the opinion that in those cases which belong to the *ius personarum*, the *actio fiduciae* was not available, but the only remedy was direct coercion by the praetor[2]. It is at least true to say that we cannot safely infer an *actio fiduciae* wherever in the law of persons we find an allusion to *fiducia*. The fiduciary clause was not embodied in the *nuncupatio* of the *mancipatio*: it was a separate and subsequent informal agreement, though it is clear that the *nuncupatio* might itself advert to the fiduciary nature of the transaction[3]. The actionability of the *pactum fiduciae* is of much later development: there is reason to think that it is subsequent to the establishment of the Formulary system.

We have been considering *Fiducia* in connexion with

[1] See Girard, Manuel (4) 518.

[2] See, however, Bechmann, Kauf, 1. 285; Pernice, Labeo, 3. 122 *sqq.*

[3] Bruns, Fontes, 1. 332.

mancipatio alone, but it must not be forgotten that it was equally applicable to *cessio in iure.* If we do not find much reference to it under that head, this is probably due to the fact that *cessio in iure* was never, at least so far as can be proved, at all a usual method of transfer of *dominium* in individual things. Its main applications, as known to us, are not transfers of *dominium* of specific things, but of rights and duties, and groups of rights and duties which are incapable of *mancipatio* or *traditio.*

48. The aspect of *Cessio in iure* is that of litigation, and it is commonly spoken of as a case of fictitious litigation. The view has however recently been propounded that it is not litigation even in form, but from the beginning an avowed act of conveyance confirmed by the praetor. The *Addictio* which it contains does not occur in a *vindicatio* by *Legis Actio* where the claim is admitted: in fact the whole theory of *confessio in iure* has been declared to have no application at all to a *legis actio in rem.* According to this view, the *addictio* by the praetor is an official adhesion to, and confirmation of, a transaction which is essentially *inter partes.* But this matter is much too controversial to be considered here[1].

Whether the process is properly called fictitious litigation or not, it is clearly modelled on the form of a *legis actio per sacramentum*, and borrows from that source some of its characteristics. Some of the rules which are given in the texts suggest interesting questions from this point of view. It is a familiar idea that a judgment is binding and conclusive as between the parties. We regard it indeed as the most binding of all obligations, and if we wish to speak of an obligation as perfectly binding we are apt to say that it is as binding as a judgment. The classical Roman law shews the same habit of thought. *Res iudicata pro veritate accipitur*, they say, and, *confessus pro iudicato est*[2]. But the Romans like ourselves consider a judgment as a matter *inter partes*, having no effect, in ordinary cases, on the rights

[1] Wlassak, Zeitsch. der Sav. Stift. 25. 102 *sqq.*
[2] D. 1. 5. 25; D. 42. 2. 1; P. *Sent.* 5. 5a. 2.

of independent third parties. There are however a number of rules in connexion with *Cessio in iure* which raise questions as to the extent of the binding force of such a transaction. A few of them are worth our consideration. In the *cessio in iure* which constituted the last step in *Adoptio*, and also in the case of manumission *Vindicta*, essentially a *cessio in iure*, the right acquired by the person to whom the *cessio in iure* was made was quite different from that lost by the *in iure cedens*, a state of things not easy to reconcile logically with the view that *cessio in iure* is essentially a pure conveyance. If a *tutor cessicius* attempted to cede his *tutela* to another, the effect, according to Ulpian, was to end it and to cause the *tutela* to revert to the *tutor legitimus*[1]. Here too it is hardly treated purely as a conveyance, for an attempted alienation which fails merely because of the inalienability of the subject-matter is not an abandonment. Nor is it treated exactly as a judgment, for as such it would presumably have covered all the right of the *cedens*, and the right could not have reverted. It is clear that some effect is attributed to the solemnity itself. But if we look at another similar case we shall see still more difficulty in regarding it as a judgment. If a *heres legitimus* attempted after entry to cede the *hereditas*, the *cessio* failed as to debts due either to or by the estate, obligations being intransferable. But debtors to the estate were released. If we treat this as purely matter of alienation, we have the same difficulty as in the last case. If we regard it as a judgment, we have the anomaly that a judgment to which they were not parties releases the debtors. The Proculians thought that the same result followed where a *necessarius heres* made *cessio* of the *hereditas*, but the Sabinians considered that in this case no effect at all was produced on the debts, or indeed on the property. Here it is clear that the Proculians do not regard the case as one of abandonment, as we know that they did not regard abandonment as complete until some third party had taken advantage of it. On that view it would obviously be open to the *heres* to reclaim his right[2]. The Sabinian distinction

[1] Ulp. *Reg.* 11. 7. [2] D. 41. 7. 2. 1.

between this case and the last presumably turns on the view that a *necessarius heres* cannot by any act of his, however formal, in any way divest himself of any part of his attributes as *heres*. If we turn to *cessio in iure* of a usufruct to a third person, we find a similar conflict, but here it is between two Sabinians, Gaius who holds that the *cessio in iure* is a nullity, and Pomponius who tells us that the effect is to cause the usufruct to revert to the *dominus*.

Whatever view we may take of these conflicts, it seems safe to say that some jurists, perhaps at one time all jurists, attributed a special force which is not exactly that of judgment to the solemn *addictio* by the praetor, but that there was a steadily increasing tendency in the classical age to treat the matter as purely one of conveyance.

If it may be doubted whether the function of the praetor in *cessio in iure* is to make or merely to confirm the transfer, or neither, there is no doubt that in *adiudicatio* the conveyance is the act of the *iudex* concerned, though in this case it is not the magistrate himself, but a *iudex privatus*, who derives his authority from a *formula* issued by the praetor. It is his *adiudicatio* which creates the title to the property. No actual instance of this has been preserved, so that we do not know the actual form. It had only three applications and it probably was not a very common event.

49. The other modes of acquisition *iure civili*, such as *Lex* (which is not really a mode of acquisition at all, but only a collective term to include all cases in which the destination of property is regulated by specific statutes) and *Ius accrescendi*, which occurred only in the rare case of formal manumission of a common slave by one owner without the consent of the other (the *ius accrescendi* of the law of succession having no bearing on the present point), must have been of small practical importance. Of direct grant by the State nothing need be said.

Donatio is mentioned by Justinian, though not by Gaius, as a civil mode of acquisition. We shall have later occasion to consider why it is so treated by Justinian, notwithstanding that it is in ordinary cases not a mode of acquisition but merely a *causa traditionis.* For the present only a few other points need to be considered.

We are accustomed to think of *donatio* as a gratuitous transfer or promise to transfer property. But it may take quite other forms. It may be for instance the undertaking of a liability or the release of a claim, and the application of the principles of the institution to some of these cases is of considerable difficulty.

Donatio mortis causa is essentially a gift subject to express revocation and to implied revocation in the event of the survival by the donor of the prospect of death in view of which it is made, or, apart from this, by the pre-decease of the donee. Either of these may be expressly excluded, but if they are all excluded, the gift is not *mortis causa* in the technical sense. It may be made under a suspensive condition, *i.e.* the right whatever it may be is not to pass unless and until the death occurs. In that case the act is merely a nullity if the conditions of the gift do not arise. But there are cases in which this is impossible: there could not be, for instance, a suspensive condition on a *mancipatio* of land (though it must be admitted that if the condition were tacit there are, at least, some doubts about this). More frequently the gift was to be definitive at once, but to be null if the conditions failed. But it must be remembered that in classical law there could be no such thing as a transfer of ownership, or creation of an obligation, *ad tempus*: the act was not void, but there was a right to set it aside, a *condictio,* in case of transfer of *dominium* or the giving of a valuable security of any kind or of the release of an obligation. If the gift had been of such a nature as to give a right of action against the donor, there would be an *exceptio* in the same event. Under Justinian however it is clear that the mere non-occurrence of the death at the time or under the conditions contemplated, or express revocation, revested the ownership in the donor, so that he could bring a real action for the recovery of his property.

Donatio inter vivos is never of itself a mode of conveyance. It is a state of mind, previously declared or not, amounting to a *iusta causa traditionis*, *i.e.* enough to account for the *traditio*, to prove the existence of intention to transfer. It differs from *Donatio mortis causa* in that it is ordinarily irrevocable, except for ingratitude, and though it may be conditional, it is not necessarily so. The only point we need consider is that of restrictions on amount. In later law, gifts exceeding a certain amount (varied from time to time) were, with some exceptions, void as to any excess, unless they were registered. Not only could a promise (or the pact which sufficed under Justinian) not be enforced as to the excess, but even if the gift had been carried out the transfer was void as to the excess, so that the donor was joint owner of the whole fund or property. These rules seem to have replaced those of the *lex* Cincia. This was a very early statute, which also established a maximum, and provided that a gift in excess of this maximum could not be enforced against the donor, though, at least in later law, the *heres* had not the same defence—*Cincia morte removetur*.

The defence therefore is ineffective unless the circumstances compel the donee to take steps against the donor for the completion of the gift. A few illustrations may shew how this worked. If land had been mancipated and handed over, nothing could be done. But if there had been no delivery, though there had been *mancipatio*, the ownership had indeed passed, but if the donee sued for the land he would be met by the *exceptio*. If moveables had been transferred, however completely, it was possible for the donor, on the principles of the interdict *Utrubi*, so long as he could still plead that he had possessed the thing for a longer time than the donee in the past year, to recover the possession. If he did so, and having recovered the possession, was sued on the gift, he could use the *exceptio*. If there was a promise, not yet fulfilled, the *exceptio* was of course available, and we are told that even if it had been carried out there was a *condictio*, probably, though this is not certain, only where the payment was in error. These rules are contained in the Vatican

Fragments[1]: other texts, in the Digest[2], and therefore less trustworthy, since the institution was obsolete, and they may have been altered to suit the system of registration, give a similar *condictio* where the gift took the form of a discharge of debt by *acceptilatio*, or an assumption of liability on the donee's behalf, by *novatio* (*delegatio*). But these cases are disputed.

50. There is a well-known rule that *dominia rerum traditionibus et usucapionibus non nudis pactis transferuntur*[3]. That is to say: mere agreement is not enough to transfer a *ius in rem*. This can create only *obligatio*: there must also be an act of conveyance, of which *Traditio* is the type. This rule requiring an overt act demonstrating the transfer is not peculiar to Roman law, and needs no explanation. It may be noticed that in strictness it applied only to transactions *inter vivos*: at death all sorts of interests are transferred by nothing but a formal expression of intention, though this may be in part due to the origin of the later will in the *Mancipatio Familiae*. But even *inter vivos* the rule has a certain number of real or apparent exceptions, of which the most important are these:

(*a*) *Traditio brevi manu* and the so-called *Constitutum Possessorium*. As has been observed above[4], these are in essence the same. The idle double *traditio* is waived. There is in fact a transfer of possession, apart from the transfer of ownership, and transfer of possession is all that is needed to satisfy the principle, so that this is not a real exception.

(*b*) *Hypotheca*. Here we are told that the right *in rem* of the creditor arises by the mere agreement, but this exception, too, is only apparent. We have seen already that, from a Roman point of view, the merely possessory right which is all that the creditor gets, is not classed with the *iura* which are discussed under the head of Property or *Dominium* in a wide sense,

[1] *Vat. Frag.* 260 *sqq.*

[2] D. 44. 4. 5. 5; D. 39. 5. 21. 1. See Girard, Manuel (4) 937. See also Accarias, Précis, § 303.

[3] C. 2. 3. 20.

[4] *Ante*, § 43.

and are the subject of this rule. It is treated in the law of actions.

(*c*) *Societas omnium bonorum.* The mere agreement vests in all the partners in common the ownership of the property of each of the members of the firm. This rule constitutes a real exception, and it presents difficulties which will have to be considered later in connexion with the law of contract[1]. For the present it is enough to say that the curious rule no doubt has its origin in the ancient system of *consortium* among *coheredes*, from which this form of association in all probability descends.

(*d*) *Donatio mortis causa.* In the time of Justinian, if such a *donatio* was made on the terms that ownership passed at once on delivery, but the conveyance was to be void if the donee died before the donor, then, if the event so happened, the donor could bring a *vindicatio* for the property. That is to say, the *dominium* revested in him without any *traditio* or other form of reconveyance. That is a clear exception, but it is entirely unknown to the classical law. If the transaction is regarded as a gift *ad tempus*, or subject to a resolutive condition, that is still equally unclassical: in whatever way the rule is looked at, it evidently belongs to Justinian's way of thought. The Digest however provides us with another case of much greater difficulty. There is a text which tells us that there are certain cases in which *dominium* is acquired by *donatio mortis causa*, and couples this with legacy[2]. This is a remarkable proposition. The text must be interpolated, since it is certain that the agreement to give never transferred *dominium* in classical times. Even in the time of Justinian nearly every text which deals with *donatio mortis causa* assumes, or states, a delivery. Opinion has been a good deal divided as to whether this is a mere mistake of Justinian's, or whether, in his time, the mere agreement to give, *mortis causa*, transferred *dominium* without *traditio*. There is a provision in the Code[3] which has been adduced as supplying the answer to the question. In this text Justinian prescribes a form for *donatio mortis causa*

[1] *Post*, § 124. [2] D. 6. 2. 2. [3] C. 8. 56. 4.

if it exceeds a certain amount, which is, in fact, precisely the same as that for written *codicilli*, and he adds that gifts made in this form are to have all the effects of legacies. One of these effects is, as we know, the transfer of ownership on death without any delivery. Hence we can deduce the rule that, in the time of Justinian, a *donatio mortis causa*, if made in a particular form, transferred ownership on the death of the donor without any delivery, being in fact hardly distinguishable from a *fideicommissum*, which at that time did the same. It has been suggested that this not only explains the text under discussion, but also accounts for Justinian's treatment of *donatio* as a mode of acquisition, which it ordinarily is not, since in all *donatio inter vivos*, and in all *donatio mortis causa* which is not in the above-mentioned form, the *donatio* itself is not the transfer, but nothing more than a *iusta causa traditionis*. However, so far as his motive is concerned, a probable explanation is that he so treats it merely as a convenient way of grouping together the rather numerous rules which refer to gratuitous alienations, whatever their form.

(*e*) Creation of certain servitudes. There are a number of texts of later law which tell us that servitudes could be created by stipulation and by pact and stipulation[1], and there are others which speak of them as created by *quasi traditio*[2]. We are also told by Gaius that in the provinces, where the land had not italic right, and civil modes of conveyance were not applicable, servitudes, or rather quasi-servitudes, were created by pact and stipulation. The original form of these agreements seems to have been an informal agreement—a *pactum*—containing the terms of the right intended to be created, followed by a stipulation for a penalty to be paid in the event of failure to allow the servitude to be enjoyed. In later times however the usual form seems to have been a single stipulation embodying the terms: the difference, which turns it seems on the freer use of stipulation for promises other than those of money, is indifferent for our purpose. If the mere agreement was itself

[1] *e.g.*, D. 7. 1. 3. *pr.*

[2] *e.g.*, D. 8. 1. 20.

enough to create the servitude, how are we to account for the texts which mention and seem to require *quasi traditio*, a process much more troublesome in itself, inasmuch as it requires the parties to go to the spot? One view is that the two institutions were entirely independent, that the system of pact and stipulation is carried over through the praetor to the civil law, just as *hypotheca* and some other institutions of the same type were. *Quasi traditio*, on the other hand, is also an introduction of the praetor, being an extension of *traditio* analogous to the extension of *longi temporis possessio* to servitudes in the form of *longi temporis quasi possessio*[1]. But in reply to this it has been contended that the acquisition of *iura in rem* by pacts and stipulations, being strikingly abnormal, would have been more specifically emphasised if it had been admitted, and that the texts which speak of it are too loosely expressed. This however is hard to accept in view of the fact that these texts are not merely allusive, but purport to state the mode of creation expressly. It should be noted that there are many servitudes in relation to which *quasi traditio* is inconceivable. In any negative servitude there is no step which can amount to *quasi traditio*—no act which can be done, so as to amount to a demonstration of beginning of enjoyment. In a servitude *non altius tollendi* the agreement not to build is all the *quasi traditio* of which the facts admit. The indistinguishable fact of not doing anything contrary to the servitude is hardly capable of being regarded as *quasi traditio*. The rule may possibly therefore have been that servitudes were created by stipulation, followed in the case of positive servitudes by *quasi traditio*, an actual beginning of enjoyment, and in negative servitudes by nothing but *patientia*. But the whole question is still very controversial.

51. It may be convenient to group together at this point some subsidiary rules affecting transfers of property. It has already been pointed out that neither *cessio in iure* nor *mancipatio* admitted of express conditions: they were *actus legitimi*

[1] See Girard, Manuel (4) 372, 373.

which were totally avoided by the addition of any such thing. The same may be said of *dies*: such an act could not be expressly made to operate only on a future day, certain or uncertain. As to tacit conditions there is somewhat more difficulty. In the case of *cessio in iure* it is not easy to imagine such a thing. Of course the conveyance was ineffective if the transferor had no right in the thing, but the question may be asked whether the *cessio* was in a real sense tacitly conditional on his acquiring a right. What would happen if a *cessio in iure* was made by one who had no title but, after the *cessio*, became *heres* to the true owner? From the fact that in the case of *traditio* by a non-owner who afterwards acquires title there is no transfer of ownership under Justinian, though nothing would be easier than to imply such a condition in *traditio*, it seems certain that the *cessio in iure* would be a nullity, especially as some of the texts which lay down the rule were written of *mancipatio* or *cessio in iure*. It is true that they give the holder bonitary ownership, but this is due to the fact that there has been a delivery[1]: it does not appear that the *cessio* as such would have produced any effect.

There is some difficulty in the case of *mancipatio*. There is one clear case of a tacit condition which did not apply to *cessio in iure*: the XII Tables provide that in Sale the transfer of ownership is, apart from special agreement, conditional on payment of the price. Apart from this there are texts which are commonly understood to shew that tacit conditions were possible[2]. Discussion of these texts would carry us too far: it must suffice to say that neither affords any direct evidence and that the most important, that which says that an *acceptilatio* of a conditional debt is tacitly suspended till the debt has become simple, gives, if applied to *mancipatio*, results inconsistent with the conclusions drawn from the texts above cited. It would at least give the result that if land had been left to me under a condition I could mancipate it before the condition was satisfied.

It is on the other hand clear that there was no difficulty in

[1] D. 6. 1. 72; D. 21. 2. 17, *etc.*

[2] D. 50. 17. 77; *Vat. Frag.* 329.

applying *conditio* and *dies* to *traditio*, and on the other hand that a resolutive condition or a *dies ad quem* was quite impossible in any case until the time of Justinian.

The topic of error in connexion with transfers of property is somewhat intractable. There is little direct authority, and such as there is refers to *traditio*, while it is by no means clear that civil law methods would be covered by the same principle. We have seen that where there was intent to convey, but the parties had different *causae* in mind, there was disagreement as to the validity of the *traditio*[1], but it may be taken for granted that in *mancipatio* or *cessio in iure*, such error was immaterial, so far as the passing of property was concerned. Where a man conveyed property, which was in fact his own, but he was acting as agent for the supposed owner, the better view is that the *dominium* did not pass[2], but this kind of case could not occur in *mancipatio* or *cessio in iure*. Where there was mistake as to the identity of the property transferred, which might easily occur in *traditio brevi* or *longa manu*, there was no transfer[3], but it by no means follows that this would also be the case in *mancipatio* of land at a distance. It is generally held that in these ancient formal transactions the form was everything and that the intent of the parties may well have been immaterial[4]. Thus it seems that a manumission *vindicta* by one who did not know that he was owner was valid[5]. *Traditio* where there was a mistake as to the nature of the transaction, and no intent to transfer ownership at all was void, but, here too, it is doubtful if the same rule is to be applied to the formal methods.

52. It is this conception of *dominium*, as unlimited and illimitable, which made it impossible for a vendor of land to impose restrictions on dealings with the property, outside the region of servitudes. There was of course no difficulty in imposing such restrictions as a matter of contract, but any breach of the contract would not itself be a void act or annul

[1] *Ante*, § 43.
[2] D. 41. 1. 35: *cf.* D. 17. 1. 49.
[3] D. 41. 2. 34. *pr.*
[4] See P. *Sent.* 1. 7. 6, 8; G. 4. 177.
[5] D. 40. 2. 4. 1.

the conveyance: it would give only a right of action for damages. It is true that in the case of sales of slaves it was possible to impose restrictions which operated *in rem*, for instance, that the slave should be kept away from Rome, or should or should not be freed[1]. These were effective *in rem*: in some cases the attempted breach was simply a nullity, in others the act of breach vested the slave in the original transferor, but all these cases are exceptional, and have no bearing on the general law. Thus it was not possible to prevent alienation by imposing a prohibition as one of the terms of the sale. Here too however Justinian may have altered the law: there are two texts which as they stand shew clearly that a conveyance with a prohibition of alienation operated to annul any attempted sale by the transferee, though not by his successors[2]. It is also clear that Justinian allowed resolutive conditions, so that, on this view, it was possible in his time to transfer property with a condition that the transfer should be void if there was any attempt to alienate.

The desire to keep property together which causes the imposition of such restrictions had not much encouragement in Roman Law, so far as conveyances *inter vivos* were concerned. Beyond creating a usufruct, which was essentially inalienable, there was not much that a settlor of property could do. It was not possible to settle property, for instance on a marriage, so as to keep it in the family. The case was somewhat different in the law of wills, as we shall see later, but *inter vivos* there was no such power. On the other hand the recorded documents and inscriptions leave no doubt of the frequency of gifts which are difficult to reconcile with this[3]. It was a very common thing to establish, *inter vivos*, funds for charitable or public purposes which were intended to be perpetual, and some of which unquestionably had a considerable permanence. There were several ways of effecting this object. One way was to

[1] D. 18. 7. 6, 9; D. 40. 1. 20. 2.

[2] D. 20. 5. 7. 2; C. 4. 51. 7. But most writers refuse, for various reasons, to accept the texts as expressing the law.

[3] The following remarks are from Pernice, Labeo, 3. 150 *sqq*.

contract with a transferee under heavy penalties that he would in his will devote the property to the desired object and would impose *fideicommissa* in turn on his successors. This brought the resources of the law of wills to the help of the living settlor, and it was equally applicable to public purposes and to the private purpose of keeping the property in the family. But it is precarious, since it ultimately rests only on contract. Another way was to vest the property in a *collegium*, who were to distribute the property as directed. But here too there was no effect *in rem*. If at a later date the *collegium* made away with the fund, it was difficult to find a remedy. The most effective way seems to have been to transfer the property to a municipality, with directions as to what is to be done with the proceeds, and, in some cases, a gift over to some other body if the directions are not obeyed. Neither the gift over, nor indeed the directions, could have any force in strict law, though so far as the directions were concerned it might have been possible to provide for them by taking security. But there was an official called the *curator reipublicae*, whose duty it was to supervise the local administration, and it seems likely, though it cannot be proved, that on an appeal to him, administrative machinery would be set at work to enforce the discharge of the trust. But this applies mainly to gifts for public purposes.

53. The general theory of Servitudes is simple and logical, but it presents some points of interest, mainly historical. The terminology which is adopted in modern treatises is not exactly that of the Sources. The expression *Servitus Praedialis* is not found in Roman texts, these rights being almost invariably called *iura praediorum*, though the term *servitus* is commonly applied as a collective term. But it is a secondary name: *iura praediorum urbanorum et rusticorum*, says Gaius, to which Justinian adds *quae etiam servitutes vocantur*. The word is of course not new. Gaius himself speaks of *servitutes praediorum*. The names start from different points of view. The description of them as *iura* considers them as rights. The name *servitus* considers them as burdens. One name considers them from the point of view of the holder of the servitude, the other from that of the owner of the servient property, or rather, perhaps, from that of the servient property itself. The fact that a servitude can exist where there is no ownership brings the former view into prominence. A right of way does not cease to exist because the owner of the land over which it is exercised abandons his property. A *servus sine domino* may be subject to usufruct[1]. This is rendered less readily visible in relation to praedial servitudes by the fact that the Roman terminology attributes the right to the land itself and not to the owner of the land as such.

Personal servitudes, which differ at almost all points from praedial servitudes, in duration and in character, are unquestionably of much later introduction. It is a noticeable fact that neither Gaius nor Justinian in the Institutes tells us that these rights are servitudes at all. In those books, and also in the Digest and the Code, there are a number of texts which distinguish sharply between servitudes and usufruct. The Rubrics *de servitutibus* and *de usufructu* are quite distinct, and the titles of the Digest which deal *ex professo* with usufruct[2] do not anywhere speak of it as a servitude. But there are many texts which do so call it, and the title on servitudes enumerates the familiar personal servitudes as such.

The notion of *servitus* as a general conception was of course of only gradual development, proceeding in all probability, *pari passu*, with the acceptance of a settled theory of the nature of *dominium*. To the rights of way and water, which certainly existed in the time of the XII Tables, and which betray their antiquity by the fact that they are *res mancipi*, clearly regarded as rights rather than as burdens, there are first added other rustic servitudes, and then the urban servitudes which last are not *res mancipi*. Then comes the recognition of *ususfructus* and *usus*, and thereafter their recognition as servitudes, this last step being a great one which could hardly have been taken till it was fully recognised that *dominium* was the ultimate right in a thing. It is probable that the imposing list of

[1] Ulp. *Reg.* 1. 19. *Dos. Frag.* 10. Czyhlarz, Eigentumserwerbsarten, 129.
[2] D. Bk. 7.

servitudes, rustic and urban, which we meet in the texts is gradually evolved, and it is certain that *habitatio* is only recognised as a distinct servitude very late[1].

The relation of usufruct to *dominium* is somewhat uncertainly handled even in later law. There are several texts in the Digest which give, as the reason for the rule they lay down, the fact that usufruct is *pars dominii*, and there are others which, equally definitely, draw conclusions from the fact that it is not *pars dominii*[2]. To a certain extent the divergence may be explained on the view that the writers are not using words in quite the same sense. When they say that usufruct is a *pars dominii*, they mean that it consists of certain rights which, with others, make up *dominium*. They are thinking of ownership as a bundle of rights. When they say that it is not a *pars dominii*, they mean that ownership, or rather *dominium*, is none the less *dominium* because rights are carved out of it. They are thinking of ownership as the ultimate right, and usufruct as a mere servitude. Some of the texts, however, cannot readily be disposed of by this treatment, but appear to indicate a real conflict of opinion. Thus Julian tells us that one who stipulates for land, and then for a usufruct in it, or *vice versa*, is like one who stipulates for the whole and then for a part, or *vice versa*, and holds the stipulation for the usufruct a mere nullity[3]. Ulpian, on the other hand, tells us that one who, having stipulated for land, gives a release of the usufruct produces no effect, since the usufruct is not a part, but a mere servitude[4]. It hardly seems possible for Julian, on the lines of the opinion just stated, to have come to the same opinion. If the stipulation for the usufruct was void, because the usufruct was part of the land, the release of the usufruct must have been valid for the same reason. Paul[5] tells us that a pact not to sue for land bars any action for the usufruct of it, and compares the case with others in a way which shews that he regards it as a part.

[1] Girard, Manuel (4) 369.
[2] See, for these texts, Roby, De Usufructu, 42.
[3] D. 45. 1. 58. [4] D. 46. 4. 13. 2. [5] D. 2. 14. 27. 8.

54. Among the many classifications of servitudes there is one which has given rise to much discussion. Praedial servitudes are either Rustic or Urban. The Digest does not help us to a clear distinction between these (perhaps because the most striking result of the difference, the fact that the former alone were *res mancipi*, was obsolete), though the general nature of the distinction is clear enough. Into the various definitions that have been given it is not necessary to go: it will suffice to point out some considerations which must be borne in mind, when one is attempting to frame such a definition. One has already been pointed out: such an expression as rustic servitude is not really Roman. The proper expression is *ius rustici praedii*. This of course leaves entirely open the question, what is a rustic *praedium*, but it seems clearly to associate the labelling of the servitude with some characteristic of the dominant *praedium*, that to which the right attaches.

The common enumeration of rustic servitudes, justified indeed by the sources, ignores a distinction also justified by them. Many texts draw a sharp distinction between the rights of way and water and other rustic servitudes. These are spoken of as *in rusticis computanda*[1]. In one text in the Institutes it is said: *in rusticorum praediorum servitutes quidam computari recte putant aquae haustus, etc.* The word *recte* can hardly have formed part of the original text, the passage having been apparently taken by the compilers of the Institutes from the Institutes of Ulpian. Many texts, stating the rules of rustic servitudes, state them as applying simply to the ancient four[2]. It seems plain that the extension to others is relatively late, and it is suggested as a corollary to this that only the ancient four were really *res mancipi*.

In general the texts treat the two classes as fixed and distinct. A servitude is always urban or it is always rustic. But there are in the texts some exceptions to this. Thus the *ius aquaeductus*, which is in most texts called rustic, is at least

[1] D. 8. 3. 1. 1.

[2] *e.g.* D. 8. 1. 17. See Elvers, Servitutenlehre, 11.

once called urban[1], and it is plain that there is little in common between the runnel which you may lead to your field across that of your neighbour and the imposing structures which were built across land for the supply of houses. So too the *ius altius tollendi*, rarely named, is commonly regarded as urban, but in one text it is called rustic[2]. It is of course possible here too to think in the one case of access of light to a house, and in the other of access of light to vegetation, but unfortunately the text in which it is rustic plainly contemplates a house as entitled. A still more remarkable departure from the ordinary classification has been found. In one text we are told by Papinian that though the rights to water and of pasture are praedial servitudes, yet if a testator *personam demonstravit cui servitutem praestari voluit, emptori vel heredi non eadem praestabitur servitus*[3]. And there are other texts expressing much the same notion. But all these exceptional cases must not obscure the fact that the two types of praedial servitudes are standing classes. It must however be admitted that many, if not most, modern writers hold on the evidence of these texts that we cannot say that the character of the *praedium* in connexion with which they are ordinarily found is decisive of the class to which the servitude belongs, but that, for instance, a right of way is urban if it is attached to an urban *praedium*[4]. It is not worth while to pursue further the question as to what is on this view exactly the meaning of the word Urban.

Servitudes have been classified as Continuous, those which do not involve action for their enjoyment, and Discontinuous, those which consist in doing something and cannot be enjoyed without action. This distinction gives two lists which agree very closely with the lists we have of urban and rustic servitudes. It also agrees very closely, though perhaps not exactly, with the usual distinction between positive and negative servitudes. Most continuous servitudes are negative, but *aquaeductus* and *ius tigni immittendi* would appear to be positive.

[1] D. 6. 2. 11. 1. See also D. 8. 2. 18.
[2] D. 8. 3. 2.
[3] D. 8. 3. 4; see *h. t.* 36, 37.
[4] See, *e.g.*, Girard, Manuel (4) 360.

It seems that, to some at least of the jurists, the urban and the continuous, or at least the negative, servitudes are the same class, for we are told that urban servitudes are not lost by non-user, but only by the doing of something by the servient owner inconsistent with the servitude, and the sufferance of this by the holder of the servitude[1]. This distinction, as applied to urban servitudes, in any ordinary sense which that distinction may have, seems absurd, but it is intelligible as applied to negative and continuous servitudes, for as their use does not consist in doing anything, non-use *per se* could hardly be shewn. But if the owner of the servient land does what is inconsistent with the servitude, non-use is clear. It may be this confusion, or attraction, which makes Neratius class the *ius altius tollendi*, and the right to have a projecting balcony, as rustic servitudes[2]. Building higher involves action, and a projecting balcony is in the nature of a positive easement, as most rustic servitudes are. But the general result seems to be that there was not sufficient consistency in Roman views to justify any attempt at exact definition, and that those that are found in text-books can be no more than rough approximations.

55. Gaius and Justinian end their discussion of the law of property with a short account of what may be called representation for the purpose of alienation and acquisition. Most of the topics there considered are more conveniently treated elsewhere, but there are two which can be discussed here. The first is that of acquisition and alienation through the intermediation of a free agent. The Roman law was very slow to admit the principle of representation in legal acts: indeed in connexion with formal civil law acts it never did admit it. The case of acquisition by sons and slaves and of alienation by them, under authorisation, is hardly an exception: it rests on grounds other than representation. But the existence of these rendered the inconvenience of the strict rule much less than it would otherwise have been, and it was not until the employment of freemen had made much progress that any relaxation was seen.

[1] See, *e.g.*, D. 8. 2. 6.

[2] D. 8. 3. 2.

The course of the development is to be made out by a comparison of the language of Gaius with that of Paul and with that of the Institutes. Gaius says that we can acquire nothing *per extraneam personam,* but adds that the question has been raised whether possession can be acquired through them. Paul is clear that we can acquire possession through them, but no more[1]. This is settled it seems by an enactment of Severus which is preserved in the Code[2]. Justinian tells us in the Institutes that, as a logical consequence of this, we can acquire ownership by *traditio* if the transferor was the owner of the thing. The rule at first applied probably only to procurators, but in later law it is true for other men. There is however the difference that for a procurator knowledge of the principal was not needed, while for other persons the principal's possession was not completed till he was informed. Some of these conclusions are however controverted.

Neither Gaius nor Justinian says anything at this point as to alienation by a free agent. Here the rule was stricter. Even under Justinian, for voluntary alienation of ownership it was necessary to have either express or general authority.

It is however important to realise exactly what is meant by the expression alienation or acquisition *per extraneam personam.* For the act to have been through him, he must be the actual negotiating party[3]. If I, having sold a thing, hand it over to anyone to take to the buyer, he is merely a messenger: there is no acquisition till the thing is delivered, and the transfer is not through him. If, having bought a thing, I send a friend to fetch it, and the thing is delivered to him by my instructions, there is no acquisition through him. No doubt it is mine when he has received it, but it is no more acquired through him than it would be acquired through my land if the vendor of the thing, say a plough, had at my orders left it in my field, when I was not there. It is a good *traditio* to put the property in my power, no matter in what way this is done. But if I asked my friend to buy a plough for me, and he did so, saying that he had bought it for me, and taking delivery, then under the older

[1] D. 41. 2. 1. 20. [2] C. 7. 32. 1. [3] 41. 1. 13.

law, the plough would be, for the time being, his own property, under the new law it would at once become mine. These are all clear cases, but the scanty way in which the texts deal with this important matter, while it shews that the institution is rather post-classical, leaves us much in the dark as to a number of questions. Thus, in relation to the first cases mentioned, there is a text which speaks of the intermediary, who was no more than a messenger, as acquiring for me[1], but the foregoing seems the correct analysis of the facts. It is the sort of case on which there might be differences of opinion, and indeed the texts shew signs of these. The cases discussed are those in which the intermediary was in fact also a *procurator*, and it is easy to see that the view that he was actually acquiring for us rather than acting as a mere receptacle would be more readily taken than when he was a mere outsider. But in fact it is easy to formulate cases in which the court would have to determine whether the intermediary was a mere messenger or the negotiative party and might have considerable difficulty in deciding. It should however be noted that the actual receiver need not have been the person who made the contract out of which the transfer of *dominium* arose. Thus, if I have agreed for the purchase of a thing, and the vendor, knowing that Titius is my *procurator*, gives the thing to him, as acting for me, the thing becomes mine at once and is acquired through him.

If these rules have been correctly stated they still leave many difficult questions. What will be the resulting situation if a person entirely unauthorised by me visits a shop and in my name buys goods on credit and receives delivery of them for me, acting all the time in perfectly good faith? It may be presumed, though no text unequivocally tells us so, that under Justinian the property vests in me. But as to what the resulting contractual relation is, the only certain thing is that I am bound by no contract.

56. The other topic to mention is acquisition and alienation by slaves and *filiifamilias*. It is not possible to deal with

[1] 41. 1. 20. 2.

more than a few points. Acquisition by subordinate members of the *familia* does not rest on representation, since it takes effect even if the acquisition was forbidden[1]. It is a recognition, not so much of the individuality of these persons, as of their nullity: the only possible holder of property rights is a *paterfamilias.* There is no inroad on this principle till the time of Augustus. Then and thereafter by the successive introductions of *peculium castrense, peculium quasi castrense, bona materna* and *bona adventitia,* the face of things is completely changed. The *filiusfamilias* of Justinian's time is economically an almost independent figure.

None of these changes affects the slave. All that is transferred to him vests at once in his master[2]. But the existence of lesser rights than ownership in the slave led to the development of rules as to the distribution of his acquisitions which are not without difficulty. The broad rule expressed by the texts is that what is acquired through his labour (*ex operis*) or in the affairs of his holder (*ex re*) goes to the holder (*sc.* usufructuary or *bona fide possessor*), everything else to his owner. The notion, *ex operis,* is a very narrow one: so far as can be seen it applies only where the slave hires himself out to a third person. If the holder had hired him out the hire would not be acquired through the slave at all, and the ownership of the ordinary results of his labour is not acquisition through him either. *Ex re* means "in the affairs of the holder"—a fairly simple idea, but leaving room for doubts as to what are the affairs of the holder. There was for instance debate as to acquisition of a *hereditas*[3]. If the holder told the man to enter, might it not be said that this was *ex operis?* No. The act of labour involved in the entry is not that contained in the notion of acquisition *ex operis,* it is rather using the services of the slave, as where he is ordered to make something. Might it not be *ex re,* where there was intent to benefit the holder? Julian, who was clear that there was no question of acquisition *ex operis,* was inclined to accept this view, but the opinion that

[1] D. 41. 1. 32. [2] D. 29. 2. 79.
[3] D. 41. 1. 19.

prevailed was that the usufructuary or *bona fide possessor* could not acquire such things at all[1].

The acquisition of possession is a conscious act, and where it is through a subordinate member of the family, it is not complete apart from previous authorisation till the *paterfamilias* is aware of it. Hence, as the subordinate must also be conscious of it, two consciousnesses are involved. Convenience dictated some relaxations of the rule, notably in the case of *peculium*, where the *paterfamilias* need not know, and in cases where the *paterfamilias* was of defective capacity[2]. But possession could never be acquired through a slave who was himself incapable of conscious action.

[1] D. 6. 1. 20. [2] D. 41. 2. 1. 5; D. 41. 3. 28.

CHAPTER IV

UNIVERSITATES IURIS. SUCCESSION BY WILL

57. A MAN'S *Universitas Iuris* is the sum total of his assets and liabilities: it consists of the various elements which would go to make up his financial, or economic, balance sheet. In general the law is concerned with it only when it is passing from him, an event which happens most obviously at death, but occurs also at other times. In such cases this mass of rights and duties, with the exception of those that are destroyed by the event which occasions the transfer, pass to some sort of successor, but each case has its own peculiar rules and some of these are worth statement. Some of the cases belong to the civil law, as for instance Adrogation, or entry into *manus*, others are of praetorian origin, as for instance *Bonorum venditio*. It is hardly correct to say that this transfer of a *universitas* occurs in every case of *capitis deminutio*, since a subordinate member of a family has no *universitas* to be transferred: in an ordinary case of *adoptio*, no patrimonial rights pass from the subject of the adoption. The *peculium castrense* and *quasi castrense* pass with the *adoptatus*, whose rights are thus unaffected. So far as the *bona adventitia* are concerned, they do not wholly pass. Some remain with the father on adoption. But it must be remembered that the usufruct and management of this fund belong to the father: the son has only a deferred right in it, which does not become operative till he is *sui iuris*. There is no question of any transfer of a *universitas*.

In the case of *Adrogatio*, the rights of the *adrogatus* pass automatically to the *adrogator*, as if he were *heres*, except the few which are destroyed by the *capitis deminutio*, but the law as to his liabilities is not so simple. The principle apparently is that he is to be treated as if he had always been in the *potestas* of the *adrogator*, so that his acquisitions would have enured to the latter. But the obligations of a *filiusfamilias* do not bind his father, and these therefore do not pass automatically. In so far indeed as these debts were due from the *adrogatus* as *heres*, they bind the *adrogator*, since the *hereditas* would have been acquired by him if the *adrogatus* had been in his *potestas*, and he would thus have been fully liable. He is not *heres* to the *adrogatus*, but he is *heres* to the person to whom the *adrogatus* was *heres*. This we have already mentioned. His liabilities *ex delicto* do not cease to bind the *adrogatus*, though, as he has, or may have, no property of any kind, the remedy of the creditor is precarious. But a father would have been noxally liable, and the *adrogator* is similarly liable—*noxa caput sequitur*. So far as contractual liabilities are concerned, the father would be under no liability at civil law, nor therefore is the *adrogator*. Such debts are indeed extinguished at civil law by the *capitis deminutio*. The injustice of this may have been prevented in early law, as has indeed been suggested, by a refusal on the part of the officials charged with the preliminary investigation, to allow the adrogation to proceed except subject to undertakings by the *adrogator* as to these liabilities. But, in any case, the praetor dealt with the matter in another way. The edict gave the creditor of the *adrogatus* an *actio fictitia* against him, in which the *iudex* was directed to proceed as if there had been no adrogation, and thus no *capitis deminutio*. In this action the *adrogator* was required to undertake the defence, and to give the ordinary securities. If he failed to do so, the creditor was entitled to seize the goods which formerly belonged to the *adrogatus*, and sell them to satisfy his claim. This gives a result not unlike that arrived at by the *actio de peculio*, and it might have been thought that this action itself would suffice to meet the case. But it may well have been that there was no *peculium*, the *adrogator* having made no grant. Even if he had done so, it is far from certain that the *actio de peculio* would have been available in such a case, except, indeed, if the principle can be generalised that the *adrogatus* had always been in his *potestas*. The only text which raises the point speaks of doubt, and it is noteworthy that the case is not within the terms of the edict, as we know it. The edict speaks only of contracts made with one in the *potestas* of another, which would not cover contracts made with a *paterfamilias* who was afterwards adrogated. In fact it is probable that the text is really considering the different question whether, where the *adrogatus* was liable on a contract made by his slave, the action is available against the *adrogator*[1].

The case of *bonorum emptio* in insolvency is one of purely praetorian succession. In fact it is not a case of universal succession at all, for the debtor has not suffered any *capitis deminutio*, and still remains liable for his old debts. Moreover, while the goods pass to the *bonorum emptor*, it is not absolutely certain that it is he whom the creditors sue. He has contracted with the *magister bonorum*, and it is possible that it is his duty to hand over the amount for which he has made himself liable to the *magister*, who in turn is sued by the creditors. But as it is clear that the *bonorum emptor* sues the debtors, there is no obvious reason why he should not be liable directly to creditors, and it is now generally held that he was, though it can hardly be proved on our imperfect information[2]. Though both Gaius and Justinian speak of this as a case of succession, the conception of *universitas* is of little help in relation to this topic, to which we shall recur in another connexion.

The case of *cessio in iure hereditatis* is remarkable in that it is the transfer not of the *universitas* of the contracting party, but of a *universitas* to which he has an inchoate legal title. We have already considered some of the doubts and difficulties which the subject presents, in connexion with our discussion of the essential nature of *cessio in iure*[3]. There are

[1] D. 15. 1. 42.
[2] *Post*, §§ 163, 164.
[3] *Ante*, § 48.

other points of some interest. Gaius tells us that while an agnate *heres* on intestacy could cede before entry, a *heres scriptus* in a will had no such right, but if he purported to cede, produced no effect at all. He suggests no reason for the difference, and very different reasons have been assigned by conjecture. According to one view, any assignment by him before entry would be an intolerable departure from the expressed intention of the testator. According to another view, the *heres scriptus* has nothing to cede before entry, since all his right depends on a disposition which is of no force at all unless he accepts the *hereditas*, while the agnate has a right defined by statute. The disputes which arose in some of the other cases have been considered, but a word or two may be said of them. In the case of the *necessarius*, Gaius states the Sabinian view that a cession by him is a mere nullity, but himself apparently prefers the view of the other school, which was that the effect was the same as if a *heres* under a will attempted to cede after entry. The position is the same, they argue, in both cases: the man cannot cease to be *heres*, but he is the owner of the property, and can thus cede it. The other view presumably rests on the notion that one on whom the law casts the *hereditas* with no power of refusal does not produce any effect by an act which on the face of it purports to be exactly what the law forbids him to do. But in fact this would apply with equal force to the *heres* under a will who has accepted[1].

The case of *Adsignatio liberti* is even more remarkable. It is a transfer by will of a *universitas* in which the transferor has not even what can fairly be called an inchoate right. For the *libertus* is still alive. It rests on a provision by *senatusconsult*[2] that a patron may, by his will, assign the prospective succession of a particular *libertus* to a particular child. If the *libertus* is dead before the patron's will operates by his death, this is merely a disposal of his own property, and would need no authorisation by *senatusconsult*. The case contemplated

[1] See also Roby, Rom. Priv. Law, 1. 228.

[2] D. 38. 4. 1. *pr.*

is however that of a living *libertus*, whose succession passes to the *liberi patroni*, if the patron is already dead. Their rights of succession are not inherited from the patron: they are an express creation of the XII Tables. They are wholly independent of the patron, and thus, though the patron should have disinherited a child, this would not of itself in any way affect the child's right to the succession of a *libertus* who outlived the patron. The present provision therefore is an enactment entitling him to dispose of property which is not his own, a thing which apart from some such provision would be impossible. It may be compared with a power of appointment vested in a person who has no devisable interest in the property.

58. Far more important however than any of these is succession upon death. To the general proposition that the rights and obligations pass to the *heres* there are of course some obvious exceptions. The political and family rights of the deceased are extinguished. Usufructs and the like are ended, and the same is true of contractual rights for personal service, and obligations of the same nature. So too, a man's liabilities on *delict* in general die with him, as also do some of his rights of action on *delict*. Those rights and duties which survive the death pass to the *heres*, except so far as legacy *per vindicationem*, under which the ownership passes directly to the legatee, may be said to constitute an exception.

The only topic in the general theory of *hereditas* which we need consider is the *Hereditas Iacens*. We know that this was an incomplete personification of the *hereditas*, and that it arose only in those cases in which there was no *heres necessarius*, and where, therefore, there would be an interval of time between the death and the entry of the *heres*. It is said indeed by some writers that if a *suus heres* is unborn at the death, or if a *heres necessarius* is instituted under a condition, the *hereditas* is *iacens* for a time. There does not however seem to be any text which definitely applies the theory of *hereditas iacens* to cases of this kind, and some of the texts seem to make *hereditas iacens* and *heres extraneus* inseparable ideas[1]. No doubt many of the rules must have been the same, but, in fact, we have very little discussion of the questions which one would think must have arisen. We can therefore deal here only with the case of *heres extraneus*.

The notion of quasi-personality of the *hereditas* was invented to obviate the very great inconveniences which would plainly result from the fact that in the meantime the inheritance belonged to no one. Its business could not be carried on, since there was no one qualified to acquire rights for it, or to undertake obligations on its behalf. It might be seized or damaged with impunity. It is observable that many of these inconveniences were disposed of by methods which have no connexion with our present subject, methods so diverse as to shew, when coupled with the doubts and difficulties which arose in connexion with the conception of *hereditas iacens* itself, that this is only one of many practical devices by means of which the difficulties of an awkward legal situation were evaded. These devices cannot be expected to form a coherent whole, or even to conform individually very closely to logical requirements. There could be no theft of *res hereditariae*, as they belonged to no one and were not in any one's possession. Accordingly a special procedure was invented: the *crimen expilatae hereditatis*[2]. On the other hand, for *damnum* to the *hereditas* the *heres* was allowed to proceed by the Aquilian action, on the ground, not elsewhere supported, that the *lex* by the word 'owner' did not necessarily mean the owner at the time of the wrong[3]. There was a special procedure for dealing with any freed slaves who pillaged the *hereditas* before their liberty took effect[4]. But the quasi-personification of the *hereditas* is more important than these devices, and gave rise to several interesting questions.

It is inexact to speak of the *hereditas* as a *persona ficta*: the Roman lawyers themselves do not go quite so far. In fact,

[1] *.eg.* D. 43. 24. 13. 5. [2] D. 47. 19. 1. [3] D. 9. 2. 43.

[4] D. 47. 4. 1. *pr.* For many other illustrations see Pernice, Labeo, 1. 360 *sqq.*

as we have seen, they nowhere use this conception. What they say is that the inheritance *personae vicem sustinet*, or the like. As might be expected the compilers of the Digest are not very particular on this kind of point, and in fact the modern technical conception of *persona* is developing in their age. Thus there are two or three texts in which the *hereditas* is spoken of as actually being the *dominus* of the *servi hereditarii*[1]. But these texts usually contain very clear evidence of their Byzantine origin, and even so, there does not seem to be any text which goes the length of saying that the *hereditas* is a person. Justinian in the Institutes expressly says that it is not.

The *hereditas* represents a *persona*, but whose *persona* does it represent? Upon this question there are obvious signs of a disagreement among the classical lawyers. It is laid down by some jurists, not exclusively representative of either of the two schools, that it represents the *persona* of the future *heres*, and, in conformity with this, that the entry of the *heres* is retrospective, so as to date from the opening of the succession. It is clear however that the view which prevailed was that the inheritance represented the *persona* of the deceased, since this is plainly dominant in the Digest. There are not however wanting texts which express the opposite view. Thus on the question whether a *servus hereditarius* could stipulate in the name of the future *heres*, both opinions are several times expressed[2], and it seems to be now generally held that for most purposes the later jurists were prepared to accept the view that the entry of the *heres* was retrospective, on the ground of convenience, however difficult it might be to reconcile this opinion with the view, which was undoubtedly also dominant, that the *hereditas* represented the *persona* of the deceased.

The *hereditas* did not however represent the *persona* of the deceased for all purposes. The Institutes definitely express a limitation in the words: *in plerisque personam defuncti*

[1] See, *e.g.*, D. 9. 2. 13. 2; D. 28. 5. 31. 1.

[2] D. 2. 14. 27. 10; D. 45. 3. 16, 28. 4, 35.

sustinet. The text does not indeed clearly say what is the limitation that it is intended to express. It might indeed merely mean that the *hereditas* did not take up the political, social, and family rights of the dead man, as we know that it did not. But the restriction is important in many ways more significant than this. It finds its practical application mainly in numerous restrictions on the activity of *servi hereditarii,* who are the only people capable of acting on behalf of the *hereditas*[1] (and who are themselves so capable only through the principle we are considering), since ordinary mandates were ended by the death. Though these restrictions all express the fact that representation by the *hereditas* is incomplete, they do not all turn on one principle. In most cases there is an excellent reason for them quite apart from this incompleteness of representation. Thus the *servus hereditarius* cannot acquire a *hereditas* to which he has been instituted, for the benefit of the *hereditas* to which he belongs, since that *hereditas* is incapable of giving the necessary authorisation[2]. But there is in addition the important practical reason that, if the slave could accept without authorisation, the *heres* of the inheritance to which he belonged might find himself bound to this other *hereditas* which might well be *damnosa.* The extension of the same rule to legacy[3] might seem to be merely one of the analogical extensions of which there are many, but there is the same practical point. If the slave could accept, the legatee would find himself barred from attacking the will, as he has accepted a benefit under it. The slave cannot stipulate for a usufruct for the *hereditas*: there is in fact no life to which it can attach. He cannot stipulate in the name of his late master, since no such person exists, nor, in the opinion of most jurists, though not of all, can he stipulate in the name of the future *heres,* in view of the fact that this *heres* is as yet an *extranea persona.* On the other hand, he can be examined as a witness in litigation affecting the *hereditas,* though a slave cannot be heard where his master

[1] See however D. 14. 3. 17. 3 and *post,* § 125 *fin.*

[2] D. 41. 1. 61. *pr.*

[3] D. 31. 55. 1.

is concerned. The *hereditas*, it is said, is not his master[1]. It is plain that in all these matters there was no strict adherence to any theory. The rules were determined by considerations of convenience: any logical or theoretical justification is, for the later law at least, little more than an excuse.

However far we may go towards endowing a *hereditas* with the attributes of personality, there are limits which we cannot pass. It can do nothing which involves a conscious act. It cannot commit a *delict* or a crime, and it cannot authorise any one to commit such a thing. It cannot authorise a contract, appoint an *institor*, or grant a *peculium*. In strictness an *institor* would cease to serve, and a *peculium* to exist, but in practice this was not the case. It seems clear that a contract made with the *institor* even by one who knew of the death of his principal would bind the *heres*[2], and it is also clear that the *peculium* continued to exist as such. This last fact is important in relation to the history of the changes in the law as to the acquisition of possession. As a *hereditas* has no *animus*, it cannot possess, since *animus* of some sort is essential to possession. Nor can it acquire possession through the medium of a slave, for it is clear that even where possession is taken by a slave for a living owner, the owner has not possession in ordinary cases, until he knows of it. These restrictions are demanded by logic, but it is plain that the resulting rules were too inconvenient to stand. The first inroad made on strict principle was, naturally, within the field of *peculium*. The evidences of dispute and change of rule are clear on the texts. It is clear also that a *servus hereditarius* could in classical law continue an existing possession, and even complete it for the purpose of usucapion. But as to the beginning of possession, the law is not clear even in the case of *peculium*. Papinian expresses, or is made to express, conflicting views on the question whether a *servus hereditarius* can acquire possession for the purpose of usucapion, even in affairs of the *peculium*. But the view now most generally accepted, and supported by certain emendations, is that the

[1] D. 1. 8. 1. *pr.*; D. 48. 18. 2. [2] D. 14. 3. 17. 3.

classical law allowed a *servus hereditarius* to begin possession, for the purpose of usucapion, in connexion with his *peculium*, but that it is only Justinian who allows it in a wider field[1]. There is no authority on the question whether under such circumstances interdict possession could be acquired in the classical law. Probably it could not, until the time of Justinian. It is noticeable that the texts on the possessory interdicts do not mention any cases of dispossessed *servi hereditarii*, or discuss any cases in which they had begun possession.

Although the *servus hereditarius* plays for the moment a very important economic rôle, the facts do not in any way alter his essential character, or increase his faculties. His powers are still dependent, and purely derivative. This point becomes important if the *hereditas* is not accepted. If no *heres* enters under the will or on intestacy, all that the slave has done is void. Thus the *Fiscus*, which takes the property subject to the rights of creditors, will ignore obligations incurred since the death[2].

59. It appears to be not uncommonly thought among students that it was a difficult matter for a Roman to make a will, that the rules he had to satisfy were extremely complex, and that on the whole he was a lucky man, or had an exceptionally good lawyer if he did not break one or more of them. A corollary to this is the opinion that the introduction of *codicilli* and *fideicommissa* was a kind of relief from these intolerable rules of form, and that thereafter things were changed in this respect. All this seems to turn on a misconception. Many modern legislations impose similar restrictions, but these do not seem to be regarded as creating great difficulties of form, however oppressive they may be thought to be in substance. In view of the extreme dislike of intestacy which certainly prevailed from very far back in Roman history, it is in the highest degree unlikely that the rules of form would have remained substantially unchanged till the time of Augustus, if the effect of the rules had been to make testation

[1] The chief texts are D. 41. 3. 20, 31. 5, 40, 44. 3, 45. 1.

[2] D. 45. 1. 73. 1

precarious. In the recorded will of Dasumius (A.D. 108[1]) there are institutions, substitutions and substitutions to substitutes, but all this very short, and by far the greater part of the lengthy document is made up of various legacies and directions. Of course, if a man had children over age and others under age, and one insane, and grandchildren by a deceased son, and he wanted to disinherit some of these, and to provide different substitutes for others, to give *praelegata* to some, and to impose *fideicommissa* on others, he would have to be very careful or some of his instructions would fail to take effect. But so far as the validity of his institutions and therefore of his will was concerned, a very small amount of precaution would be all that was needed. The exceptional case is of course always a difficult case: an English will to produce the corresponding effect would not be very easy to draw. The real value of the codicil and *fideicommissa* was the release not so much from rules of form as from substantive restrictions on the power of devise, restrictions which had been found oppressive.

60. As to the power of testation, *testamenti factio activa*, as it is called, it should be pointed out that there were persons who were incapable of testation, but whose wills made before their incapacitation were nevertheless valid. This seems to have been so from the earliest times in the case of *furiosi* and *prodigi interdicti*[2], but in that of *captivi* the rule resulted from a certain *lex* Cornelia[3]. In the first two cases there is no technical difficulty; *furiosus* and *prodigus interdictus* are both *cives sui iuris*. But *captivus* is for the time being regarded as a slave, so that apart from legislative relief his will must have been void. It may also be said that while testation was in general a privilege of *cives sui iuris*, *filiifamilias* could devise *peculium castrense*, and there was a curious rule that public slaves could devise half their *peculium*. As to the right to be instituted in a will—the so-called *testamenti factio passiva*—we need not discuss the numerous statutory restrictions or

[1] Bruns, Fontes, 1. 304.
[2] D. 28. 1. 6. 1.
[3] See Buckland, Slavery, 299.

their gradual disappearance. It may however be worth while to say a word or two on the distinction between *testamenti factio* and *ius capiendi*. There were two classes of person, the junian latin and the *coelebs* who, while they had *testamenti factio*, and thus could be validly instituted, were barred from taking their gift, by express statute, and thus were said not to have the *ius capiendi*. There were others, the *orbus* and the *pater solitarius*, who could take only part of what was left to them. The point of the rule that the latin has *testamenti factio* is that the institution of such a man is not simply void. The *heres* must have *testamenti factio* both when the will is made and at the death. Thus if a peregrine and a latin are instituted, neither can take, but if, before it is too late to claim under the will, they receive grants of *civitas*, the latin can now take, but the peregrine is still excluded, since he had not *testamenti factio* when the will was made. The distinction disappeared, as to *coelibes* and *orbi*, when their disability was taken away by Constantine, but as to latins only when they were abolished by Justinian. The expression *ius capiendi* occurs under Justinian, but it now means no more than *testamenti factio passiva*.

61. The law as to the exclusion of certain witnesses has some points of interest. English law takes exception to attestation by persons interested in the will on obvious grounds of prudence, and prevents it by the expedient of avoiding the gift to the witness. The classical Roman rules excluding attestation by persons in the same family group as the testator do not turn on any such idea, but, as they are found in the old Mancipatory Will, exclude these as well as those in the same family group as the *familiae emptor*, though these last at least have, as such, no interest. No doubt the ultimate origin of the rule may be conceived of as of the same order, but as the exclusions appear in the law of wills they rest on the fact that the will is a *mancipatio*, and there is a formal rule that no one can be a witness of a *mancipatio* to which a member of his family group is a party on either side. The conception of the family as a unit no doubt plays its part in this exclusion. The principle excluding, for fear of fraud, persons beneficially interested in the will was not clearly recognised in the classical law. Gaius indeed goes so far as to say that it is undesirable to have such a person as a witness. Justinian definitely excludes the *heres* and his family. But even then the rule goes no further. A legatee is not excluded, nor is a *fideicommissarius*. They may be even more interested than the *heres*, while the children of the *heres*, who are excluded, may very well not be interested at all.

It may be worth noting that the function of a witness to a will in Roman law was not quite the same as that of the witness to the execution of an English will. All that such a witness has to attest, at least in modern law, is the due execution of the will. It does not appear to be necessary that he should know that the document is a will. The Roman witness attests not merely, or even mainly, the execution of the document, but the genuineness of the whole transaction. Paul tells us that the witnesses need not know the language in which the will is written, but that they must know that it is a will[1], though they need not, it seems, know anything about its contents. All this seems to have been a survival from the principles of *mancipatio*, in which the witnesses are there to attest the fact of conveyance, and to have been transferred through the mancipatory will to the later forms. The principle is shewn by the exclusion of those who were either deaf or dumb, who could have attested a signature perfectly well. There is in existence a document of A.D. 474, which records the proceedings in the opening of a will, proceedings which are provided for in the Edict. The witnesses in turn acknowledge their signatures, and say *in hoc testamento interfui*[2]. This is far from being the only case in which the rules of the mancipatory will, which themselves result from its origin in *mancipatio*, were carried over to other forms of will. The rules as to the number of witnesses come from it. So does the requirement that institutions must be at the beginning, the original *familiae emptor* having been *in loco heredis*, and so far as form goes, the

[1] P. *Sent.* 3. 4*a*. 13. [2] Bruns, Fontes, 1. 317.

active party from the beginning. The rule that a man cannot be partly testate, and those excluding institution *ex die* or *in diem*, have the same origin. The representation of the deceased by the *extraneus heres* is from the same source, and there are many other illustrations.

62. To discuss at length the original forms of Roman Will is outside the purpose of these pages, but a word or two must be said about them. The most important of the ancient forms appears to have been that *in Comitiis Calatis* of which it may be said that, although it is not absolutely certain that there was a vote on it, which would make it practically a legislative act, its character shews clearly that testation was not, as it became in later law, a matter of course. Probably wills were rare in primitive Rome. The other form of will, *in procinctu*, a will made on the opening of a campaign, before the testator's comrades under arms, is sometimes regarded as an equally formal act, done before the nation assembled in *centuriae* instead of *curiae*, and sometimes as a mere informal relaxation of law for urgent circumstances, analogous to the relaxations of form which our own law provides to a certain extent in the case of a will of a soldier under arms. In any case its existence affords some evidence that in the *Comitia Calata* the *populus* were witnesses rather than legislators[1], though they might presumably have refused their attestation. It does not appear that this will *in procinctu* plays much part in the later evolution. On the whole it seems best to regard the will *in Comitiis* as the normal will, from which descend the notions which dominate the later law, especially the rule that it is the main purpose of a will to provide a *Heres*.

The history of forms of will during the Empire is a fairly straightforward story, though there are a number of difficulties of detail, not of much importance. The most remarkable of the recorded forms of will is the nuncupative will before seven witnesses which appears at latest in the 3rd century[2]. It was in no way restricted to circumstances

[1] Karlowa, Röm. R. G. 2. 848. [2] C. 6. 11. 2.

of urgency, and it might seem that such a simple method would have superseded the elaborate machinery of the tripartite will. In fact however it does not seem to have been much used, and it is easy to see that a will of which the provisions were left at the mercy of the good faith and accurate memories of a few men, all of whom might be dead before the testator, was rather a precarious thing. The nuncupative will before a magistrate seems to have needed no other witnesses, but it, too, is of little importance.

The history of the development of the mancipatory will belongs to a stage of Roman history earlier than that we are considering. Some remarks on the form of the developed will have been made on an earlier page, but a little should be said here. As we have it, the *nuncupatio* contains nothing analogous to the assertion of ownership with which the ordinary form of *mancipatio* is begun. This omission is entirely consistent with the view that the assertion was required to secure a remedy in case of defective title[1]: there could be no need for this here. It must be admitted however that some editors suppose it to have been omitted by error, and add words to represent it. On the other hand, we have in the mancipatory will what we do not find in *mancipatio* proper—a form of words spoken by the transferor, in which he calls on the witnesses to note that the purpose of the transaction is the disposition of his property. The declaration of the receiver is not that he has bought the property as his own, but that he has received it into his custody, in order that the testator may make his will of it. There can be no doubt that such a formula as this, stating the purpose and unreality of the transfer, was only gradually arrived at.

The praetorian will seems to have disappeared with the creation of the tripartite will. Properly speaking it was hardly a will at all. It did not effectively appoint a *heres*, though it may have done so in terms. But this point became a mere technicality without practical importance at the time when, and in the cases in which, *bonorum possessio* under the praetorian will became *cum re*. But, apart from this, the edicts

[1] *Ante*, § 46.

setting forth the remedies under this will, which may however be only imperfectly known[1], suggest that much that could be done by an ordinary will could not be done in this way. The document operates under certain edicts which provide that possession of the property affected will be given to persons who can shew gifts to them either by way of universal succession or by way of legacy, under such a document duly attested by seven witnesses. What was the effect of the appointment of a *tutor* by such a document? We are nowhere told, but it is likely that it would be confirmed by the praetor. What was the effect of a direction to the quasi *heres* to perform some service? What was the effect of a manumission in such a will? There seems to be no answer to these and similar questions.

The tripartite will, or more accurately, the will based on *ius tripertitum,* is the will of the Digest. The seven witnesses are derived remotely from the civil law, as also is the rule that it must be *uno contextu*[2]. From the praetor come the seals, and from the new imperial law the signatures. Its rules thus give a picture of the development of modes of authenticating transactions, as civilisation progresses.

The high value which the Romans set on the right of testation is evidenced by many texts and by the rules of the institution itself. In no other case was so much care taken to secure the validity of the transaction. The special rules applied in the case of impossible conditions, and of *institutio ex die*, or to specific things, are well-known illustrations of this. If the *institutio* is not at the beginning it is not the *institutio* which fails, but the provision which precedes it. Apparently the only serious limitation is found in the very natural rules for the protection of the rights of children, for the rules requiring the use of specific words are intended to secure that what was not meant to be an *institutio* shall not be so regarded.

The privilege was jealously guarded. In classical law the testator must be a *civis sui iuris.* There were many exclusions

[1] Lenel, Ed. Perp. (2) 330 *sqq.*

[2] D. 28. 1. 21. 3.

from testation; in some cases these rested on permanent obvious considerations, in others on reasons which disappeared with the mancipatory will, though some of the prohibitions seem to have remained. Till Hadrian's time a woman in *legitima tutela* could not make a will even with her tutor's consent, a rule resting on reasons which are much debated, and on which something has already been said[1]. Peregrines and Colonary Latins had no right to make wills by Roman Law, though this is not to say that they could not do so under the laws of their own community[2]. Junian Latins were barred from testation by express legislation: *dediticii* by the fact that they were not *cives* and did not, at least the *dediticii* of the Empire, belong to any peregrine community.

Nothing need be said of the cases in which persons not *cives sui iuris* could make wills, but that of the *captivus* should be mentioned. His will made before his capture was valid if he returned, by the ordinary rules of *Postliminium*. But it was also valid if he died in captivity, a rule resulting from a provision in a *lex* Cornelia. It is probable that this is a direct provision and not as has been suggested a mere inference. But the exact nature of the provision, and even the identity of the *lex* remain unsolved problems.

63. The institution of the *heres*, having originally been the whole of the will, remained throughout Roman history its principal and indispensable part. It is not, strictly speaking, a gift of property: it is rather a gift of the patrimonial aspect of the personality—the *universitas* of rights and duties. The *institutio* of the *heres* must therefore cover the whole: a man cannot die partly testate. The *heres* or *heredes* must represent him completely. Hence follows the rule that though 12 is the customary number of *Unciae* into which the testamentary *As* is divided, still, if in any case less than that number are given, the lesser number will still cover the whole inheritance. It is true that under the principles of the *Querela inofficiosi testamenti* there were, as we shall see later, cases in which the

[1] *Ante*, § 18. [2] Ulp. *Reg*. 20. 14.

effect of a successful *querela* was that a part and a part only of the *hereditas* was distributed as on intestacy, but this was admitted to be an anomaly, and was justified by a text which seems to mean that the testator did not in fact die intestate *pro parte*, but became so as the result of certain proceedings after his death[1]. In the latest system, that of the Novels, there was an even greater anomaly. When a will was upset for *inofficiositas*, the whole might stand good except the institutions[2], but this is wholly without parallel in the earlier law.

The rule that the *institutio* must be in express and imperative terms (not *precative*, *jubeo*, not *volo*), and that it must come at the beginning, both descend from the mancipatory will. More accurately stated, the rule is that any provisions before the *institutio* are void if they are such as in any way lessen what will be coming to the *heres*. Such for instance are manumissions and legacies, but there was a dispute as to appointment of a *tutor*. The Sabinian view that it must not precede may have been based on the notion that if no appointment were made the *heres* might in many cases be the *tutor*. Curious questions arose where a legacy followed one set of institutions and preceded others, but they can best be considered in connexion with the law of legacy[3]. In any case all these rules of form and place affecting institutions are obsolete under Justinian. The rule *semel heres semper heres* bars any institution for a certain time—*institutio in diem*. It is not so obvious why, in view of the permissibility of conditions, an institution from a certain time—*ex die*—was also barred. It may be that it is too definite and precise a breach of the continuity of ownership between the deceased and the *heres*, which a condition does not necessarily produce. It may be that it was disregarded as being meaningless in view of the fact that the destination of the *hereditas* is irrevocably fixed[4].

The law of conditional institutions is rather complex. For the decision of questions which arise on actual wills it is necessary to be clear as to what constitutes a Condition.

[1] D. 5. 2. 15. 2. [2] *Nov*. 115. 3, 4. [3] *Post*, § 74.
[4] Dernburg, Pandekten, 3. § 82. *n*. 1.

Properly speaking, a gift is conditional when it is made to depend upon some event which is both future and uncertain. A gift to *X* "if he was born in Italy" is not conditional. There is nothing future or uncertain about it, there is only an ascertainable fact as to which the testator was not informed. A gift to *X* "if he shall become Consul" is conditional. A gift on an event which must happen, but as to which the time at which it will happen is uncertain, is not properly speaking a condition: it is *dies, certus an, incertus quando.* In documents *inter vivos,* such a modality is treated as *dies,* but in a will it is put on a level with conditions[1], the principal importance of which is that it may be valid in an institution, and that a legacy under such a modality does not vest (*dies non cedit*) until the event happens. Of such things the clause "when *T* shall die" is the commonest instance. There is another possible case. There may be events of which the occurrence is uncertain, but as to which, if they do occur, they must occur at a certain time—*dies, incertus an, certus quando.* Such is the case of a gift to *X* when he shall reach the age of 25. This is sometimes treated as conditional on his attaining that age, and sometimes as mere *dies,* so that if *X* never reaches the age, the gift is due when he would have done so had he lived. It appears to be *dies* in manumission, condition in legacy[2].

64. We know that impossible conditions (with some others) were void: they did not vitiate the institution as they would a contract, but were simply struck out of the gift. The object of this different treatment was to avoid intestacy, an object traceable in many other rules in the law of wills. The rule was extended to legacies, though here the same danger does not exist. It is a natural extension: the same rule of construction must be applied to different parts of the same instrument. It is important to notice what the lawyers mean by the word "impossible." They mean what is impossible in the nature of things, what we may call inconceivable. To touch the sky with one's finger is impossible in this sense. But the "nature of

[1] D. 35. 1. 75. [2] D. 40. 4. 16; D. 40. 7. 19.

things" is not a very exact idea, and the line must shift with every advance in scientific knowledge. In one case the jurists declare, after some hesitation indeed, that a condition "if he build a tomb within three days" must be treated as impossible[1]. But actual impossibility to the person concerned is immaterial. If a gift is left to Titius provided he paints a picture as good as one by Apelles, this is not a case of impossibility, though Titius will certainly not be able to satisfy the condition. Moreover it must be initial impossibility. Supervening impossibility is not on the same footing. It is true that it often releases the donee from the obligation to satisfy the condition, but this, though it gives a similar result, rests on an entirely different notion: it is discharge by *casus*, not by impossibility. A condition which assumes a non-existent state of facts is actually impossible, but it gives rise to very difficult questions of construction. Thus a gift "when my daughter reaches 21" may give different results, according as the testator never had a daughter, or had one but she was dead when the will was made, or had one who died after he made his will but before he did, or who survived him and either did or did not reach the age of 21. There are many texts dealing with such points, but they are too full of questions of intent and construction for us to enter on the discussion of them[2].

It has been said above that impossibility to the person concerned is not material, but there is one case in which this is not true. We know that if a son in *potestas* was omitted he could upset the will, absolutely, and that, even if formally disinherited, he could, if there had been no sufficient cause, attack the will by the *Querela inofficiosi testamenti*. Someone appears to have hit upon a device for evading these two rules. He instituted his son for his proper share, subject however to a condition. This condition was not technically impossible, but it was of such a character that there was not the smallest likelihood of his being able to satisfy it. The condition might for instance have been "provided my son becomes praetor at the

[1] D. 28. 7. 6.

[2] *e.g.*, D. 40. 4. 16; D. 40. 7. 19, 28. *pr.*; D. 28. 5. 46.

earliest possible age." A son so dealt with cannot say that he is omitted: he is actually instituted. He cannot say that he is unjustly disinherited, so as to entitle him to bring the *Querela*, since he is not disinherited at all. But he is quite effectually excluded. Accordingly the rule was laid down that a son in *potestas* might not be instituted conditionally, except upon a condition within his own power. Any other condition was treated as an omission. If however the condition was in his power, but he simply neglected it, he was excluded but the will remained valid. What was or was not in his power was a question of fact. Even if it was in his power it was laid down that it must not outrage natural affection: if it did, it vitiated the institution and the will was void[1]. These rules do not appear to have been applied in the case of other *sui heredes*, though in later law they were in exactly the same position.

65. The classification of *heredes* as *Sui et necessarii*, *Necessarii* and *Extranei*, the first two classes being those who are *heredes* by direct operation of law, irrespective of their consent, and the last those who may accept or reject the *hereditas* as they think fit, leaves out of account, it has been pointed out, the case of a grandson who has been instituted by a grandfather who has disinherited the father. Such a person does not come within the definitions of *sui* or of simple *necessarii*. The former are those who become *sui iuris* by the testator's death: the latter are slaves. The grandson in such a case is regarded as a *necessarius*, though the exclusion of his father does not give him the rights of a *suus*: if he is omitted he cannot attack the will[2]. The cause of the defective terminology is presumably that the conception of *exheredatio*, ancient as it unquestionably is, is not primitive, but is superimposed on the existing classification. In classical law, such an institution would simply benefit the disinherited father, but under Justinian it seems that this inheritance would form part of the *bona adventitia* in which the father had only a limited interest.

[1] D. 28. 2. 28. *pr.*; D. 28. 5. 4. *pr.*; D. 28. 7. 15. [2] D. 28. 3. 6. *pr.*

It is laid down that *Extranei heredes* must have passive *testamenti factio*, i.e., they must have the capacity of inheriting under a will. It should be noted that the word *heres* is much wider than the English word heir. It covers any universal successor on death, while the English word applies only to the person who takes the beneficial interest in real property on intestacy. The *heres* must have had this *testamenti factio* not only at the date of the making of the will, but also at the time of the death (or in the case of conditional institutions, at the time when the condition is satisfied) and from that time until the actual acceptance. Loss of capacity between the making of the will and the opening of the succession was not material, provided that the capacity was recovered before the latter date, while loss after that date but before entry was always fatal. The reason of this difference of treatment is that the requirement of capacity at the time when the will was made is an accidental result or survival from the fact that wills were made by *mancipatio*. The *familiae emptor* must of course have been *capax* at the time of the *mancipatio*. The rule which requires capacity from the opening of the succession till the actual acceptance depends on another idea altogether, namely, the principle that the *hereditas* is *delata* to him throughout this time, and if this *delatio* becomes from any cause impossible the whole gift fails.

66. The word *cretio*, which primarily means the formal declaration of intention to accept, is also used in a secondary sense to denote the clause in the will by which the testator expresses the requirement of such formal acceptance. Gaius tells us that two forms were in use, either *cretio perfecta* or *cretio imperfecta*. The rules which he proceeds to give as to the difference in effect, where there is a *substitutio*, form an admirable illustration of the logical exactness with which stated forms of words were interpreted by the lawyers. If the testator says "Let Titius be *heres*, if he do not make *cretio* let Balbus be *heres*," the formula does not exclude Titius in any case. There are no words actually requiring Titius to make *cretio.* In the absence of any such express direction, the classical law regarded acting as *heres* (*pro herede gestio*), shewing, in any way, intention to take the inheritance, as equivalent to *cretio.* In our case *cretio* is not expressly directed. Its non-occurrence is simply a condition on the institution of Balbus. The words are in effect "Let Titius be *heres,* and on a certain condition let Balbus be *heres.*" As Titius did not make *cretio,* this condition is satisfied, and accordingly both institutions are valid, and Titius and Balbus share. But where the testator used the form "Let Titius be *heres*: if he does not make *cretio* let him be disinherited and Balbus be *heres,*" then, if Titius does not make *cretio,* even though he does act as *heres,* and informally shew his intention to take, he is excluded and Balbus is sole *heres.* The statutory modifications of this rule, stated by Gaius and Ulpian, go a long way towards breaking down this logical system. Thus the rule laid down by Marcus Aurelius that, even where the fuller form is used, informal acts, *pro herede gestio,* shall be as good as *cretio,* turns the case into one of simple *substitutio.*

The act of entry, or acceptance, vests at once in the *heres* the property rights and obligations of the deceased. Property becomes his, and he can bring *vindicatio* for it. Debts whether on delict or on contract are due to him and his action requires no fiction or other device. He has stepped into the dead man's shoes, and he is, broadly speaking, liable in the same way. The injustice which might result where the *heres* was insolvent, while the inheritance was not, was met by the device of *beneficium separationis*: the creditors of the deceased could claim to have the inheritance administered distinctly from the estate of the *heres*[1]. It may be worth noting that one exceptional right did not pass to the *heres,* of necessity. The right of action for interference with the family sepulchre was available not only to those who had accepted the *hereditas,* but also to *sui heredes* who had abstained. It may be said that they were still *heredes* at civil law, but they were not *heredes* for any practical purpose beyond this, and there is the noticeable rule

[1] D. 42. 6. 1; as to *separatio* on behalf of slaves instituted, *h. t.* 1. 18.

that where such a person brought the action and recovered damages these damages were not assets available for the creditors of the deceased. They are not contemplated as forming part of the *hereditas*[1].

Justinian's introduction of the Inventory system by which a *heres* could, by making an inventory of the property, secure himself from liability beyond the assets, was intended to do away with the *spatium deliberandi*, as appears from the disadvantages which he imposed on those who still preferred to rely on it, and failed to make an inventory. The right to the limitation of legacies under the *lex* Falcidia was denied to them, and they remained liable for all the debts no matter how small the assets. And if they allowed the time to pass without declaring their intention, they were regarded as having accepted. But there must have been many *hereditates* in respect of which none of these disadvantages were material. Probably the majority of testators were obviously solvent, and it may be supposed that it was exceptional for a testator to give away the greater part of his property in legacies, to the detriment of a person he had appointed *heres*. It may be that there were many cases in which no inventory was made, and though the enactment instituting the inventory was passed in A.D. 431[2], the Digest contains a short title on the *spatium deliberandi*.

Each of several *heredes* is entitled and liable *pro rata*: the XII Tables contain an express rule that each *heres* is to be liable on each debt only in proportion to his share[3]. But it is possible for the testator to vary this by imposing particular debts on particular *heredes*, and in connexion with this there are certain difficulties. Papinian lays down the rule that this must not be done to the exclusion of that *heres*[4]. A restriction is arrived at by treating such a charge as a kind of legacy. It must be ascertained what would be the share of that *heres* in the nett estate assuming that debts were distributed proportionally, and then the total burden of debts imposed on him must not be more than three-quarters of that amount. A

[1] D. 47. 12. 6, 10.
[2] C. 6. 30. 22. *pr.*
[3] Bruns, Fontes, 1. 24.
[4] D. 10. 2. 20. 5.

simple illustration will make this clear. *A*, *B* and *C* are instituted *heredes* in equal shares, and all the debts are charged on *A*. The assets are worth 1000, and the debts amount to 400, so that the nett value of the estate is 600. Each share is therefore 200. Not more than 150 may be charged on *A*, so that upon these facts he will get 50 and the other two will get 275 each. The same result will be arrived at by stating the matter in a different way. Each share of the gross estate amounts to $333\frac{1}{3}$. Each normal share of the debts amounts to $133\frac{1}{3}$. It follows that each gets 200. But *A*, having been charged by the testator with all the debts is bound to pay the others so much as the *lex* Falcidia allows, as if it were a legacy to them. This is 150, making 75 each. Accordingly *A* receives 50 and *B* and *C* get 275 each. It is easy to see that if the different *heredes* are charged with debts in various proportions the arithmetic involved might be somewhat complicated.

67. The institution of slaves is very prominent in the texts. No doubt in many cases there is intention to benefit the slave, the idea of the testator being that the master will allow this *hereditas* to remain in the *peculium*. But this he could not of course be compelled to do, and perhaps a more common purpose was to provide an indirect way of making the *hereditas* alienable. If an instituted slave is alienated before entry on the *hereditas*, he takes the right with him[1]. Thus, if his owner sells him, before the entry, and contracts for his restoration after he has entered, the practical effect of the transaction will be a transfer of the inchoate right of inheritance, and substantially nothing more.

If a man instituted his own slave as his *heres*, this was a nullity unless there was also an express gift of freedom, until Justinian enacted that such a gift should be implied. The reason for this somewhat severe rule may perhaps be that the benefit to the *heres* (and in such a case there may be other *heredes*) is not to be diminished by implication, a principle of which there is an analogous application in the rule that if a man is

[1] D. 37. 11. 2. 9.

freed *inter vivos* he keeps his *peculium* unless it is expressly reserved, but if it is by will he does not take it unless it is expressly given[1].

The institution of another man's slave does not require, indeed it does not admit of, a gift of liberty, though it may be conditional on his being freed. Apart from this, *testamenti factio* in the master is the chief requirement, and it must be noted that at least in classical law, if the master had no *testamenti factio*, the gift could not be saved by alienation before entry. The institution of a slave common to the testator and another may be *ut alienus* or *ut suus.* If there is no gift of liberty, this is *ut alienus* and it simply benefits the other master[2]. If there is a gift of liberty coupled with an institution we are nowhere told what happens, but it is commonly supposed that, till Justinian, the effect was the same as in the last case and in that of manumission without institution. There are logical difficulties, but we need not enter into these, and the effect of Justinian's changes is familiar.

The testator might appoint a single *heres* or he might distribute the succession among any number. It was the practice to state the share taken as one or more twelfths, *unciae*, the whole *hereditas* being contemplated as an *as.* Though this mode of division was not compulsory, but the testator might divide the estate as he liked, it was so far usual that it was presumed to have been intended if no other was clearly stated. Hence comes the rule that if less than 12 shares or *unciae* were allotted and there was a *heres* whose share was not definitely stated, he, or they, if more than one, took all that were unallotted out of twelve, and if this number had been reached or exceeded, then all that were unallotted out of 24, the double *as* (*dupundius*) and so on. Clearly large estates might call for further subdivision and Volusius Maecianus[3] has recorded for us the names of a number of the subdivisions. Each of the names may be accompanied, or perhaps replaced by a symbol, which he also gives us, the smallest fraction

[1] D. 15. 1. 53; D. 33. 8. 8. 7. [2] Ulp. *Reg.* 22. 10.
[3] See Huschke, *Jurisprudentia Anteiustiniana*, 411.

he mentions being the *Scriptula*, the symbol of which is *X*, representing the 24th part of an *uncia*, the 288th part of the *hereditas*.

68. *Substitutio vulgaris*, the institution of a *heres* to take if the first institution fails to take effect is essentially a sub-institution. Its rules are simple and need not be stated here. In the texts the substitutions in a will are commonly called institutions of a second, or, as the case may be, of a third grade, and there is a good deal of law as to the extent to which subordinate provisions associated with the institutions of the first grade are to be understood as applying also to those of the second grade, or need to be repeated if they are to operate on the substitutions[1]. It was usual to substitute *coheredes* to each other. This would produce much the same result as the old *ius accrescendi*, but, apart from the fact that the testator might vary the shares and conditions in such substitutions, it must be remembered that such substitution is an express gift and not a lapse. Thus if one of the *coheredes* died after he had entered, and one of the others then lapsed, his representatives might have taken their share of the lapse, but if there had been reciprocal substitutions all would go to the surviving *heredes*, since the dead *heres* had not lived to the time when the share in question was *delata* to him. Moreover the *leges caducariae* practically abolished the old *ius accrescendi*; collateral relatives were excluded from the operation of those laws so far as there was an express gift to them, so that they could take by substitution a share which fell in, but not one which lapsed.

Substitutio pupillaris, the provision of a *heres* to a child in *potestas* who should survive the testator but die too young to make a will for himself, is a rather more complicated institution. Its rules are not wholly coherent since there is a certain wavering between the conception of it as a provision in the father's will, and as itself an independent will. It deals with the child's inheritance, not the father's, and thus such a *sub-*

[1] See, *e.g.*, D. 28. 6. 36, 46.

stitutio might be effectively made in the case of a disinherited child, and it covered property which came in no way from the father. On the other hand it required validity of the father's own will, and where the pupillary substitute and the father's *heres* were the same person he could not accept one institution and refuse the other[1].

Substitutio quasi-pupillaris or *exemplaris* is not an institution of the classical law: it is first erected into a system by Justinian. He provides that any ascendant, having no other children, who has left property to a descendant who is insane, may appoint a substitute to take what is so left to him if he dies without having ever recovered his sanity, no matter at what age. He has not a free choice, but must choose from among the relatives of the *mente captus*, in an order laid down in the enactment. If several ancestors appoint, it seems that each takes what comes from the ascendant who appointed him, but we are not told who takes what comes from neither[2]. The whole institution is difficult to fit in with the ordinary conceptions of the law of succession.

69. The *sui heredes* are regarded as so far entitled to succeed to the *paterfamilias* that if he desires to exclude them he must do so by an express provision in the will—*exheredatio.* There are many points of interest in the law of this topic. If any *suus heres* other than a son is omitted, *i.e.*, is neither instituted or disinherited, the will is not void at civil law, but the omitted person is entitled to come in and take his share by what is called the *ius accrescendi.* This has no resemblance to any other *ius accrescendi*, and seems indeed rather to resemble a *ius diminuendi.* The language of Gaius and Ulpian[3] seems to shew that these persons are contemplated as increasing the number of *heredes.* Their right is to take a *pars virilis* as against *sui instituti*, and half the *hereditas* as against *extranei instituti.* It is not altogether clear whether, if there are two such *omissi*, each is entitled to a *pars virilis* or they

[1] See Girard, Manuel (5), 834.
[2] C. 6. 26. 9.
[3] Ulp. *Reg.* 22. 17.

are entitled to one between them, though the former view is the most probable, while it is clear that as against *extranei* they share the half. The rule as stated leads to an odd result, for an omitted daughter will in all cases in which a *suus* and an *extraneus* are instituted, get more than the *suus institutus*, and if there are two *sui instituti* and an *extraneus institutus*, she will get more than she would have got on intestacy. Thus if the *instituti* are two *sui* and two *extranei*, and all the shares are equal, and a daughter is omitted, she will get half of what would go to the *extranei*, that is a quarter, together with one-third of what is given to the *sui*, that is one-sixth, so that she will get, in all, five-twelfths, while her brothers get only one-sixth each, and she herself would have taken on intestacy only one-third. The Praetors, by allowing all such persons to claim *bonorum possessio contra tabulas*, and thus, practically to set aside the will, so far, at least, as its main provisions were concerned, introduced a more reasonable rule, the practical difference being that the *extranei instituti* were excluded altogether, and the whole estate was divided between the *sui instituti* and the *omissi*. In view of the nature of the rule it is somewhat odd to find that Antoninus Pius enacted that a woman should in no case be entitled, under the new rules, to more than she would have received under the civil law rules. In the majority of cases this could not occur: she would not be entitled to more under the new rule. The total fund to be divided would be increased by the failure of some, but by no means all, legacies, but that would not ordinarily be of very great importance. If the *instituti* were all *sui*, she would, subject to this, get the same under the two rules. If there were both *sui heredes* and *extranei* instituted, she might get less and could not possibly get more under the new rule. It was apparently only where *extranei* alone were instituted that she would get more under the new rule, and the provision of Antoninus Pius would be operative. The question may be asked and does not seem to have any certain answer, what, in this case, happened to the excess which the woman could not take. There could be no other *sui*, entitled to claim, for they could have upset the will altogether if they had existed, since on the hypothesis they are neither instituted nor disinherited. It seems possible therefore that the institution of the *extraneus heres* remained good for a half. There is however one small point in which, apart from this, the rule of Antoninus Pius may have produced a change. If a woman obtained *bonorum possessio contra tabulas*, she would under his rule have to pay all legacies which would have fallen on her had she come in by *ius accrescendi*, though in general such *bonorum possessio* destroyed some legacies, though not all.

It will be remembered that the Praetor made another important change in this connexion: he equalised *emancipati* with *sui* for the purpose of *bonorum possessio contra tabulas*. As however they had been in a position to acquire property of their own, which was not the case with *sui*, and as moreover the enfranchisement was probably often accompanied with a gift of money, he laid down the reasonable rule that an *emancipatus* who claimed to come in and take with the *sui* must bring into the fund for division any property which he possessed. This forced contribution is called *Collatio Bonorum*. But the purpose of the rule indicates some reasonable restrictions. The *collatio* could be demanded only where the *institutus* was a *suus heres*, where the coming in of the *emancipatus* was to his own benefit, and where it injured the *institutus suus*. A few cases will illustrate these restrictions.

(*a*) Where a *suus heres* was instituted for a quarter, and an *extraneus* for three-quarters, the *suus* cannot complain, for he has his *pars legitima*. But if an *emancipatus* was omitted and claims *bonorum possessio contra tabulas* he will not have to make *collatio bonorum*, for the *suus heres* will now take half and is actually benefited. If however the figures had been reversed there would have been a case for *collatio*, since the *suus heres* would only get one-half instead of three-quarters.

(*b*) Anyone who attacked a will lost all benefit under it. If then by his action the *emancipatus* upset the will, and lost legacies to as great a value as the amount he could claim, there was no case for *collatio bonorum*, as he had not in any way benefited.

(*c*) There were two sons, *S* and *E*. *E*, having been emancipated, left *C* and *D*, his children, in the *potestas* of *P* their grandfather. *S* is instituted to a half, and *C* and *D* are instituted to the other half between them. *E* claims *bonorum possessio contra tabulas*. There is no *collatio* in favour of *S* who is in no way affected as he still takes half. But on such facts the emancipated father is entitled to half of what his children took and they divide the rest. As their interest is thus reduced they can claim *collatio*[1].

It appears also, though the evidence is not quite clear, that in no case of *collatio* was the *emancipatus* compelled to bring in more than would balance the loss which his claim caused to the *sui*.

There is one case in which even in classical law a member of the *familia* may be compelled to make *collatio*. A daughter who has received a *dos* may be required to make *collatio dotis* if she claims *bonorum possessio contra tabulas*[2].

It should be observed that the gradual extension, under the Empire, of property rights to *filiifamilias* led to many new developments in the rule of *collatio*, so that *filiifamilias* had to make *collatio* so far as their *peculium castrense* or presumably *quasi castrense* had been provided in the first instance by the father. But the texts on the matter as stated by Justinian are obscure and conflicting[3]. The whole law of *exheredatio* is indeed much simplified in his law. All disherison must be *nominatim*: there is now no question of the *ceteri* clause, and the effect is the same in all cases.

70. These restrictions are formal, *i.e.*, if certain steps are taken in the will the rules are satisfied and there is no question of *bonorum possessio contra tabulas*. But the *Querela inofficiosi testamenti* provides a protection of a different kind. *Exheredatio*, however formal, may be unjust, and the *Querela* provided a remedy. It had a much wider field of operation. It was available not only to children of a man who were unjustly

[1] D. 37. 8. 1. [2] D. 37. 7.

[3] D. 37. 7. 1. 7; C. 6. 20. 21, 19. 1, 20. 1, 21.

disinherited, but to those of a woman who were unjustly omitted (for there could be no question of *exheredatio* in a woman's will), to parents unjustly omitted, and even to brothers and sisters so treated, provided in this case that a *turpis persona* is instituted. The remedy is regarded as in some way reflecting on the testator and thus is not allowed if there is any other remedy. Thus a *suus omissus* cannot bring it: he had his remedy under the rules of *exheredatio*.

It is not necessary to state the rules in detail, but there are some points presenting difficulties which are worth mentioning. The general rule is that this remedy is available to certain relatives who have received under the will less than a certain fraction of what they would have received on intestacy, and thus it follows that no one could bring the *querela* unless he had a claim on intestacy. On the other hand we are told that a person who has no claim on intestacy, but who brings the *querela* successfully, benefits, not himself but the *heres ab intestato*[1], whoever that may be. These two propositions are not really inconsistent. The *querela* is not necessarily an arraignment of the whole will: it is a litigation between two persons, of whom one asks to have the institution of the other set aside on the ground that he himself is unjustly dealt with, in the will, either by *exheredatio* or by omission as the case may be. In such an action he may get judgment even though he had really no claim, either by an error of the judge, or because at the time he was the person supposed to be the *heres ab intestato*, or, an equally likely case, because the defendant sets up no reply to the claim, as he knows that, though the present claim is unfounded, there are others to follow in which he must inevitably lose. His institution is thus upset, but this litigation cannot prejudice the rights of the true *heres ab intestato*, who is in no way party to it, and who thus is still entitled to claim. There were however certain cases in which the claimant might bring the *querela* successfully and for his own benefit, even though he was not the *heres ab intestato*. Thus, if the nearest claimant failed, on the ground that he

[1] D. 5. 2. 6. 1.

was justly excluded, the next might now bring it for his own benefit, provided of course that he was one of those near relatives enumerated above who alone were entitled to the *querela* in any case. This is laid down as a general rule[1].

This fact that the *querela* is not an arraignment of the whole will, but a mere litigation *inter partes*, coupled with the rule that one who pushes a *querela* to judgment and fails, loses any benefits he may have received under the will, causes the proceeding to produce different results according to the state of the facts. Thus, if of two persons whose claims are equal, one brings the *querela* and fails, he alone suffers, while if he succeeds he benefits both, since the will is avoided. If a single claimant brings it against only one of several *instituti*, because only one of them is open to attack, the will remains partly good. For instance, the *instituti* may be a *suus*, instituted for his right share, and an *extraneus*. On such facts the disinherited *suus* will attack only the *extraneus*, and, accordingly, the *suus institutus* will be quite unaffected. The Digest records a certain number of cases in which a claimant succeeds against one *institutus* and fails against the other. As his claim rests so to speak on his own merits it may not at first sight be obvious how this could happen. But the case just given would provide an instance, if the *suus exheredatus* indiscreetly made the *suus* a party to the suit. And there is another obvious case. A brother proceeds against two *instituti heredes*, and fails against one of them because he is not a *turpis persona*. Again, a claimant might conceivably bring the *querela* independently against two *instituti* before different *iudices* of whom one might give judgment in his favour, while the other thought him justly excluded. There is another case in which the will may stand partly good. It may be that there are two persons *prima facie* entitled to claim. Here it seems that if one alone proceeds, the will is upset, provided the other was really entitled. If however the other expressly repudiated his right, or was justly excluded, the will stands good *pro parte*, so that minor provisions, such as manumissions, are good except so

[1] D. 5. 2. 14, 31. *pr.*

far as they are expressly charged on the *institutio* which is destroyed. A similar result is said by some writers to follow if both proceed and one fails, but the texts on this matter are obscure and conflicting[1]. It is to be observed that all cases in which this partial testacy is shewn are irreconcilable with the nominal basis of the proceeding, *i.e.*, that the testator was insane.

The rules of the *querela*, like other positive provisions, were liable to change. This was made manifest in connexion with the amount which would exclude it. In the classical law it was a quarter of the statutory share. Under the Institutes (though one text retains the old language) any benefit excluded it, the injured person being thrown back on the *actio ad supplendam legitimam*, which left the will standing, but had previously been used only where the testator had directed that shares which were too small were to be made up. There were also changes as to the kinds of gifts which were to count towards exclusion, the changes, up to the time of Justinian, being in the direction of extension. Not long after the publication of the Institutes a fresh minimum was established for the case of children. They were to have one-third of the *hereditas* if there were four or less, and one-half if there were five or more, a somewhat hasty piece of legislation which gives the odd result that if there were four they could claim one-twelfth each, while if there were five the legal minimum was one-tenth[2].

About ten years after the publication of the Institutes, Justinian completely remodelled the *querela*, so far at least as concerned the claims of ascendants and descendants, brothers and sisters being left under the older law. In estimating the *pars legitima* nothing was to count unless the claimant was actually instituted *heres* for some share but, if he was, all *mortis causa capiones* were reckoned. The will was to be treated as *inofficiosum* unless the exclusion was on one of certain grounds

[1] The chief texts are D. 5. 2. 6. 1. 16, 17, 19, 23. 2, 25. 1. See Windscheid, Lehrbuch, § 584, n. 24.

[2] *Nov.* 18.

stated in the enactment, and the ground was expressed. If the rules were broken the institution went, but minor provisions stood good, a complete breach with old ideas which made a valid *institutio* a *sine qua non* of a will[1]. There has been some doubt as to the exact effect of this change. Some writers have held that after this legislation the rules of the *querela* and those of *exheredatio* were fused, the new system in fact superseding them both. But those who take this view are not of one mind as to the proper way in which to state the result. According to one opinion the real practical result was the survival of a system based on the principles of the *querela*, and the substantial disappearance of the old law of *exheredatio*. Another opinion exactly reverses this. The new rules supersede the *querela* altogether and are in fact a remodelled set of rules of *exheredatio*. The main practical difference would be that if the surviving rules were those of the *querela*, the proceedings would ordinarily have to be brought within five years, while if they were the rules of *exheredatio* the claim would not be barred by anything short of the ordinary period of limitations, *i.e.*, thirty years. It is impossible to go into the arguments in favour of this view in either of its forms. The other opinion seems much more probable in view of the language of the Novel itself, namely, that both sets of rules still survived, that absolute omission of a *suus heres* or an *emancipatus* still entitled him to *bonorum possessio contra tabulas*, the new rules applying only in cases which in earlier days would have given rise to the *querela*.

71. The entry into the family of a new *suus heres* after the will was made would cause it to fail, by reason of the rules of *exheredatio*, unless the person concerned had been disinherited or instituted by anticipation. Such persons are defined by Justinian, in another connexion, as those who would have been *sui heredes*, if they had been born soon enough, a definition which has the interest of being one of the very few cases in which Tribonian has corrected loose language which he found

[1] *Nov.* 115.

in Gaius. (Gaius says "would have been in *potestas*" and a little reflexion will shew that this is too wide.) The event may happen in several ways. A child may be born after the will was made, even after the death (such a child being called a *postumus*, a name which has no reference to death and burial as the English form of the word suggests, but is merely a superlative of *post*). Or it may happen that remoter issue born either before or after the will, or after the death, become *sui heredes* at some date after the making of the will, by the death of their father, the essential point being that they will not come into this class, unless the father predeceased the grandfather. Hence the form of the definition: it covers those who would be *sui* if born soon enough, not those who would have been *sui* if the testator had lived long enough. That would bring in a number of cases which the law excludes from consideration, *e.g.*, a posthumous son of a son who survived the testator. Or the event which makes the remoter issue a *suus heres* may have been, not the death of the father, but his passing out of the family by emancipation or adoption. There was a great deal of legislation and juristic construction by which it was rendered possible to provide for these various cases one after another. It is not necessary to set out this development, but the final state of the classical law is stated by Tryphoninus who lays down the rule that it is permitted to institute or disinherit by anticipation all persons who become *sui heredes* in the course of nature after the will is made[1]. This expression appears to mean by some fact which does not involve their incurring a *capitis deminutio*, for it is clear on the texts that the rule does cover the case in which the intervening father passes out of the family otherwise than by death[2]. The case is very different with those who are introduced into the family by a voluntary act of the *paterfamilias*, such as adoption, legitimation, *anniculi probatio, erroris causae probatio, etc.* Previous *exheredatio* of such persons would be a mere nullity, and it does not seem that previous institution of them would save the will. Hadrian allowed it to do so in one exceptional case of *anniculi probatio*,

[1] D. 28. 2. 28. 1, *in fin.*

[2] *Ib.*; D. 28. 2. 29. 5.

and it seems that in course of time his rule was generalised, so that the rule was that previous institution of such persons would save the will, but that previous *exheredatio* of them would not[1]. It is plain however that this previous institution is a prophetic act which cannot always have been possible, but there is no particular hardship in requiring a man, who does such an act as adoption, to reconsider his will.

72. The law as the causes and effects of failure of gifts, in a will, was the subject of great changes. Almost the only rule in the matter which was never altered was the rule that if an institution or other gift was absolutely void at civil law because the beneficiary had not *testamenti factio*, it was simply struck out, and the will was construed without it. Apart from this the ancient rule of *ius accrescendi* was that if a share lapsed from any cause, it passed to the other *heredes*, *pro rata*, and legacies specially charged on it failed: it passed necessarily, but *sine onere*[2]. *Substitutio* prevented this lapse, and the rule itself was almost modified out of existence during the Empire. Where a gift failed by reason of *indignitas*, *i.e.*, unworthy conduct in the donee, it usually, but not always, went to the *fiscus*[3]. The cases of lapse were lessened in number by successive enactments providing for specific cases in which a *heres* died without claiming, before it was too late to claim, culminating in an enactment of Justinian, who laid it down in general terms that if any *heres* so died his successors might claim in his place, so long as his time was unexpired.

But the most profound alteration was that caused by the *leges caducariae*. By the *lex* Iulia *et* Papia Poppaea all *caduca* and the like went to those *heredes* who satisfied the requirements of the *leges*, *i.e.*, had children or were ascendants or descendants of the testator. Failing these they went to legatees with children and failing these to the *aerarium*, to the exclusion of other *heredes*. Caracalla substituted the *fiscus* for the *aerarium*, and perhaps excluded any but

[1] D. 28. 2. 23. 1. See Girard, Manuel (5), 858.
[2] D. 31. 61. [3] D. 34. 9; C. 6. 35.

ascendants and descendants from taking *caduca*[1]. The aim of these provisions is the encouragement of marriage and paternity. To the existing causes of lapse they added celibacy between certain ages, and they provided that childless persons could take only half their gift. The application of these drastic rules is however subject to two important exceptions. Ascendants and descendants of the testator are said to have *ius antiquum*, that is to say, they are entirely unaffected by the *leges*: they retain the rights they had under the older law, whether they have children or not, so that childlessness or celibacy does not cause their share to lapse or prevent them from taking their part of shares which do lapse. Other relatives are said to have *solidi capacitas*, *i.e.*, a gift to them does not fail merely because they are childless or unmarried, but they do not share in lapsed gifts as would ascendants in the same position. They can only take what is expressly given to them. The distinction between the two cases is well illustrated in the case of reciprocal substitution. *A*, *B*, and *C* are instituted *heredes*. *A* refuses his share. *B* is an *extraneus* with children who accepts the *hereditas*. *C* is a cousin with no children, who also accepts. *A*'s share will go wholly to *B*, *C* having *solidi capacitas*, but no right to claim *caduca*. If the *heredes* had been reciprocally substituted, *C* would have shared in the gift which *A* refused, since there was an express gift to him in the event which happened. If *C* had been the testator's father he would have shared what *A* refused, whether there had been reciprocal substitutions or not. It should be added that students will find an allusion to *pater solitarius*[2]. This appears to mean a widower, or divorcing or divorced husband, who has not remarried. It is fairly clear that he was to some extent penalised by these *leges*, but it is not known to what extent.

Gifts originally validly made, which from any cause fail to take effect, are classed as *caduca* or *in causa caduci*. The latter are, according to Justinian, those which have failed before the death of the testator. The former are those which fail by

[1] Ulp. 17. 3. [2] Ulp. 13.

the operation of the *leges caducariae*, or by repudiation or incapacitation after the death of the testator. These are treated as true *caduca* because it was only the *leges caducariae* which, by postponing the right to claim to the opening of the will prevented them from being accepted immediately after the death, before the incapacitating event had taken place. The distinction does not seem very important, since, apart from some small details, the two classes seem to have been dealt with in the same way, though modern opinion is not quite unanimous on this point.

The rules under the *leges caducariae* were a good deal modified from time to time. Justinian swept away the whole system, the most oppressive parts having indeed long since been abolished, especially by Constantine's repeal of the provisions imposing penalties on childlessness and celibacy[1], provisions which could not of course be maintained when a church which made celibacy its chief virtue had become dominant in the State. Under Justinian's system, the rules were simple. Lapsed shares were to go to those who would have taken them under the old law. But they need not take them unless they liked, and if they did take them they took with them all burdens which had been charged on them: the lapse was *cum onere*[2].

73. The various defects which may cause a will to be *ab initio* void or which may cause the failure of a will originally validly made have each its epithet, applied to the will affected. The former need not be stated here, though they are a good illustration of the careful terminology of the Roman lawyers. But something must be said of the latter class. There were *testamentum irritum* (a name which, while it might apply to any cause of failure, was conventionally limited to the cases in which the testator suffered *capitis deminutio*, and that in which no *heres* entered, which last case was also called *testamentum destitutum*) and *testamentum ruptum*, where the will was destroyed by the addition of members to the family, not provided

[1] C. 8. 57. 1. [2] C. 6. 51. 1.

for by anticipation, or was revoked. The subject of revocation calls for some discussion.

Mancipatio was essentially an irrevocable act, and thus the testator could not undo it. But the written instructions to the *familiae emptor* had not this irrevocable character, and thus there was nothing to prevent the testator from varying them. Hence arose the rule of the classical law, that at civil law a will could not be revoked except by the making of a second one, but failure of the second from any cause would not revive the first, though the Emperor on application allowed exceptions to this rule. Conversely a man who had once made a will could not thereafter, of his own wish, die intestate, though he might produce much the same result by making a new will, creating no legacies and appointing as *heredes* those who would come in on intestacy. If in the second will the *heres* was instituted to specific things only, this was, as we know, a good institution and in the ordinary way the restriction to specific things was simply ignored. But in the present case, it was provided by Severus that the first will should indeed be revoked, but the *heres* under the second will must be regarded as under a *fideicommissum* to give to those interested in the first will all but the things mentioned, with enough added to make up a quarter of the *hereditas*.

The Praetor however took a different line. He would refuse to give *bonorum possessio* under a will, if the will or its essential parts had been destroyed by the testator, and also of course if a revoking will had been made. But here, if the second will was revoked, he would give *bonorum possessio* under the first. In the later law, the mancipatory will being gone, there was a change. Theodosius the Great laid down the strange rule that a will should be revoked *ipso iure* by the lapse of ten years. Justinian substituted the more rational provision that it could be revoked after ten years by any declaration in court or before three witnesses[1]. And it appears that the praetorian rules as to destruction were still fully operative[2].

[1] C. Th. 4. 4. 6; C. 6. 23. 27. 2.

[2] See Girard, Manuel (5), 839.

74. The subject of legacy is on the whole simple, though even as stated in an elementary way by Gaius and Justinian, the amount of detail is surprising. Apart from these details there are several points which call for some discussion. A *legatum* is a direct gift by will, otherwise than by way of *hereditas*, having an ascertainable money value. Hence it follows that since liberty is inestimable, manumission by will is not a legacy, and in fact it is always carefully distinguished from legacy in the text, though of course a great many of the rules are the same.

We have already seen that minor gifts might not precede the institution in early law, manumissions and legacies being on the same level in this respect. The institution was good, but the minor gift failed. The rule gave rise to some difficulty where there were two institutions and the minor gift was placed between them. If the second institution failed from any cause, the minor gift would be good, but it was void if the second institution took effect. The *leges caducariae* however altered the situation. Under their rules an institution which failed was not a mere nullity. They established an order of devolution of such lapsed gifts. They would go, primarily, to other *heredes* with children. If the first institution was of such a *heres*, or of one of those who though childless had the *ius antiquum*, *e.g.*, a grandfather, there was no difficulty: the minor gift was good. But if he was a childless cousin, with *solidi capacitas*, he could not take this lapse: the legatees with children would take it, and we are told that they took it as *heredes*. It follows, according to Ulpian, that there is a subsequent institution, and the minor gift fails[1]. He adds that some lawyers disagreed with this conclusion, which is indeed not inevitable, since the will contained no institution of these legatees. In any case the *leges caducariae* and the rule as to position alike disappeared under Justinian.

Of the four forms of *legatum* described by Gaius it is plain that those *per vindicationem* and *per damnationem* are by far the most important. By the first form there was a direct

[1] Ulp. *Reg.* 4. 21, 24. 15.

transfer of the ownership to the legatee, at the moment of the acceptance by the *heres*, and this was probably the usual form. The curious doubt or difference of opinion between the two schools as to the ownership in the meantime, where the legacy was on a condition not yet fulfilled, was of some practical importance, though it must not be supposed that the Proculians, who thought it a *res nullius* in the meantime, held that it was open to *occupatio*. The chief practical point would be the interim right to the fruits. The Sabinians held that it was in the meantime the property of the *heres*, who would thus be entitled to the fruits. On either view the arrival of the condition would vest the property in the legatee, and at least so far retrospectively as to destroy any alienations or charges created by the *heres*. The Proculians also held that in any case it was a *res nullius* till the legatee had actually accepted it, but the view which prevailed was that of the Sabinians, *i.e.*, that it vested in the legatee at once, but devested if he refused the gift. Here, as elsewhere, it is difficult to say that the difference of opinion rests on any real principle.

The original form of the *legatum per damnationem* was *Heres meus damnas esto dare* (*etc.*) and it appears to owe to this form its special characteristic of creating a liability to double damages in certain cases. But in the classical law any words sufficed which imposed the obligation on the *heres* in peremptory words. It is not easy to see why this form was used in an ordinary gift of property, but its special use was in gifts of a third person's property which could not be directly given, or of services of any kind.

Legatum sinendi modo and *per praeceptionem* have both a somewhat exceptional look, a fact which explains the number of elementary points about which doubts arose, especially in connexion with the last named. These disputes, which turn mainly on the question whether it is, or is not, anything more than a variety of *legatum per vindicationem*, are familiar, and need not be entered on, but the form is interesting, as having been apparently the origin of the *praelegatum* of the later law. This is in all cases a legacy to one or more of the *heredes*. Its most noticeable rule is the obvious one that since a legacy to the *heres* of what would be his in any event is void, a *praelegatum* must necessarily fail, in so far as it is charged on the share which the legatee takes as *heres*. The effect of this is illustrated in several texts. Thus where *A* was *heres ex uncia*, *i.e.*, to one-twelfth, and *B* was *heres ex deunce, i.e.*, to eleven-twelfths, a farm was left to them jointly by *praelegatum*[1]. It follows from principle that the more either of these persons takes as *heres*, the less he can take as legatee, and thus *A* is entitled to eleven-twelfths of the farm as legatee while *B* is entitled only to one-twelfth. Where *A* and *B* were *heredes* in equal shares, a farm was left to *A*, *X* and *Y* in equal shares. *A* can claim only half his share, since half is chargeable on his own institution. As *A*'s share in full would be one-third, he can thus claim only one-sixth. *X* and *Y* can claim all the rest, taking from *B* what is charged on him in their favour, that is to say, two-thirds of his half, or one-third of the farm, and from *A* the one-third charged on him in the same way, and, on the ground of lapse, the one-sixth of the legacy which has failed by reason of being a legacy to the *heres*[2]. It may be noted that these points have some importance in relation to the *lex* Falcidia. Thus if the legacy is simply to one of two *heredes*, the other may charge the fraction of it which is charged on him towards the Falcidian limit of three-quarters[3].

By the *Sc.* Neronianum of A.D. 64, the difference between these forms was made much less important. This enactment provided that where a gift was made in a form not suited to it (*minus aptis verbis*) it should be construed, if it could be valid at all, as if it had been in the most favourable form, *i.e.*, *per damnationem*, since in this form any kind of benefit could be conferred. This piece of legislation did not however destroy the importance of the forms: Gaius still finds it necessary to distinguish very clearly between them. The point is that if a legacy is given in its proper form, the rules of that form still apply to it, and the incidental rules, especially as to joint

[1] D. 30. 34. 12. [2] D. 30. 116. 1.
[3] See on these points Dernburg, Pandekten 3. § 116.

legacy and lapse were different in the different cases. In A.D. 339 it was enacted that the differences of form should be of no importance[1]; they accordingly dropped out of usage, and Justinian formally suppressed them. In his day the rules are in general those of *legatum per vindicationem.*

75. The texts discuss at some length the case of joint legacies, cases in which the same thing is given to different persons. One case, that in which it is given to them in definite shares (*verbis tantum coniuncti*), is joint only in appearance: each is entitled to a share and is in no way concerned with the other share. But there are difficulties where the thing is given to two or more *coniunctim* (*re et verbis coniuncti*): "I give the *fundum* Cornelianum to *X* and *Y*," or *disiunctim* (*re tantum coniuncti*): "I give the *fundum* Cornelianum to *X*, I give the same land to *Y*."

If the gift were by vindication or preception, either *coniunctim* or *disiunctim*, the legatees shared and if one failed to take the other benefited. If the gift had been to *X* and *Y* *coniunctim*, followed by a gift of the same thing to *Z disiunctim*, *Z* took none of the lapsed share of *X* or *Y*, unless they both failed to take. On the other hand, if there is no lapse, *X* and *Y* will take only one-half between them. These various rules are not arbitrary: they follow from the two facts that there is in favour of each of the two donees a gift, in form, of the whole thing, the only circumstance capable of depriving him of it is the concurrent gift to another. If that is extinguished in any way the whole will come to him. In *legatum per damnationem* the rule is very different. If it is *coniunctim*, *i.e.*, "be my *heres* bound to give the thing to *X* and *Y*," this is an obligation on the *heres*, and like other joint debts it is divided, so that if one fails to take his share the *heres* benefits. If it is *disiunctim*, there are two distinct obligations each covering the whole thing, so that whether *X* takes or not, *Y* is entitled to the whole value. The rules were the same in *sinendi modo*, except that in the case of gift *disiunctim*, it was doubted whether the *heres* was

[1] C. 6. 23. 15. 2.

not absolutely discharged by allowing one to take it. The decision was ultimately made to depend on the intent of the testator.

Here too the *leges caducariae* introduced great changes. The rules are almost exactly the same as those in institutions, except that the first right to a lapsed gift is in a joint legatee with children. Under Justinian the old system is reintroduced with some modifications. Apart from joint gifts lapsed legacies go to the *heres* with their burdens. All joint legatees take in shares and lapsed gifts go to the colegatee. But there is a curious distinction. If it had been *disiunctim*, the colegatee having accepted his own part must take the lapse but holds it free of its burdens. If it was *coniunctim* he can refuse it, but if he takes it, must assume its burdens too. Justinian bases this distinction on the view that in a gift *disiunctim* the intention to give the whole to each if the other does not take is more certain than in the form *coniunctim*[1]. This is perhaps true, but to leave it to the choice of the legatees *coniunctim* whether they will take the lapsed gift or not is hardly a logical consequence of the difference.

76. The rules as to modalities in legacies do not greatly differ from those in institutions and a few words will suffice. Resolutive conditions, *i.e.*, those which determine the gift on the occurrence of some event, were struck out till the time of Justinian, but much the same result could be arrived at by the use of negative conditions. There is not much practical difference between a gift "till he does so and so," and a gift "provided he does not do so and so," but the former was an absolute gift, while under the latter the donee would be compelled to give the *cautio* Muciana, *i.e.*, security for return of the property if he did the forbidden thing[2]. This principle applied however only where the event depended on the volition of the beneficiary, *i.e.*, it was some course of conduct on his part to be abstained from, while the forbidden resolutive condition might of course cover a much wider field.

[1] C. 6. 51. 1. 11.

[2] D. 35. 1. 7. *pr*.

It is important to distinguish *modus* from *condicio*. A gift *sub modo* is an absolute gift with a direction as to its application. It vests at once in the legatee, but he cannot compel the *heres* to deliver it till he has given security for its proper application[1].

The rules as to *dies* in legacy are noticeably different from those in institutions. A *legatum* might always be given *ex die*, from a future day. The notion of legacy does not imply that continuity which is required in institutions and which appears to be infringed by such a modality. The restrictions on gifts after, or so many days before, the death of the *heres* or legatee were all swept away by Justinian. Something will be said of them in connexion with the law of contract[2].

77. Space is lacking for the discussion of the various different types of legacy which are considered in the texts, but it is desirable to distinguish one or two cases which can readily be confused, bearing in mind that as the testator may use what words expressive of the gift he likes, a distinction which may be made clearly enough in dealing with a typical case, may often have been very difficult to make in practice, where the words employed are infinitely variable and the testator's expressed intention is the governing factor. A *legatum generis* is a gift of a thing of a certain kind, *e.g.*, a horse, but not any particular horse. Here we have the rather clumsy rule that the legatee may choose, if there are things of the kind in the *hereditas*, but may not choose the absolute best, while if there are no such things in the *hereditas*, the *heres* may procure one at his choice, but it must not be of very bad quality[3]. Where the choice is expressly given to the legatee, this is *legatum optionis*, and here he has an unhampered choice, though even here, if the testator directs a third person to choose, Justinian does not allow him to choose the best. Until the time of Justinian a *legatum optionis* was conditional on personal choice by the legatee, at least to the

[1] *e.g.*, D. 40. 4. 17; D. 32. 19.
[2] *Post*, § 112.
[3] D. 30. 37. *pr.*

extent that it failed if he died without having chosen. There are however signs of dispute in the texts and it is by no means clear that it was regarded as conditional for all purposes. It is clear that such gifts might differ in form. Thus it might be *servi optionem do* as in *tutoris optio*, or *Stichum aut Pamphilum utrum eorum volet do* and so forth. The disputes may perhaps turn in part on these differences. The first form is less obviously conditional than the other. It may be added that though such gifts might be made of any kind of property, they were far more frequent in the case of slaves than of anything else.

A legacy of a thing pledged by the testator or held by him subject to a charge (*legatum rei obligatae*), was construed according to the state of the testator's knowledge. If the testator knew of the charge the *heres* must free it: if he did not it passed subject to the charge. A *legatum debiti* is a legacy of the testator's debt, to the creditor, and it is void unless it in some way increases the creditor's right, *e.g.*, it was absolute, while the debt was conditional. If valid it superseded the debt. A *legatum nominis* on the other hand is a legacy of a debt due to the testator. If it is a debt due from a third person, the legatee can require the *heres* to transfer his rights of action. If it is from the legatee himself, it is also called a *legatum liberationis*, and is a reply to any action on the debt, as well as entitling the legatee to a formal discharge. A *legatum liberationis* may also be from a debt by the legatee to a third person: here the legatee can require the *heres* to procure his release from the creditor[1].

The rules as to *legatum dotis* illustrate several principles. A legacy of her *dos* to the wife was valid even in the common case in which it would be hers in any case, though a legacy of a debt to the creditor was void unless it gave him in some way a better position. The point is that a legacy of *dos* can, like any other legacy, be recovered at once, while the recovery of *dos* by the ordinary action involved considerable delay. A legacy of *dos* in a case in which there had been no *dos* was

[1] D. 46. 1. 49. *pr.*

of course void. But where a testator left his wife a certain sum, or thing, describing it as *dos*, when in fact there was no *dos*, this was a valid legacy, on the principle that misdescription will not invalidate a clearly expressed gift—*falsa demonstratio non nocet*. This is, it seems, first laid down by Julian[1], and is twice confirmed by imperial rescripts within the next century.

Legatum peculii is subject to the rule that where it is to an *extraneus* the legatee is entitled to it as it is at the time of the death, while if it is to the slave himself he is entitled to it as it is at the time when he is free, *i.e.*, in ordinary cases, the entry of the *heres*. At first sight this looks like the ordinary rule, that a legatee is entitled to the thing as it was at *dies cedens*. But the texts shew that it is not this conception which underlies them. They speak of it as based on the probable intent of the testator[2]. The *peculium* differs from other unities, in that its constitution may vary from day to day, and thus changes in it are of a different kind from those which occur in a specific thing. The rule is thus in effect that in the case of the slave it is to retain its artificial unity till the entry of the *heres*, or any later date at which the slave is free, while where it is left to an *extraneus* it loses this character at the death of the testator, so that the legatee is entitled to the things which it contained at that time.

A *legatum partitionis* is a legacy of an aliquot part of the *hereditas*. One who has such a gift is quite distinct from a *heres*. He does not in any way represent the deceased and thus cannot sue or be sued on any debts. It was the practice therefore for agreements to be made between the *heres* and the legatee under which the *heres* would be bound to hand over the proper share of the assets, while the legatee agreed to pay his proper share of the burdens. Such agreements were called *stipulationes partis et pro parte*, and it will be remembered that they recur in connexion with transfers of part of the *hereditas* under a *fideicommissum*.

78. The expressions *dies cedit* and *dies venit* are used in

[1] D. 30. 75. 1. [2] *e.g.*, D. 15. 1. 57.

connexion with legacy, to express the arrival of two critical points of time in the acquisition of the legacy. The opposition is purely one of tense. *Dies cedit* means: the day is coming[1]. *Dies venit* means: the day has come. It is on the occurrence of the first that the gift may be said to have vested, to use an English technicality, so that though the donee should now die his representatives will still be able to claim the gift. The arrival of this day also determines in some cases the extent of the gift, for where specific property, or an aggregate, such as a flock of sheep or a slave's *peculium* is left, it is its value on that day which is due. It may determine the destination of a gift, for where a legacy is made to a slave whose ownership chances to be transferred, it is his owner on that day who is entitled to the gift. When *dies venit*, the legacy is recoverable by action. But though the opposition is purely one of tense, and the different verbs seem to be used merely because in writing, the present and the perfect of the verb *venire* are, in the third person, identical, this is obscured by the fact that past tenses of *cedere* are found in the texts in this connexion[2]. *Dies cessit* properly means exactly the same as *dies venit*, but it is not so used: it is a convenient way of expressing the fact that the time called *dies cedit* has passed. It is of course possible for the gift to fail even after *dies cedit*, since if no *heres* enters under the will, the whole thing will be void.

In general *dies cedit*, in *legata pura* and *sub modo*, and *ex die*, on the death, and in *legata sub condicione* on the arrival of the condition. *Dies venit* at the entry of the *heres*, or the arrival of the *dies*, or the occurrence of the condition, whichever be the last. There are a few cases, notably *legatum usufructus* and *legatum peculii* to the slave himself in which *dies cedit* only on the entry of the *heres*, and under the *leges caducariae*, ultimately repealed by Justinian, *dies cedit* in no case before the opening of the will. It is clear, in later law, that *dies cedit* without the knowledge of the legatee.

79. The *Regula* Catoniana is a rule which presents some

[1] D. 50. 16. 213. [2] *e.g.* D. 36. 2. 8; *h.t.* 16. 2.

difficulties of application. It provides, as ordinarily expressed, that a gift which would have been absolutely void if the testator had died immediately after he made it, cannot become good by subsequent events. Such a case would be that of a legacy to a man of what was already his own. It will not be valid because he sells the property after the will is made but before the death. The same would be true of a legacy to a *peregrinus* who afterwards acquires *civitas*, or one of materials which at the time of the will are part of an existing building[1]. This rule has been a favourite subject of commentary and interpretation from Roman times onward. It is expressly laid down that it does not apply to institutions, though as we know they are subject to a somewhat similar rule.

Some rules which look as if they were connected with the *Regula* Catoniana have really nothing to do with it. Thus the rule that a *legatum per vindicationem* requires that the thing shall have been the property of the testator at the time when the will was made looks like a direct application of the *regula*, but in fact it is independent, as is shewn by the fact that that rule applies equally to conditional gifts while the *regula* Catoniana does not.

The question how the *regula* was affected by the *leges caducariae* has been much discussed. It has indeed been said, by some writers, that they swept it away, a view which rests on a text from which we learn that the *regula* does not apply to any legacies in which *dies cedit* later than the death[2]. This, as we have just seen, was the case with all legacies after the enactment of these *leges*, for they deferred *dies cedens* to the opening of the will. Moreover the fact that the legatee was a *caelebs* or a *latinus* did not make the gift *ab initio* void, as it might seem that it should have, on the principles of the *regula*. But notwithstanding these appearances it is perfectly clear that the *regula* still existed. The rule as to *coelebs etc.* is explained by a text which tells us that the disabilities created by the *leges caducariae* were specially excluded from the operation of the *regula*[3]. And the other text, which creates the difficulty,

[1] D. 30. 41. 1. [2] D. 34. 7. 3. [3] D. 34. 7. 5.

merely means, as indeed it says, that the *regula* did not apply to legacies of which *dies cedit* only on the entry of the *heres* or arrival of a condition. Again it has been said that Justinian abolished the *regula* Catoniana by his enactment which provided that legacies and *fideicommissa* were to be assimilated and that each form of gift was to have all the advantages of the other. But the Digest contains a title on the *regula*, though a very short one, which shews clearly enough that it still existed. The alternative seems therefore to be that the *regula* was thereafter to be applied to *fideicommissa*, which were certainly not affected by it in earlier days. It seems indeed hardly likely that Justinian's enactment was meant to extend the restrictions of either form to both, since such a piece of legislation would have been restrictive, and indeed almost impossible to apply. Yet this is what must have happened in respect of the *regula* Catoniana[1]. It is indeed extremely difficult to say what Justinian did mean by this piece of legislation: the commissioners seem indeed to have decided somewhat capriciously what rules were to disappear and what were to be extended to both kinds of gift.

We know that the *regula* did not apply to conditional gifts. It did however apply to gifts which had originally been conditional, but which had become simple or unconditional by the occurrence of the condition before the death of the testator. This led to a question which seems to have caused the jurists some trouble. A legacy is left to Titius "provided he marries Claudia." At the time when the will was made Claudia was under marriageable age. Before the death of the testator Titius has in fact married Claudia. It is not now a conditional gift. It follows therefore that the *regula* Catoniana must apply to it. But if it does, will it not make the legacy inevitably void, since it is clear that if the testator had died at the moment of making his will this legacy could not have taken effect? The answer given by the jurists, obvious enough as it would seem, but not arrived at without hesitation, is, that the legacy

[1] See on these points and on the *regula* generally, Machelard, Dissertations, 472 *sqq*.

would not have been invalid if the testator had died at the moment when it was made, though it could not have taken effect there and then. It is not the words of the *regula* which are the law: the rule really is that a legacy cannot take effect by virtue of subsequent events if it was of such a nature that it might have taken effect at once but for some legal obstacle to the legacy. There seems to be some clumsiness about this, but the resulting rule is rational. The same difficulty is raised in perhaps a more subtle form in a text which discusses a legacy "to Titius, if I die after the Kalends of June," where the testator does so die. It is indeed in connexion with this case that the meaning of the rule is discussed[1].

The converse case may also occur. Suppose a legacy is given simply, *i.e.*, without any condition, and is such that it would be void if the testator now died. Such a gift cannot convalesce: the *regula* Catoniana applies. At a later date the testator by a codicil, duly confirmed, makes a conditional ademption of this legacy, *i.e.*, he provides that in a certain event this legacy is not to take effect. The result of this is that the legacy now becomes conditional on the non-occurrence of a certain event. It is therefore a conditional legacy. Is the effect of this to relieve it from the operation of the *regula* Catoniana? We are told that this effect is not produced, the reason assigned being that an ademption, being designed to take away or lessen the legatee's right, cannot in any case be construed as increasing it[2].

A simple legacy to the slave of the *heres* is plainly bad by the *regula*, since it is a gift to the *heres* of what is his own already. The case however is one which gave rise to much dispute, as can be seen from Gaius. The chief interest in the dispute is that Servius, in declaring all gifts to the slave of the *heres* good, appears to ignore the *regula* Catoniana altogether. On the other hand the Proculian view that all such gifts are bad cannot rest on the *regula*, since their rule covers conditional gifts and the *regula* does not. Gaius tells us that the opinion rests on the view that the *heres* cannot owe conditionally, any

[1] D. 34. 7. 1. *Cf. h.t.* 2.

[2] D. 34. 4. 14; D. 34. 2. 6.

more than he can simply, a gift to one in his own *potestas*. But this is little more than giving the rule as a reason for itself, and this Proculian rule did not prevail. The doctrine of the later law is that a simple gift is bad by the *regula*, while a conditional one may be good, as the *regula* does not apply to it, but will fail, as being meaningless, if at the time when the condition is satisfied the slave is still in the *potestas* of the *heres*.

It is a somewhat remarkable fact that while a gift of his own property to a man is void, and therefore a simple gift to a slave of the *heres* is void, by the *regula* Catoniana, a gift of the property of a third person to that person's slave is perfectly good, even though unconditional. This seems to infringe the *regula* Catoniana, since it would be ineffective if the testator died at once. It is a strong expression of the individuality of the slave. It imposes on the *heres* the duty to give the slave the value of the thing and is not thus a mere empty form as must be a legacy to the slave of the *heres*. It should be noticed that the validity of it does not depend on any alienation of the slave. The gift is absolutely good: it is not contemplated as affected by the *regula* in any way[1].

There is a difficulty in interpreting these texts in which gifts to slaves are concerned, owing to the fact that there is a progressive tendency to accentuate the duality of the slave and his master, considering the latter only so far as *testamenti factio* is concerned. But into this we cannot well enter.

A few words may be said as to the effect on a legacy of the destruction of its subject-matter. Apart from fault of the *heres* the loss falls on the legatee. Loss of one of several things left does not bar a claim for the rest, but if they are clearly principal and accessory and the principal thing is destroyed, the legatee cannot claim the accessory. Thus we are told that if a slave is bequeathed with his *peculium*, and the slave dies, the legatee does not get the *peculium*, while if it had been an *ancilla* with her children, these can never be accessories, and thus the death of the *ancilla* will not bar a claim for the children. It is not always easy to say what is an accessory, and much turns on the

[1] D. 31. 82. 2.

language of the will. Thus we are told that in a legacy of a *fundus cum instrumento*, the *instrumentum* is an accessory, but if it had been of a *fundus et instrumenta*, the construction would be different[1].

80. The remedies available to a legatee were much developed by Justinian. In early law he had either an *actio in rem* for the thing or an *actio in personam* against the *heres* according to the form of the gift, though even in the later classical law it was possible for the legatee *per vindicationem* to bring an *actio in personam* against the *heres* if he preferred. It should also be noted that even a legacy *per vindicationem* imposes a duty on the *heres*: the ownership passes, but he is under a duty to transfer possession, a fact which creates some difficulty in interpreting texts which speak of the *heres* as under an obligation. We cannot always infer from this form that the legacy concerned was *per damnationem*. Justinian provided that all legacies were to have one and the same nature and to be recoverable by the same actions. These were:

(*a*) *Actio in rem*, varying of course with the nature of the gift, *e.g.*, *vindicatio*, in an ordinary gift of property, *actio confessoria* in a legacy of a servitude, and so forth.

(*b*) *Actio in personam*, asserting a duty in the *heres* to transfer the property.

(*c*) *Actio hypothecaria*. He provided that all the property of the testator should be under a charge for the payment of legacies. So long as there had been no partition he provided that no *heres* should be liable under this action for more than his share, but after partition, as a particular *heres* might not have this thing, and in that case would not be liable to be sued by the *actio in rem*, and would be liable by the *actio in personam* only to the extent of his share, the *actio hypothecaria* gave the best remedy, since any *heres* could be sued by it for the whole amount of the gift, as all the property of the *hereditas* was pledged for it. He could of course claim reimbursement from the other *heredes*[2].

[1] D. 33. 7. 5.

[2] C. 6. 43. 1.

There were some cases in which no action *in rem* was conceivable, *e.g.*, where what was left was a mere *ius in personam* as in *legatum nominis* or *liberationis*, or where it was a service to be rendered, or the property left did not belong to the testator, or it was a legacy of *res fungibiles* and there were none of them in the *hereditas*.

81. It is clear as has been said above, that the primary purpose of *fideicommissa* was the making of gifts by will to persons who had not *testamenti factio* with the testator. Such gifts were common in the later days of the Republic, but they were not in any way enforceable, resting entirely on the good faith of the *heres*. Augustus ordered them in a few cases to be carried out by the administrative authority of the Consuls, not exactly as juristic institutions, in some cases because the testator had begged the beneficiary to carry them out *per salutem principis*, and in others because of the perfidy of some beneficiaries. Gradually they came to be a recognised legal institution and a special *praetor*, the *praetor fideicommissarius*, was appointed to adjudicate on them. There is no necessary connexion between *fideicommissa* and informal codicils; at first they were always in wills. But a certain Lucius Lentulus having made Augustus one of his *heredes*, as it seems, imposed certain *fideicommissa* on him and others by codicil. Augustus ordered his to be carried out, and the other fiduciaries, or some of them, then did the same. Augustus then invited the opinion of lawyers as to whether these codicils ought to be legally recognised. Trebatius thought they should be, as being very convenient, for instance, when a man was travelling in remote regions. Labeo actually made codicils, and they were thereafter accepted as legal. It does not appear that these codicils of Lentulus were the first *fideicommissa* to be enforced. It is to be observed that there is nothing about the *praetor* in these developments. If we ask what was the authority on which they rested, no doubt the really correct answer is that they were established by the will of the Emperor. But Augustus could not make law, and they must technically be regarded as civil law institutions—juristic creations. At first such *fideicommissa* could be created by codicil only if there was a will, though before Gaius the further step had been taken of validating *codicilli* in which *fideicommissa* were imposed on the *heres ab intestato.* But it was still true that if there was a will codicils failed if they were not confirmed actually or by anticipation by it, and also if the will itself failed. Severus and Caracalla provided, however, that even an unconfirmed codicil could make *fideicommissa* though it could do nothing else.

Though *fideicommissa* could benefit those who could not have taken direct gifts, they required *testamenti factio* in the maker: no one could make a codicil who could not have made a will. The further things which could be done by a confirmed codicil and the various rules of form which gradually developed need not be considered here.

Restrictions soon began to be imposed as to the persons who could benefit. The *Sc.* Pegasianum (A.D. 73) made them subject to the ordinary law as to *coelebes* and *orbi,* and Hadrian excluded *peregrini, postumi alieni* and *incertae personae.* But they were still a great extension of the powers of testation: it was possible by their means to evade practically the rules preventing institutions *ex die* and *in diem.* Junian latins could still take and other details can be found in Gaius of the same kind.

Fideicommissa of the *hereditas* or part of it seem to have been the most usual, as they were certainly the most important, form. To avoid the liability for debts, which attached necessarily to the *heres* (*semel heres semper heres*), notwithstanding transfer, it was customary for agreements to be made as on the sale of an inheritance, under which the *fideicommissarius* undertook to satisfy the debts or his share of them and the *heres* to transfer his rights of action. The *heres* if afterwards sued had an *exceptio restitutae hereditatis.* But the Roman law did not recognise the principle that a trust ought not to fail for want of a trustee, and thus if a *heres,* who was to take no profit, saved himself trouble by refusing to enter, the *fideicommissum* would be destroyed. A *Sc.* Trebellianum did something towards creating a remedy by a provision that if a *heres* handed over the *hereditas* or part of it under such a trust, the actions should pass wholly or *pro rata*, by the mere fact of the handing over, a process which did not need any form, but might be done by mere declaration.

It is probable that this system did not work satisfactorily, perhaps *heredes* insisted on being paid for their complaisance. At any rate about eleven years later (A.D. 73) the *Sc.* Pegasianum authorised the *heres* to keep a quarter of the *hereditas*, as he could against legatees, and it provided also that if the *heres* still refused to enter he could be made to do so, taking in that case no profit and incurring no loss. The act of entry was not simply dispensed with: the magistrate compelled the *heres* to enter and transfer, refusal being no doubt met by the ordinary methods of magisterial *coercitio*. But we are told that, if in any case the *heres* who entered cut down the *fideicommissa*, the *Sc.* Trebellianum did not apply to the case and it was necessary to fall back on mutual stipulations, in a slightly different form, those being used which had been employed in the case of a *legatarius partiarius*—*stipulationes partis et pro parte*. (It is said, though the texts are in conflict, that these stipulations were needed where there was a right to cut down the *fideicommissa* even though it was not exercised.) No rational basis has ever been assigned for this remarkable rule. The language of Ulpian and Paul suggests that it was due to something in the *Sc.* Pegasianum itself[1]. It was the practice, perhaps necessary, to declare under which *senatus consultum* one was surrendering, and this suggests, as indeed Paul expressly says, that one entitled to keep back a quarter but intending not to do so, might declare himself to surrender under the *Sc.* Trebellianum, in which case actions would pass *ipso facto*. The probability is that the language of Gaius reflects that of the senatusconsult itself, and that its provision was that the gifts should be cut down as in the case of legacies, and in the case of legacies, even *legata partis hereditatis*, there could be no question of actions passing *ipso facto*.

Justinian simplified the system, repealing the *Sc.* Pegasianum

[1] Ulp. *Reg.* 25. 15; Paul, *Sent.* 4. 3. 2.

and grafting its rules, as to compulsory *aditio* and the right to cut down the gift, on the *Sc.* Trebellianum, of which he declares his rules to be a recast. He thus gets rid of the notion that the case is to be dealt with as one of legacy, and actions now pass *ipso facto* without any need for stipulations. The rules as to cutting them down if they exceeded three quarters applied also to *fideicommissa* of single things, but there was no compulsion on the *heres* to enter on their account[1], and there could thus be no question, in their case, of any transfer of actions. Justinian provided also that such gifts and legacies were to be assimilated, but there were still important differences in gifts of freedom, which as we have seen were not, properly speaking, legacies. A direct gift of freedom could apply only to the testator's own slave, and made him a *libertus orcinus*, having no living patron. A *fideicommissum* of liberty could be made in favour of another man's slave and made him the *libertus* of the *fiduciarius*, subject, however, to some restrictions.

It will be noticed that *fideicommissa* of specific things have some resemblance to *legata per damnationem*: in classical law the rules of such *legata* were applied to them in certain cases, particularly in settling the claims of joint beneficiaries.

82. There is one very important kind of question, arising in connexion with *fideicommissa*, to which the Institutes provide no answer. If a *fideicommissarius* is himself subjected to a *fideicommissum*, how far can he deduct the *quarta Pegasiana*? In the same case, if there are legacies, and the *heres* has handed over the whole *hereditas* to the *fideicommissarius*, how far can the *fideicommissarius* deduct the *quarta Falcidia*? The questions are quite distinct and both are somewhat difficult, the numerous texts in the Digest having been altered in such a way that they can hardly represent accurately any of the *strata* of law which the subject presents, so that no clear answer can be got from them. As to the first question, the rules seem to be these. If the *heres* could not have deducted anything when he handed over the *hereditas*, the *fideicommissarius* can deduct

[1] D. 36. 1. 17. 2.

nothing. If he could have done so, but did not, the *fideicommissarius* can deduct, at any rate if the *heres* refrained from doing it in order that he might. If the *heres* did deduct, he can do so too, unless he was a freedman of the deceased, or there was some evidence that the testator did not mean him to have any such right. Leaving the case of the freedman and evidence of intent out of account, the principle seems to be that, as the right of the *fideicommissarius* is derived wholly from the *fiduciarius*, he can have no right that the latter had not.

The other question gives rise to many questions of construction, and its difficulty can be at once realised by anyone who turns to the titles in the Digest on the *Lex* Falcidia and the *Sc.* Trebellianum. It must first be determined whether the testator intended legacies to be charged on the *heres* or on the *fideicommissarius*, there being a general presumption in favour of the latter view, at least where the duty to transfer was not postponed. Without going into details the principle may be roughly stated as follows. If they were to be chargeable on the *heres*, the legacies and the *fideicommissa* are treated as a whole, and cut down *pro rata*, the *heres* keeping a quarter and there being no question of any deduction by the *fideicommissarius*. If the *heres* only entered under compulsion, under the provisions of the *Sc.* Pegasianum, a *fideicommissarius* of the whole may cut down legacies to three quarters. If legacies were to be chargeable on the *fideicommissarius*, his *fideicommissum* of the whole is regarded as being one of the whole, less the amount of the legacies. The *heres* keeps a quarter and the rest is distributed *pro rata*. Thus, if the whole *hereditas* was worth four and there were legacies of three and a *fideicommissum* of the whole, the *heres* will keep a quarter, and of the rest the legatees will take three quarters and the *fideicommissarius* will take one quarter. If the *heres* entered only under compulsion (*coactus*) the *fideicommissarius* will also get the quarter which the *heres* might have retained had he entered voluntarily. There is, it will be noticed, a rule, covering all cases, that the fact that the *heres* entered only under compulsion is not to entitle the legatees to get more than they would have received if the *heres* had entered voluntarily. If the *heres* enters voluntarily, and refuses the quarter, this does not of itself entitle the *fideicommissarius* to take more at the cost of the legatees, but we are told that he may do so, *i.e.*, may deduct the quarter of the *heres* also, if the intent of the latter in refusing the quarter was to benefit the *fideicommissarius*[1].

Where the *fideicommissum* is only of a share of the *hereditas*, there are a number of complicated cases which we cannot discuss. It must also be borne in mind that the refusal of the *heres* to enter, even under the system of Justinian, may be an entirely rational act. If the estate should be insolvent, even though the fideicommissary has undertaken to accept transfer, he may refuse to do so, the fact of the insolvency having come out after the entry of the *heres*. The latter will then be liable—*semel heres semper heres*—and his remedy, if he has one, against the fideicommissary, may on readily imagined circumstances be very illusory. He can of course protect himself by an inventory, but, if he is to get nothing, it is not worth his while.

83. A question of some general interest is that as to the extent to which a Roman testator could create limited interests by his will. It is plain that the desire to do so existed: how far could it be gratified? How far could a testator tie up his property and determine its future devolution after his death? Apart from *fideicommissa* the power seems to have been very small. No *incerta persona* could be instituted *heres* or receive a legacy, and thus, though a testator might create a series of usufructs they must all be to existing persons, or at any rate to persons conceived, and thus property could hardly be effectively "settled" for more than existing lives and the period of gestation. The right to institute *postumi* is not a real extension of this power. All such *postumi* must have been born or conceived at the time of the testator's death, whether they are the *postumi sui* of the civil law or the praetorian *postumi alieni*. It must

[1] See for an account of this matter and references to the principal texts, Poste's Gaius (ed. Whittuck), 256 *sqq*.

be borne in mind that the power to institute *postumi sui* was not primarily intended to increase the power of testation and settlement, but to prevent the intestacy which would otherwise result from the agnation of a *postumus*. The rule as to *postumi alieni* is an analogous extension so far as it goes. But this is not very far: the institution was not good at civil law, though the *institutus* could obtain a grant of *bonorum possessio secundum tabulas*. What the primary purpose of this praetorian extension may have been is not very clear. It may have been in order to be able to provide for the posthumous children of *emancipati*, or it may have been a mere development from the rule recognised at civil law, that the slave of a *postumus alienus* could be instituted. Just as *servi hereditarii* could be instituted where the *hereditas* was *iacens*, so in the same way, where it was in an analogous position because a *suus heres* entitled to succeed was not yet born, it was recognised as early as Labeo that an institution of a slave in that *hereditas*[1], by the will of a third party, was perfectly good, though the slave had in strictness no existing owner. The praetor may well have thought it reasonable to recognise the possibility of instituting a person whose slave could be instituted. But all these provisions come to very little: the possibility of holding over the *delatio hereditatis*, for more than the period of gestation, does not seem to have been contemplated.

Fideicommissa however afforded a means of going very much further in this direction. They could at first be made in favour of *incertae personae* and, as there could be *fideicommissa* on *fideicommissa*, it was possible to burden each successive beneficiary with a trust to hand over the property at his death to his son, and so on in perpetuity. We know indeed that such things were done. The will of Dasumius, made in A.D. 108, is still in existence[2]. It gives certain lands to his *liberti* with no power to sell or pledge them, with a right of accrual or survivorship, and a direction that on the death of the last survivor, the lands are to go to the *posteri* on the same terms. The last of these is to have the power of alienation. This is substantially

[1] D. 28. 5. 65.
[2] Bruns, Fontes (7) 1. 304.

a complete "perpetuity." It is not possible to say whether such things were usual or not. Probably the will in question owes its partial preservation to the fact that it was inscribed on marble, otherwise we might suppose that its peculiar provisions had something to do with it. In any case, Hadrian forbade *fideicommissa* in favour of *incertae personae*, so that the power ceased.

Thereafter testators inserted in their will directions not to alienate. If these were valid they would produce much the same result, but Severus and Caracalla provided that such a direction was a nullity unless it was combined with a *fideicommissum*[1]. Such a *fideicommissum* would usually be for members of the family, and the Digest gives many illustrations of such family trusts. They could not however be perpetual—they were not it would seem binding in classical law, except on donees alive at the testator's death and their immediate issue. Such restrictions seem to have had a certain operation *in rem*, *i.e.*, they not merely imposed a duty on the *heres* and successors, but they vitiated any sale by the fiduciary, at any rate if there was an express prohibition of sale. If there was no express prohibition of sale, but only a *fideicommissum* in favour of the *familia*, we are told that the *fideicommissarius* could get *missio in possessionem* against a buyer who had notice of the trust. But Justinian in abolishing this remedy tells us that it was ineffective and obscure[2]. No doubt there might be difficulties in proving notice and there were the rights of a *bona fide* purchaser from the first buyer to consider. Under Justinian it seems that all property subject to a *fideicommissum* was by that fact rendered absolutely inalienable.

But there was another change under Justinian of much greater importance. All sorts of gifts could now be made to *incertae personae*, but as institutions were still confined to persons conceived at the time of the death, and *ususfructus sine persona constitui non potest*, neither of these could well be used to establish perpetuities. But, as in earlier days, *fideicommissa* were available, and they were used for the purpose. It was

[1] D. 30. 114. 14.

[2] C. 6. 43. 3. 2.

possible to direct the *heres* to hand over the property on his death to his son, to direct the latter to do the same, and so on for ever. The only difficulty was the quarter which the *heres* was entitled to retain. If he was old his usufruct might not be worth so much. But it was easy to reserve enough to satisfy this, and, in any case, Justinian allowed the testator to forbid the keeping of this. In Novel 159, Justinian states a case in which such a perpetuity had been created. The novel shews that a certain testator Hierios, evidently a man of mark, had in his will enumerated certain specific estates and given them each to a different son, on the terms that the donee was not to alienate it away from his name and family. Those of them who died leaving issue were to leave the property to their issue. The shares of those who died without issue were to go to the survivors on the same terms. In a codicil, he transferred a suburban property to a grandson on similar terms, but adding a direction that it was to remain for ever in the family. The directions in the will applied only to the heirs themselves, but that in the codicil was perpetual. The grandson obeyed the directions of the codicil, but his son left the property to a posthumous child, and in the event, which happened, of the child dying under puberty, to his wife and mother jointly. A surviving *heres* of the original testator claimed the property, on the ground that the wife and mother were not of the family. The actual decision is that, for the then present purpose, they were, so that there has been no breach. It further points out that it is only in the codicil that there is any perpetual restriction, and then by way of *ex post facto* legislation lays it down that it has been going on long enough, and that the present holders are to be free to do what they like with the property. It then adds as a general rule for the future that no such prohibition is to hold good for more than four generations. It may be added that this restriction of what have come to be called fideicommissary substitutions to four generations is still in force in several parts of the British empire, and played an important part in the case of Strickland *v.* Strickland, from Malta, a few years ago[1].

[1] 1908 App. Ca. 551.

CHAPTER V

SUCCESSION ON INTESTACY. BONORUM POSSESSIO

84. WE know that in early law the will was exceptional, and we know also that, long before classical times, the state of things had entirely changed, and intestacy had become unusual. It had come to be regarded as a great misfortune, and even as early as Plautus a feeling had developed which has been called a horror of intestacy. The very artificial state of the law of succession on intestacy may account for the desire to make a will, but hardly for the intensity of this feeling. Accordingly there have been many attempts to explain it in other ways. These are little more than conjectures: here, as in many other cases, it is difficult to be sure of the historical origin of a social sentiment. Maine[1] suggests that emancipation is really a reward, but has the unfortunate effect of excluding the emancipated son from the succession, and for this state of things the will provides a remedy. This hardly seems enough to account for a state of opinion in which "May you die intestate" was a curse to hurl at your enemies. Another explanation is that the stern Roman mind saw a duty and a responsibility involved in the right of testation. Another is that the power of testation was prized by the plebeians as their most striking triumph over the patricians, and that as the plebeians in course of time became the dominant element, what had formerly been a mere plebeian sentiment became a Roman sentiment. Another explanation is that there was no power of giving legacies or of appointing *tutores* without a will[2]. But all these forms of the

[1] Ancient Law, 222.

[2] Girard, Manuel (5) 795.

proposition that everyone likes to extend his influence beyond his life do not seem enough to account for the strength of the feeling in question. It has accordingly been suggested that there must be something religious at the bottom of it, and that it may have been due to the fact that a *heres legitimus* could cede the *hereditas*, and thus shift the *sacra* to other, uninterested, keeping, while a *heres ex testamento* could not[1].

Many of what may be called the subsidiary rules of succession apply to succession on intestacy as well as to succession by will. Such are the rules as to *beneficium abstinendi*, *spatium deliberandi*, inventory, *collatio bonorum*, *fideicommissa* and so forth. But there is one very important exception. The rules of the *leges caducariae* as to *coelibes* and *orbi* have no application whatever in cases of intestacy. Even if they had applied, they could not have been of very great importance, since some relatives are wholly excluded from their operation and almost all are so far excluded that they can take what is expressly given to them, and the *heres ab intestato* is a relative. But they do not apply where, for instance, an agnate refuses. Accrual applies in favour of the others in the same degree, whether they are married or not, while if it has been a case of gift by will, they would have been wholly excluded from sharing in *caduca* or the like, in such a case. Moreover there could be no question of a *heres necessarius* (other than *suus*) in a case of intestacy[2].

85. The rules of succession on intestacy constitute a great mass of detail, undergoing constant change. These changes are nearly all in one direction. A system resting absolutely on the idea of agnation is gradually superseded, at first under the influence of the Praetor, but at least as early as the time of Hadrian, by express legislation, by one in which the natural blood relationship is more and more considered, until, in Justinian's final legislation, that which is embodied in Novels 118 and 127, there is no longer any trace of the old civil law ideas. Nothing is said therein of *potestas* or of agnation: the order is in the main governed by modern-looking notions,

[1] Accarius, Précis, 1. 840. [2] See, however, *ante* § 65.

so modern indeed that it has passed with more or less modification into most modern systems of law, even our own, for it underlies the provisions of the Statutes of Distribution of personal property.

The word 'heir' of English law is much narrower in scope than the word *heres* of Roman law. The former applies only to the beneficial successor to real estate on intestacy: the latter covers all universal successors on death at civil law, either by will or on intestacy. But though it no doubt applied to successors by will as soon as wills came into existence, the name does not seem to have been applied in the earliest times to all successors on intestacy. There are two well known texts of the Twelve Tables which lay down the rules of succession on intestacy:

Si intestato moritur cui suus heres nec escit agnatus proximus familiam habeto. Si agnatus nec escit gentiles familiam habento[1]. No text survives, and probably none existed, laying down in express terms the right of succession of the *suus heres*. It is taken for granted in the first of these texts. The word *heres* indeed means, as it seems, owner: the *suus heres* is not exactly inheriting, but assuming control of what was in a sense his already. More significant is the fact that the agnates and the gentiles are not said to become *heredes*. The words are not *heredes sunto*, but *familiam habento*. They were not in fact *heredes* as they became in the more developed law. They do not appear to have been under any personal liability for the debts of the deceased, and they were certainly under no obligation as to the *sacra*. When in course of time, and still very early, agnates did become liable for the *sacra* and for the debts, they equally came to be considered as *heredes*. But though the succession of the *gentiles* may have continued until nearly the end of the Republic, the conception of *hereditas* never seems to have been extended to their right. Little is indeed really known about their case, but it seems always to have been considered not so much one of succession as one of reversion to a common stock, an idea which also colours some of the texts which deal

[1] Bruns, Fontes, 1. 23.

with agnatic succession. But the rights of the *gentiles* have so little bearing on later developments that we need not discuss them.

The language of the texts above cited is interesting from another point of view, as it expresses another very striking principle of the old law of succession. It admits neither *successio graduum* nor *successio ordinum.* If the nearest in any degree does not take, a point which can arise only in connexion with agnates, since there can be no question of degrees among *sui heredes*, or of refusal at civil law, the language of the *lex* expressly excludes the next in succession: *proximus agnatus familiam habeto.* These words give no right to any agnates but the *proximus*, and whether, as some suppose, the succession of agnates was introduced by the Twelve Tables or not, that enactment was always regarded as expressing the fundamental law of the matter. So also, in the same case, it seems that a refusal by the agnates does not let in the *gentiles*: it is only if there are no agnates that they come in: *si agnatus nec escit.* In the praetorian law the principle is very different. So far as *successio ordinum* is concerned, that is, the right of the next class to come in if those entitled under the earlier class refuse, the Praetor's rule is that this latter class can now claim[1]. It often happens indeed that those included in one class are also covered by another, so that they have two chances to claim. Thus *liberi* who have allowed their time to pass may be the nearest *legitimi*, or *cognati.* As to *successio graduum* he applies in general the same principle. If the nearest *cognati* allow the time to pass, or even if they repudiate the succession, the next *cognati* may now claim[2]. This is not so indeed in the case of *Agnati*, in regard to whom the Praetor does not let in any claim but those admitted at civil law. This is expressed in the words of the edict: the persons entitled are the *legitimi*, *i.e.*, those entitled under the *lex.* This is clearly because it is no part of his scheme to extend the operation of the agnatic idea. Justinian admits *successio graduum* even among agnates, and

[1] See, *e.g.*, D. 38. 9. 1. 11.

[2] D. 38. 8. 1. 10.

in his final rules under the Novels he freely allows devolution[1].

It is important to notice that the succession may not be immediate on the death. The most important date is not that of the death, but that on which the succession "opens." This may be described shortly as being the date at which it is clear that there will be no *heres* under any will[2]. It is obvious that this may not be till long after the death. A *heres institutus* may refuse only at the end of the *spatium deliberandi*, or it may be long before it is certain that a condition on an institution will not be satisfied. The statement that there is intestacy where there is no *heres* under any will is not absolutely correct. The *heres* is a civil law successor and intestacy will be excluded by any sort of successor under any sort of will, *i.e.*, by the existence of any *bonorum possessor secundum tabulas*, at any rate *cum re*. The importance of the date of opening is that it is the person entitled at that date who takes, who is not necessarily the person who was nearest at the time of the death. If my brother survives me, but dies before a *heres institutus* has refused, my cousin may be my nearest agnate though he was not so at my death. The date of the death is however material in another way. No one can succeed on intestacy unless he was born or conceived at the time of the death[3].

86. It was said above that the changes were in the direction of lessening the importance of the agnatic connexion. One rule is however something like an exception to this. Late in the Republic the rule developed that no woman could succeed as an agnate except a *consanguinea*, a sister. This would of course have the effect of keeping the property in the male side of the family and is so far an expression of the agnatic idea. It is said to be based on *Voconiana ratio*, and it is obviously similar in principle to the rule of the *lex Voconia* (B.C. 168) by which a person of the wealthy class was prevented from

[1] See Girard, Manuel (5) 885 *sqq.*

[2] D. 29. 2. 39.

[3] D. 37. 9. 1. 1.

instituting a woman as his *heres*. It is a civil law rule, but the mode of its development is unknown.

The Praetor's changes are all in the direction of recognising cognation. He gives the first claim to *bonorum possessio* to *liberi*, a class which includes besides *sui* and *emancipati*, children of deceased *emancipati*, and children of the deceased who had been left in a family from which he had been emancipated. It should be noted that in the praetorian scheme the distribution among *liberi*, who replace for him the *sui* of civil law, is somewhat more complicated than the civil law rule had been. Even at civil law *sui* had not necessarily taken equally, for grandchildren through a son who had died or suffered *capitis deminutio* would divide his share between them. But when the Praetor admitted *emancipati*, it is obvious that the claims of an emancipated son and those of his children left in the family would clash. Logically it would seem that the rule ought to have been that if the emancipated son claimed, his children in the family ought to have been excluded. But they were *sui heredes*, and a special rule in the Edict so far respects their right as to make them share with their father. It is a remarkable fact that this rule was not laid down till the time of Julian. How the matter was settled in earlier days we do not know. This rule had the result that as the coming in of the father injured no *heres* but his own children, for he merely took part of their share, he had no *collatio bonorum* to make as against other *sui*, but only as against these children of his[1]. After these came the *legitimi* who were those entitled at civil law, and after these the important new class of *cognati*. Relationship for this purpose was not recognised beyond the sixth degree, or in one case (second cousins once removed), the seventh, but subject to this any kind of relationship counted. Thus it covered besides relatives through females, all agnates, male or female, children not born *ex iustis nuptiis*, and, in the case of women, children born *incerto patre*, etc. It was the Praetor also who gave reciprocal right of succession to the husband and wife, in the absence of blood relatives.

[1] D. 37. 8. 3; D. *h.t.* 1. *pr.*

The Imperial changes were nearly all in the same direction. Of the important rules laid down by the *Scc.* Orphitianum and Tertullianum, and later legislation extending their principle, we shall have to speak shortly. But apart from them there were many changes. Anastasius allowed brothers and sisters who had been emancipated to rank as agnates, with a certain deduction. Justinian extended this to their issue and to half-blood brothers and sisters through the mother[1]. Justinian broke with the Twelve Tables by allowing devolution among agnates: if the nearest refused, the next took. And he also abolished the rule excluding from the class of agnates women more remote than sisters.

87. The earlier law of succession on intestacy is stated almost entirely from the point of view of the *paterfamilias.* The rules of succession to the property of a woman are of course implicitly contained in what is said, but they have to be picked out. It is the position of a woman in the agnatic group which leads to the absurd looking result that the children could not succeed to their mother at all at civil law, and only remotely, as cognates, even at praetorian law. It must be remembered of course that we are concerned with marriage without *manus,* the only one which is important in the classical law. Issue of an ordinary marriage had no claim to succeed to their mother if she had any agnates, however remote. This was not remedied till A.D. 178, and then not by the Praetor, whose powers of legislation had disappeared under Hadrian, but by the *senatusconsultum* Orphitianum. It is at first sight somewhat surprising to note that the simple rule that children can succeed in the first instance to their mother comes historically later than the provision for what must have been a much rarer case, namely that of a mother succeeding to her children, which was provided for by the *senatusconsultum* Tertullianum, the date of which is not known, but which was certainly enacted at some time in the reign of Hadrian. The reason of this is said to be that the two pieces of legislation are based on entirely different ideas. The *Sc.* Tertullianum is a late part of that elaborate

[1] C. 6. 58. 15.

legislation for the encouragement of marriage of which the *leges caducariae* are the earliest and best known part. The *Sc.* Orphitianum on the other hand is an early part of that legislation which in the long run superseded the agnatic idea altogether, so far as succession was concerned. It is to be noticed that it is not until the time of Justinian that the rules under the *Sc.* Tertullianum are wholly dissociated from the *ius liberorum*, so that the rights are given to all mothers.

The rules under this enactment are deserving of some attention. We know that they underwent changes from time to time, always in the direction of improving the position of the mother. Her claim at first depended on her having the *ius liberorum*, *i.e.*, having three children (four if she was a *libertina*), and in the order established by the enactment she was excluded by brothers of the deceased. Constantine improved her position and, in particular, gave her a reduced share even without the *ius liberorum*. There was further legislation with the same tendency in A.D. 369 and 426, and Justinian, besides sweeping away the *ius liberorum*, provided that she should share with brothers. The actual order at different times need not be stated.

The important point to note is that while the order under the senatusconsult differs widely from the existing rules it appears to leave these unaffected. There is no hint, and no reason to think, that this enactment in any way superseded the older law. The rules are a direct creation of the senatusconsult and do not in any way depend on the older law. There are some near relatives who have rights of succession and who are not mentioned in the order laid down in the senatusconsult. What rule is to be applied if in the given case there are such persons? The answer to questions of this kind is to be found in two great governing principles which control the application of the senatusconsult. The first is that the senatusconsult is to be applied only where the claimants are those which it mentions, that is to say, it is not to be applied if there exists a person who is not mentioned in its order, and who would, at common law, take before the person who is entitled under its provisions. There is also the further and perhaps still more important principle that the enactment is not meant to give any person other than the mother any greater rights than he or she would have had under the ordinary law. If in the given case there exist persons who on the terms of the senatusconsult are preferred to the mother, then the enactment has no application at all: the common law is applied.

These principles are freely illustrated in the texts, but the cases are in some respects difficult because of the uncertainty whether the order mentioned in them is that operative under Justinian or that operative in the time of the original author. In one case a grandfather emancipated a grandson, who died leaving, surviving him, this grandfather and his own father and mother. The senatusconsult prefers the mother to any grandfather, but it prefers the father to the mother. The mother being thus excluded, the senatusconsult has no application to the case: the common law is applied and the grandfather, as being *parens manumissor*, takes the succession[1]. A deceased left a mother, certain agnates, and a father who had been given in adoption by the grandfather. Such a father did not exclude the mother, under the senatusconsult, as fathers in another family are expressly excepted. Agnates are not mentioned in the senatusconsult as having a place in the order, and it might be thought that on our rule they would take, as agnates have a better claim at common law than the mother. But as Justinian states the enactment mothers are preferred to all *legitimae personae* (which means agnates and those at that time grouped with them), except brothers and sisters. It follows that the mother excludes them and takes the property[2]. A person died leaving a mother, children given in adoption and an agnatic cousin. Agnates exclude children given in adoption, at common law, and are not expressly postponed to them in the senatusconsult. They exclude the children, but the mother excludes them under the senatusconsult, and thus takes the property[3]. Other cases are more complicated but these seem to express the principle sufficiently.

[1] D. 38. 17. 5. 2. [2] D. *h. t.* 2. 17.

[3] See Demangeat, Cours de Droit Romain, 2. 49.

Where a woman died leaving both a mother and children it is plain that there might be difficulties in applying the *Scc.* Tertullianum and Orphitianum. If there were other claims that were preferred to the mother, *e.g.*, under the original scheme of the *Sc.* Tertullianum, brothers, then the children took the property on the principles we have laid down, for as brothers exclude the mother the *Sc.* Tertullianum has no application, and the *Sc.* Orphitianum gives the property to the children. But where there was no other claim than those of the mother and child their rights are equal as cognates at praetorian law, and they have no rights at civil law. The *Sc.* Tertullianum standing alone would give the property to the mother, while the *Sc.* Orphitianum standing alone would give it to the children, so that they shared, until in the later Empire it was provided that in any case children should succeed to their mother notwithstanding anything in the *Sc.* Tertullianum[1].

The *Sc.* Orphitianum gave no rights to remoter issue. This was remedied by legislation of 389 A.D. which provided on the one hand for grandchildren of a man through a deceased daughter, and on the other for grandchildren of a woman through a son or a daughter. In the first case they were to take two-thirds of the share their mother would have taken, as against surviving *sui heredes*, and three-quarters of the estate as against agnates. The rule was the same in the second case except that it is not clear that there was any deduction for surviving children of the woman, though there was for the agnates of the deceased[2]. This deduction was however removed by Justinian.

88. In the Institutes can be seen a number of small changes made by Justinian or his legal advisers always in the direction of making the rules of succession more rational. But these changes are unsystematic, tentative and half hearted, and must, it would seem, have rendered the law still more confusing and difficult than it was before. Ten years later a new start was made. A completely new system of rules was introduced, with

[1] C. 6. 55. 11. [2] C. Th. 5. 1. 4.

the definite aim, as Justinian tells us, of doing away with the unfair distinctions between males and females which filled the older law. They shew a complete breach with old notions: there is not a word about *sui heredes*, agnation and so forth. The rules look extremely modern, and have indeed found their way, of course much modified, into practically every modern western legislation. In our own law the rules as to the distribution of personal property, as opposed to land, though they rest on a statute are the descendants of these rules, through the Ecclesiastical Law. The rules, contained in Novels 118 and 127, are approximately as follows:

1. Descendants, without distinction of sex, remoter issue taking their deceased parent's share.

2. Ascendants, the nearer excluding the more remote. If there are several in the same degree but in different lines, *e.g.*, two grandfathers and one grandmother, each line takes half irrespective of number. Brothers and sisters of the whole blood share with ascendants, and in this case it seems that all take equally. Children of deceased brothers and sisters represent their parents, if there survive other brothers or sisters with whom to take. That is, the right of representation is allowed if there is some existing person who keeps the class alive. Thus if I leave a father a brother and a nephew by a deceased brother each will take a third. If I leave only the father and the nephew, the father takes all. If I leave a number of nephews by different brothers and sisters all of whom are dead, the nephews and nieces will divide equally: if a brother survives, what does not go to him will be divided *per stirpes*.

3. Brothers and sisters, with the same rule of representation.

4. Half-brothers and sisters in the same way.

5. The nearest relatives, *per capita*.

The right of husband or wife to take in the absence of relatives is not mentioned, but appears to have survived.

89. The notion that a *filiusfamilias* can have a succession is of course quite strange to the older law. We know however that there were in the Empire a certain number of cases in which a *filiusfamilias* could make a will, but, in all of them, if he did not do so, the property reverted, as *peculium*, to the person in whose *potestas* he had been. This remained the law, with slight exceptions, till the time of Justinian. Under his legislation however there was a great change, highly important in practice, and, in theory, completely destructive of the old ideas. It was provided by Justinian that, if a *filiusfamilias* did not make a will of his *peculium castrense*, it should pass, as a succession, to his children, or, failing them, to his brothers and sisters. In the absence of any of these, it was to go to his *paterfamilias, iure communi*. In all probability the *peculium quasi castrense* was dealt with on the same lines, though it is clear that *bona adventitia* were differently handled. The meaning, however, of this expression *iure communi* is not very clear. Does it mean that he took it as inheritance, which had, by Justinian's time, become the common method of dealing with such funds, or does it mean that in the absence of the preferred claims mentioned, the fund reverted to the *paterfamilias*, as ordinary *peculium*? The main arguments in favour of the former view are that it is quite clear that, already, before the time of Justinian, the father's rights in *bona adventitia* on the death of the *filiusfamilias* had come to be regarded as *hereditas*[1], and that the enactment we are considering does not in any way suggest that the *paterfamilias* is to take in a way different from that in which the children and the brothers and sisters take, which is clearly succession. In favour of the latter view are some texts of the Digest which plainly treat it as a case of reversion of *peculium*[2], while there seem to be none contradicting them, and the fact that Theophilus, in his Greek paraphrase or commentary on the Institutes, definitely so treats it. Theophilus is a better authority for the rules of his own time than he is for earlier conceptions, but he is far from trustworthy, and the texts in the Digest may be no more than survivals of an obsolete doctrine, a thing by no means uncommon. Neither view can be considered certain.

[1] Accarias, Précis, 1. 772. [2] *e.g.*, D. 30. 44. *pr.*

The distinction is one of considerable practical importance, as can be readily seen.

1. If the fund was *peculium*, there was no question of *aditio* or acceptance. It belonged to the *paterfamilias*: he could not refuse it, though he could of course abandon it as he could any other property.

2. If it was *peculium*, he would not be liable for the debts of the *filiusfamilias*, except under the edictal actions, *de peculio* and the like, and within their limits, while, if it was a *hereditas*, he would on acceptance, be liable absolutely apart from inventory.

3. If it was *peculium* he would not have a general action for the recovery of the fund from holders without title, as the *peculium* is not a *universitas* for this purpose. He would have, in case of need, to 'vindicate' the objects specifically. If it was *hereditas* he would have the general action, *hereditatis petitio*, to recover it as a whole.

4. If it was *peculium*, theft of it after the death would be a *furtum*, and would make the stolen property *furtiva*. In the other case there would only be the *crimen expilatae hereditatis*.

5. If the father was himself under *potestas*, the grandfather would take it if it was *peculium*. If it was *hereditas* the father would take it, and in his hands it would be *bona adventitia*, as it did not come from his father.

Other differences might be stated but these are sufficient to shew the practical importance of the question.

90. The law of succession to freedmen *cives* underwent changes in the same direction, *i.e.* in favour of cognatic claims. As the freedman could have no relatives but *liberi*, the possible claims are fewer, and the most important changes seem to be in relation to the relatives of the patron. It is not necessary to state the rules in detail, but some remarks may be useful.

There is in this case no question of reversion of *peculium*: it is always true succession. The children, the patron and so forth are *heredes*. The civil law right of the children of the patron is in no way inherited from the patron: it is an independent right expressly created by the Statute. We saw one effect of this in the law as to *assignatio liberti*[1]. The exclusion of the *extranei heredes* of the patron is due to the same consideration. There can be no question of anyone succeeding to the patron's right. If the *extranei* were to have a claim it must be on the ground of mention in the Statute, and they are not mentioned there. The Praetor's scheme of succession for these cases expresses the cognatic idea, by admitting *emancipati* and so forth, but it is also noteworthy that it completely breaks with this severe limitation of the Twelve Tables. We shall have to deal with it in discussing *Bonorum possessio* in detail: it is obscure in some points, but it is certain that he did give rights to remoter relatives of the patron. The *Lex* Papia Poppaea established a much more elaborate scheme in which the rights of the various parties differ according as the claimant is a patron or *patrona* or patron's son or patron's daughter. In the case of the patron and his son the rights vary according to the wealth of the *libertus*, in the other cases according to the number of their children, the rights of a *patrona* being larger than those of a *patroni filia* with the same number of children. They vary also according as the deceased was a man or a woman with similar subordinate variations. No purpose would be served by stating the details[2]. A singular fact connected with this legislation is that it gives what are, on the face of them, praetorian rights. It declares that for instance, a *patrona*, mother of two children, is to have the edictal rights of a patron. It is somewhat surprising to find civil law institutions dealing in praetorian conceptions in this way, and it leaves no doubt that *bonorum possessio* on intestacy was at this time ordinarily *cum re*. Justinian, of course, abolished all this elaborate scheme, and adopts a somewhat simpler form of the praetorian scheme.

These rules are accompanied by restrictions on the power of devise, of a kind peculiar to freedmen. It is singular that the Twelve Tables impose no such restrictions: it is the Praetor who interferes to protect the patron, and in the same connexion the

[1] *Ante*, § 57. [2] Ulp. *Reg*. 29. 3—7.

fact may be adverted to that, while an ordinary *ingenua* could in early law make no will, whether her tutors were willing that she should or not, a *libertina* could do so with her patron's consent.

In the case of a junian latin there can be no question of succession. His property becomes *peculium* at his death: it reverts to his patron as if the patron had been still his *dominus*. He becomes, we are told, a slave at his death. If the patron is dead, the *heredes* of the patron, whoever they may be, take the property as representing him. Thus a disinherited child of the patron could take nothing, and of course the children of the latin had in no case any claim. All this is an inevitable result of the conception of the fund as being no more than *peculium*. The exclusion of the child of the latin seems cruel, but it must be remembered that it was so easy for a latin with children to acquire *civitas*, or rather for him to marry in such a way as to be entitled to acquire it, that this was probably not a very common case. Upon this logical interpretation the *Sc.* Largianum makes an inroad, though it in no way benefits the child of the latin. It provides, rather illogically, that if the patron is dead any issue of his, not expressly disinherited, will take to the exclusion of the *extranei heredes*. The practical effect of this seems to be to give the rights to those disinherited by the *ceteri* clause, and to issue who from any cause had refused their share in the patron's estate.

As to the goods of a *dediticius* it may be said, shortly, that there are no special rules. His property goes in any case to the patron, and the children of the *dediticius* never have any claim. If he would have been a *civis* but for the misconduct that caused him to become only a *dediticius* on manumission, *i.e.*, if his manumission was formally perfect, the property goes to the patron as if he had been a *civis*, that is to say by way of succession. If the manumission would otherwise have made him a latin, the property goes as does that of a latin, *i.e.* it reverts to the patron as *peculium*. It may be supposed, though it does not appear to be capable of proof, that claims posterior to those of the patron himself were admitted in this case as much as in the case of actual latins.

Some of the practical results of the distinction between succession and reversion have been considered in the case of a son's *peculium*, but there are some others which can occur only in the case of a freedman, and are set out by Gaius. They need not be repeated here, but two or three may be stated by way of illustration. The patron's *extranei heredes* might have a claim if it was by way of reversion, but not if it was a *hereditas*. If there were two patrons they would take equally if they were taking as *heredes*, but if they were sharing the fund as a *peculium* they would take in proportion to their shares in the slave, which might not be equal. If one of two patrons was dead, the survivor would be the sole *heres* if it was a case of succession, *iure accrescendi*, while in the case of reversion of a *peculium* he would share with the representatives of the deceased patron.

91. The actual working of an ordinary case of succession at civil law, the remedies open to the *heres*, the steps he has to take, and so forth, are very simple, but the corresponding rules in a case of praetorian succession are of such a special kind that it seems desirable to give a systematic account of the principles of *Bonorum Possessio*. It is not within the present purpose to consider the controversial question of the origin of *Bonorum possessio*, and though we shall have to consider the order of claims it will be necessary to ignore, or to touch very lightly on, the doubts and controversies which exist in some of the cases as to the persons who were entitled to claim under a particular rubric. Moreover the subject of treatment is the ordinary praetorian succession—*Bonorum Possessio Edictalis*, not *Bonorum Possessio Decretalis*.

The Praetor grants *Bonorum Possessio* to claimants in a certain order which is not that of the civil law. If, as it happens, the person who receives a grant of *bonorum possessio* is also entitled at civil law, his possession will be effective succession and it is said to be *Bonorum Possessio cum re*. If, however, he is not entitled at civil law, it may be effective against the civil law claimant or not, *cum re* or *sine re*. The circumstances under which it is the one or the other will be considered later on.

Where *bonorum possessio* is given to one who is also civil law *heres* it is said to be given "*iuris civilis confirmandi* (or *adiuvandi*) *gratia*." If it is given to others with the *heres*, it is "*supplendi iuris civilis gratia*," *e.g.*, where an *emancipatus* comes in with *sui*. If it is given in disregard of a civil law claim it is said to be "*corrigendi* (or *emendandi* or *impugnandi*) *iuris civilis gratia*," *e.g.*, where it is given to the cognates to the exclusion of the *gentiles*.

There is of course a system of priority or order of claims, and a certain time is allowed within which each of these claims is to be made. If a person has not claimed within the right time he is excluded, and the next claim can come in, but we shall see shortly that a person may conceivably have a claim under more than one head, so that although he has failed to claim in the first place, he may still have an opportunity of coming in. It may however chance that he would have stood alone under the first head, but may now have to share with others. The general notions of the order have been considered at various points in our short discussion of the law of succession, but they must now be set forth systematically as they appear to have stood in the Edict.

92. In administering the estate of a dead man it is plain that the first question to be asked is whether there is or is not a will. And if a will is produced, it cannot be acted on under a system of laws which imposes restrictions on devise, unless it is clear that there is no one who has a right to object to its provisions. Accordingly the first *Bonorum Possessio* is:

A. *Bonorum Possessio contra tabulas*. We have seen where this was available among *ingenui*, in general, though it may be noted that there are cases in which if there was one of the *liberi* omitted, his bringing this claim would let in to share with him children who had been given in adoption and thus could not have claimed on their own account[1]. It was also available to a patron whose rights were disregarded. It must

[1] D. 37. 4. 8. 11. Possibly a rule only of late law.

be observed that the resulting state of things is not intestacy. Some parts of the will are good, *e.g.*, *exheredationes* and legacies to near relatives. This is the reason why this *bonorum possessio* has to be stated as a distinct case and cannot be fused with *unde liberi* and the like. If there is no one who can thus attack the will, there is

B. *Bonorum Possessio secundum tabulas.* This involves the production of a will which satisfies the praetorian requirements of form whether it satisfies those of the civil law or not. If there is no such will or no one claims *Bonorum Possessio* under it, the case is one for

C. *Bonorum Possessio ab intestato.* Here there is a lengthy list of cases set out in the order of priority.

i. *B. P. Unde Liberi.* The word *unde* here as in other cases does not belong to the Edict. It is used by the jurists in referring to "that part of the edict in which" *liberi* are authorised to claim. We have already considered what persons were entitled to succeed under this head. The only things that need be observed are that a child who was entitled to upset a will but had failed to claim *Bonorum Possessio contra tabulas,* and had thus let in the claimants under the will, could not afterwards obtain a valid grant *unde liberi,* and that if no one had claimed under the will, so that he could still come in *unde liberi,* he would be liable to pay all legacies which would have been valid had he claimed *bonorum possessio contra tabulas*[1].

ii. *B. P. Unde Legitimi.* This applied to all cases of statutory claim, *e.g.*, to agnates and those in later law entitled to claim with them, to the patron and his children, and to cases under the *Scc.* Tertullianum and Orphitianum, and their later extensions. As it extends to all who are *heredes* at civil law, it covers *sui* as well as the remoter claimants, from which it follows that if a *suus* has refused to claim *bonorum possessio unde liberi,* and no others have claimed it, he may still be entitled to come in under the present head to the exclusion of the agnates, provided he was nearer in degree. This he would usually be,

[1] D. 38. 6. 2; D. 29. 4. 6. 9, so where one entitled by will and on intestacy claims only on intestacy, *h. t.* 1. *pr.*

but it might well happen that he had only an equal claim with others in this case, for instance, a grandson is no nearer than a brother. He might even be excluded: a great grandson is more remote than a brother.

iii. *B. P. Unde Decem Personae.* This is a special case. Where an *ingenuus* in being emancipated, had, after the third sale, been finally manumitted by the *extraneus* without resale to the father, the *extraneus* was his civil law *heres*, and therefore was *prima facie* entitled to *bonorum possessio unde legitimi*. But the Praetor by a special clause in the Edict preferred certain near relatives to him. The list and order are given in the *Collatio* and in the Institutes, not however quite identically. They are roughly ascendants, descendants and brothers and sisters, of the whole or half blood. As this mode of emancipation could not occur under Justinian, the institution is obsolete. It is remarkable that this *bonorum possessio* should have been placed in the edict after that *unde legitimi*, of which, in the only case in which it could arise, it clearly takes precedence. It is therefore supposed by Lenel, relying on a text in Ulpian's *Regulae*, that it was not an independent clause of the Edict constituting a definite class of *Bonorum possessio*, as Justinian states it, but a subordinate clause in the provision creating *Bonorum Possessio unde legitimi*[1].

iv. *Unde Cognati.* This was a right of purely praetorian creation. We have already considered who were included under the head of *Cognati*. It need only be noted that persons who were entitled to claim as *legitimi* but had failed to do so, might still be, alone or with others, the nearest *cognati*.

v. *Unde familia patroni* (also alluded to as "*tum quem ex familia patroni*"). The purpose of this *bonorum possessio* is not certainly known. So far as it is known it appears to give rights to persons who might have come in earlier, and this without adding to the class. But this is so apparently useless, and even unfair, that it can hardly be the right explanation of its purpose. Of the many explanations that of Lenel[2] is supported by some textual authority. It is that the class

[1] Lenel, Ed. Perp. (2) 343. [2] Lenel, op. cit. 344.

includes a *patronus* who had suffered *capitis deminutio*, the emancipated children of the patron, and perhaps the *parens manumissor* of the patron. It is clear that the Praetor did give these a right, and that they had none at civil law, and there is no other obvious class under which they could come in. There is however the difficulty that the texts which can be shewn with certainty to refer to this case do not hint at any but the civil law sense of the word *familia*. Other writers hold therefore that it refers to agnates of the patron. They had no civil law claim to the property of the freedman, and Theophilus definitely tells us that they came in here[1]. A long text discussing the meaning of the word *familia*, and contained in a work commenting on this particular edict observes, allusively, that "*communi iure familiam dicimus omnium agnatorum.*" But the whole question is too controversial for discussion in this place.

vi. *B. P. Unde Patronus patrona liberi et parentes eorum.* This case presents at first sight the same difficulty as the last. It seems mainly to refer to persons who have earlier claims. The *parentes* would on this view constitute the only extension. There is however some evidence that the case contemplated is that of a patron who was himself a freedman, and on that view this clause gives a right of succession to the patron's patron (or *patrona*) and the issue and ascendants of the latter. This interpretation leaves a good deal obscure, but it is supported by the language of a Greek constitution of Justinian in which he reorganises all this matter. It is however not wholly free from difficulties[2].

vii. *B. P. Unde Vir et Uxor.* In the absence of relatives the Praetor gives *bonorum possessio*, reciprocally, to the husband and wife of the deceased. It is clear that this applied, like "*unde liberi*," "*unde legitimi*," and "*unde cognati*," to *ingenui* and *libertini* alike. But it seems strange in view of this, that the right of cognates of the patron is postponed to it.

viii. *B. P. Unde Cognati manumissoris.* In this last grade

[1] See Roby, Rom. Pr. Law, 1. 278.
[2] Lenel, op. cit. 346.

the Praetor gives succession to the cognates of the patron of the freedman.

There is another case of edictal *bonorum possessio* which cannot be placed in this scheme, because it is a single provision of the Edict, applying to a number of possible claims. This is *bonorum possessio uti ex legibus.* There are certain cases in which *bonorum possessio* is given by statute: we have already adverted to this peculiarity in dealing with the rules of succession to freedmen, under the *Lex* Papia Poppaea[1], which is the best known case. It was placed in the edict after the others, but detached from them, some subsidiary provisions being interposed between them. Not very much is known about it, but we are told that no previous grant of *bonorum possessio* prevented a grant of it under this head[2].

Under Justinian the order is considerably simplified. The case of *unde decem personae* is rendered obsolete by the change in the form of emancipation, and *tum quem ex familia, unde patronus patroni*, and *unde cognati manumissoris* are brought under *unde cognati*, so that besides those under wills there are left only *unde liberi, unde legitimi, unde cognati* and *unde vir et uxor*, with the exceptional *uti ex legibus.* The change seems to have the effect of changing the relative positions of *unde vir et uxor* and *unde cognati manumissoris*: indeed it does not seem clear that the former survived Justinian's changes, in the case of freedmen. It is also noteworthy that while, in general, cognation was reckoned to the sixth degree, Justinian confined it to five degrees, in the case of cognates of a patron claiming the estate of a *libertus.*

93. In considering the actual working of this system it is necessary to bear in mind certain points which have already been mentioned, but which it will be well to recall. Though the order established by the Praetor is not the same as that of the civil law, there are points at which they agree. There are cases in which he admits only those who have a civil law claim (*legitimi*). There are cases in which he admits

[1] *Ante*, § 90. [2] D. 38. 14. 1. 1.

persons who have no civil law claim to share with those who have (*e.g.*, *liberi*), and there are others in which he excludes persons with a civil law claim (*gentiles*). We must remember also that it did not follow that a person who had obtained a valid grant of *bonorum possessio* would in the long run be entitled to keep the property: there was such a thing as *bonorum possessio sine re*. What this meant and how it came about we shall have to consider later.

We are told that *Bonorum Possessio* was granted by the Praetor to claimants in a certain order, and that a fixed number of days was allowed within which the claimant in any class must apply. For a grant of *bonorum possessio* the time allowed was, in general, 100 days, but, in the case of ascendants and children whether claiming under a will or on intestacy a year was allowed. In considering what this means we must bear in mind that the days are *dies utiles* and that in each *bonorum possessio* the time runs only from the expiration of the time allowed for the previous claim. These facts have three important results.

i. Only those days counted on which a demand of *bonorum possessio* could lawfully be made. This however does not mean very much, as the Praetor heard and granted such applications *de plano*, and without the use of the formal words "*do, dico, addico*," which involved the sitting of a court.

ii. The days ran only from the time when the claimant was *certus* of his right, *i.e.*, on matters of fact[1], and was able to take the necessary steps.

iii. If, after the time had begun to run he became *incertus* of his right, *i.e.*, as before, not on any point of law involved, but on the facts of the case, or if he became incapable, the running of the time was suspended[2].

All this looks as if, in a case in which there was no will, and there were no near relatives, it might be a long time before remoter claims, such, for instance, as those of wife or husband (*unde vir et uxor*), could be put in. This might indeed be so,

[1] D. 37. 1. 10.

[2] See Roby, Rom. Pr. Law, 1. 265.

and the resulting inconvenience led to the adoption of a number of rules and devices for shortening the time. Thus if a particular class was actually non-existent, the time for that class would be disregarded so that if, for example, a man had died intestate and unmarried, *bonorum possessio unde legitimi* could be validly given at once. Again, if all the members of any class repudiated the succession, the time for that class stopped at once, and claims by the next class became admissible, the repudiation once made being irrevocable. In the case of those persons who had an *annus utilis* within which to claim, the persons entitled in the next place could summon them to court and ask them if they repudiated. They were not bound to answer the question, but if they did, and repudiated the claim, the next in order could claim. So too if a whole class died out while its time was running, or was excluded from any cause, the same effect followed. Of course if any single member of the class died or repudiated the effect was merely, in intestacy, and, apart from the *leges caducariae*, under wills, to cause accrual in favour of the other members of the class[1]. The general result then of all this is that in an ordinary case no very long time would elapse before the claim, however remote, could come in. A word of warning is necessary at this point. We must remember that any *bonorum possessio* can in fact be given at any time. The Praetor can, and will, give it at any time without any serious enquiry, to any applicant for it, who sets up a *prima facie* claim on *ex parte* evidence. The Praetor knows nothing about the parties or the facts of the case. But, as we shall see later, such a grant will be a mere nullity, for all purposes, unless the person to whom the grant is made is the person, or one of the persons, entitled to it at that time or, as the technical expression ran, unless he has it "*ex edicto*," *i.e.*, in accordance with the terms of the Edict.

94. The demand for *bonorum possessio* would be made to the magistrate, and granted by him. It is sometimes spoken of as a judicial proceeding, but in classical law, though there

[1] D. 38. 9. 1. 1, 8, 12; D. 37. 1. 3. 9—5.

appear still to be formal terms in which the application must be made, there is very little that is judicial about it, whatever may have been the case in earlier days. Even a slave may obtain a grant for his master[1], though it is a commonplace that he can take no part in judicial proceedings. In later law, though probably not in classical times, the magistrate may grant it without any application at all, and the class of magistrates who may grant it extends as time goes on and form becomes less important. The truth is that while the grant is essential to the further proceedings, it has no other significance. The real question at the later stages will be not so much whether he has received a grant of *Bonorum possessio*, but whether he was entitled to it, whether the grant was "*ex edicto.*"

In ordinary cases there was no enquiry, merely an *ex parte* statement, shewing a *prima facie* case, or hardly even that. Thus, on proof that there was a will, *bonorum possessio secundum tabulas* could be given without opening it[2], though no one can say without looking at it that the person who has the grant is the person entitled under the will. It follows that it might often be given to one who was not entitled to it at all, and a number of such cases are recorded in the Digest. It might be given, for instance, under a will which was forged, or revoked by a later will, or on intestacy where there really was a will, but the Praetor had been told that there was none. So *legitimi* might get it by pretending that there were no *liberi*, when in fact there were, and their time was still running, or under a mistaken notion that the *liberi* had repudiated the claim. Such a wrongful claim might be innocent or fraudulent, but in either case, a *bonorum possessio* thus obtained, granted, that is to say, to one who was not at the time entitled to it under the Edict, was worth nothing: it did not entitle the holder of the grant to go further to any purpose. It was merely like the issue of a writ to one who has no sort of claim. The grantee will not succeed in the interdict *Quorum Bonorum*, or be able to use effectively any of the edictal remedies. The emptiness of such a *bonorum possessio* is shewn by a text which speaks of

[1] D. 37. 1. 7. [2] D. 37. 11. 1. 2.

a certain legatee who has obtained a grant of *bonorum possessio contra tabulas* as an omitted child. In fact however he is not an omitted child, but he is one of those persons legacies to whom stand good even though a will is upset by *bonorum possessio contra tabulas.* He will get his legacy whether the will stands or is in fact upset by some other person who is an omitted child. The point is that though a person who attacks a will, and loses, loses also any benefit to which he may be entitled under the will, his attack is a mere nullity. The text shews that this strong decision was not arrived at without doubts[1].

It is plain that as *bonorum possessio* is granted without serious enquiry, a grant to one who is not entitled to it, a grant not *ex edicto,* does not in the least bar a grant of it to one who is entitled to it, in the same or any other class, and it may be presumed that one who has a grant conferred out of due season is not thereby barred from applying later on for a valid one. As these later grants will also be made without enquiry, the rule practically is that no grant of *bonorum possessio* is any bar to any other grant, though we shall see shortly that this does not mean so much as it seems to mean. It should be added that a grant to one or some of a class is not a grant to all the class. Each person who wants *bonorum possessio* must ask for it. Hence arise cases of accrual. If, for example, one of several *liberi* has made a claim and received a grant, and the others have taken no steps, when their time has expired he will have received a grant of *bonorum possessio* of the whole[2].

Where *bonorum possessio* has been granted to anyone in accordance with the terms of the edict, *ex edicto,* it cannot be validly granted to anybody else, adversely to him, which means practically to anyone in another class, so long as the grant to him stands. Such a second grant may indeed be made, as we have just seen, but it is a mere nullity, it cannot be *ex edicto.* Thus if a man has a valid grant *unde liberi,* this does not prevent others from obtaining a valid grant *unde liberi,* but it renders nugatory any grant *unde legitimi,* unless and until all valid

[1] D. 37. 5. 5. 3. [2] 37. 1. 3. 9, 4, 5.

grants *unde liberi* are revoked. The considerations set forth in these two paragraphs explain the fact that it may be said, and is said by modern commentators, with perfect accuracy, both that one grant of *bonorum possessio* bars any other, and that it does no such thing.

95. The claim and grant of *bonorum possessio* operate somewhat like *aditio* at civil law: they entitle the beneficiary to take steps to recover the property, but they do not of themselves give him the possession of it. This is a question of physical control, *inter alia*, and the grant cannot give him this: there is no magic in it. We have therefore now to consider what are the ways in which it can be made effective. We must remember that there are two kinds of *bonorum possessio*—*cum re* and *sine re*, to say nothing of the man whose *possessio* is not *ex edicto*: he is neither *cum re* nor *sine re*—he has no right at all. We shall deal first with the *bonorum possessor cum re*, the true praetorian successor. His remedies and liabilities are as follows:

I. He may proceed by the Interdict *Quorum Bonorum*. It is important to notice the exact effect of this interdict. It is by no means a universal remedy. It applies only to matters of which possession is possible, or at least, *possessio iuris*, as in case of usufruct, and thus it is not a means for the recovery of debts. But it has a still more important and less obvious restriction. It is available only against those who hold *pro herede* or *pro possessore*, that is to say, those who claim to be *heredes* or refuse to state any title at all[1]. Thus, if I am *bonorum possessor*, and you are in possession of a house which had belonged to the deceased, which you allege to have been sold to you, and which you thus hold *pro emptore*, the interdict *quorum bonorum* is of no avail against you. On the other hand, as against a holder *pro herede* or *pro possessore*, it is available, as to things of which he has fraudulently parted with possession, or which he has even usucapted. It must be remembered that by a senatusconsult of Hadrian *usucapio pro herede* was made

[1] See Lenel, Ed. Perp. (2) 436.

ineffective against claimants of the *hereditas* whether it had been in good or bad faith. The *usucapio pro herede* which figures in the Digest[1] appears to be only *usucapio* by an actual *heres* of what did not really belong to the deceased. To recover under the interdict, the mere issue of which, like the grant of *bonorum possessio*, is made, as of course, without real enquiry, the *bonorum possessor* must shew that he was entitled to it, and it is at this point that the validity of the grant to him of *bonorum possessio* will be considered. The wording of the interdict brings out this point. It orders the goods to be handed over to the claimant, who has a grant of the *bonorum possessio ex edicto, i.e.*, in accordance with the terms of the edict. If, for instance, the grant was *unde liberi*, then it must appear that he was one of that class, that the grant was made within the proper limits of time, that there had been no previous valid grant still in force, that the goods formed part of the estate of the deceased, and that the defendant sets up, *i.e.*, alleges, no title otherwise than as *heres*. We need not consider the burden of proof.

It must now be noted that this interdict, like all possessory interdicts, is merely provisional. If the claimant proves his right to the interdict, against the defendant, the goods are, as the result of a procedure the details of which do not here concern us, handed over to him. But no question of title is thereby determined. It by no means follows that he will be able to keep the property in the long run. The whole legal effect is that anyone who wishes to recover the property from him must bring the appropriate action against him and prove his case. We shall see hereafter how this works in the case of *bonorum possessio sine re*.

Before leaving this interdict it should be noted that there was another interdict of similar type, but of less importance, called *Quod legatorum*, available to the *bonorum possessor* against one who had taken possession of property alleging that there was a legacy of it to him, without the consent of the *bonorum*

[1] D. 41. 5.

possessor. The *bonorum possessor* must in this case give security for the restoration of the legacy, if it should prove to be due. We need not discuss this institution[1].

II. He is entitled to *Hereditatis Petitio Possessoria.* This is a praetorian extension of the *hereditatis petitio* of the *heres* to the *bonorum possessor.* Like the interdict it is available only against possessors *pro herede* or *pro possessore,* and it covers in general the same assets, *i.e.,* the various *iura in rem* of the estate of which he had possession or quasi possession or had fraudulently ceased to hold. Where they had been replaced by other assets, by sales and so forth, there were rules determining the liability of the holder, varying according as he was in good or bad faith, but into these we need not go. It must be noted however that in one case debts could be recovered by it. If a person claimed to be *heres* and refused to pay on that account, this action lay to co-recover these debts even though, as might happen, the debtor did not at the moment hold any positive assets of the estate[2]. The action follows the same principles as the ordinary *hereditatis petitio,* with the details of which we need not deal. To recover under it the plaintiff must shew that he is entitled to *bonorum possessio,* and has received a grant of it, but he need not shew, as has been sometimes alleged, that he is entitled to it *cum re.* The judgment in this action differs in force from that on the interdict. It is not merely provisional: it is final. It deals not merely with the question of possession; but also with that of property, or rather of substantive hereditary right. As it calls for the same proof as the interdict, covers almost exactly the same property, and a little more, is available against the same persons, and gives a more definitive result, it is not easy at first sight to tell why the *bonorum possessor cum re* ever thought it the wiser course to proceed by way of *quorum bonorum.* Various solutions of this problem have been proposed: the following considerations seem sufficient.

(*a*) A *bonorum possessor* does not always know whether he is *cum re* or *sine re.* The texts speak of *bonorum possessio* as

[1] Lenel, Ed. Perp. (2) 436.

[2] D. 5. 3. 13. 15.

being granted *cum* or *sine re*[1], but of course it is not so stated in the grant, and it is possible that no party concerned may know which it is. If the possession was *sine re*, and the opponent was in fact the *heres*, the possessor would fail in the *hereditatis petitio possessoria*, but he would win in the interdict *quorum bonorum*. If he has any doubt on the point he will bring the interdict, and leave the *heres* to proceed against him afterwards by the *hereditatis petitio*. As an illustration of the kind of doubt here intended, the case may be taken of an *extraneus* who is claiming under a praetorian will. He knows that in point of fact no one has actually claimed *bonorum possessio contra tabulas*. But this in no way proves that there is no child: there may very well be one who is content to rest on his civil law claim. The *bonorum possessio* will be no answer to *hereditatis petitio* brought by such a child, but the interdict will give him the advantage of actual possession and the position of defendant. So also he may not know whether the defendant is the true *heres* or not: this is indifferent in the interdict. Similar doubts may arise in a number of ways.

(*b*) Up to the time of Hadrian the *hereditatis petitio* was not available against one who had fraudulently ceased to possess. The interdict was. But this of course would not account for its use in cases where there was no question of this, or for its survival in later law[2].

(*c*) The interdict being prohibitory, the procedure involved *sponsiones*. The payments under these were actually enforced: they were not merely formal. Thus success in the interdict would involve a profit.

(*d*) Even in later law, the interdict had the advantage of being subject to restrictions in the matter of appeal.

III. If, having obtained the possession he is now sued by the *heres*, by the *hereditatis petitio*, he has of course no defence at civil law, but the Praetor gives the *bonorum possessor cum re* an *exceptio doli*.

IV. He can recover property of the estate held by persons who are claiming by some title other than inheritance, and who

[1] *e.g.* Ulp. *Regulae*, 28. 13.

[2] D. 5. 3. 20. 6 b, 11; *h.t.* 25. 9.

are thus not to be reached by the interdict or the *hereditatis petitio possessoria*. His remedy in this case is an *actio fictitia*, in which the fiction is that he is *heres, i.e.*, the *iudex* is directed to condemn, if the plaintiff would be entitled "*si heres esset.*"

V. He can sue and be sued on account of debts, by actions with a similar fiction. As these actions cover liabilities which have arisen after the death (*e.g.*, from damage to the *hereditas*), they form a complete scheme. Here, however, a certain difficulty arises. Gaius gives us the *intentio* of these actions, under this and the last head, and the *intentio* says nothing about the fact that the plaintiff is a *bonorum possessor*. What then is there to prevent anyone from bringing such actions against the debtor, since the question whether he is a *bonorum possessor* or not is not put in issue? The fact of the grant of *bonorum possessio* would of course be on record, and no doubt a *formula* would not be issued except to a person who had such a grant. But he might have got it wrongly, and the fact that he was not entitled to it would not be known to the Praetor at any rate till after the interdict or *hereditatis petitio possessoria* had been brought, and there is nothing to shew that these *actiones fictitiae* could not be brought in the first instance. The way in which this very material point was raised in the *formula* is not known. Lenel thinks that it was by means of an *exceptio* expressly raising the question whether the *bonorum possessio* was *ex edicto*, but this cannot be proved from the texts[1].

VI. The acquisition of possession under the interdict, or under the *hereditatis petitio possessoria*, does not of itself confer *dominium*, though Ulpian, at least in the Digest, speaks of the resulting right as *dominium*[2]. The *bonorum possessor* will however acquire *dominium* by *usucapio*: in the meantime he has the protections which are available to other praetorian owners, with which we need not deal. Under Justinian *bonorum possessio* and *hereditas* are almost fused, and the two systems of remedies coexist almost as alternative remedies for the same end. There is no longer such a thing as praetorian ownership, so that these distinctions cease to exist.

[1] Lenel, op. cit. 178.

[2] D. 37. 1. 1; *cf.* D. 50. 16. 70 (Paul).

96. We can now turn to the *bonorum possessor sine re*, that is to say, to one who has obtained a valid grant of *bonorum possessio ex edicto*, in accordance with the terms of the edict, but who is not one of those whom the Praetor will in the long run protect against the civil law *heres*. We can schedule his various rights and remedies as in the other case.

I. He has the interdicts *quorum bonorum* and *quod legatorum*, and, so far as these remedies are concerned, he is in precisely the same position as the *bonorum possessor cum re*. The interdicts are effective even against the true *heres*.

II. He has the *hereditatis petitio possessoria* against any one who holds *pro herede* or *pro possessore*, except the *heres* himself. The *intentio* of it does not in terms exclude even him, for we have just seen that in *bonorum possessio cum re* it was effective against the *heres*, and at the time of the issue of the formula the Praetor cannot ordinarily have known which it was. Though we do not possess the actual *formula*, it seems fairly certain that the *heres* met the claim by an *exceptio*. But we do not know what this *exceptio* was, though it is thought by some writers to have been an *exceptio doli*.

III. If the *heres* sues him by the *hereditatis petitio* he has no reply whatsoever, and the action will cover all the property he has recovered by means of the interdict, and the *hereditatis petitio*, or by the various *actiones fictitiae*, or without litigation —in fact everything which he holds as *bonorum possessor* and in some cases what he has made away with[1].

IV. He has the same *actiones fictitiae* against debtors and detainers of property as if he had been a *bonorum possessor cum re*. But he is of course liable to be called on to restore what he has recovered, to the *heres*, by the action last mentioned. This situation gives rise to one curious question. If a *bonorum possessor* has thus handed over all that he has recovered, he is still a *bonorum possessor ex edicto*. The grant of *bonorum possessio* to him was valid and has not been revoked. Is it still possible for him to sue debtors? The texts give us no answer, but analogy suggests that in such a case he would be met by an *exceptio doli*.

[1] D. 5. 3. 25. 18.

V. He might be sued by creditors in the same way as if he were *cum re*. If after he has paid certain debts, he is ejected by the *heres*, he can deduct the amount of these payments from what he hands over[1]. But here too a difficulty may arise. If, having obtained a grant of *bonorum possessio*, he proceeds to pay debts out of his own pocket, intending to recoup himself out of the estate which he expects to be able to get in and retain, it may be that his expectation is disappointed. The *heres* may step in and recover the various assets from those who are holding them, so that nothing gets into the hands of the *bonorum possessor*. Can the *bonorum possessor* claim an indemnity from the *heres*? It was not a case of *negotiorum gestio*, for the *bonorum possessor* was plainly acting on his own account. One or two texts suggest, but are far from proving, that he had a *condictio indebiti*[2]. There is however the difficulty that a *bonorum possessor ex edicto* is liable for debts, so that it was not an *indebitum*. The fact that in the long run he gets no benefit out of his *bonorum possessio* does not alter that and make his act a payment in error of what was not due. Perhaps the solution is that, as he is still *bonorum possessor*, he can put pressure on the *heres* to indemnify him, since it is possible for him to recover the goods from the *heres* by the interdict *quorum bonorum*, and then, when sued by him in the *hereditatis petitio*, or any other proprietary action, he can set off the debts which he had paid. But this is conjecture. If the *bonorum possessor* is sued for debts after the *heres* has recovered the *hereditas* from him, he can defend by means of an *exceptio doli*.

VI. He will usucapt in the same way as the *bonorum possessor cum re*, but he is of course liable to see his usucapion interrupted by the intervention of the *heres*.

97. It has been assumed in the foregoing observations that the distinction between *bonorum possessio cum re* and *sine re* was understood. The nature of the distinction ought indeed to be clear, but we have now to pass to the consideration of the question when it was *cum re* and when *sine re*. It must first be observed that although we have treated *heres* and *bonorum*

[1] D. 5. 3. 31. [2] *e.g.*, D. 12. 6. 2.

possessor as distinct persons, they are not necessarily such. The *heres* is often the person entitled by *bonorum possessio* also. A *suus heres* on intestacy is also entitled to *bonorum possessio unde liberi.* A claimant under a sealed mancipatory will can claim *bonorum possessio secundum tabulas.* A *suus heres omissus*, it would seem, can proceed either by *hereditatis petitio* or by obtaining *bonorum possessio contra tabulas.* It would however be wiser to proceed by the civil law method, as *bonorum possessio contra tabulas* leaves some legacies valid. An agnate might claim at civil law as such, or he might take *bonorum possessio unde legitimi*, and so forth.

In Justinian's time all *bonorum possessiones* are in the normal way *cum re*, a fact which accounts for some doubts in details as to *bonorum possessio sine re*, since nearly the whole of our information comes from the Digest, which of course is intended to set forth the law of Justinian. The civil law *heres* and the person entitled to *bonorum possessio* are usually the same, and he may make his claim either by *aditio* and *hereditatis petitio* or by *bonorum possessio* with *quorum bonorum* and *hereditatis petitio possessoria.* The difference is now mainly one of form. It may be noted that the Digest, though it gives a title to *quorum bonorum* and another to *hereditatis petitio possessoria*[1], has only a word or two to say about each, a fact which indicates that they had been important and still existed, but had ceased to be of much importance. There are, nevertheless, some cases, even under Justinian's law, which give rise to some difficulty and must therefore be mentioned.

i. As to those entitled both to *hereditas* and to *bonorum possessio* it mattered little in which of the forms they cast their claim. The times within which they would have to act were not the same, but if too late for one, there was nothing to prevent their falling back on the other. There still remained however certain cases in which a claim of *bonorum possessio* was the only possible course, and it is the accepted opinion that if the time for *bonorum possessio* had gone by the result was complete exclusion even in the time of Justinian. But such cases

[1] D. 5. 5; D. 43. 2.

were much rarer than they had been. The praetorian will was substantially abolished by the legislation which established the so-called tripartite will. The enactments extending the class of *legitimi* expressly gave all the rights of agnates to the new additions, that is to say, *hereditas* as well as *bonorum possessio*. On the other hand Justinian expressly confines *emancipati* and *emancipatae* who attack a will to *bonorum possessio contra tabulas*, and *bonorum possessio unde cognati* and *unde vir et uxor* still remain purely edictal. The claimants are *bonorum possessores*, but not *heredes*.

ii. If anyone who was entitled to *bonorum possessio* let the time pass, it is clear on the terms of the edict, or rather of the commentaries on it by the jurists, that the person next entitled could come in. Suppose an intestate under Justinian leaves *sui heredes* and agnates. The *sui heredes*, relying on their civil law title, do not ask for *bonorum possessio unde liberi*. When the time within which they could claim has expired, can the agnates now claim *bonorum possessio unde legitimi*? They certainly could have done so under the old law, though their *bonorum possessio* would of course be *sine re*. There is nothing in the law as stated in the Digest or the Code to prevent their still doing so. But if they still could claim, there might still be cases of *bonorum possessio sine re*[1]. But the Digest expressly says (the text is put down to Ulpian, but has probably been altered) that *bonorum possessores* have the right of getting and retaining the goods. This fact, coupled with the further fact that the *Corpus iuris* nowhere says that *quorum bonorum* was available against the *heres*, even in a passage in which the writer might have been expected to say it if it was true, has led to the opinion[2] that the interdict *quorum bonorum* would be absolutely refused in such a case, or rather, since the interdict (or the possessory action which has superseded the interdict) was given on an *ex parte* application without real enquiry, that the form of it was now such that it was ineffective against the *heres*.

[1] Windscheid, Lehrbuch, § 532, n. 6, cites D. 37. 4. 14. *pr.*; D. 37. 5. 15. 2; D. 37. 6. 10.

[2] Accarias, Précis, 1. 1280.

There are however some reasons for thinking that the claimant was still entitled in strictness to the interdict, but that his claim was paralysed by the *exceptio doli*, so that substantially he had no *bonorum possessio* at all. This seems to be suggested by the fact that the interdict as given by Justinian is substantially the same as that given by Gaius, but the question hardly admits of solution and is of little practical import.

Upon another point of detail in Justinian's law there is much controversy. He tells us that there was no longer any reason to demand *bonorum possessio*, but that it could be obtained by any expression of wish. The point of dispute is whether this means that there was now no need to go before the magistrate. This is the natural meaning of his words, and would put the matter on the same footing as acceptance of the civil law *hereditas*. But as he says that the rule was laid down by earlier emperors, and such a rule certainly was not, it is supposed by some writers that all that he means is that, as was certainly already the law, no particular words were needed, and the grant might be made by any magistrate[1].

98. In classical times it is important to note that every *bonorum possessio* would be *cum re* if the claimant was the *heres*, or there was no *heres*, and thus any *bonorum possessio* might be *cum re* under certain circumstances. Some were always *cum re*. Others were *cum re* or *sine re* according to epoch (for there is a good deal of historical development in this matter), and circumstances, of which circumstances the Praetor would not, and the parties well might not, be informed at the time of the grant of *bonorum possessio*. We will now consider the various *bonorum possessiones* in order to shew, so far as we can, how far they were *cum re* and when they became so[2].

Bonorum possessio contra tabulas appears to have been *cum re* in the time of Gaius, though it must be admitted that this is nowhere expressly stated. But the language which is used about it in many texts is not such as could possibly be used if

[1] See C. 6. 9. 8, 9. [2] See as to this Girard, Manuel (5), 888.

there were any normal cases in which it was *sine re.* Indeed the whole system of *collatio bonorum* would be unintelligible, if the *bonorum possessio* of the *emancipatus omissus* was *sine re,* liable to be defeated by a claim on the part of the *sui heredes,* or other *instituti.* And it would hardly have been necessary for Antoninus Pius to provide that a woman should not get more under the system of *bonorum possessio contra tabulas* than she would have got at civil law, if in the former case she could not keep what she got. It is more difficult to say when first it became *cum re,* or by whose authority. It is clear that it was so when Julian revised the edict under Hadrian, since the *bonorum possessor* was liable to pay certain legacies under that system[1]. *Collatio bonorum* was already a subject of discussion among the jurists as early as Cassius, about a century before Hadrian. There is some evidence that *bonorum possessio contra tabulas* obtained by a patron or his issue against the will of a *libertinus* was *cum re* in the time of Cicero. If that is so it is at least possible that ordinary *bonorum possessio contra tabulas* was *cum re* from the time of its inception, which seems to have been about the close of the Republic. In any case it cannot have been long before it became so.

As to *Bonorum possessio secundum tabulas,* there are a great many possible cases. If the will is valid at civil as well as at praetorian law, then the *bonorum possessio* obtained under it is of course *cum re.* If the will is defective in point of form, *i.e.*, is an ordinary praetorian will, the *bonorum possessio* is still *cum re* if the persons entitled by it are also entitled at civil law, or there are no *sui* or *legitimi.* If however there are adverse claims of agnates, it seems to have been *sine re* until Antoninus Pius made it *cum re* against them, though it is possible on the language of the texts that it may have been *cum re* as against agnates remoter than *frater et patruus* even before this enactment. Hadrian made it *cum re* where the only defect in the will was that there was a *postumus praeteritus,* and he had died before the testator. Where the defect of the will was that it was a woman's will made without

[1] D. 37. 5. 2.

the consent of her *tutor fiduciarius*, the same enactment probably made it *cum re* whether it satisfied civil law rules of form or not. But if the tutor was *legitimus* it was still *sine re*.

Other cases of *bonorum possessio secundum tabulas* are discussed by the jurists, but we need not consider them. Enough has been said to shew that there were many factors to be considered before it could be said with certainty whether in a particular case *bonorum possessio secundum tabulas* would be *cum re* or *sine re*, that the Praetor could not be informed of these factors when he issued the interdict, and that up to the latest age of the classical law such a *bonorum possessio* was, *prima facie*, *sine re*.

Bonorum possessio unde legitimi, *unde cognati* and *unde vir et uxor* were at all times normally *cum re*. They excluded no one but the *gentiles* and these were disregarded. If however these cases of *bonorum possessio* took effect, as they might, merely because earlier claimants, entitled at civil law as well, had simply not taken the trouble to obtain *bonorum possessio*, then it seems clear that the *bonorum possessio* would be *sine re*, if these other claimants had made *aditio*, or had still time to do so, and actually did so after the grant of *bonorum possessio*. If however they had renounced the *hereditas* or were excluded by the lapse of the *spatium deliberandi*, the *bonorum possessio* would be *cum re*. Similar distinctions must be taken in relation to *bonorum possessiones* given to the patron and his relatives in succession to a freedman. We know that the *Lex* Papia Poppaea gave a statutory basis to some of them, which would of itself indicate that they were *cum re*, and therefore realities, in normal cases.

We are nowhere told that *bonorum possessio unde liberi* was *cum re*, but as *bonorum possessio contra tabulas* was so from very early times, and this case affects the same persons, and is of earlier date, it may be taken for granted that, here too, it was *cum re*. The case is not quite so clear in the case of *bonorum possessio unde decem personae*, but it is *à priori* most probable that it was *cum re*, and this is somewhat confirmed by the language of the *Collatio* which says, purporting to quote Ulpian, that the Twelve Tables gave the *hereditas* to the *extraneus manumissor*, but the Praetor, on grounds of equity, preferred the *decem personae* to him[1].

It will appear from what has been said that in some cases at least it was not the Praetor but express legislation by the sovereign authority which made a particular *bonorum possessio cum re.* This is the case for instance with Hadrian's enactment as to the will which fails technically because of a *postumus praeteritus*, who is however in fact dead. It is the case with *bonorum possessio contra tabulas*, made *cum re* as against agnates by Antoninus Pius. It is true of the *bonorum possessio* relative to the goods of a *libertinus*, under the *Lex* Papia Poppaea, and, of course, of Justinian's sweeping changes. How stands the matter with those *bonorum possessiones* which were *cum re* before the foundation of the imperial system? Some writers go so far as to say that the Praetor never of his own authority made *bonorum possessio cum re*, except where there was no *heres* to set up an adverse claim. But the state of our information does not warrant any such general statement. *Unde liberi*, *unde decem personae* seem to be republican, and it is most probable that they owe their efficacy to the edict alone. The language of Cicero certainly implies that the edict could give an effective right as against civil law *heredes*[2].

Before leaving this point the warning must be repeated that all these distinctions between *bonorum possessio cum re* and *sine re* are quite foreign to those cases which we have mentioned of *bonorum possessio* not in accordance with the edict. Grants not *ex edicto*, grants, that is, to one not entitled to the grant under the terms of the edict, must have been common enough, since, as we know, the grant is a matter of form, and is made by an officer who has in most cases never heard of any of the parties till they come before him with their demand. Such a *bonorum possessio* is neither *cum re* nor *sine re*: it is not for any practical purpose *bonorum possessio* at all.

[1] Coll. 16. 9. 2.

[2] Cicero, *In Verrem*, 2. 1. 48.

99. The foregoing statement of the rules of *bonorum possessio* suggests a number of questions, some of which call for an answer. Why does a claimant take the trouble to obtain a grant of *bonorum possessio sine re?* To this question there are obvious answers. A man who is entitled to *bonorum possessio*, or who thinks he is, may not know on the facts whether it will prove to be *cum re* or *sine re*. We have seen that the determination of this point depends on circumstances which are not necessarily, even in some cases not possibly, within his knowledge. Moreover, though it may be technically *sine re*, and he knows this, it may yet be effective because from various causes the person entitled does not take steps against the *bonorum possessor*. Again, we are told that the *bonorum possessor* who has obtained actual possession under the interdict *quorum bonorum*, for which result it is immaterial whether his *bonorum possessio* is *cum re* or *sine re*, has the advantage of being defendant if the property is claimed from him by the civil law *heres*. This means a good deal: the burden of proof is on the plaintiff. He may have a good title but be unable to prove it. This does not express a very lofty morality, but no doubt it operated often enough as a motive for claiming *bonorum possessio*.

The question may also be asked: why did the Praetor grant *bonorum possessio sine re?* Why did he give possession to one to whom, on the principles of his own system, the property in question was not ultimately to belong? There are several answers. So far as the original grant of *bonorum possessio* was concerned, the Praetor could not possibly know whether it would prove to be *cum re* or *sine re*. Under appropriate circumstances any *bonorum possessio* might be *cum re*, and the Praetor has ordinarily never heard of the deceased until the demand of *bonorum possessio* is made, and knows nothing of his family or affairs. Again, the fact that a particular *bonorum possessio* is *sine re* is no evidence of the wish of the Praetor that it should be so. No doubt every *bonorum possessio* was originally *sine re*, if there was a civil law *heres*, unless it was actually granted to him. The first step in the evolution of a new praetorian right of succession would be to grant *bonorum possessio* and no more. This would be *sine re*. Later on the Praetor, or very commonly some other agency, might turn it into *bonorum possessio cum re*, by giving the *bonorum possessor* an *exceptio doli* if he was sued by the *heres*, and in due course the *hereditatis petitio possessoria* against him. That is to say, the *exceptio doli* of the *heres* would be excluded. Again, when the person to whom such a *bonorum possessio* was given brought the interdict *quorum bonorum*, we have seen that even where the *bonorum possessio* was *sine re*, the *heres* who was really entitled was not allowed to plead and prove that fact in the interdictal procedure, but must let the *bonorum possessor* win in that procedure, and, if he thought fit, bring the *hereditatis petitio* later, although the facts that he will then have to prove might, one would think, just as well have been proved, under an appropriate *exceptio*, in the proceedings under the interdict itself. That is to say, the plea of title was not admitted in the possessory procedure. This restriction is not in any way peculiar to *bonorum possessio* and *quorum bonorum*: it runs through all the possessory remedies. Taking this accepted principle as a starting-point, it is clear that *bonorum possessio* was necessarily granted without reference to the question whether it would ultimately prove to be *cum* or *sine re*.

If we go further and ask why title might not be pleaded in reply to a possessory claim, we may find ourselves in difficulties. The most fundamental answer will certainly have nothing to do with succession, probably it will have nothing to do with the Roman law itself at all, for exactly the same principle is found in the ancient system of possessory remedies in English law, which do not seem to be in any way connected with the Roman system, or to owe anything to it. Any attempt to answer the question may be deferred till we are considering the interdictal procedure in general. Here however it may be suggested that if *bonorum possessio sine re* was only a first step towards *bonorum possessio cum re*, there is an obvious reason for not facilitating proof of title. But the Praetor's aims in originating the system of *bonorum possessio* are a matter which we have expressly excluded from discussion.

We have seen that the demand for *bonorum possessio* was analogous in nature and effect to *aditio*. The periods within which it might be claimed, though not the same, are somewhat similar. A period of one hundred days or even a year seems very short as a period of limitation, and yet a man who has let these times pass can never claim either *hereditas* or *bonorum possessio*. But it must be remembered that where the Praetor fixes a *spatium deliberandi*, and usually, where it is fixed by will, and always in the case of praetorian *bonorum possessio*, the time runs only from the date at which the claimant has notice of his right, and that all he is called on to do is to make a certain formal, or in some cases (and always in later law) informal, declaration. When once he has done that, his right is an ordinary right of action, subject to no rules of limitation or adverse prescription except such as affect all actions alike.

CHAPTER VI

THE LAW OF OBLIGATIONS. GENERALIA. SPECIFIC CONTRACTS

100. It has already been pointed out that obligation is essentially a relation between two persons, a debtor and a creditor, and that thus it can be looked at from the point of view of either, so that in one aspect it is a duty, and in the other a right. In the classification of *res*, where obligation appears as a *res incorporalis*, it is clearly the right which is in view, while in the definition of obligation in Book III, where it is declared to be a bond of law, imposing a duty, it is the other aspect which is explicitly brought out. In the detailed treatment of the matter however this point of view is again abandoned, and the right reverted to, with results to which it will be necessary to call attention later. The conception of obligation as a relation between two persons is sufficiently clearly expressed in the name, which denotes a tying together, and the same idea is expressed in the name of one of the oldest of all obligations, obligation by *nexum*. It is scarcely less obvious in the forms *contrahere* and *contractus*, of which words the latter is the general name of that kind of obligation which is created by agreement, subject to small limitations not now material. It should however be noticed that the word *contrahere* is not limited in its force in the same way. A man can contract an obligation in a variety of ways of which contract is only one. Thus Gaius, in explaining "*quibus modis re contrahitur obligatio*," points out the nature of the confusion, which he could hardly avoid making, since he has no place in his institutional scheme for *obligatio quasi ex contractu.* It is characteristic of Justinian's method, or lack of method, that though he has a place for such obligations, he faithfully follows the exposition of Gaius, including the apologetic part, and then, when he comes to deal with *obligatio quasi ex contractu,* states the law again.

101. From the fact that, in the preliminary discussion of obligation, it is regarded primarily as a right (properly enough, since the subject of discussion is *res*) appears to result the omission of certain matters which ought logically to find a place in any treatment of the subject. Thus we are told how rights of obligation are acquired for us by others, but we are not told how the acts of others can put us under an obligation at law. No doubt, so far as contract is concerned, the case could not occur at civil law, but this is by no means true of delict, since the Twelve Tables and the *Lex* Aquilia both recognise noxal liability. But our liability for the contracts and delicts of subordinate members of our family (and in some cases *extranei*) are both discussed under the law of actions. It may be noted that though a confusion between procedure and rights of action, both being denoted by the word *actio,* may have something to do with this, yet, for the most part, these rights of action are discussed in Book IV only by way of illustration of special types of action there explained.

Noxal liability is not properly speaking an exception to the rule that a *paterfamilias* is not bound by the acts of the subordinate members of his household: it is primarily considered as a right of ransom of the actual wrongdoer, and thus is a right rather than a liability. It is important to keep clear of any notion of representation: the contracting slave is not really regarded as an outpost of the master's personality, though this may well appear a convenient way in which to express the result. The idea seems to be that, just as the results of the slave's handiwork benefit him as owner of the slave, so must the results of his activity in any other field. The owner is the only person to whom they can enure. Thus the principle is not that the slave is an expression of him, but only that the slave is his. This mere idea of ownership would afford no basis for the view that the master ought to be liable for his acts, and thus every such liability whether in contract or in delict is the effect of an express piece of legislation.

102. The intensely personal nature of *obligatio*, as conceived in Roman theory, is shewn by some of its most familiar rules. Thus it is well known that rights of contract or the like could not be assigned. Similar results could of course be arrived at by means of a system of substituted contracts, by way of *novatio*, and to a certain extent by giving a person who is for practical purposes an assignee, authority to sue on behalf of the assignor (*procurator in rem suam*). These evasions merely illustrate the principle itself, which however is less significant than at first sight it appears to be, since, in this respect, obligation does not differ from other rights: it has often been pointed out that in Roman law rights were in general not assignable. In classical law ownership was practically the only property right which could be directly transferred. The difficulty of assigning incorporeal rights has been felt in other systems. Our own law did not recognise assignments of obligations and found relief in evasions very similar to those of the Roman law. But English law ultimately attained a statutory rule providing for direct assignment and Roman law never got so far. Even where the contract affected the enjoyment of land, the benefit of it did not pass with the land, as it does in our modern law. Where a man let a farm with agreements as to proper cultivation and died leaving the land away from the *heres*, the legatee could not enforce the covenants, nor could the *heres*, for lack, in his case, of *interesse*. If the legatee prevented the tenant from using the land, his remedy was nevertheless against the *heres*: it was one of the obligations of the deceased[1]. No doubt this kind of case was dealt with by a system of precautionary securities.

Another rule illustrating the personal nature of obligations is the well-known principle that rights of obligation could not

[1] D. 19. 2. 32.

be acquired through the acts of a third party. In early law indeed no rights could be so acquired: *per extraneam personam nihil adquiri posse.* But this general rule proved too inconvenient to be retained in that absolute form in a commercial age, and we know that about the time of Gaius it became possible for a free agent to acquire ownership for his employer, by informal modes of transfer. But no such change occurred in the law of obligation. Up to the time of Justinian, and under his legislation, it still remained true that a contract by an *extraneus,* even if he was a *procurator,* a general agent, gave his employer no right to sue except by one of the evasions of principle which we have mentioned in connexion with assignment.

There is another kind of question which brings out this attitude of the Roman law very clearly. If a slave makes a contract, for example, of hire, and the master deals negligently with the property hired, or *vice versa,* what are the resulting liabilities? One of them made the contract: how can the other of them break it? *Obligatio* is personal. So far as the first case is concerned there is but little authority, but the rule deducible from the few texts seems to be that the master's *culpa* could not make him liable to any action on the contract, though if his negligence had resulted in physical damage to the property no doubt there might be an *actio e lege* Aquilia. If he was guilty of *dolus,* this would of course, in the absence of any other remedy, make him liable under the *actio doli* (since *dolus* is a delict in itself), to compensate for the damage done. But it seems clear that the law went a step further, and, in *bonae fidei* actions, allowed this *dolus* to come into account, under the clause in the *intentio* "*ex fide bona.*" In *stricti iuris* contracts the classical law knew no remedy but the *actio doli,* but later law gave an *actio utilis* on the contract itself. The other, no doubt far commoner case, that of negligence of a slave in carrying out a contract made by his master, was the subject of a great deal of controversy. The earlier view clearly was that this gave no action on the contract, but only, in the case of actual damage to the property, an Aquilian action, which would be noxal since the damage was done by a slave. There were however from early times some supporters of another view, namely, that an action on the contract would lie, but that the master could avoid liability thereunder by handing over the slave. This is not exactly noxal surrender, since the action is not delictal, but it gives much the same result. This view, which does not seem to have fully prevailed till the time of Justinian, is itself an acknowledgment of the principle we are discussing[1].

103. In his treatment of obligation Justinian follows in the main the order and method of Gaius, except that while Gaius strictly excludes all reference to *obligationes honorariae* (reserving them for Book IV, where he gives many of them in illustrating the different types of *actio honoraria*), Justinian does occasionally refer to them. Indeed he does more: at the very opening of his discussion he states his main classification of *obligationes* as being in two classes: civil and praetorian. But he at once proceeds to state what he calls a *sequens divisio* which is in fact the well-known classification of Gaius, based on the nature of the fact which creates the *obligatio*, amplified by the addition of the headings of quasi-contract and quasi-delict. The odd result is that while he mentions praetorian obligations as one of the two main types, and proceeds to discuss the distinction with some care, they are not specially marked off in his detailed treatment and indeed are only very imperfectly treated at all. So far as delict and quasi-delict are concerned we do get a good many praetorian obligations discussed, *e.g.*, the subsidiary actions in *furtum*, the extensions of the *lex* Aquilia, praetorian rules in *iniuria*, and so forth. But there is little or nothing about them in contract. The rules as to praetorian pacts and the liabilities *de peculio* and so forth are discussed, under the influence of Gaius, in Book IV. The treatment of the distinction between civil and praetorian obligations as the principal one is no doubt due to some other book which Tribonian used, though it does not seem that its origin has been traced.

[1] Buckland, Roman Law of Slavery, 161 *sqq*.

In discussing the forms of contract individually, Justinian follows the order adopted by Gaius. The order is: Contracts *re*, *verbis*, *literis* and *consensu*, and it is difficult to see any good reason for taking them in this order. Many explanations and justifications of the arrangement have been given, and a few of them may be mentioned here. According to one view the order is chronological, *mutuum* being the oldest contract and drawing the other contracts *re* with it. The chief objection to this view is that there is no evidence for the antecedently improbable extreme antiquity of the informal contract of *mutuum*. Another view is that they are taken in the order of relative simplicity, but a moment's consideration will shew that this does not accord with the facts. It has been said, again, that the order proceeds from that which has the most obvious external sign to that which has the least. But apart from the extremely artificial nature of this distinction, it is open to the same objection as the last. Again it has been said to be merely arbitrary: this is a most unlikely view, since Gaius adopts the order in both of his institutional works. It has also been said to be a traditional order, which is probably the case, but that is no explanation. It leaves open the question on what the traditional practice rested. Another, and somewhat more satisfactory, opinion is that the arrangement is suggested by the Edict. The treatment of contract under the heading "*de rebus creditis*" in the Edict brings close together *mutuum* and stipulation. *Mutuum* as being the typical *certum creditum* comes first: it is not in fact distinguished from stipulation in the Edict, as both forms of contract have the same remedy. *Mutuum* takes with it all the other contracts *re*, since they are *credita* of the same type. In support of this close association of *mutuum* and stipulation it may be observed that the *formula* in what is called *condictio certi*, which was the appropriate remedy, does not mention the "*causa*" in the *intentio*: it is not necessary to say therein whether the money was due on *mutuum* or on stipulation. But though this opinion is at least plausible, neither this nor any of the others is proven: they are all conjectural[1].

[1] See Accarias, Précis, 2. 15; Moyle, Inst. of Just. ad *In*. 3. 13. 2.

Apart from the points which were plainly borrowed by Justinian from earlier writers there is little that is of much value in Justinian's classification of obligations. It has been pointed out that it is a very artificial affair, which may not have any very close relation to actual practice. A little analysis of it will make this clear. There are, he says, four sources of obligation, contract, quasi contract, delict and quasi delict. But if quasi delict is made a fourth head on account of its vicarious character, one would have expected a heading of some kind for vicarious liability in contract. Of contract there are four classes, but this is really to omit the innominate contracts and the *pacta vestita*. Of contracts *re* there are four, but *commodatum* and *depositum* might equally well have been treated as one contract. Of contracts *consensu* there are four, but the *pacta praetoria* and *legitima* might have been called consensual contracts. There are four delicts, but this is arrived at by making theft and aggravated theft distinct delicts and by ignoring a number of delicts altogether. There seem also to be four quasi delicts, though this is not so clearly brought out. This recurrence of the number four gives a very false air of symmetry; it is plain that the whole scheme might be made to wear a very different aspect[1].

104. As has been observed there were some cases of agreement in the later Roman law which were actionable, but were never called contracts, *pacta praetoria* and *pacta legitima*, and we know that these were specially created exceptions to a principle which remained throughout the history of the law, *i.e.* that a mere informal agreement could not as such be sued upon. This principle is expressed in certain well-known maxims, "*nuda pactio non parit obligationem, sed parit exceptionem,*" "*cum nulla subest causa praeter* (or *propter*) *conventionem constat non posse constitui obligationem*[2]." In these passages the word *obligatio* means, of course, actionable obligation, and in the second the arising of this obligation is declared to depend on

[1] Goudy, Studi Fadda; Roby, Rom. Priv. Law, 2. 2.
[2] D. 2. 14. 7. 4, 5.

the existence of a *causa* over and above the mere fact of agreement. This word, *causa*, is a most unreliable instrument. Even where it is used to express a basis of right it does not always mean the same thing. We have already seen that the *iusta causa traditionis* is not exactly the same as the *iusta causa* or *iustus titulus usucapionis*, though in each case it means some pre-existing state of facts on which the legal result of other facts is to depend. Its meaning is similar in the words of the *sacramentum—secundum suam causam*, though here it seems to include all the facts of title, the conveyance as well as any *iusta causa* leading up to it. But it also means many things which have little or nothing to do with a legal basis of right. It means a law suit, as in the expression *causam perdere*. It means the accessories of property recovered by action: the plantiff is entitled to *rem cum sua causa*. It means also cause, and indeed the lexicons give an enormous number of meanings and shades of meaning. In the present connexion the word is commonly taken to mean a pre-existing fact, giving title, and it is used to justify the principle, or rather dogma, that in the Roman law an action on contract arises from agreement to which is added *causa*. The *causa* is, it appears, some characteristic of the transaction. It is of course usually the form employed. But in consensual contracts there is the difficulty that they have no necessary form. All that they require is the mere *conventio*, and this is, in the main text on which this principle is based, expressly stated to be insufficient. Sir Henry Maine surmounted the difficulty by finding the *causa* not in the individual transaction, but in the frequency or importance of such transactions as a class. There is however the further difficulty that if agreement and *causa* together make up an actionable contract, all agreements which have any of these *causae* ought to have been actionable. But this is not the case. Gratuitous delivery of an article for any temporary purpose would not make a contract *re* unless it was one of the recognised cases. It is true that, as the texts shew, many of these cases can be brought within the conception of mandate, but for that purpose it is quite indifferent, from the point of view of contractual liability, whether there has been any delivery of a chattel or not. It is very doubtful whether there is any importance in all this. The whole notion depends on giving a significance which it does not deserve to the use of the word "*causa*" by Ulpian[1], and to that of the expression "*causa civilis*" in quite another context by Pomponius[2]. All that Ulpian means is that you cannot in general sue on a mere pact as such: you must shew that your agreement is one of those which the law makes actionable. His way of putting the matter expresses the great difference which exists between the Roman attitude towards agreement and that of our law. With us an agreement is actionable unless there is some reason why it should not be so. With the Romans an agreement was not actionable unless there was some reason why it should be so. The result is that, in these texts, *causa* means merely actionability, and does not denote anything else, independent of actionability, which creates that important characteristic. If we treat agreement together with *causa* as creative of contract, *i.e.*, agreement with a civil action, we cannot easily shew why *permutatio*, which, as we know, involved delivery, did not give a civil law action. If we make contract mean merely actionable agreement, we cannot find any *causa* in connexion with such things as *pacta legitima*, except that they were in fact made actionable. The truth is that it is only in connexion with the formal contracts that this conception of *causa* can be made to work at all.

If this theory can neither be regarded as convincing in itself nor, as a statement of the principle of obligation by agreement, be credited to the Romans, still less can either of these be said of a classification found in some modern books, according to which Roman contracts can be divided into three classes, formal, equitable and consideration contracts. It is difficult to give any real sense to the word equitable which is used to group together the contracts *re*, including *mutuum*, and a consensual contract, *mandatum*. They are neither more nor less equitable than other contracts, less so, one would be inclined to say, than

[1] D. 2. 14. 7. 4. [2] D. 15. 1. 49. 2.

sale and hire. Most of them, but not all, are of praetorian origin, but though the Praetor introduced many equitable notions, it does not follow that all his introductions have a special claim to be called equitable or, if not, why these should be singled out for that distinction.

105. The contract of *Nexum*, obsolete so early that our legal texts say very little about it, finds of course no place in the classification of Gaius, but we get some help towards an understanding of it from the fact that discharge *per aes et libram* survived to his time, and from what he tells us about its rules we can draw some inferences for the contract of *nexum* itself, for which, as being contracted *per aes et libram*, this mode of discharge was peculiarly appropriate. *Nexum* played a large part in the economic and social life of Rome for some centuries. The sufferings of the *Nexi*, the resulting disaffection, and the legislation which, by destroying the specific and severe remedies of the nexal creditor, caused the disuse of the contract of *nexum* are recorded by the historians. But as these accounts are not the work of lawyers, much obscurity has reigned, and, it may be said, still reigns, as to the exact juristic nature of the transaction. The view rendered dominant by Huschke, long practically universally accepted, and still the most widely held, is shortly as follows. *Nexum* was a contract, made with *aes et libra*, like *mancipatio*, with a *nuncupatio* by the creditor, analogous to that in *mancipatio*, in which the debtor was declared to be "*damnas*" if he failed to fulfil his obligation. The significance of this *damnatio* in early law, whether it occurred in a legislative act, or in a will or in a solemn contract, was, *inter alia*, to entitle the injured party, in our case the unpaid creditor, to seize the other party by *manus iniectio* without judgment, and carry him into confinement. At first used only as the protection of otherwise informal loans of money it was ultimately applied to other cases, but always, so far as can be seen, to cases in which the obligation was for a certain sum of money. By a *lex* Poetelia, the date of which appears to be a little before 300 B.C., it was made necessary for the creditor in such a transaction to obtain actual judgment before proceeding to execution. In the result *nexum* passed rapidly out of use, having no longer any advantages to the creditor to compensate for its somewhat clumsy form.

This brilliant hypothesis received striking confirmation when, years later, a re-reading of Gaius by Studemund disclosed the fact that in the form of *manus iniectio* as given by Gaius, which had not, hitherto, been fully made out, the word *condemnatus* was found to occur just where Huschke's theory required it[1]. Nevertheless the theory has not remained unchallenged. It was strongly attacked by Mitteis in 1901, and since that date there has been a steady and still continuing stream of literature on the subject[2].

It is not possible to go into detail as to the controversies, but a general indication of the tendencies of the attack on Huschke's theory may be given in a few words[3]. Mitteis emphasises the well-known fact that *Nexum* is not mentioned by Gaius in his historical account of the various cases of *manus iniectio.* He points out that in at least one non-juristic text the seizure under *Nexum* is treated as not based on any *addictio,* though it is clear that this was an essential of *manus iniectio.* He shews that there are several texts which speak of one who binds himself by *Nexum* as having already incurred his indebtedness. He holds also that Huschke's association of the right of seizure with the use of the word *damnas* is an error, since, as he shews, there are several *leges* in which this word is used, where it is certain that there was no *manus iniectio.* He arrives therefore at the conclusion that, while the loan *per aes et libram* no doubt existed, it gave no right of seizure, but like any other contract would be enforced by an ordinary action, *actio sacramenti in personam.* The right of seizure, he says, depended on another step, also *per aes et libram,* a mancipation of the man by himself, in order that he might work out the debt, a step which he considers to have been taken in order to

[1] Gai. 3. 174.

[2] The latest contributor is Eisele, Studien. He gives references to the earlier literature.

[3] See Roby, Rom. Priv. Law, 2. 296 *sqq.* for a collection and examination of the principal texts.

avoid the capital consequences which would have resulted if the original debt had been allowed to lead to a judgment and *condemnatio* which the debtor was unable to satisfy. The negative or destructive part of Mitteis' essay met at once with very wide, though not universal, acceptance. But there was more hesitation as to his own explanation of the texts. The double transaction *per aes et libram* has not been thought acceptable. Lenel, while agreeing that Huschke's view is untenable, simplifies the matter by the suggestion that there is no evidence for the view that loans of money were made *per aes et libram*, so that he gets rid of one of the transactions *per aes et libram*. He seems to regard the *nexi* as vendors who have become liable to the *actio auctoritatis* and double damages for defect in title to the thing sold. Mommsen adheres more closely to Mitteis, but gets rid of the double transaction by supposing the transaction *per aes et libram* to have occurred at the time of the loan, but to be in effect a *mancipatio* of the man by himself, to be operative only if he makes default in payment. Other variations may be found in Girard[1].

Huschke's theory found however defenders from the first publication of Mitteis' article and their number is tending to increase. The principal counter-arguments are briefly and clearly set out by Girard, and need not be here repeated. The general result is that it is extremely unsafe to regard Huschke's notions as having been completely overthrown.

106. Another form of contract which existed in the time of Gaius, and even later, but is not mentioned in his scheme of contracts, though he refers to it incidentally at several points, is *Fiducia*. It has the peculiar characteristic that it is, so to speak, parasitic; it can occur only as a subsidiary transaction in connexion with a transfer of property, and it is perhaps for this reason that it was not called expressly a *contractus*. The only recorded instances of it are in connexion with *mancipatio*, and though we are told by Gaius and later authority that it was applicable to *cessio in iure*, it does not seem to have been

[1] Manuel (5), 481 *sqq*.

possible to attach a *fiducia* to a *traditio*. It is an informal pact, added to the actual conveyance, but not forming part of the *nuncupatio*. It may have several parts. Thus in two instances which we have, both referring to *fiducia* as security for a debt, one being apparently a blank form for use as a model, there are provisions for a power of sale, and in one there are agreements as to the event of sale for more or less than the debt. The agreements contain an express declaration that the property is held in *fiducia* till the debt is fully paid, but in neither is it expressly said that it is then to be returned[1]. The main purpose of the agreement is always to regulate the ultimate disposal of the subject-matter of the conveyance. The transaction has certain well-known applications in the law of persons, *e.g.*, *coemptio cum fiducia*, emancipation and *tutela fiduciaria*, with others not so prominent, *e.g.*, transfer of a slave with a *fiducia* for manumission. Its applications in the law of things are of two types: *cum amico*, *e.g.*, conveyance for safe custody, or by way of loan, or for disposal in various ways, and *cum creditore*, by way of security for a loan. The former purposes were in classical law attained more simply by *depositum*, *commodatum* and *mandatum*, so that *fiducia cum amico* was probably obsolete by the time of Gaius. But *fiducia cum creditore* was a very powerful form of security, and appears to have remained in use till the fifth century. It has been made clear that many of the texts, even of the later jurists, which in the Digest speak of *pignus*, were originally written of *fiducia* and have been altered by the compilers[2].

The *actio fiduciae* was *bonae fidei*, but it is a controverted point whether there was an alternative *formula in factum*. It is also matter of dispute whether the *formula*, of which alone we know anything, was the first remedy or whether there was an *actio fiduciae* under the system of *legis actiones*. It has been suggested that the very archaic form of part of the formula preserved to us is an indication that the Praetor is adopting the form used in the *legis actio*, as he did in the *actio furti*. On the other hand there is no real evidence for this earlier action,

[1] Bruns, Fontes, 1. 332.

[2] *Ante*, § 1.

and it is by no means incredible that the obligation, resting on *fides*, was without direct legal protection in earlier law. As in the case of the other contracts *re*, there was an *actio contraria*.

The fact must be noted that there is a complete conveyance apart from the *pactum fiduciae*. This makes the transferee owner, and gives him the ordinary rights of an owner. The pact cannot restrict these, but it may make the exercise of them a breach of the obligation, giving rise to the *actio fiduciae*. This will be more conveniently considered in connexion with pledge[1]. But there is an interesting and eminently practical question which may be mentioned here. It may happen that the person who has handed over a thing on trust to be given to a third person, or a slave on trust for manumission, changes his mind before the act is completed, and gives notice to that effect to the transferee. What is the effect? There has been a good deal of discussion of the matter: the general result seems to be that the *fiducia* may not be carried out after notice of revocation. The *actio fiduciae* will lie, and thus there is an implied *fiducia* to restore the subject-matter on revocation of the instructions. In late law, after the disappearance of the *actio fiduciae*, the remedy is a certain *condictio ex poenitentia* and this *condictio* is the remedy mentioned in the Digest, in such cases of revocation. But it is fairly clear that these texts are interpolated, and that this *condictio ex poenitentia* is, in this connexion at least, if not an invention of the compilers, at any rate post-classical.

107. For the sake of completeness it may be well to mention another group of actionable agreements which find no place in the scheme of Gaius. They are the actionable pacts. One group, rendered actionable by the Praetor, and on that account called *pacta praetoria*, are sometimes described as contracts based on consideration, and, though there is no reason to suppose any conscious adoption of this as a test by the Praetor, they all have their *quid pro quo*. The oldest of them are hypothec and the banker's agreement giving rise to the *actio*

[1] *Post*, § 110.

receptitia, if this is, as Girard holds, a praetorian pact, and not, as is more commonly thought, an ancient civil law institution[1] They are all protected by exceptions and by actions *in factum*, and it is probably the absence of an *actio in ius* which causes Gaius, to whom they were familiar, to exclude them from his scheme of contracts. The few *pacta legitima*, made actionable by late emperors, *pactum dotis*, *pactum donationis*, and the agreement to submit a question to arbitration do not rest on consideration, and it may be noted that Justinian, who made the last binding, required a note in writing as a condition of validity[2].

108. The contracts *re* are disposed of by Gaius, and by Justinian, following him, in very few words. We have already noted the fact that Gaius is discussing *obligatio re contracta* rather than contract *re*, and thus is compelled to discuss the rules of *condictio indebiti* in connexion with these contracts.

Mutuum differs from the others in being unilateral, *i.e.*, binding only one, and giving rights only to the other, and in giving rise to a *strictum iudicium*, a characteristic of unilateral contracts, and of no others. It must have been of considerable importance, for though it was in itself gratuitous, it might be, and no doubt usually was, accompanied by a promise of interest for which a stipulation would usually be necessary, though in a few privileged cases a mere pact sufficed. It may indeed be doubted whether *mutuum* standing alone was ever a common form of contract. As we know it, it was created by mere delivery of the money lent and needed no witnesses. It is plain that if there were in fact no witnesses, the creditor had but poor guaranty for the return of his money. From what is said by the historians it seems probable that commercial loans were usually fortified by *nexum*, so long as *nexum* served a purpose, and from the Digest it is clear that it was not only usual, but almost a matter of course, to accompany a *mutuum* with a stipulation, not merely for interest, but for the return of the capital

[1] See for discussion and references, Lenel, Ed. Perp. § 50.

[2] C. 2. 55. 4. 1.

sum. This stipulation would, in ordinary practice, be embodied in a written *cautio*, as indeed the fact of the loan itself would commonly be. In *mutuum* the one duty of the borrower is to return what is lent. There can be no question of *culpa*: his liability is absolute. The contract imposes no obligation on the lender. If, for instance, the loan is of seed, and the seed lent contains other seeds of such a nature as to cause damage when the whole is sown, the only remedy will be by a delictal action.

It was a rule of *mutuum* that there must be an actual transfer of *dominium* from the lender to the borrower, so that, if what was handed over was not the property of the lender, there was no *mutuum*. But the exigencies of commerce compelled relaxation of this strict rule, in ways analogous to those with which we are familiar in the case of *traditio*. Thus there is a *mutuum* if you, under an arrangement with me, sell property of mine to hold the proceeds as a loan. If *A*, by arrangement, lends his own money to *B* as being *C*'s, there are two cases of *mutuum*. If I tell my debtor to pay his debt to you, and he does so, there is a *mutuum* to you. Some of these cases might be brought into line with help of the conception of acquisition through a *procurator*, and of *traditio brevi manu*. But the jurists make it clear that they do not contemplate the property as having ever been in the lender, and some of them are of an earlier date than that of the development of acquisition of *dominium* by a procurator. They are cases of departure from strict principle on grounds of general convenience.

109. The contracts of deposit and *commodatum* are of no great commercial importance. The rules are in general simple, though there are certain small difficulties of detail. They do not seem to have attracted the attention of the jurists very closely and it is perhaps this which accounts for the fact that, in *commodatum*, there survived to the time of the compilers under Justinian a great number of doubts on small points which were then settled by legislation[1]. These contracts are imperfectly bilateral, *i.e.*, they bind primarily one party, the

[1] C. 6. 2. 22.

depositee and the borrower, and only incidentally and by means of an *actio contraria* the depositor and the lender. It will be remembered that the same characteristic exists in the case of *fiducia*, from which they both descend.

The case commonly called *depositum irregulare*[1] is a remarkable juristic development. It is deposit of money, usually with a banker, on the terms that he may use it. It is distinguishable from *mutuum* only by the intent of the parties, but the distinction has important results, most of which turn on the fact that it gives rise to the *bonae fidei* action of deposit, and not to *condictio*. They need not be stated. It does not appear on the texts whether, if the money was destroyed by accident before the banker had in any way dealt with it, the loss fell on the depositor or on the banker.

Another exceptional case of deposit is *Sequestratio*[2], deposit for safe custody pending the settlement of a dispute concerning the right to it. Its chief peculiarity is that the *sequester* has possession, entitling him to proceed by way of interdict against any person who deprives him of the possession, and not a mere *ius in personam*, such as that of an ordinary depositee. Since one main purpose of the transaction is to prevent either disputant from acquiring the thing by usucapion, it is plain that its economic purpose would not be served unless the *sequester* had had possession. The rule may be regarded not so much as a special privilege invented for this case as a survival from the regime of *fiducia*.

It must be noted that the sharp distinction in the texts between *depositum* and *commodatum*, and again between these contracts and *mandatum*, would not be so clearly made in practice. If I ask you to take care of my silver in my absence and tell you that you may use it if on any occasion of a dinner party your own silver falls short, it would seem that while there is clearly only one contract it would have to be governed by the rules of *commodatum* on any such occasion, and by those of deposit at other times. If *A* and *B* have become common owners of a thing and *A* asks *B* to take care of it, with

[1] D. 19. 2. 31.

[2] D. 16. 3. 6, 12. 2, 17 *pr.*

permission to use it, but he is to miss no opportunity of selling it, all three contracts appear to be present and perhaps *Societas* as well.

110. *Pignus* is of far greater importance. Like the foregoing, it is a descendant of *fiducia*, and, as in those cases, the changed position of the parties in respect of ownership has fundamentally altered their relations. The creditor who held a *fiducia* was owner of it and thus could realise his security at any time, so that it became necessary to come to agreements restricting his power of sale, or even barring it altogether. The pledgee is in a very different position. He is not owner, and has not therefore, on ordinary legal principles, any power of sale whatever. It is therefore necessary to say a few words as to the development of his various remedies. Some of the rules affecting the relation of the parties to a *pignus* are difficult to account for logically, but find their explanation in the fact that they have come over from the system of fiduciary mancipation, in which they were appropriate enough. In *pignus*, as in *sequestratio*, the purpose of the transaction requires that the holder shall have *possessio*, or at any rate be able to recover the possession from any third person. The history of this right is somewhat obscure. It is commonly held, though the textual authority is very slight, that *pignus* gave a right to the possessory interdicts from the earliest times. They would apparently be *Uti Possidetis* and *Utrubi*, and a remark of Javolenus[1] that the pledge creditor, though he has not possession for *usucapio* has it for all other purposes, and may add the debtor's possession to his own, perhaps refers to the latter. However this may be it is after the introduction of hypothec, *i.e.* pledge without transfer of actual possession, that we get any detailed information. The *interdictum* Salvianum, which was available only in respect of hypothec for rent, did not go very far. It was at first available only against the debtor himself, and though it was afterwards extended against third persons, it was never applied to any other cases of hypothec, and it was

[1] D. 41. 3. 16.

never available except for the first taking of possession. A landlord who had taken possession of the property pledged for the rent of a farm, and afterwards lost possession, could not bring the *interdictum* Salvianum[1]. Another remedy was more effective. This was the *actio* Serviana, available to the same class of creditors, introduced probably not long before Augustus, and extended, early in the Empire, to all hypothecary creditors, under the name *actio quasi* Serviana. These gave a right to recover possession from third parties—a complete possessory right. This protection of a purely possessory right by an action, which in procedure and incidents was modelled on *vindicatio rei* suggests a connexion with *fiducia* in which the remedy of the creditor was a *vindicatio*. But in view of the date at which this remedy developed, and of its connexion with *hypotheca*, it is generally held that it was an importation through the *jurisdictio* of the *praetor peregrinus*.

The mere power of keeping the pledged property, with no right to profit by it, is of little use to the creditor if he cannot get his debt paid. He must have some means of realising his security. His most obvious means of putting pressure on the debtor is by having a clause inserted in the agreement to the effect that the property is to be his at a price, to be settled at that date, if the debt is not paid in full by a certain date, so that the whole transaction would be a sort of conditional *traditio brevi manu*, as well as a pledge[2]. The creditor cannot sell the pledged property, since he is not its owner. But here too it became the practice to provide, in the agreement, that the creditor should have the power to sell the pledged property if default was made in payment, in order to pay himself out of the proceeds. But alienation by a non-owner is contrary to general principle, at least till a relatively late date, and it is easy to see that such a machinery could be used collusively to create a power of alienation by agent. Such a power of sale seems to be referred to by Labeo[3], as edited by Paul, but it is difficult to believe that it can have been admitted so early: the text may

[1] See on the controversies as to its scope, Girard, Manuel (5), 780.

[2] D. 20. 1. 16. 9.

[3] D. 20. 1. 35.

well have been written of fiduciary mancipation. This was the usual form of pledge in the time of Labeo, and commonly contained such a pact, not that the creditor could not have sold without it, but that the pact makes it clear under what circumstances the sale will not be a breach of contract. Another text takes it back to Servius[1], but here too there is nothing to shew that the case was not one of *fiducia*. In any case it is clear from the language of Gaius that the power of sale under a pact entered into at the time of the pledge was older than any general power of sale by agent. By a very natural evolution there developed in late classical law a power of sale without express agreement, a power which could however be excluded by agreement, though even where there was such an understanding it seems that the creditor could sell if he three times gave the debtor notice of his intention so to do. On the other hand agreements for "foreclosure," *i.e.* that the property shall belong to the creditor if the debt is not paid by a certain day, were forbidden by Constantine, their place having been taken more reasonably by a system introduced under Severus under which the creditor can obtain a decree vesting the property in him, after delays and preliminary steps, varied from time to time and elaborately regulated by Justinian, mainly in the interest of the debtor[2].

It must be borne in mind that pledge is something more than a possessory right. Such a right is essentially null against a claimant by *vindicatio* proving his title, but the pledge creditor will prevail against the debtor or those claiming under him, even proceeding by way of *vindicatio*. This *ius retentionis*, coupled with the power of sale and the possibility of foreclosure, and the usual *pactum antichresis* by which the creditor could take fruits in lieu of interest, gives it rather the appearance of a *ius in rem*, and though the Romans did not, as modern writers do, treat it under *iura in rem*, they did in practice consider it from some points of view as an independent right, and not a mere burden on the owner. Thus we hear of pledge of a pledge[3], though there is some controversy as to whether this is

[1] 47. 10. 15. 32.
[2] See Moyle, Inst. of Just. Exc. 2.
[3] D. 20. 1. 13. 2.

a pledge of the right of pledge, or a second pledge of the subject-matter, analogous to the sale of it. As an independent right it is essentially a right *in rem*, but here too there arose in practice an institution difficult to reconcile with this notion: the pledge of a debt. Into the mode of enforcement of this and the curious theoretical questions to which it might give rise we cannot go.

The introduction of *hypotheca* rendered possible successive pledges of the same thing to different persons. This gave rise to rules of priority, the earliest hypothec being preferred irrespective of actual possession, subject, on the one hand, to the special priorities given to particular charges, such as those of the *fiscus* for taxes and of a widow for her *dos*, and, on the other, to a system of registration, introduced in late law, under which priority was given to the hypothec first registered, irrespective of its date.

Besides the hypothec resulting from express agreement, there were hypothecs created by law, tacit hypothecs, sometimes over specific property, such as those of rural and urban landlords for their rent, sometimes over the whole of a man's property, such as that given to a legatee by Justinian. General hypothecs might of course also be created by agreement. It was possible indeed to create what in modern English law is called a floating charge, that is to say, a charge over present and future assets. A business man could give a charge over his stock-in-trade, which was to affect all new stock as it was acquired, but on the other hand was to cease to apply to goods which were disposed of in the ordinary way of business[1]. It is noticeable that while this form of charge appears to be playing an increasingly important part in English law, it has disappeared, as the result of their codifications, from the laws of France and Germany.

111. Unlike the contracts *re*, which were applications of a particular form to a narrow range of transactions, the verbal contract of *Stipulatio* was a form which could be applied to any kind of transaction. It was made by question and answer,

[1] D. 20. 1. 34. *pr.*

which had at first to be in Latin, perhaps at one time required the use of specific words, and certainly required the most exact correspondence between the question and the reply. There was a progressive relaxation of these rules, and by the time of Justinian all that was needed was substantial correspondence. Indeed even this was not required, for if what was promised was more or less than what was asked, the contract was good for what was common to both, at least where it was a question of quantities, and probably more generally[1]. There was no need of writing or witnesses, a rule which affords a striking contrast with that of Attic law which appears to have required writing for all transactions, as a condition of enforceability. The contrast throws light on the difference between the standards of commercial morality which prevailed at Rome and Athens respectively. Of course it became usual to make a note in writing and in later law, where such a signed note declared that a stipulation had been made, the signer could not dispute the fact that the question had been actually spoken, though the note was not in the form of question and answer. So too if it gave time and place, this raised a presumption that, as the law required, the parties had been present together, rebuttable only by proof that one of them had been in another town all that day. A word may be said here as to the form of these memoranda of transactions, to which the name *cautio* is given. The practice is not for the parties to draw up a statement of their transaction and sign it, with or without witnesses, but to go before some third person, not necessarily or usually an official, but often a *tabularius*, a person who makes it his business to make this sort of memorandum, called by Justinian a *publica persona*. This person makes, from their statement, a note of the transaction and authenticates it by his own signature, in some cases having the custody of the document.

With the vexed questions as to the origin of the contract and of the significance to be attached to the rule that the form "*Spondes-ne?*" "*Spondeo*" was confined to *cives* we will not deal, but it may be well to remark that there can be no doubt

[1] See D. 45. 1. 1. 4, 83. 3.

but that in its earliest days it was of a far narrower scope than was the *stipulatio* of the classical law. There is indeed some reason to think that originally it was employed only for promises of specific sums of money, or at any rate of specific quantities, and it will be remembered that the *legis actio per condictionem* dealt with these alone. At that time it operated only indirectly for the enforcement of obligations of a different kind, namely, by the addition to the bargain, whatever it might be, of a stipulation for a penalty in the event of breach of the undertaking. Of these the most familiar illustration is in connexion with the creation of servitudes or quasi-servitudes on provincial land. There was a pact to grant the servitude, followed by a stipulation for a penalty, not as in later law, a stipulation to grant the servitude[1].

The general rules of *stipulatio* though elaborately worked out in the texts are in the main simple, and only one or two of them call for discussion. It is observable that *stipulatio* is treated to a certain extent as the typical contract, so that many rules are stated as rules of *stipulatio* though they are applicable to contracts generally. This is for instance the case with the rule that a *stipulatio* cannot be made to bind or benefit a third party, and with the rule that a *stipulatio* by a lunatic is void. But the rule that a deaf man cannot stipulate has no bearing on the contract of Sale. It is, however, usually very easy to tell to which group a rule belongs, and we need not discuss the matter.

The effect of impossibility, illegality or immorality in a *stipulatio* (or other contract) or in its conditions, is not the same as in the case of an institution of a *heres*. In that case the inadmissible provisions are struck out: in a contract the whole transaction is void.

112. The rule "*ad diem deberi non posse*" is in itself rational. An agreement under which I am to owe you a sum of money until some future day, which is certain to come, looks upon the face of it absurd, and the rule is laid down that

[1] *Ante*, § 50.

mere lapse of time, apart from limitation of actions, cannot operate as discharge from liability. Yet cases can readily be conceived in which such an agreement might serve a real purpose. Assume that I have money in hand which I intend to invest in goods on a certain day: it is for instance my practice to invest all balances at the end of the month. You are thinking of making a purchase and you ask me whether I will lend you the necessary money. I undertake to do so if you will ask for it before the day on which I have arranged to invest my available funds. We embody the arrangement in a *stipulatio.* It is evident that my promise is in effect a *promissio ad diem.* The jurists get out of the difficulty by treating the obligation as perpetual, but giving me, the *promissor,* an *exceptio pacti conventi* if I am sued on a demand made after the agreed day. In the Digest the same thing is said of a *stipulatio,* "*decem aureos quoad vivam*[1]," the remark being made that the object of the parties is that the *heres* shall not be able to enforce the obligation. This also is clear enough. But in the Institutes this agreement appears in the form, "*decem aureos annuos quoad vivam.*" Here too the same rule is laid down, namely, that it is perpetual, subject to *exceptio,* as otherwise it would break the rule that we are considering. It will be observed however that this is a very different agreement: and does not in the least imply that the *heres* is not meant to be liable for instalments which have accrued due before the death. So far as these are concerned there is no infringement of the rule; in fact the writer is obscure and fails to distinguish between action for instalments already due and actions for instalments accruing due after the death.

The rule that a *stipulatio* in favour of a third party, or a promise of an act on the part of a third party, is void, is fully illustrated in the Institutes, and is a simple expression of the personal nature of *Obligatio.* Clearly such an agreement could not benefit or bind the third party, but it is not so clear that the first could not have been regarded as the promise of a service to me in the form of a payment to another, and the

[1] D. 45. 1. 56. 4.

latter as an undertaking to procure that the third party should pay. Indeed, so far as the first case is concerned, it did so operate in practice, though, at least so far as *stricti iuris* transactions were concerned, not till rather late. If the *stipulator* had any *interesse* in the payment, the *stipulatio* was valid. Thus, to take a very simple case, if you promised to pay my creditor and failed to do so, I could sue you on the stipulation, not necessarily for the amount which you agreed to pay, but for the value of that payment to me, which might well be not the same thing. And of course the promise might always be validated by expressing in the alternative a penalty payable to me. As to promises that a third person should act, the liberal construction above-mentioned was freely adopted in *bonae fidei* transactions, but not in stipulations. Here, the personal undertaking that the third party should act had to be express[1].

The stipulations for payment to the *stipulator* or a third person, under which only the *stipulator* can sue, but payment may be made to either, are not unpractical. Where the *stipulator* is likely to be away it is convenient to have some one else to whom payment can validly be made. The *solutionis causa adiectus* would often be an *argentarius*, so that the contract is to pay to me or into my bank account. It is equally easy to formulate cases in which it is convenient to arrange that money due from me shall be paid either by me or, in my absence, by some one on my behalf. The hypothesis of stipulations for payment to or by the contracting party and a third person does not seem so practical, and it may be that the discussion on them was largely academic, which may account for the fact that the Proculian view that the contracting party was liable or entitled only to a half, was made settled law only by an enactment of Justinian. This rule does not apply, as it seems, to consensual contracts[2].

The rule that a *stipulatio* for payment so many days before the death of either party is void is a mere application of the rule as to *stipulationes praepostere conceptae* and disappears

[1] See for details and discussion Moyle, Inst. of Just. ad 3. 19. 3.
[2] D. 18. 1. 64.

under Justinian, who validates them, omitting the impossible or preposterous part. The rule against stipulations for payment after the death, which also disappears under Justinian, may be an application of the rule that a stipulation for the *heres*, simply, is a stipulation for a third party, or the rule *obligatio in heredem vel in herede incipere non posse* may be regarded as independent. It was evaded by the use of *adstipulatores*, to whom the identical promise was made and who on recovery accounted to the *heres*. There was no objection to a promise after the death of a third party and in the adstipulator's contract the principal was a third party. But a promise of payment at the moment of death was always valid, though it is plain that it can be enforced only by the *heres*. It is in fact what is called a "limiting case" and the jurists, plainly on grounds of convenience, answer the scholastic question whether at the moment of his death a man is alive or dead, in the sense that he is alive.

Like all the ancient contracts, *stipulatio* is unilateral and *stricti iuris*, and it must be remembered that it is not until nearly the close of the Republic that fraud becomes any defence in an action on a *stipulatio*.

113. In Roman law, where several persons were liable or entitled to payment of a debt, the obligation was commonly divided between them: each was liable or entitled *pro parte*, and what happened in respect of one part was without any importance to the other creditors or debtors. On the other hand there were cases in which several persons were liable to pay a penalty in respect of some common wrong-doing. Here each of them was liable to pay the full penalty, and his liability was not in any way diminished by the fact that other people had to pay, or had already paid, or been sued for, the full penalty. Each of a band of thieves had to pay, by way of penalty, irrespective of the liability to restore the property, a certain multiple of its value[1], a fact which no doubt would involve a heavy profit to the victim of the theft, but for the fact that thieves have not usually the money to pay with. Neither of these cases presents

[1] C. 4. 8. 1.

any difficulty. There are however cases of a different kind. There are cases in which there are several persons each of whom is liable or entitled to the whole of a certain claim, but it is due only once, so that satisfaction by or to one of them destroys the whole obligation. This is what is commonly called "Solidary Obligation," a name coined from the Roman expression, *in solidum*, an expression which has in itself no special technical meaning, but is applied whenever it is desired to emphasise the fact that one person owes the whole of a debt. (Thus one who is liable on his own debt as opposed to one incurred by his slave is said to be liable *in solidum*.) This solidary obligation occurs in two forms.

I. Correal Obligation, a name formed out of the Roman expression, *correi*. Where an obligation is correal, it may be so either on the creditors' side (*correi credendi*), or on the debtors' (*correi debendi*), or on both. The main effect of correality where it occurs is that not only does satisfaction by or to one of the *correi* end the whole obligation, but so does the bringing of an action in respect of it. *Litis contestatio* in an action puts an end to the whole obligation. That fact raises another important question. If one of the *correi* liable has been sued on the claim, or has paid it, and has thus released the others, has he a right to claim contribution from them? And where one of correal creditors has received the whole amount, is he under an obligation to account to the others? The matter is disputed, but the view most generally held is that the relation of correality gave no such right, but did not exclude it if it existed on some other ground. This somewhat harsh-looking rule does not in reality mean very much: people do not join together in a correal obligation by mere chance without any previous negotiation with each other. It will usually be in pursuance of some common undertaking, in respect of which they have already made their arrangements. If they are partners, as they very often, perhaps usually, would be, the obligation to account is clear, as an incident of the *societas*, and even if they are not partners an agreement would naturally be made. Where this right to contribution or account exists it rests on some other contract between the *correi*: the actual correal contract is regarded as a relation between them as a body and the party on the other side.

The question now arises: under what circumstances is an obligation correal? The answer seems to be that this state of things arises only by consent. If the parties intend the obligation to be correal they say so at the moment of making the contract. Justinian gives us the form for the case of *stipulatio*, and though it is probable that in later law any words would suffice, if embodied in the *stipulatio*, provided they made the intent clear, it is plain that the form given is intended to express the point that on the facts there is only one *stipulatio*, and not as many *stipulationes* as there are parties. Thus, if it is clear that there is only one *stipulatio* the two parties on one side will always be correal, and the expression *duo rei stipulandi* is equivalent to *correi stipulandi*. The institution is not confined to stipulation: it might occur in any *stricti iuris* contract and there is one text which unequivocally says that it might arise in *bonae fidei* transactions[1]. But this text has been suspected of interpolation, and it may express only the law of Justinian. If that is so, and there is certainly one passage which suggests that, at any rate, correality did not necessarily follow where there were several parties on one side in a single sale[2], the result is that in classical law the obligation would be divided as if there had been distinct transactions.

On the other hand we shall see shortly that the most noticeable rules of correality are mere applications of ordinary principle, and it is clear that similar results follow in cases which cannot be called contract. Thus the possibly interpolated text abovementioned applies the rule itself to a case in which a testator gives a legacy in the form "*Titius et* (*aut* is a generally accepted emendation) *Maevius Sempronio decem dato*."

There are other cases which will be mentioned shortly. It must be noted that in Justinian's time the novatory effect of *litis contestatio* is gone: it no longer destroys a correal obligation.

[1] D. 45. 2. 9. *pr.* See also D. 19. 2. 13. 9.

[2] D. 18. 2. 11—13.

II. Simple Solidary Obligation. There is another type of solidary obligation commonly called by this name. The main difference in effect is that even in classical law the mere *litis contestatio* in an action against one had no effect on the obligation of the others: release resulted only from satisfaction, but as soon as satisfaction had once been made, the whole obligation was *ipso facto* discharged. Upon the question when an obligation was solidary in this sense, the first point to be made is that there is very little textual authority for the view that it ever occurred at all on the creditor's side. Several cases have indeed been suggested, from the texts, but the only one of these which has not been repudiated by writers of authority is that of a promise of *dos* to the husband, followed by a legacy of it to the wife. Here payment on either account discharges the other and the bringing of one action does not affect the right to bring the other, even in classical law[1]. But the case is not treated quite like solidarity, for Julian says that if both sue the *heres* has an *exceptio doli*, and they must agree as to which action shall be brought. However these doubtful cases are looked at it is clear that the really important field of simple solidarity is "passive," *i.e.* on the side of the debtors. From the cases mentioned in the texts it has been inferred that this kind of liability arises where several persons are liable to make good some damage or injury resulting from their neglect or other misconduct. It is not possible to give all the cases: among those which have been cited are those of several persons liable to the *actio doli*, or to *condictio furtiva* or for carelessly losing a thing lent to them. The liability may be in connexion with contract, but it need not. All the cases however have this common quality, that it is not a question of paying a penalty, but of making good the damage done. Thus it does not arise in the *actio furti*, but it does in the *condictio furtiva*. It has been shewn that in every case in which this solidary liability is declared to exist in *bonae fidei* contracts there has either been common misconduct, or the subject-matter of the contract is indivisible[2]. The principle that in contract the

[1] D. 23. 3. 29. See Girard, Manuel (5), 746. [2] Girard, *loc. cit.*

obligation is divided apart from special agreement is not infringed.

114. The next point to consider is the reason why *litis contestatio* discharges in the one case and not in the other. The view most generally accepted, and clearly stated by Dr Moyle[1], is that in correality there is only one obligation, which is necessarily ended by any fact which ends it for any of the persons liable, as *litis contestatio*, by its novatory effect, unquestionably does. In simple solidarity, on the other hand, there are several obligations but only one subject-matter of the obligations, so that what affects the obligation of one does not necessarily affect the others, while satisfaction does. Apart from certain objections which have been taken to the proposition on which this opinion rests, *i.e.* to the unity of the obligation, it is open to the serious criticism that it does not in reality explain the matter at all. It is indeed little more than giving the rule as the reason for itself. It does not in the least shew why in the one case there is only one obligation while in the other there are many. Why should a common act constituting a breach of duty under a contract create a number of distinct obligations while the common speech by which the contract was made created only one? It seems better to fall back on a simpler explanation which has distinguished support. Whether there is one obligation or more, there is at any rate only one sum of money due, and there is a very ancient rule expressed in the maxim "*non bis in idem*": the same thing must not be claimed twice. Where for instance a slave had two masters, a creditor on the slave's contract could sue either *de peculio*, but, if he had sued one, the strict law did not allow him to fall back on the other. In this case, indeed, and in many others, the Praetor relieved plaintiffs against this strict rule, but no one is a *correus* without his own consent, and that of the other party. There is consequently no need for relief. Thus the rule in cases of correality is not a special rule, but only an application of general principles. It is the rule applied in simple solidarity,

[1] Moyle, Inst. of Just. Exc. 7.

so-called, which needs explanation. The repeated action is "*bis in idem*," for it is certainly *eadem res*. It seems more probable therefore that, as is now held by many writers, it is idle to look for any logical explanation. According to this opinion the rule in this case is an illogical relaxation, probably a very gradual historical development expressing the idea that people who do wrong ought not to be released from their duty to compensate except by paying compensation, but that only one satisfaction is needed. One result of the acceptance of this view would be that if the classical law allowed any force at all to a convention in a *bonae fidei* contract that the liability, or right, should be *in solidum*, the result must be correality and not simple solidarity.

It is obvious that other things may happen to the obligation besides *litis contestatio* and satisfaction. The thing due may cease to exist with or without the fault of one of the debtors. The action against one of the debtors may be barred by lapse of time. One of the debtors may have a set off. The creditor may make a *pactum de non petendo* with one of them. Analogous incidents may occur on the side of correal creditors. The question naturally arises how far these affect the position of the other *correi*. An *acceptilatio* or *novatio* made with one discharges the whole obligation, but a *pactum de non petendo* made with one does not affect the others, as it still leaves the obligation existing, *iure civili*. But the result of a rather confusing set of texts by Paul[1] seems to be that even in this case, if the pact is *in rem*, *i.e.* not specially confined to him, but expressed as a general undertaking not to sue on the debt, it is available to the other *correi*, on the general principle of *pacta in rem*, *i.e.* in the case in which action against them would involve an ultimate liability of the person with whom the pact has been made. That is to say, a *pactum in rem* is available here if some circumstance extraneous to the actual correal contract have created a right to contribution. There is much controversy as to the results of the other facts mentioned, the texts giving either no answer or one which is inconclusive,

[1] D. 2. 14. 21—27.

while the various answers given by modern writers are of course determined by their various conceptions of the principle underlying correality. It would not be possible adequately to discuss these points in the space available[1].

It should be added that, in correality, it is possible that where there was no relation giving a right to the one who has paid to fall back on the others he may have had a right to take *cessio actionum*, a transfer of his rights of action, from the creditor. There is however little or no evidence for this right, except where they have become sureties for each other, a practice which became very usual in later law, having apparently been borrowed from the Greek provinces[2]. There is also evidence that in the later classical law, at least in some cases of simple solidary obligation resulting from negligence, the person sued was entitled to claim the *beneficium divisionis*, as sureties could[3].

The subject of solidarity may be left with two further observations. It has been said above that correality results only from consent and occurs only in contract. There are however a few cases in which the main characteristic of correality occurs, *i.e.* two persons each liable in full, and each discharged by action against the other, but there is no express consent to be *correi*. Thus a principal and his *institor* are *correi* in this sense. So too, action against either owner of a common slave, *de peculio*, on his contract releases the other. The same is true of noxal liability of common owners, which has no relation to contract at all. These, and some others which might be mentioned, are all cases of vicarious responsibility, and may safely be neglected in considering the general principle. In some of the cases the Praetor relieved against the strict rule. The other observation to be made is that while we are accustomed to speak of correality and solidarity as cases in which there are several persons entitled or liable as principals, and to contrast this case with that of persons whose liability is subordinate, *e.g.* sureties, it

[1] See Girard, Manuel (5) 744.

[2] D. 45. 2. 11. Cf. Mitteis, Reichsrecht und Volksrecht, 184.

[3] Girard, *op. cit.*, 748.

must not be forgotten that the cases overlap. We have just seen that it became the practice for *correi* to become sureties for each other. In like manner an *adpromissor* and the principal debtor are practically *correi*, since either can be sued for the whole debt, and action against one frees the other, in classical law, and in the same way joint *adpromissores* are *correi* with each other, though, as we shall see, their position in these matters was fundamentally altered by elaborate legislation.

115. We can now pass to the case of accessory parties to the stipulation, either *Adstipulatores*, on the side of the *stipulator*, or *Adpromissores*, who are sureties for the *promissor*. *Adstipulatio* is a very ancient institution, but it is obsolete under Justinian. The device of employing an *adstipulator* to make a contract identical with that of his principal, on which he could sue if the principal, from absence, was unable to sue on his own contract, became unnecessary very early, when it became possible to appoint a *procurator ad litem*. The other case in which they were used, to validate promises for payment after death, remained till Justinian rendered such contracts valid. This case presents some difficulty, in view of the fact that an *adstipulator* is appointed by mandate, and a mandate for performance after death is void in principle. To this we shall have to recur[1].

The right of the *adstipulator* is of an intensely personal nature. His right of action does not pass to his *heres*, perhaps because the mandate to him is ended by his death, though this would logically lead to an *exceptio doli*, rather than to a denial of an action, since the *adstipulator*'s contract is a distinct one. *Adstipulatio* by a slave is a nullity. If the man was a slave of the principal, the right would vest in the principal and the desired result would not be produced. But the same rule applies to a third person's slave. So too, an *adstipulatio* by a *filiusfamilias* cannot be sued on by his *paterfamilias*, but is dormant till he become *sui iuris*. These peculiarities have

[1] *Post*, § 125.

been explained as being due to the fact that he is acting as a *mandatarius*, but this seems hardly enough to account for such a rule as that an action acquired by a *filiusfamilias* does not vest in his *paterfamilias*. In general where a son contracts under a mandate to do so, given by a third party, his *paterfamilias* acquires the right of action, for instance, where he acts as *magister navis*[1]. Altogether it seems more likely that the explanation is to be looked for in some ancient characteristic of the transaction, giving it an intensely personal character, and this view is strengthened by the fact that the rule that his right does not pass to his *heres* is paralleled by the rule that the obligation of a *sponsor* or a *fidepromissor* does not bind the *heres* while that of the *fideiussor* does, though he is equally a *mandatarius*. But *sponsor* and *adstipulator* were introduced and had acquired their marked characteristics before the conceptions proper to *mandatum* had developed.

116. The three cases of surety of which we hear in connexion with verbal contracts—*Adpromissores*—are far from exhausting the forms of surety known to the Roman law. There are for instance the ancient *praedes* and *vades*, the extent of whose application is matter of controversy; there is also the *pactum de constituto*, which is surety wherever the *constituens* is not the original debtor; there is also the so-called *mandatum qualificatum*, of which we shall have to speak later. Moreover in every case of correality or solidarity in which there is a right of contribution, those who pay are practically acting as sureties for the others to the extent at least of their shares. In fact, surety, the undertaking of a third party to meet the liability, if the debtor does not, was always more prominent than what is called real security.

The law concerning *adpromissores* consists for the most part of statutory rules and praetorian innovations, which it is impossible to set forth in detail, though some account of it must be given. The earliest of these forms of surety, the

[1] D. 14. 1. 5. *pr*.

Sponsor (who must be a *civis*, does not bind his *heres*, and can be used only to reinforce a verbal obligation), has no obvious means of obtaining reimbursement, since he antedates the notions of *mandatum*. Accordingly a *lex* Publilia gives him, if he is not reimbursed within six months, an *actio depensi* for double damages, involving a right of *manus iniectio pro iudicato*. The *fidepromissor*, who need not be a *civis*, is clearly somewhat later, but still ancient, since he too is available only where the contract is verbal, and he does not bind his *heres*. We hear nothing of any special remedy against the debtor, from which it has been inferred that he appears only after the introduction of mandate. With his appearance comes however fresh legislation, applying both to him and the *sponsor*, and dealing especially with joint sureties. The *l.* Apuleia gives an action against his co-sureties to one who has paid more than his share, a necessary provision, since they have not in any way contracted with him. The *l.* Furia de sponsu, which applies only to sureties taken in Italy, releases any such surety by the lapse of two years from the day when the debt was due, and limits his liability to the amount of the debt divided by the number of sureties living when the debt falls due. Its original remedy is worth attention. His promise is of the whole, and he can thus be sued for the whole, but he will have *manus iniectio pro iudicato* against the creditor who has exacted from him more than his share. In later times this clumsy method has given way to an *exceptio* in the original claim. The *l.* Cicereia requires the creditor to inform each surety, before he binds himself, as to the amount of the debt and the number of sureties. There is much discussion and no certainty about the dates of these *leges*. All are earlier than Sulla. The *l.* Furia is after 240 B.C. (since it assumes provinces) and probably before the *l.* Aebutia[1].

The *Fideiussor* marks a step in advance. He binds his *heres* and, though his undertaking, like the others, is by *stipulatio*, he is used to guarantee *obligationes* of any kind. The *l.* Cornelia (46 B.C.), the first statute to apply to all three

[1] See Girard, Manuel (5), 758.

(though the *l.* Cicereia seems to have been applied in practice to the *fideiussor*), restricts the amount for which a surety can be liable for one man to one man, in one year. The *Sc.* Velleianum (A.D. 46) prohibits surety or any other form of *intercessio* by a woman, with some exceptions.

Three other rules appear which need special mention. The *l.* Furia does not apply to *fideiussores*, and thus any one of them is liable for the whole debt. He has of course a claim against the debtor, but under these circumstances the debtor is probably a man without money, and he has no claim against other sureties, since their contract is distinct from his. The practice therefore grew of inducing the creditor at the time of payment, to cede to the paying surety his rights of action against the debtor and other sureties, and any securities he may have. The difficulty that, as he is paid, he has no rights to cede, is met by treating the payment not as discharge but as purchase of the debt. The practice became a rule of law, probably in the first century of the Empire: the surety was entitled, as a condition of his payment, to require this cession of actions to be made. This is the *Beneficium Cedendarum Actionum*[1]. But he must actually secure the *cessio*: at no time was there any implied cession in such cases.

Hadrian provides a better system (which however does not supersede this, since the new rule applies only to remedies against other sureties) in the *Beneficium Divisionis*. This is a rule that each surety is to be liable only to the extent of the debt divided by the number of then solvent sureties. There is some doubt as to the machinery of this protection, but it need not be discussed. It was introduced specially for *fideiussores*, but appears from the language of Gaius to have been extended to the decaying *sponsores* and *fidepromissores*, and it was certainly extended in later law to some other cases of surety.

The third rule to mention is the *Beneficium Ordinis* or *Excussionis*. The novatory effect of *litis contestatio* and the rule "*non bis in idem*" produce the result that the creditor has to choose between the debtor and the surety, and, the liability

[1] See Girard, *op. cit.* 762.

of the surety being absolute, he cannot complain if the creditor sues him first. The difficulty is evaded by adopting the form of *fideiussio indemnitatis*[1], the *fideiussor* promising only what the creditor cannot recover from the principal debtor, so that the latter must be sued first and the action against him does not bar action against the surety. In later law, after the disappearance of *iudicia legitima,* it was usual for the surety to agree that if the principal was sued first he would not avail himself of the *exceptio rei iudicatae*[2]. Justinian systematised the matter by providing that *litis contestatio* against one should not release the other or others, and, a little later, that the creditor must sue the principal first if he was within the jurisdiction[3].

117. The exact form of the contract *literis* has been the subject of much controversy, but is of itself of so little importance in the development of the law that we need not discuss it. It was at any rate created by a formal entry in an account book of some kind, of a loan of money, the entry being assented to by the debtor. The entry does not really represent the facts: if it did, if there was a real loan of which the entry was merely the record, this was a *nomen arcarium*: there was a liability on *mutuum,* and no contract *literis* in the case. The *nomina transscriptitia* were entries of fictitious loans. A liability already existing in some other way, *e.g.*, on a sale, was entered up in this way as a loan, and thereupon the old liability ceased to exist, and liability on the entry took its place: *transscriptio a re in personam.* Or a sum due from *A* was so entered as due from *B* with a similar result: *transscriptio a persona in personam.* The exact method of the *transscriptio* to which the contract owes one of its names we need not consider. The important point is that the entry so made was not mere evidence, rebuttable like other evidence; it was the contract itself, and there was no possibility of going behind it. It was a written contract binding by its form, and almost as elastic as

[1] D. 46. 2. 6. *pr.* [2] C. 8. 40. 28. 1.
[3] C. *loc. cit.*; *Nov.* 4.

stipulatio, except that in the nature of things it applied only to specific sums, a restriction which at one time applied to *stipulatio* also. Even fraud was no answer to a claim on it, except by a relatively late, apparently praetorian innovation, in the time of Cicero, the *exceptio doli*[1].

The contract *literis* existed in the time of Gaius, but seems to have disappeared not long after, and with it disappeared the last trace of an obligation in an absolutely binding writing, *i.e.*, in which the written document is the binding contract. In a famous passage in the Institutes Justinian disputes this, and argues that there is still in his day such an obligation. His argument, though unsound, is very plausible, and it is worth while to look closely at it. His contention put in a slightly more general form is as follows. *A* executes a written *cautio* (a word which is used to denote any kind of memorandum, whether in connexion with security or not), in which he records the fact that he has made a promise to *B* in a stipulation, that he will repay to *B* 100 *asses* which *B* has lent to him, or merely that *B* has in fact lent him 100 *asses*. There has been in fact no loan, and he has never said the words of the stipulation. The obvious question arises: why should a man do this? An equally obvious answer is that it might well occur, as a novation of some previous transactions, and also that a creditor about to make a loan might often require the acknowledgement before he handed over the money. Let it be assumed that in this case the loan was never actually completed. If, now, the debtor is sued, either on the stipulation or the loan, he has the *exceptio non numeratae pecuniae*, which will compel the creditor to prove the actual loan, notwithstanding the acknowledgement. It will be remembered that under Justinian, if there was an actual express acknowledgement of the loan, this *exceptio* was barred, and in any case, it was available only within certain limits of time, which were not the same at all epochs. If now he is barred, either by his express acknowledgement, or by lapse of time, from using this *exceptio*, he is absolutely bound. But by what contract is he bound? It

[1] See on the whole subject Roby, Roman Priv. Law, 2. 279.

cannot be, says Justinian's argument, by the *mutuum*, for on the facts there has not been a *mutuum*. It cannot be by the *promissio*, for he has not made one. Consequently, says Justinian, we must say that he is bound by his writing, which is thus a binding written contract. There is however a defect in this reasoning. He will be sued on the *stipulatio* or the *mutuum* as the case may be, and his acknowledgement will be put in as evidence of the promise or loan. He is not allowed to contradict the evidence he has provided, though in fact the contract was never made. The written document is thus not the contract but mere evidence of it, evidence which in the actual circumstances is irrebuttable.

These rules as to the *exceptio non numeratae pecuniae* give rise however to a curious point of procedure. We are told that the defendant can, for a certain time, meet the acknowledgement by the *exceptio* mentioned. This imposes on the plaintiff the burden of proving that the money has been handed over. This curious rule involves infringement of two fundamental rules of procedure, the one infringement perhaps explaining the other. In *exceptiones* the defendant is *pro actore*, and the proof is on him, not as here on the actual plaintiff. And since a *mutuum* does not exist unless the money has been handed over, this defence negatives the contract altogether: it is strange that it should be raised by *exceptio*, this being in principle a defence which does not amount to a denial of the primary allegation in the *intentio*. In effect the rule is that such a *cautio* is not admissible in evidence, without the consent of the defendant, unless a certain time has elapsed, or, in the time of Justinian, the acknowledgement of the loan is express.

118. The so-called innominate contracts are commonly treated as analogous to the contracts *re*, but the analogy is rather remote. It rests on the fact that just as the contracts *re* are only complete by the handing over of the subject-matter of the contract, so these are complete and enforceable only when one party has rendered his service. But the essential part of the contracts *re* is not so much part performance as the transfer of a physical thing. The *commodator* and *depositor* have not necessarily done all their part[1]: the very existence of the *actiones contrariae* is proof of that. The service basing the liability in the present case is not necessarily the delivery of a chattel, though it often may be. Again, the service rendered is the *quid pro quo*, or as we should say, the consideration for the undertaking, enforcement of which is claimed, and no one will say that the handing over of the deposit is the consideration for the undertaking to look after it, though it is true that English law has been compelled to say something of the kind in an analogous case.

Research has been busy in recent years with the history of these contracts. The view now most generally held as to the course of their development is somewhat as follows. There were some cases in which it was clear that there was a contract, but not so clear what contract it was; cases in which it might be looked on as sale or as *locatio*, and so on. No doubt in many such cases the action on one or other of these contracts was given. But the case was met as early as Labeo, by the employment of a formula for a *bonae fidei* contract, but not specifying which it was (called, it seems, *actio civilis incerti*), and having prefixed to it a statement of the facts (*praescripta verba*[2]). This may be called *agere praescriptis verbis*[3], but it is not the general action called *actio praescriptis verbis.* That is a later idea. The cases which really raised difficulty were those transactions which presented an analogy with some existing type of contract but were not in fact within the definition of it or of any. There was always of course the *actio doli*, if one had done his part and the other failed to carry out his share of the bargain, and if what he had done was the transfer of a right or the surrender of a security, there was a *condictio ob rem dati* for its restitution[4]. But neither of these remedies amounts to enforcement of the contract. They undo the damage which has

[1] D. 16. 3. 5; D. 13. 6. 18. 2.

[2] D. 2. 14. 7. 2. *etc.* Lenel, Ed. Perp. (2) 292.

[3] D. 19. 5. 19. *pr.* Whether '*actio*' *praescriptis verbis* is ever classical is disputed, Lenel, *loc. cit.*

[4] D. 19. 5. 5. 3; C. 4. 6. 6.

been done: they put the parties, so far as possible, in the position in which they would have been if the agreement had not been carried out at all. A further step was however taken in the classical age. The Praetor gave an action *in factum* on such facts, and this amounted to enforcement of the bargain, for it put the parties, so far as money could do it, in the position in which they would have been, had the agreement been carried out on both sides[1]. But there was no general action *in factum* in such cases; apparently only a few specific cases were so provided for. Then the *formula* above mentioned, with *praescripta verba*, was applied to a certain, and as it seems an increasing, number of such cases. Finally, but not till after the classical age, and perhaps not till the time of Justinian, the rule is applied, that, wherever an agreement has been made for mutual services, and one has done all his part, this action will lie, in which the facts are stated in a preliminary clause. Then, and then only, the name *actio praescriptis verbis* comes into use as descriptive of a general type of action. The action is also sometimes called in later law, the *actio civilis in factum: in factum* (though it is not *in factum concepta*, but *in ius*) because of the preliminary clause stating the facts: *civilis*, because it alleges an obligation, being formulated *in ius*. Whether this name already exists in the classical law is disputed[2].

The innominate contracts are commonly grouped after Paul (or Tribonian) under four types: "*do ut des*," "*do ut facias*," "*facio ut des*," "*facio ut facias*[3]," and it must be borne in mind that these are to be understood as including their negatives: *non facio*, and so forth. No doubt the different types were not recognised all at once, and there are signs in the texts from which a certain order has been inferred, but all this is very uncertain. It is obvious that such bargains may be innumerable, but only a few of them assumed enough importance to call for exposition in the juristic texts. Of these *Permutatio*, *Precarium* and *Aestimatum* are the most important. *Permutatio*, or Barter, needs no comment. *Precarium*, regarded as a contract,

[1] D. 19. 5. 1. *pr*.

[2] Lenel, *loc. cit.*

[3] D. 19. 5. 5. *pr*.

seems to be a very late introduction, though the institution itself is extremely ancient. In classical times it seems to have been mainly applied in connexion with land; its chief uses having been in *Fiducia*, where the creditor often allowed the debtor to hold the land *in precario*, and in Sale, where the unpaid vendor sometimes handed the possession over to the buyer in this way[1]. It is a tenancy at will, revocable at any time even though there is an agreement to the contrary, and necessarily determined by death. It is, in essence, a gift, though not technically a *donatio*, the holder not being liable for negligence but only for *dolus*. The only remedies therefore are the *actio doli* and the interdict *de precario*, for restitution. In late law however, in a text credited to Julian, but as to this part clearly due to Justinian, there is an *actio praescriptis verbis* against the *precario tenens*[2]. The *condictio incerti* mentioned in this text and confused with the *actio praescriptis verbis* is merely a *condictio* for restitution[3].

Of *Aestimatum*, or the *contractus aestimatoria*, it is necessary to speak at somewhat greater length. This is essentially an agreement under which a thing is handed over by the owner to another person on the terms that he is to restore the thing, or an agreed price, usually within a certain time. The agreement may vary in detail: in particular, the profit of the undertaker may consist entirely in the difference between the price he gets and that he has agreed to give if he keeps the thing, or he may get some reward. He may either keep the thing, or return it, or sell it, this last being the real intention of the transaction. The institution is very similar to the delivery of goods "on sale or return," which is a common practice now-a-days between manufacturers and retailers of jewellery, and in the book trade. It is the only instance, so far as is known, in which the Praetor's Edict expressly gives the action with *praescripta verba*. It may indeed be mentioned only as the type, but it was in any case probably the first to be recognised[4]. It has obvious and close affinities with all the consensual contracts, with *locatio*

[1] D. 43. 26. 20.

[2] D. 43. 26. 19. 2.

[3] Gradenwitz, Interpolationen, 128.

[4] Lenel, Ed. Perp. (2) 290.

operarum, with *societas* and with *mandatum*, no less than with sale, and one can easily see how questions may have arisen, as to whether it could be properly placed under either of these heads, and if so, under which. The absence of any actual obligation to sell, or to get the best price obtainable, differentiates it from both *locatio operarum* and *mandatum*. The absence of joint exploitation distinguishes it from *societas*. Nothing but the fact that the primary intention is not purchase by the receiver differentiates it from Sale, and some modern commentators actually treat it as essentially a conditional sale. It is clear that, as in such a sale, the ownership does not pass to the dealer, if he may be so called, but the texts are in conflict on the subject of risk, a conflict which may be due to variations in the actual agreement. They agree however that the risk is with the dealer if he originated the business, a rule which is contrary to the principles of sale under a suspensive condition[1].

119. The consensual contracts, in which the mere informal agreement constitutes a binding contract, are of a commercial importance much greater than that of most of the contracts *re*, a fact which is reflected in the comparatively detailed treatment which they, and particularly Sale, receive in the Institutes. It will be noticed that two of them: Sale and Hire, have double names, *Emptio Venditio*, and *Locatio Conductio*, a characteristic which is shared by no other contracts. The reason is a simple one. Each of these contracts is perfectly bilateral; that is to say, it binds both parties equally, there is no question of a primary action and an *actio contraria*. The contracts which do not set up any mutual obligation, but bind one party only, *i.e.*, *mutuum*, *expensilatio*, *stipulatio*, and the other less important verbal contracts, have, of course, only one name. The same is true of those contracts which primarily bind one party only, those which are said to be imperfectly bilateral, the remaining contracts *re* and *mandatum*. *Societas* resembles Sale in that it is perfectly bilateral, but it has only one name, a fact which is explained by the circumstance that the duties on each side are

[1] D. 19. 3. 1. 1; D. 19. 5. 17. 2. Windscheid, Lehrbuch, § 383.

the same. It is no very hazardous guess that this duplicity of name indicates an original conception of the contract as consisting of two independent contracts. Before the consensual contract was recognised such agreements were probably made by reciprocal stipulations.

The consensual contracts, though earlier in date, represent in respect to the principle of consideration, *i.e.*, the notion that liability may reasonably depend on a *quid pro quo*, a further step than the innominate contracts. Those require a completed service, "executed consideration." The consensual contracts need only an undertaking of service. From another point of view however, the innominate contracts are a long step forward; the consensual contracts apply the notion of consideration only within a very narrow range of specific cases, while the innominate contracts, in later law, apply it generally to bargains of any kind.

120. The detailed treatment accorded in the sources to the law of Sale, an indication of its practical importance, does not involve the establishment of a complete scheme of law on the subject, free from doubts and difficulties: it means rather a multiplication of such doubts. The possible combinations of fact are so infinitely various that every new rule gives rise to new questions. They are for the most part difficulties of detail, which we cannot consider here, but there are several of them which call for discussion.

The rule that the price or part of it must be in money, denied by the Sabinians but adopted in later law, is almost the only thing in the negotiations between the parties which distinguishes sale from *permutatio*, which would be binding only by part performance. The rule that it must be *certum*, as to which there was the same history, is wide enough to cover cases in which its certainty rests merely on further enquiry, *e.g.*, "at the price which Titius gave for the other field." Indeed in later law the rule was still more relaxed. A purchase for so much and whatever more I may sell it for was held good[1]. A sale at

[1] D. 18. 1. 7. 2.

such price as *T* shall fix was conditional till *T* did fix a price, but a sale "at such a price as a reasonable man would fix" was no sale at all. Such a negotiation might however have its importance, since if the goods were delivered under it, there would certainly be in later law an *actio praescriptis verbis*.

The primary duty of the vendor is to give the buyer undisturbed possession of the property. He is not bound to make him owner, though the requirement to guarantee him against disturbance comes to much the same thing. The reason for this way of stating the obligation is not certainly known. It has been suggested that the rule is so put in order to facilitate dealings with peregrine buyers and with provincial land and property held only *in bonis*, since in all these cases it is impossible to transfer the *dominium*. This however is difficult to reconcile with the fact that in *permutatio*, where the same difficulty arose, and which must have been common with peregrines, the obligation is stated as being to transfer ownership. It is also suggested that it was in order to relieve the owner from the obligation, which might be very troublesome, of proving a title which in fact was perfectly good, unless and until it was effectively disputed by some third person. This, in view of the commercial importance of facilitating dealings in open market, seems a more likely origin[1]. The buyer had to make the vendor owner of the price, but this would not present the same difficulty.

The point that the vendor is not bound to make the buyer owner is apt to be confused with a different one: was the vendor bound to do what in him lay to make the buyer owner? In practice this means: was the vendor of a *res mancipi* bound to mancipate it, apart from agreement? It is a question to which the texts give no clear answer, and the opinion of modern writers is divided[2].

We are accustomed to think of sale as concerned with a piece of property, but it covers a much wider field. Any transferable right might be sold; and though servitudes were inalienable, the creation of a praedial servitude was no doubt

[1] Moyle, Sale in Roman Law, 103. [2] Girard, Manuel (5), 553.

often initiated by a contract of sale, and we know that the enjoyment of usufruct might be sold[1]. Inheritances might be sold, though apparently they must be existing: there could be no sale of the inheritance of a living man[2]. But future things might be sold and the distinction between *emptio spei* and *emptio rei speratae* is familiar. On the same principle, the sale of a third person's property was perfectly valid as a contract, and the vendor would be bound to procure the transfer of it[3]. The sale of a thing not *in commercio* was in principle a nullity, but there was a certain relaxation of this rule on equitable grounds. If what was sold was a freeman or a piece of public land or the like and the buyer was under the impression that the man was a slave or the land *in commercio*, he had an *actio ex empto* against the vendor for an indemnity[4]. The form and arrangement of the principal texts suggest that the rule applied earliest to the man sold as a slave, and was only in late law extended to other cases. Indeed the texts are not altogether consistent as to the scope of the rule, or indeed as to the rule itself. In many of these cases in which we are told that a particular thing or right cannot be sold it is not clear whether this means merely that it will be impossible to carry out the contract or that the contract as such is utterly void. In some cases this last is clearly the right solution, but in the great majority of cases the rule would seem to be that the agreement is void if both parties were aware of the facts, but that where the buyer was in ignorance and good faith, he will have an action on the contract.

The history of the machinery of the obligation to guarantee against eviction is of some interest. Under the XII Tables there was an action, supposed to have been called the *actio auctoritatis*, for double the price paid, where a thing which had been mancipated was taken from the buyer by a third party who proved title to it (*evictio*); and at a very early date it became usual to agree expressly by *stipulatio*, for a similar

[1] D. 18. 6. 8. 2. [2] D. 18. 4. 1. See however C. 2. 3. 30.
[3] D. 18. 1. 28.
[4] D. 18. 1. 22; D. 18. 1. 4, 5, 6; D. 21. 2. 39. 3. Mackintosh, Sale, 15.

penalty, where there had been no mancipation, but the property was valuable, and it is probable that this *stipulatio* was not uncommonly made even where there had been a mancipation, in which case, except to provide another remedy, it served no great purpose. Where the matter was of small importance it was usual to stipulate merely "*habere licere*," which is, in effect, for single value. These promises could be expressly required, and, when the consensual contract of sale developed, the rule soon appeared, that even if they had not been made, good faith required that the vendor should be as liable as if he had made them, so that if an actual *evictio* occurred, the buyer could recover in the *actio ex empto* what he could have recovered in the action on the *stipulatio*, if one had actually been made[1]. And where there had been in fact no eviction but the defect of title had caused the buyer to lose the value of the thing, *e.g.*, he had had to pay off a claimant, or his defective title had been made good by some other fact (*e.g.*, a gift to him by the true owner), he was entitled to recover the amount of his loss, or potential loss[2]. It is observable that this liability for *evictio* is thus introduced into the *actio ex empto* only as it were by a side-wind.

An analogous development occurred in relation to the law as to compensation for defects in the thing sold. At civil law the vendor was bound to compensate only for defects against which he had given an express warranty, and for fraud, a requirement which covered the non-disclosure of defects of a serious kind known to him at the time of sale. The Edict of the Aediles introduced a rule that in sales of slaves or other live-stock in open market, warranties against certain defects enumerated in the Edict could be required. In course of time this was extended to sales other than those in open market and of things other than live-stock, and there was a parallel development under which the promises were regarded as binding whether they had actually been made or not. As in the case of eviction, and on similar grounds of good faith, the practice

[1] D. 19. 1. 30. 1; D. 21. 2. 2. Girard, *op. cit.* 558.
[2] D. 19. 1. 13. 15; D. 21. 2. 29. *pr.*

grew of enforcing these obligations based on the Edict, in the *actio ex empto* itself, but the texts are not at all clear as to the measure of damages. The proposition which seems to give the best account of the texts is that where there was an express warranty the vendor was liable to the extent of the whole *interesse, i.e.,* for resulting loss of any kind, but where there was no express warranty, he was liable only for the difference between value and price, unless he knew of the defect, in which case he was liable under the principles of the *actio ex empto* to the extent of the *interesse*[1].

121. Upon the transfer of property under a contract of sale of goods the Roman and the English laws have rules in absolute opposition. In English law the mere contract, without delivery or payment, transfers ownership in the thing sold: in Roman law even the delivery of the goods does not transfer the ownership, unless the price or some security for it has been given, or credit expressly agreed on, nor will payment, security or credit do so, without actual delivery. Yet the two systems arrive at identical rules on the subject of risk. In both systems accidental destruction between the making of the contract and the delivery of the goods falls on the buyer. This is a good illustration of the fact that however different the apparent structures of two systems may be, experience will provide rules which commercial convenience calls for, as well from one starting-point as from another.

The law of sale gives another illustration of the same thing. The contract of sale creates only *iura in personam.* An agreement between *A* and *B* can thus give no rights against *C.* This creates difficulty in two ways. If *C* induces *A* to break his contract with *B,* what is the remedy, since *B* has only a *ius in personam?* The Roman law could meet the difficulty by an *actio doli.* The English law meets it by a rule that there is a duty in third persons not to interfere with the performance of contracts in this way: in short, the *ius in personam* has engendered a *ius in rem.* What is to happen if *A* imposes, as a

[1] D. 18. 1. 45; D. 19. 1. 6. 4, 13. *pr.*, 21. 2. Buckland, Slavery, 63.

term in the contract of sale, certain restrictions as to what is to be done with the thing? and *B* sells the thing to *C*? If what is reserved is such a benefit to *A* or his property as can be treated as a servitude, there is of course no difficulty, but the troublesome case is that of restrictions of a different kind. English law has met the difficulty more or less by an equitable rule that subsequent buyers are, on grounds of good faith, bound by the restrictions of which they had notice, when they bought, provided they can be satisfied without expense. Roman law tried a somewhat similar method. Where a man acquired a usufruct which he knew to be subject to restrictions of this kind, it was held that to disregard them was inconsistent with the conduct of a *bonus paterfamilias*, such as is required of a usufructuary[1]. Where a man sold one of two adjoining seaside properties, and it was agreed that the buyer was not to fish in front of the property retained, and this buyer sold to a third person, it was held that though there could be no servitude over the sea, the second buyer with notice was bound by the good faith required in the contract to observe the undertaking, and it could it seems be enforced by the original vendors[2]. But these cases are isolated and it cannot be said that there was a general rule. In relation to sales of slaves, restrictions are very prominent, *e.g.*, that the slave is to be exported, or is not to be freed, or not to be prostituted. For these, special rules were applied. They were enforceable against third holders in varying degrees and ways, in some cases against holders without notice[3]. But no general rule is deducible from a special case of this kind.

122. The rules as to the incidence of Risk, above mentioned, need some further remarks. There are many cases in which the risk does not fall on the purchaser, notably where the goods have still to be completed, or, having been bought out of a larger quantity, have not yet been appropriated to the contract[4]. More important is the rule, of which indeed these

[1] D. 7. 1. 27. 5. [2] D. 8. 4. 13. *pr.* [3] D. 18. 7. *passim.*
[4] D. 18. 1. 35. 5, 7.

last stated are sometimes regarded as applications, that the risk does not pass to the buyer while the contract is still conditional, *i.e.*, is made subject to some future uncertain event, a suspensive condition as it is called in English law. On the other hand if the sale is subject to what is called a resolutive condition, *i.e.*, it is liable to be set aside in a certain event, the risk is with the buyer[1]. To the Romans such a contract is not conditional at all: they regard it, rather more logically, as an unconditional sale with a certain conditional mode of discharge: "*pura emptio quae sub conditione resolvitur*[2]."

It is evident that, as the contract need not be in any prescribed form, the words used in it may be such as to make it difficult to say which type of condition was intended. This difficulty is especially prominent in cases in which the goods are to be returned if they are not approved of[3]. There is however a *prima facie* presumption in such cases that the condition is merely resolutive, if the goods have actually been delivered, but it would be unprofitable to go into details on this matter. Indeed, on all these questions the state of the texts is very unsatisfactory. They say little about these points: in particular they do not distinguish two cases to which very different rules might apply, that of a condition entirely in the power of the buyer, of which the *pactum displicentiae*, just mentioned, is the commonest instance, and a condition not in his power at all. It is clear that where the condition is entirely in his power any rule imposing the risk on him must be nugatory. The rule applies equally both to total destruction and to partial destruction or deterioration, and it must be carefully distinguished from the rule applied to damage before the contract was made. In that case the contract is altogether void if the main subject-matter of it has absolutely ceased to exist, subject to certain rights to compensation in the buyer if the vendor knew that the thing no longer existed. As to partial destruction, the only material text has been so maltreated by the compilers, and is so nonsensical as it stands that the actual rule of the

[1] D. 18. 2. 2. 1.
[2] D. 18. 1. 3; D. 18. 2. 2. *pr.*
[3] *e.g.*, D. 21. 1. 31. 22–24.

Roman law is hard to determine. The text tells us that, at least where the subject of the sale is a house, and this is partially destroyed, if it is more than half destroyed, the sale is off, if less it is good, with a reduction in price. The text goes on to consider what rule to apply where both parties already knew that the thing had ceased to exist, a speculation no doubt due to the compilers, but not intended to be humorous[1].

It will be observed that the well-known subsidiary agreements, *i.e.*, that the sale is to be off if a better offer is received before a certain day (*in diem addictio*), or if the price is not paid by a certain day (*lex commissoria*), or if the buyer or the vendor declares it void by a certain time, are all cases of resolutive condition[2].

Before leaving the contract of Sale it is necessary to speak of the rule established by Justinian, as to the effect of an agreement that the terms should be reduced to writing[3]. To the proposition that sale is a consensual contract he introduces an important modification: he provides that if the parties agree to reduce the terms to writing, the contract shall not be binding till the document is complete. He adds that if, as was usual, the parties have given *arra*, earnest of any kind, any party withdrawing before the contract is so written shall forfeit the *arra* he has given or double the value of that he has received. It seems to be immaterial whether the agreement to reduce the bargain to writing was made before or after they had actually come to terms. So far his enactment is clear enough, but he adds that the rule as to *arra* is to apply also to unwritten agreements, as to which, earlier in the text, he says that he is making no change at all. Apparently this means that one who breaks his contract is to forfeit his *arra* as well as to be liable to damages, but in view of the contradiction, it is not worth while to discuss the exact meaning of the change.

123. The rules of *Locatio Conductio* are fairly simple, and

[1] D. 18. 1. 57.
[2] D. 18. 2. 2; D. 18. 3. 4. 4; C. 4. 54. 2.
[3] C. 4. 21. 17. 2.

a few remarks will suffice. The distinction between *locatio operis*, letting out a job, and *locatio operarum*, hiring services, is not always easy to see, since *locatio operarum* was certainly not confined to labour at a wage, though this would no doubt be the commonest case. It makes however little difference, except in terminology, the workman being *locator* in *locatio operarum*, and *conductor*, if the case is contemplated as one of *locatio operis*. There are indeed texts in the Digest in which the writer at the beginning of the passage appears to be regarding the transaction as of the one type, and later on of the other, so that the person who was the *conductor* has become the *locator*[1].

The case of *locatio* of which we hear most is in connexion with land and houses. The position of tenants of houses (*inquilini*) or of land (*coloni*) was a somewhat precarious one. Unlike tenants in our law they had no *ius in rem*: their rights rested on a contract binding only between the parties. If therefore the lessor sold the property, the agreement was in no way binding on the buyer[2]. It is to be noted however that this does not end the contract: the tenant can be turned out, but he has a right to damages from the lessor. Two other rules affecting tenants are worth mention. They are entitled to a reduction of rent, if climatic or other conditions make it impossible for them to make full use of the land[3]. On the other hand, if the landlord has urgent need of the land he is entitled in later law to retake it from the tenant, without paying full damages as for a breach of contract[4]. We are not informed as to the tenant's right to compensation for disturbance in such a case, but it is obvious that merely to release him from further liability for rent might be very far from doing justice. He might for instance have incurred heavy expenditure, in reliance on his contract, for a business to be carried on on the premises, all rendered useless by the landlord's reentry. But the whole rule rests on a single text in the Code, in which these words have been thought to be interpolated by Justinian.

[1] *e.g.*, D. 19. 2. 22. 2.
[2] D. 19. 2. 32.
[3] D. 19. 2. 15.
[4] C. 4. 65. 3.

It should be added that in all cases of *locatio rei* the risk is with the *locator*, not in the sense that the *conductor* is entitled to damages for nonfulfilment of the contract, but only, as has just been said, that the right to claim hire ceases if enjoyment is rendered impossible. The same rule applies in general to *locatio operarum*, though here there are some modifications. And in all these cases it must be remembered that the parties can vary these terms at their discretion.

In view of the large part which *locatio* plays in modern life, and, as it seems, must have played at Rome, the paucity of our information in the texts is somewhat surprising. Part of the explanation may be found in the fact that a number of the commonest cases of *locatio* were governed by special rules. The carrier, by sea or land, the innkeeper, the livery stable keeper, the wharfinger, and, in a lesser degree, the dyer and the tailor, all had special liabilities, some of which were dealt with by special provisions of the Edict and thus are treated separately[1]. Nor is this the whole matter, for there is some reason to think that these trades are mere survivals of a larger class, and that as in our law the class of "common trades," *i.e.*, of trades the setting up of which involved the acceptance of special liabilities, was much wider in early law than in later. It may well be that in the early part of the Empire, the only cases of *locatio operarum* which were governed by the ordinary law were those by persons not carrying on the business as a trade. But this is no more than conjecture.

124. *Societas* presents many points of interest, of which we can consider only a few. In view of the fact that *societas* did not necessarily aim at profit, it is not always easy to tell whether a particular relation is one of *societas* or merely of common ownership, and the difficulty is not lessened by the fact that the texts frequently use the expression *socii* to denote common owners, where there is clearly no *societas*. Apparently the distinguishing idea is common exploitation: so soon as that element is added to the fact of common ownership, there is

[1] *e.g.*, D. 4. 9; D. 11. 6; D. 47. 5.

societas. Thus where two houseowners bought a field which abutted on the houses, in common, this was *societas,* since their purpose was to keep the land unbuilt on with a view to the amenities of their houses[1].

Besides the absence of commercial aim as an essential, there is another fundamental difference between the Roman conception of *societas* and modern English partnership. The absence of agency in the modern sense in Roman law led to the giving of attention almost entirely to the relations of the *socii, inter se,* and to neglect of the firm's relations with third parties. There were in fact in ordinary cases no such relations. If the contract of one of the *socii* created rights or liabilities in the other *socii* as against third parties, as it sometimes did, this was not an immediate result of the *societas*, but must spring from some other circumstance, such as express authorisation to make the particular contract, leading to an *actio ad exemplum institoriae*, or to the appointment of that *socius* as *institor* for them all, giving rise to the *actio institoria*[2]. Our English law starts from the very different view that every partner is within certain wide limits an agent for the firm. The effect of this difference may be traced throughout the subject.

That every *socius* must contribute something in money or service and that no *socius* could be wholly excluded from profit are familiar rules. That one might be excluded from loss is perhaps not so obvious, but the cooperation of a certain person might be so valuable that it was worth buying at that price. The rule that a *socius* could take a different share in the profit from that which he took in losses, wants another detail before it is intelligible. It is necessary to know how often the account is to be taken. Let us suppose that a firm makes £1000 profit in one six months and the same loss in the second, and a *socius* is to have one-quarter of the profits and one-eighth of the losses. If the account is taken "with annual rests," *i.e.*, for the whole year, there will be neither profit nor loss. If it is taken every six months this *socius* will take £250 at the end of the first period, and will have to refund only £125 at the end of the year.

[1] D. 17. 2. 52. 13. [2] *Post*, §§ 125, 142; D. 14. 3. 1, 2.

The rule that *societas* is ended by the death of one of the *socii* may be misunderstood. It does not mean that if there was a firm of three persons, and one of them died, the business they were carrying on together came necessarily to an end. The business would ordinarily go on. It does not even mean that any new express agreement was necessary as between the survivors. It was quite open to persons joining in a business to agree at the outset that on the death of any one of them the partnership should continue for the survivors. All that the rule practically means is that at the death of a *socius* there must be a settlement of accounts, and that, if the business goes on, it must be a new firm with which the representatives of the deceased partner have nothing to do. There could not even be an initial agreement that the *heres* of any deceased *socius*, whoever he might be, should be a member of the firm[1]. If a man could not nominate a *socius* into a firm to which he belonged, still less could he do so for a firm to which he could not belong. It does not seem however that it would have been impossible for all the members of a present firm to agree with a specific outsider that on the death of any partner, or of one specific partner a new firm should come into existence, of which he should be a member. This, in easily conceived circumstances, would give a similar result. The rule that in *societas vectigalis* the death of a *socius* did not end the firm unless the one who died was the holder of the contract with the State[2] merely indicates that the other partners were in general "sleeping partners," who provided capital but not service. It does not imply any long endurance for the firm, since the State contracts farming out the taxes were only for five years[3], and thus it is likely that these contracts were also for short terms. They would not necessarily be limited to one contract, but this was probably the usual practice. It is to be noted that in this case the *heres* may, by initial agreement, be an actual partner.

Societas omnium bonorum is a rather puzzling case. Its main special rules are that the agreement vests all the *res corporales*, with some exceptions, at the time belonging to a member of

[1] D. 17. 2. 59. *pr*. [2] D. 17. 2. 59. *pr*., 63. 8. [3] D. 49. 14. 3. 6.

the firm created, in all the members in common, while subsequent acquisitions become common only on actual transfer, *i.e.*, to the *socii*. The firm (more correctly the *socii*) cannot claim the proceeds of wrongdoing, and conversely we are told that the funds of the firm are not liable for delicts of individual members[1]. If a partner in such a firm did commit a delict, the rule does not mean that no redress was to be had, but only that he could not charge this expense to the firm. This appears to be all the meaning of certain texts which seem to say that such expenses could not be paid out of the common fund at all[2]. Of course the creditor of a partner, on a delict or anything else, could ordinarily proceed only against the actual debtor: the firm is not a corporation. If the practice was to make a periodical division of the income there was no difficulty. Even apart from this, if judgment was obtained against such a *socius*, and was not satisfied, the creditor could proceed to *bonorum venditio*, which would *ipso facto* end the *societas* and make the debtor's share available. In practice there would be no need to proceed to this extreme, the amount would be paid out of the common fund and charged against the *socius* concerned. It is however difficult to resist the impression that this form of *societas* must have been very unusual in classical and later law, and that the discussion of it is largely "academic." There are indeed a good many texts which refer to *societas omnium bonorum*, but in the great majority of them it is clear that the writer is using the expression in a different sense: he is speaking of a *societas* in which all present property is thrown into the common fund, not future acquisitions, and the same interpretation is possible in nearly all the others. This is a much more reasonable sort of partnership, and it is also a much more obvious derivative from the old *consortium*, *i.e.*, an arrangement under which the *heredes* kept an inheritance in common, from which it is commonly held that this form of *societas* is descended. There seem indeed to be very few texts which unequivocally contemplate future acquisitions. Of these one contemplates only one particular future acquisition, *i.e.*, a

[1] D. 17. 2. 59. 1. [2] *e.g.*, D. 17. 2. 52. 18.

certain inheritance, and another which contemplates all future acquisitions is called *omnium fortunarum*, while the language of both of them shews that the hypothesis they are contemplating is an unusual one[1].

It has been observed above that there is nothing corporate about this form of *societas*. The firm as such is not a *persona*. The only form of *societas* in connexion with which we hear anything of corporate character is the *societas vectigalis*. There is a text which says, not exactly that they are corporations, but that it was permitted by law that they and certain other associations formed for the purpose of exploiting public undertakings might have a corporate character[2]. The exact meaning of this is uncertain and much debated. According to one opinion it does not refer to specific *societates vectigales* at all, but to larger and more permanent associations whose business it was to finance smaller firms[3] who undertook the tax-farming contracts. There is however very little evidence for this or any other opinion: all that is clear is that there is no authority for the view that all *societates vectigales* had a corporate character. It is not easy to see indeed what purpose corporate character would serve in connexion with undertakings of such a temporary character.

Of the various facts which put an end to an existing *societas* the only two which need mention are renunciation and action. That a consensual contract should be determinable by the consent of the parties to it is natural enough, but here the rule went further. Any partner could, at his own will, put an end to the existence of the *societas*, even though it had been entered on for a certain term. The rule is no doubt an expression of the fraternity which is elsewhere spoken of as a characteristic of *societas*. It is obviously inconsistent with such fraternity to compel unwilling membership of the *societas*. But the interests of the other *socii* must be safeguarded, and there is a rule that where a *socius* renounces a *societas* either before the agreed date, or, in the absence of such a date, with a view

[1] D. 17. 2. 3. 2, 73. *Cf. h.t.* 51. 16, 65. 3. [2] D. 3. 4. 1. *pr.*
[3] See Mitteis, Röm. Privatrecht, 1. 403 *sqq.*

to securing for himself some coming profit, or avoiding a loss, he is liable to the others to the extent of their loss by the renunciation, while sharing no profit subsequent to the renunciation: *liberat socios a se non se a sociis*[1]. It is this same notion of fraternity which leads to the rule that bringing an action on the contract (*actio pro socio*) ends the firm. The relations between a landlord and a tenant are not ended by litigation on the terms of the lease. But ordinary litigation is inconsistent with fraternity, and thus Proculus says that the bringing of an action is in effect a renunciation, not in consequence of any characteristic of the action itself, but by reason of the evidence afforded of desire to end the *societas*. That this is the real reason appears from the fact that if it is avowedly brought as a friendly action, to settle knotty questions of account, the *societas* is not destroyed[2].

125. *Mandatum* is a contract of very elastic nature, and is the means by which many new developments are introduced into the law. It was through *mandatum* that Roman law made its nearest approach to the idea of Agency in contract. The Praetor makes an inroad on the principle that a man's contract affects only himself, by allowing an *actio institoria* against a principal who has appointed a man to act as manager of a business and to contract in relation to it[3]. Papinian goes further: he declares the admissibility of an *actio ad exemplum institoriae*, where the *mandatum* is only for isolated transactions. Whether the third party must have known of the authorisation is not clear. In some texts this is not mentioned[4]; in two it is, but in both these cases there is another point. The person seeking the action is one who did not make the authorised transaction, but guaranteed it, so that the texts are not conclusive[5]. But his principal cannot sue on the contract, unless he has taken an assignment of the right of action from his mandatary, by being appointed by him to sue on his contract (*procurator in rem suam*), the method and history of

[1] D. 17. 2. 65. 3. [2] D. 17. 2. 65. *pr.*, 65. 15. [3] *Post*, § 142.
[4] D. 14. 3. 19. *pr.*; D. 19. 1. 13. 25. [5] D. 3. 5. 30. *pr.*; D. 17. 1. 10. 5.

which form of assignment are considered later[1]. In some cases, of great urgency, the rule is carried further: the principal can bring the action which belongs to the agent, as an *actio utilis*, and in all such cases any action by the mandatary, after this *actio utilis*, would be met, it seems, by an *exceptio doli*[2]. But at no time was the mandatary protected from being sued on his contract, so that even in Justinian's law he differs from the modern agent, who merely creates an obligation for others, acquiring no rights or duties under his own contract, in that, in the great majority of cases, he and he alone could sue, and that he could in all cases be sued on it by the person with whom he contracted. This is practically a very important point, for though he is entitled to an indemnity from his *mandator*, cases may readily be imagined in which this right was illusory.

A still more striking development is the use of *mandatum* in the classical and later law as a contract of Surety—the *mandatum credendae pecuniae*. It was of course common for *A* to give *B* a mandate to be surety for him: such a transaction would usually lie behind any case of *fideiussio* or the like. The surety recovers an indemnity from his principal by the action on *mandatum*. But that is not the present case. There is a well-known rule that a *mandator* is bound to indemnify his mandatary. It follows that if I give you a mandate to lend money to Titius, and you do so, but Titius does not repay the loan, I shall have to do so, under the principles of *mandatum*. In other words I am practically surety to you on behalf of Titius. The rules of this form of surety differ somewhat from those of *fideiussio*, in ways that are familiar, and that turn mostly on the fact that in this case the contract which creates the surety's liability is entirely distinct from that which creates the principal's liability. Thus, to take a few important illustrations, action between the creditor and the debtor never releases the *mandator*. If the debtor is a *filius familias*, the *fideiussor* is not responsible, but a *mandator*, as originator of the transaction, will be. A *fideiussor* can claim cession only of such actions as the creditor

[1] *Post*, § 130. [2] D. 14. 3. 2, *etc*. See Girard, Manuel (5), 677.

still has, but the *mandator* will be released if the creditor abandons any rights he has against the debtor—he owes a duty to his *mandator*. So the *mandator* can withdraw before the money is lent, while a *fideiussor* cannot. And the *ll.* Cornelia and Cicereia have no application to the *mandator*, nor has the *beneficium ordinis*[1]. So important is this kind of contract in the later law that the title which deals with *mandatum* in the Digest is almost entirely occupied with it.

Many of the rules of *mandatum* bring out the fact that it is essentially a confidential transaction, as its name indeed indicates. Thus it was gratuitous, though at least in the Empire this was often merely nominally so, since it was usual to agree for an *honorarium*. But it was still true that this *honorarium* could not be recovered in an ordinary action on the contract, but only by a special praetorian *cognitio*. So too, though it was gratuitous, the *mandatarius* was bound in classical and later law to shew the greatest degree of care, while *condemnatio* in the *actio mandati* involved infamy. So too, hostility arising determined the mandate.

The classification of mandates according to the persons for whose benefit they are intended is of no great significance, and is differently given in different texts. The only case worth mentioning is that of a mandate for the benefit of the *mandatarius* alone, which is declared to be mere advice and not in any way binding, unless the thing advised was one which the *mandatarius* would clearly not have done, but for the mandate, and actually was done by him, cases which are not easy to find.

The position of *mandatum* among the consensual contracts appears at first sight remarkable. It differs from all the other consensual contracts in that it is gratuitous, and only imperfectly bilateral, giving rise to the *actio mandati* and to the *actio mandati contraria*, in both which respects it resembles the contracts *re*. It resembles them also in another respect. Either party can withdraw before anything is done. It has therefore been suggested that in the institutional books the contract is misplaced, and that it should be classed with the

[1] Paul. *Sent.* 2. 17. 16; D. 17. 1. 28; D. 4. 4. 13. *pr.*; D. 46. 3. 95. 11; D. 17. 1. 56. *pr.*

real contracts. But this would involve us in serious error, for it differs from these contracts in essential ways. They have as their common quality the delivery of a chattel, but there is nothing of this sort in *mandatum.* Nor is the matter mended by regarding the delivery as a mere case of part performance, of which this is another. The mere agreement does of itself create a definite obligation, and it is for this reason that the transaction is rightly placed under the consensual contracts. This can be shewn by taking a simple case. I give Titius a mandate to make a certain contract for me. Nothing is done: he simply neglects to do what he undertook to do, to my loss. It is clear that an *actio mandati* will lie. To avoid the obligation there must be an express repudiation, and this must be made under such circumstances as not to upset my plans. So also, to use the language of the Institutes, the *mandator* can withdraw only by *revocatio,* which implies that there is something to revoke. A parallel may be drawn from the case of sale. Agreements for a right of withdrawal were not uncommon, but sale is not any the less a consensual contract, though both parties may have reserved such a right. It must be remembered that the presence of consideration is not an essential of consensual contracts: it is one of the factors which made for such recognition, but not a sole or indispensable one. Commercial importance is the real test: most commercially important contracts are consideration contracts, but not necessarily all.

The bestowal of confidence in or by a person does not necessarily extend to his *heres.* It was therefore natural that the rule should appear, and it is fully evidenced in the texts, that a mandate is ended by the death of the mandatary and by the death of the *mandator,* known to the mandatary. (It is possible that as against third persons it was ended only when they knew of the death[1].) It is possible that at one time this was a perfectly general rule, but, as we know it, it is subject to exceptions of which the principle is not perfectly clear, so that it is difficult, perhaps impossible, to state the law with exactness. There are in fact two questions. The first is: what is the effect of the death of either party, on a mandate for services

[1] D. 39. 5. 19. 3.

having no express relation to death? Here the rule is that which has just been stated, subject to the modification that the *heres* of the mandatary must see to the completion of urgent matters which the *mandatarius* left in an uncompleted state[1]. The other question is: what was the effect of death of either party, on a mandate for services to be rendered after the death of the mandator? As to the death of the mandatary the rule is no doubt exactly as in the last case. But there are difficulties in the case of the death of the *mandator*. A mandate for a service which clearly cannot be rendered in any way till after the death was void till the time of Justinian, as a breach of the rule that an obligation cannot begin in the *heres*. But Gaius says that a mandate to an *adstipulator* to validate a *stipulatio post mortem*, by *adstipulatio*, so that he can sue on his *adstipulatio* after the death of the *mandator*, is good, and we are told in the Digest that a mandate to build a tomb for the *mandator*, or to buy land for the *heres*, after the death, is valid[2]. As to the *adstipulator* there is no great difficulty: he must make his *adstipulatio* at once, so that the obligation does not begin in the *heres*. The text dealing with the tomb justifies its decision on the ground that preparatory acts of various kinds may be done before the death, and Gaius says in the following text that the same is true of the mandate to buy land. But, apart from the fact that these explanations look rather like the work of the compilers, the extension of the principle from cases in which something *must* be done before the death to cases in which something *can be* so done, is to reduce the rule to a triviality, for it is hardly possible to conceive a case in which no preparatory acts could be so done. It may be that in the later classical law there was an increasing list of cases in which the rule was disregarded where there were reasons, other than commercial, for obeying the wish of the *mandator*. Perhaps for Justinian's law the nearest thing to a general rule was that a mandate was ended by the death of the *mandator*, subject to notice, unless the nature of the mandate itself showed a contrary intention.

[1] See Accarias, Précis, 2, 377.

[2] D. 17. 1. 12. 17, 13.

CHAPTER VII

THE LAW OF OBLIGATIONS (*concluded*)

126. FROM the fundamental distinction between the Roman and the English conceptions of contract, already pointed out, springs the result that there can scarcely be said to be any general theory of contract in Roman law. There is a classification of actionable agreements into groups, each of which has its appropriate rules, separately laid down. It is this which makes it difficult to say what the law was on such subjects as impossibility or mistake[1]. It is by no means clear that the same rule will apply to, for example, sale and stipulation. However, if contracts are divided into two groups, the *stricti iuris* transactions and those *bonae fidei*, something like general rules may be arrived at. So far as initial impossibility is concerned, it may be said that an agreement to do anything which was impossible in the nature of things was void. And the same is true of things legally impossible. But where the thing undertaken, though in fact impossible in the nature of things, was not obviously so, and, in particular, in cases of legal impossibility, there were certain modifications, especially in *bonae fidei* transactions, and most fully expressed in the case of sale. If one party was not aware of the impossibility, he had a remedy against the other party[1]. In sale, and perhaps in the other *bonae fidei* contracts, he had the action on the contract, apparently even though the other party was equally ignorant, his state of mind affecting only the measure of damages. In practice this means that the buyer, or hirer, of the property had such a remedy against the vendor or letter; the latter need

[1] See Girard, Manuel (5), 444, 460.

no remedy as they have suffered no loss. In contracts *stricti iuris* there was no remedy but, possibly, the *actio doli*, if damage resulted; that is to say, there was no remedy at all against the other party ignorant of the impossibility. As to supervening impossibility, impossibility arising after the contract was made (which was in the Roman law more usually called not impossibility but *casus*), the general rule was that the party whose performance was made impossible, without any fault or fraud, was released[1]—*lex non cogit ad impossibilia*. It is in conformity with this principle that the vendor is released by the accidental destruction of the thing sold before delivery, while the buyer is still liable to pay the price.

127. With regard to Error, it seems impossible with the available material to arrive at a general rule. The rule may indeed be laid down that such mistake as excluded real consent prevented a contract from arising. But such a proposition is of no real value: it leaves open the question, what sort or degree of mistake was enough to exclude real consent. Mistake may occur in relation to many factors, but the only factors which seem to be material are identity of parties, nature of the transaction, and subject-matter. Mistake as to the nature of the transaction cannot have been common, but will clearly exclude consent to a transaction, *e.g.* where a thing is handed over and one party thinks it is a gift, while the other intends a sale, or where one party accepts the thing as a *commodatum*, while the other party intended to make a *depositum*. But although the texts lay this down perfectly generally[2], it is very doubtful whether a person who had made a promise in a *stipulatio* would have been allowed to prove as a defence that he did not know that it was a *stipulatio*. Such transactions if of any importance were commonly embodied in a *cautio*, prepared by and attested by a *tabellio*, and it may be that the enactment forbidding any party to such a *cautio* to dispute the fact of the question and answer was introduced precisely to avoid defences of this kind. A man who had definitely gone through the

[1] D. 50. 17. 23. [2] D. 12. 1. 18; D. 44. 7. 3. 1.

promissory form could of course not be heard to allege that he did not know it bound him: he was presumed to know the law.

As to identity of person, the only case mentioned in which this was material was where the contract rested on a transfer of property (*mutuum*), and the mistake of identity prevented the property from passing[1]. Strictly speaking there can be no mistake of identity where the parties are contracting face to face. There is no evidence, indeed it is hardly probable, that where I had agreed to buy goods of a person called Balbus, I could back out of my bargain merely because I thought he was Titius, to whom I had been recommended.

Error in connexion with the subject-matter may take many forms. In the case of error as to the identity of the subject-matter the few and well-known texts create some little difficulty. In regard to sale we are told that if I think I am buying the farm *A* and you think you are selling the farm *B*, or I think I am buying Stichus and you think you are selling Pamphilus, there is no sale for lack of consent[2]. So far as this proposition goes there is no difficulty: there is nothing in the text to shew that the property sold was designated by name—*tu* Pamphilum *absentem vendere putasti*. So far as appears it is a simple case of ambiguity, each party is thinking of a different slave, to whom the description used will equally apply. It does not follow from anything said in the text that if they had expressly agreed on Pamphilus by name, either party could afterwards have been heard to say that he meant Stichus. The same rule is applied in stipulation, and here too so far as the texts in the Digest go[3], there is nothing to shew that if I had expressly promised Pamphilus by name, I could be heard to say that I had meant Stichus. But in the Institutes we have another and much stranger rule. If in a stipulation I promised Pamphilus and was thinking of Stichus there is no contract. This is of course consistent with the conception of contract as based on mutual consent, but it is difficult to see how anyone could be held to any contract under such a rule. He must know

[1] D. 12. 1. 32. [2] D. 18. 1. 9. *pr.*
[3] D. 45. 1. 83. 1, 137. 1.

best what he was thinking of. This is however generally accepted as having been the Roman law.

As to other forms of error it is laid down that in *bonae fidei* contracts fundamental error (*error in substantia, error essentialis*) prevents a contract from arising, but error in detail (*error accidentalis*) does not. But when we come to consider what was essential and what was not, the possible complexity of the facts makes it useless to attempt to lay down a rule. In *stricti iuris* contracts it seems that, subject to what is said above, neither of these forms of error is material. The difficulty of dealing with these questions is increased by the fact that some of the forms discussed are very ambiguous. The hypothesis *si aes pro auro venditur*[1] may denote any of several very different states of mind and of fact, and many cases which look like mistake are really cases of incurable ambiguity[2].

128. A party to a contract is bound to shew a certain amount of care in carrying it out; that is to say, he is liable to the other party for any damage which results from want of due care on his part. But the amount of care necessary is not the same in all contracts. The difference is commonly expressed in the texts by the use of terms expressing different degrees of negligence: *culpa levis, culpa lata.* But it is also frequently stated in another way. The contract is declared to call for a certain degree of care (*diligentia*), and failure to shew that degree of care involves liability under the contract, if damage results. This gives the same practical result, and perhaps it is more rational to refer the gradations to the amount of care needed than to the amount of carelessness shewn. The general rules are very simple, or at least can be stated in a simple form. In *bonae fidei* contracts *diligentia maxima* is required from any party who benefits, *i.e.*, the care which would be taken by a *bonus paterfamilias* on such facts, and failure to shew this (*culpa levis*) creates liability if damage results. From one who does not benefit, a less degree of care is required: he is liable if he shews less care than any reasonable man would shew—*non intelligere*

[1] D. 18. 1. 9. 2.

[2] See on this Moyle, Sale, 50 *sqq.*

quod omnes intelligunt—failure in which is *culpa lata.* Finally there are several cases in which the necessary degree of care is stated in a different way. There are certain cases in which a party is bound to shew in the transaction the care which he ordinarily does in his own affairs, which may of course, in the case of any given man, be less or more than either of the foregoing standards. Failure in this, which is also called *culpa levis,* is distinguished by modern writers as *culpa levis in concreto* to mark it off from failure to shew the ordinary *diligentia maxima,* which they have called *culpa levis in abstracto.* In *stipulatio* the rule seems to be that in a *stipulatio* to give the *promissor* is not liable if impossibility is caused by his negligent omission, but is if it is caused by his negligent act. In a *stipulatio* to do something the *promissor* seems to be bound to shew *diligentia maxima*[1]. On these rules there are several remarks to be made.

(i) The texts do not tell us an absolutely consistent story; a fact which is to be explained in part as resting on differences of opinion, and in part on historical development of doctrine. Thus we are told in most texts that a depositee is liable only for *culpa lata,* but in one or two texts we are told that he must shew the same care that he does in his own affairs. It is of course possible to harmonise these texts, as one text[2] is inclined to do, by the view that one who is less careful of what is entrusted to him than he is of his own property is shewing less care than any reasonable man would. It is held indeed by many writers that the only difference between *culpa lata* and this *culpa levis* (*in concreto*) is in the matter of proof. If it is called *culpa levis* the burden of proof is on the defendant: in *culpa lata,* the negligence must be proved. But this does not remove the conflict which is found in the texts[3].

(ii) *Culpa lata* is repeatedly declared to be on a level with *dolus,* which does not of course mean that the state of mind is the same, but only that when we are told that a party to a contract is liable only for *dolus,* it must be understood that

[1] D. 45. 1. 91. *pr.*; D. 45. 1. 137. 2, 3.
[2] D. 16. 3. 32.
[3] D. 13. 6. 5. 2; D. 44. 7. 5. 2; D. 16. 3. 32.

this involves liability for *culpa lata.* The liability of a depositee is frequently so stated. There is indeed another way of looking at this matter. We may consider negligence as a state or habit of mind leading to a certain kind of conduct, but since legal standards are necessarily external, the state of mind has to be inferred from the course of conduct. Where a man's conduct falls very far short of what we expect in ordinary intercourse, this may be due to mere carelessness, or it may be wilful. In the first case it is *culpa lata* and in the second it is *dolus.* As to which it may be the *indicia* are very uncertain, and there is no reason for presuming the one rather than the other, so that the practical course is to put them on the same level. But where the departure from the proper standard is only slight, it is far more likely to be due to such a lapse in carefulness as we know that all men are subject to. Hence it is attributed to negligence, *culpa levis.* So too, since people are prone to slight negligence, damage which results to your property in the course of my contractual dealings with it is presumed to have been due to my carelessness, and it is for me to exculpate myself if I can, while, since *culpa lata* and *dolus* are more exceptional, they are never presumed.

(iii) The rule that a party to a contract who does not benefit under it is liable only for *culpa lata* and *dolus* has many exceptions. It may have been absolute in early times, but there was, as is clearly shewn by a comparison of the texts, a progressive raising of the standard of care required in cases having an element of trust or confidence, so that in later law there are many cases in which one who does not benefit is bound nevertheless to shew *diligentia maxima.* It is not necessary to enumerate them: *mandatarius* and *tutor* are familiar instances[1]. Conversely, the holder *in precario* benefits but is not liable for *culpa levis*[2].

(iv) The cases in which a man is bound to shew the same degree of care that he shews in his own affairs, in which, that is to say, the standard is relative to him, and not absolute, look at first sight a rather heterogeneous group. There is however

[1] Coll. 10. 2. 3; D. 50. 17. 23; D. 27. 7. 1. *pr.*

[2] D. 43. 26. 8. 6.

a common characteristic. With the exception of one or two cases, *e.g.* deposit and *tutela*, in which other texts shew that this was in reality not the standard applied to the case, they are all transactions in which in some very real sense it is his own affair. This is obviously so in the cases of *socii*, common owners and the husband in relation to the *dos*, and less obviously, but technically, in the case of a holder *in fiducia*[1].

(v) The foregoing account of *culpa* is properly speaking applicable only to the contractual and quasi-contractual obligations discussed in the Institutes under the heading of obligation. But there is a heterogeneous mass of obligations under praetorian law as to which it does not seem possible to lay down any general rules as to the treatment of negligence. The *iudex* in any action would be guided by the instructions in the *formula* of the *actio in factum* by which these obligations were enforced, and there is some reason to think that these were of very various form.

(vi) Many texts speak of a duty *custodiam praestare*. The exact nature of this obligation cannot be made out from the texts, many of which have been altered by the compilers. The primary meaning seems to be liability if the property is stolen, irrespective of negligence. The holder is so to speak an insurer against theft, though not against robbery. At first this liability seems to have existed in a great number of cases. It is not indeed impossible that it existed in all cases in which the holder benefited: it certainly existed where the benefit was gratuitous as in *commodatum*. But in course of time this liability in its extreme form seems to have been gradually limited to a few cases. Even in Justinian's law it still applied to *nauta, stabularius, horrearius* and some others. It may be indeed that it still applied to all cases in which the article was received to be taken care of or to be worked on, as a part of the ordinary business of the receiver, that is to say, wherever a man "held himself out" as carrying on that kind of business, though not in the case of casual service, even for reward. However this may be, the result is that texts dealing with other cases have been

[1] D. 10. 2. 25. 16; D. 23. 3. 17. *pr.*; Coll. 10. 2. 2.

altered in such a way as to confuse this absolute liability with the duty to take extreme care. In effect *custodia* is treated as identical with one aspect of *diligentia maxima*, and thus the expression *custodia diligens* is found here and there in the texts. This at least seems the most probable explanation of the rather intractable texts, though other explanations are offered. Thus it has recently been maintained, not without some textual support, that the whole conception had disappeared in the time of Justinian, and that allusions to *custodia* in his texts, as implying anything more than *diligentia maxima*, are mere survivals[1].

129. Upon the subject of *Naturalis obligatio* some remarks are necessary. The conception is by no means ancient. It seems to have originated about the beginning of the Christian era under Greek influence and to have found its first application in the case of transactions by slaves[2]. It is a mistake to suppose that *obligatio naturalis* and moral obligation are equivalent expressions. No doubt the moral obligation is at the bottom of them, but, in fact, the *obligationes naturales* are a rather narrow class, fairly well defined. There is no general principle by which it can be determined whether a *naturalis obligatio* has been created or not. They are only a certain number of specific cases, and they were not all recognised at once: indeed the class seems to have been expanding throughout the classical age. It would serve no purpose to enumerate the various recorded cases. They may be grouped under two heads: (i) those that depend on incapacity of the parties, either absolute, as in the case of contract by a slave, or relative, as in contracts between *paterfamilias* and his *filiusfamilias*, and either existing at the time of the contract or supervening, as by *capitis deminutio*, and (ii) those that depend on some statutory rule which forbids an action on an obligation *prima facie* valid. The most familiar instance under this head is that of the *filiusfamilias* who has borrowed money contrary to the provisions

[1] See Schultze, Zeitschrift der Sav. Stiftung, 32. 23.

[2] Pernice, Labeo, 1. 150.

of the *Sc.* Macedonianum[1], but there are several others, while as to some cases the question whether an *obligatio naturalis* existed is still disputed as, for instance, where a debt is barred by lapse of time[2].

The selection seems to have been somewhat haphazard. It is not obvious why the *Sc.* Velleianum, which forbade a woman to be surety, did not allow a *naturalis obligatio* to arise. A more remarkable case is that of the *pactum nudum.* It seems to be clear that a mere pact did not, except in certain cases of pact to pay interest[3], create even a *naturalis obligatio.* Its only force is that it can be used as a defence, and the recognition of this force is older than the conception of *naturalis obligatio.* It is a generalisation by the praetor of the rule of the XII Tables which allows a pact as to compensation, or ransom, to be pleaded in defence to an action on delict.

It is a mistake to suppose that all *obligationes naturales* were alike in their effects. The only characteristic which seems to have been common to them all was that money paid under them could not be recovered—*solutum non repeti*[4]. Even the rule that they could be used by way of set off was not absolutely general[5]. Again an ordinary result of *naturalis obligatio* was that it might be the basis of a valid surety, but this was not so in the case of a loan contrary to the *Sc.* Macedonianum, except where the surety had for some reason no right to demand indemnity from the principal, the reason being that to make the surety pay was indirectly to make his principal, the *filius-familias,* liable[6]. These are only instances of diversities altogether too numerous to be entered on.

130. Something has been said above as to the assignment of contract. In strictness such a thing is inconceivable in Roman law: contract is a personal relation and cannot be transferred. Novation, the discharge of an obligation by the substitution of another by consent of parties, may amount to an

[1] D. 12. 6. 40. *pr.*
[2] See for this and other cases Girard, *op. cit.* 641.
[3] D. 46. 3. 5. 2.
[4] D. 44. 7. 10.
[5] Arg. D. 16. 2. 14.
[6] D. 14. 6. 9. 5.

assignment either of rights or obligations or both, but apart from this, obligations under a contract cannot be got rid of by transfer. On the other hand means were found by which rights under contracts could be practically assigned[1]. Under the formulary system it was possible to appoint representatives to sue on behalf of the creditor (*cognitor, procurator*). Such a person is appointed by *mandatum*, to bring the action, and it is plain that if he is expressly relieved of the duty to account to his principal, this is very like an assignment of the claim to him, and he is called *procurator in rem suam.* But the fact that this rests on a mandate creates several weak points. Thus it can be revoked by the mandator, or renounced by the mandatary before anything is done. It will be revoked by death of the principal, and so forth. But as the real nature of the transaction as an assignment became more fully realised, these weak points were gradually removed. In the later classical law it is clear that where death or revocation has ended the mandate, so that the assignee has no longer the right to sue as *procurator*, he is allowed to bring an *actio utilis* at any rate in all cases in which the assignment had been in some way for value: the rule was not applied as it seems till Justinian in a case of pure gift[2]. The principle was carried still further: if there had been a contract to assign the debt, but the actual mandate to sue had never been given, the same *actio utilis* was allowed, although, at earliest, this institution is post-classical[3]. It was formerly held that this *actio utilis* rested on a fiction that there had actually been, and still existed, a mandate to sue, and the name *cessio legis* was invented to denote these cases in which a legal rule presumed the existence of the valid cession of action. But it is now more usually thought that this *actio utilis* does not rest on any such fiction, that it is an independent action in which, probably with a fiction, the plaintiff sues in his own name and not in that of the original principal.

A further step is necessary for the protection of the

[1] See Girard, Manuel (5), 731 *sqq.*

[2] C. 4. 10. 1; C. 8. 53. 33.

[3] C. 4. 10. 2.

transferee. To give him an *actio utilis* is not to destroy the action in the hand of the principal or his successors. There is nothing to prevent them from suing for or receiving the debt, and so destroying the transferee's rights. The rule therefore developed that a *procuratio in rem suam* became irrevocable and binding on all parties so soon as the transferee had given notice of it to the debtor or obtained part payment from him. The rule appears in an enactment of Gordian[1], where however it may be a later insertion. It does not however appear that this rule applies where there has been no *procuratio* or *cessio* at all, but only an agreement to assign the right.

131. The modes of release from an existing *obligatio* are numerous and some of them call for a few remarks.

The maxim that an *obligatio* is to be released in the form in which it was made has ceased to be absolutely true in the later law, even in the classical law, but there was a time when it operated with what seem to modern eyes very strange results. Nothing else is so obvious a way of ending an obligation as satisfaction of it. But it is fairly clear that this of itself was not always a discharge in early law: it is not to be doubted that payment of money borrowed with *nexum* did not discharge the obligation without an actual release *per aes et libram.* It is also widely held that a promise to pay money was at one time not discharged by payment without an *acceptilatio.* The evidence for this however is not good, and we do not know enough about *nexum* to be sure that it was not some effect on the man's position produced by it which had to be discharged *per aes et libram,* so that we cannot safely assume that the principle applies in other cases. It has been ingeniously suggested that the survival in the form of *manus iniectio,* as given by Gaius, of the very archaic form *quandoc* while the formula has been carefully purged of other old forms, is really a misreading or an error of the scribe, and that the real form is not *quandoc non solvisti* but *quando te non solvisti,* expressing the fact that some personal release of the debtor is required, and it has been acutely

[1] C. 8. 41. 3.

observed that the extreme antiquity of the formal modes of discharge is against the notion that they can have been invented as modes of gratuitous discharge. But however wide or narrow the rule may have been, it is certain that performance is an *ipso iure* discharge in the classical law.

Release *per aes et libram* was the normal mode of discharge of an *obligatio* created in that way, but it is noticeable that it was also applied to release of judgment debts and legacies *per damnationem* of *res fungibiles*. The common quality of these cases is that they gave rise to *manus iniectio,* and it may be that the method was applicable wherever there was *manus iniectio.* It is to the extended applications of it that is due the survival of the mode of discharge centuries after the disappearance of the contract *per aes et libram.* Gaius remarks that release *per aes et libram* is applied in three cases, those of judgment, *legatum per damnationem,* and *obligatio per aes et libram.* It has been remarked that he speaks of this last as still existing, though he is usually careful to use the past tense when speaking of obsolete institutions. The suggestion is therefore made that the *sponsor* to be entitled to this remedy must have paid *per aes et libram,* and there is an obvious support of this in the name of the *actio depensi* and of the repeated use by Gaius of the word *dependere* in speaking of the *sponsor*[1].

Release by mere pact—*pactum de non petendo*—does not *ipso iure* destroy the obligation: it gives an *exceptio pacti conventi.* The most important effect of the distinction is that as the release operates only by *exceptio,* it can in appropriate cases be met by a *replicatio, e.g.,* the *replicatio doli.* There is however another point of interest about these pacts. A mere agreement that a person entitled will not sue leaves the obligation existing: it prevents him from effectively suing, but that is all. Thus it is not available to other persons who may be liable on the same debt, such as sureties or *correi,* or even as it seems the *heres,* unless it expressly referred to him. But this was a question of intent, and by a rather illogical concession a much wider efficacy was allowed to such a pact, if suitable

[1] Eisele, Studien, 22.

words were used. It might be framed in such a way as to make it effective for the benefit of any persons who could be sued and who, if they were sued, would have a claim against the person who made the pact, *e.g.*, sureties or *correi socii*, but not other persons[1]. In such a case the pact was said to be a *pactum in rem.* It is plain that a pact that did not produce this result would be of very little use, if any of these other liabilities existed, since the person who was actually sued would fall back on the person who had secured the pact, and thus make him liable notwithstanding it.

The rule that an obligation is to be discharged in the mode in which it was created has simple applications in the real and the consensual contracts. The former are discharged by return of the *res*: the latter by *contraria consensus.* Hence arises the rule that pacts made after a consensual contract (*pacta ex intervallo*), if they fundamentally altered the agreement could be sued upon as a part of the contract. More accurately, they have discharged the contract and substituted another for it. Apart from this, such pacts, like pacts in general, could be used only as a defence[2]. It may be remembered that pacts made at the time of the contract (*pacta continua*) were embodied in *bonae fidei* contracts and, in later law, even in *stipulatio* and *mutuum*[3].

On the same principle, the proper discharge of a *stipulatio* is *Acceptilatio,* the form of which is stated by Gaius. It is an ancient institution, owing some of its characteristics to that fact. It is an *actus legitimus* and thus admits of no conditions[4]. It may be taken by slaves and *filiifamilias* on behalf of the *paterfamilias* but cannot be given by any such person, even with authority[5]. This is commonly explained as resting on the rule that such persons cannot make his position worse, but this standing alone is hardly an adequate explanation, since there are many respects in which a son or slave, with authority, can do so. A slave, duly authorised thereto, could alienate property

[1] D. 2. 14. 27. 5; D. *h. t.* 21. 5.
[2] D. 2. 14. 7. 4–6; D. 18. 1. 72.
[3] D. 2. 14. 7. 5; D. 45. 1. 1. 3.
[4] D. 50. 17. 77.
[5] D. 46. 4. 11. 1, 22.

or novate an obligation, to say nothing of his power to bind his master by a contract made *iussu*, which is perhaps hardly in point, as this is not civil law. The point probably is that its characteristics were acquired at a very early time when other intensely personal forms of obligation, such as *sponsio*, were taking shape, and remained unaltered. No doubt the proper form of discharge of a written contract was by an *accepti relatio*, which according to analogy would be an entry in the debtor's *codex*, confirmed in some way by the creditor: the binding act is usually done by the person who benefits.

Of the obvious case of discharge by *Solutio* or performance the only things that need be said are that if the parties were agreed a thing other than that originally promised might be given, *in solutum*, and effected in that case a good discharge, at least on the Sabinian view which prevailed[1], and that there was a rule to which we shall return in discussing *negotiorum gestio*, that the *solutio* might in many cases be by a third person, even without my consent.

132. Discharge by *Novatio*, the substitution of one liability for another, calls for careful discussion, since it and its connected ideas introduce a terminology which is very easy to misunderstand. In the classical law the new contract which at once creates a new obligation and discharges the old is always so far as is known a *stipulatio*, though it is probable that the contract *literis*, where it replaced an existing liability, was also regarded as a novation.

The novation of an obligation by a *stipulatio* required, as we know it, some change in the form or the parties or the terms, but in substance the debt must remain the same. A *stipulatio* is not novated by a later *stipulatio* in the same terms: there must be some change which does not affect the identity of the debt, *condicio* or *dies* or surety added or removed, or the like. It has been doubted, on comparison of the language of Gaius and Justinian, whether in the time of Gaius the addition of a *fideiussor* was enough, or whether it must be a *sponsor*.

[1] D. 12. 1. 2. 1.

A *stipulatio* is not novated by a *stipulatio* for something in substitution: it must be the same debt. Further, there is a rule that a conditional stipulation neither novates nor can be novated: the novation is suspended till the condition is satisfied. Where the first *stipulatio* was simple and the second conditional this result is obvious, but the second is not a nullity, even before the novation is realised. We are told that, if the *promissor* was *in mora* under the first *stipulatio*, the acceptance of a new promise, even if it is conditional, purges the *mora*, so that, if, *e.g.*, a promised slave should die after the second *stipulatio*, the *promissor* will be released, since he is no longer *in mora*[1]. Where the first was conditional and the second is simple there is no novation till the condition exists, as there was no debt to novate. It does not follow that the second *stipulatio* cannot be enforced. This would appear to depend on the way in which it was framed. The form "do you promise the 10 which were the subject of such and such a *stipulatio*?" would clearly give a right of action at once. The form "do you promise to pay what is due under the first *stipulatio*?" would give no right of action till the condition was satisfied, when the old debt would become due and be novated at the same moment. On the other hand the first *stipulatio* could not be sued on, even though it was simple and the condition of the second had not yet occurred: if there was no valid novation there was at any rate a pact, and this would give an *exceptio pacti conventi*.

For novation to occur, the classical law required the *animus novandi* to be present: there must be intention to novate, but this was presumed, though it could, of course, be disproved. Under Justinian the intention to novate had to be actually expressed in the transaction[2]. It has been suggested that in pre-classical law no such intent was needed: it is said that the novation followed inevitably from the new contract for *eadem res*, the result being due to the formal act, not to the intent of the parties, the effect being thus analogous to that of *litis contestatio*, which it must be remembered is sometimes called

[1] D. 46. 2. 14; D. 46. 3. 72. 1. [2] C. 8. 41. 8.

novatio necessaria[1]. Gaius indeed does not speak of intent, but if this view is sound the new requirement of intent must have involved another change in conception. For it is hardly conceivable that the destructive effect of the new formal contract can have depended on a change of terms or parties. Of two contracts to the same effect, the second would have prevailed and destroyed the first and not have been a nullity as it was in the later law. And this change seems most improbable. It will be remembered that a new *stipulatio* in which the only change was the addition of a condition novated the old, so soon as the condition was satisfied, *i.e.* when it had become identical with the old one[2]. It is clear however that the exact principle of novation was not quite settled in early law; Gaius remarks on ancient differences of opinion as to novation by a conditional stipulation.

Although the novating *stipulatio* must be of the same debt, there is no reason why it should not cover more than one debt, and in fact one of the most important cases of novation is that known as the *stipulatio* Aquiliana. Novation provided a ready way of turning any existing debt into a debt on *stipulatio*, and the *stipulatio* Aquiliana is a device by which all the existing debts (with some exceptions) between two persons could be turned into one debt due on a stipulation. Its common application was to operate as a means of discharge, as it would be followed by an acceptilation which would end the *obligatio* which had just been created. The form is carefully drawn (no doubt it was gradually arrived at) and is expressed in such a way as to include all sorts of what may be called commercial obligations, so that an analysis of its terms is a not unprofitable exercise. No doubt it might be narrower in scope, *e.g.*, it might cover all relations arising out of a particular piece of business. It does not, as stated by Justinian, cover obligations arising out of delict, and probably it was not in the ordinary way applied to these, though it would be easy to introduce the necessary words. It must be remembered that its use is not necessarily or even ordinarily an act of charity. Men do not

[1] Girard, Manuel (5), 703.
[2] D. 46. 2. 14. *pr.*

abandon their claims for nothing. If there are a number of cross claims between two parties, it will prove when the matter is gone into, that a certain balance is due one way. The state of affairs is much simplified by *stipulationes* Aquilianae and acceptilations on the old debts and a new *stipulatio* for the balance due.

Novation by change of parties brings into use a new set of ideas, and names for them, which need statement. If *A* owes *B* money, and the obligation is novated by a *stipulatio* made by *B* with *C*, that *C* will pay the money, it will usually be the case that *C* was already indebted to *A*. What has happened is the substitution of the debtor's debtor. Such a transaction is not merely a novation: it is a *delegatio debitoris*. *C* is delegated as a debtor. But it must be noticed that the transaction has another side to it. There is also another novation, for *C*'s debt to *A* is now extinguished and replaced by a debt to *B*. This appears to be the strict technical meaning of the word *delegatio*—the substitution of your debtor for yourself in a debt of yours[1]. But the word is also used more loosely wherever *C* makes a promise for payment to *B* on behalf of *A*, whether there has been any novation or not[2]. In like manner the word *expromissio* is applied in strictness to a promise made by a debtor to his creditor's creditor, as in the illustrative case above given, by way of novation, but it is also used where the same debtor promises to a new creditor whether he was the first creditor's creditor or not[3]. In our case it is both, but there would still have been an *expromissio* in this sense if *A* had not been indebted to *B*. A man can even be *expromissor* for his own debt[4].

133. The conception of *obligatio quasi ex contractu* is a simple one. It covers those cases in which the intercourse of life sets up an *obligatio* between two persons without any contract and not resting on any wrong done. The different cases do not seem to have acquired in classical law any collective

[1] D. 46. 2. 11. [2] D. 23. 3. 5. 8.
[3] D. 23. 3. 36. [4] D. 4. 3. 7. 8.

and distinctive name. The name applied by Justinian does not seem to have been used by the great lawyers though they were of course familiar with the idea, and Gaius groups together, but not in his Institutes, quasi contracts and quasi delicts under the common name of *variae causarum figurae*. In treating some of them under the head of contract as he does in the Institutes, he may be only aiming at brevity, at a certain sacrifice of exactness of language. But the tendency to extend the notion contract to include all obligation not involving wrongdoing, by means of a fiction that there is a contract at the bottom of them, is very widespread. Thus it is only in recent times that our law has ceased to speak of obligations of this class as resting on contract implied in law, indeed it may be that it has not yet quite ceased to do so.

Of the case of money paid by mistake little need be said. The property must have been transferred under the belief that it was due, and there must have been no liability, even natural, or postponed in time, though if a conditional debt were paid before it was due, and the condition was still outstanding[1], it could be recovered. The mistake must have been reasonable and, apart from certain privileged cases, it must, at least in classical and later law, have been one of fact[2]. As the property has passed there is of course no *actio in rem*: the remedy is personal, a *condictio indebiti*, and the incidental rules of the case are much like those of *mutuum*. Thus, as we are told, money paid to a *pupillus*, when it was not due, could be recovered only under the same circumstances under which a loan to him could be recovered. These rules present of course difficulties of detail in their application, but there remains one which is interesting as it presents a problem of a different kind. This is the rule that where the supposed debt is one of those which involved a double liability in case of denial, such for instance as a liability under the *lex* Aquilia, money paid under the mistake cannot be recovered. What is the reason of this rule? It has been suggested that it is intended to prevent an evasion of the rule of double liability. The person, against

[1] D. 12. 6. 10, 13, 16. [2] D. 22. 6. 9. *pr.*–5.

whom the claim is brought, pays it, and then brings a *condictio indebiti* to recover the money, on the ground of mistake. Assuming that the money was due he would lose, but he would have succeeded in disputing the claim without incurring the risk of double damages. This may be the origin of the rule, but there are some considerations which make difficulty. In this action he will be the plaintiff. The burden of proof is on him and he will have to shew that he was not liable, while in the Aquilian action it would have been for the other party to prove the liability. He might of course have thought the saving of the risk of double damages was cheaply purchased by undertaking the burden of proof, but there is a still further difficulty. He will also have to prove that there was an error, *i.e.*, that he believed in the existence of some specific fact which did not actually exist, and was by this error induced to pay. It is difficult to see how he can do this. It may indeed be said in reply to this that the rule is an ancient one, and that the rule requiring the error to be one of fact is not necessarily or even probably extremely ancient. It is held by some writers that it belongs to the post-classical law. It is repeatedly laid down in the Code[1]. There is an alternative explanation. It is suggested that in view of the double liability he may have thought it better to pay than to run the risk. Consequently his payment is a sort of compromise, and a compromise, carried out, cannot be set aside. This seems more probable than the other, though it may be said that a compromise under which I pay all that is due is a rather odd one.

The rules of *negotiorum gestio* look rather dangerous to our eyes. A stranger is allowed to intervene in our affairs without our authority, and so long as his act is in our interest, is not prohibited by us, and is a reasonable administrative act, he is entitled to be reimbursed. A person who pays my debt can claim to be reimbursed, and yet though the debt may have been due I may have intended for various reasons to delay payment. There are however some important restrictions on this right. He must take extreme care, unless the matter was

[1] See Accarias, Précis, 2. 437.

very urgent[1]. It must have been in my interest, and if it is a matter in which we are both interested, it must be clear that he could have protected his own interests without mine, if he had not had my interests in view[2]. It must have been beneficial in its inception: there is no claim if what was done was not wanted, even though I may have benefited. And where there is the claim its measure is the benefit to me, not the cost to him[3]. It is obvious that there must have been great difficulties in applying some of these rules.

With regard to the duties of a *heres*, it must be remembered that not all his obligations come under the head of quasi-contract. His obligation to pay the debts of the deceased, and his right to recover from debtors to the estate, are on a different footing: he succeeds to these, and they have the same character in his hands as they had in the hands of the deceased. It is only the liabilities created by the will, *e.g.*, legacies, which come under this head. Indeed it is practically confined to legacies, for *fideicommissa* of whatever kind are protected by different machinery, not by an action in the ordinary sense at all. The whole conception of *fideicommissum* is indeed a puzzling one from the point of view of classification. It is still disputed whether it is or is not a praetorian institution. It is necessary to distinguish between the rights and liabilities as between the *heres* and the *fideicommissarius* and those arising between the *fideicommissarius* of the *hereditas* and the debtors and creditors to the estate. These are presumably praetorian *obligationes*, for we are told that the Praetor gave *utiles actiones* to and against the *fideicommissarius*. But this is due to the *Sc.* Trebellianum (A.D. 62) which, according to Gaius, expressly provided that the actions available at civil law to and against the *heres* should be available to and against the *fideicommissarius*. Perhaps the Senatusconsult contained directions to the Praetor, otherwise it is not plain why, if Gaius reports the enactment correctly, a civil form of action might not have been devised. As between the *heres* and the fideicommissary the

[1] D. 3. 5. 3. 9.

[2] D. 42. 5. 14. 4. See Accarias, Précis, 2. 424.

[3] D. 3. 5. 9. 1; D. 3. 4. 10.

obligation is more difficult to define. It appears that the case of Lucius Lentulus brought up together the questions of the validity of *codicilli* and of *fideicommissa*. Augustus asks Trebatius and others *an hoc possit recipi*. Trebatius replies that it is most desirable. Fortified by this opinion Augustus tells the Consul to carry out certain *fideicommissa* which affect the Emperor himself. Labeo made codicils, and then their validity was universally accepted. Not long after special officers—*praetores fideicommissarii*—were appointed to deal with such things by way of *cognitio*. This story leaves room for wide differences of opinion as to the nature of the obligation thus created. It seems to be sometimes thought of as praetorian, but the praetor had no share in the evolution, and it does not appear in the Edict. In actual fact it is of course an innovation by the Emperor, but the way in which it is made to rest on the opinions and actions of the greatest lawyers of the age indicates that it was intended to be regarded as a civil law development of which the jurists provide us with many other examples.

The duties arising under common ownership are quasi-contractual, whether the community is created by gift, purchase, legacy or death. They are enforced by the divisory actions. Justinian speaks of these actions as appearing to be *in personam* and *in rem*. They are really *in personam*, the facts that they have an *adiudicatio*, and that the parties are actually owners, give them a certain appearance of being *in rem*.

The obligations of a tutor have already been considered. There are several remedies, but that which Justinian contemplates is the *actio tutelae*, the point being that the action against sureties of the tutor rests on contract while the *actio de rationibus distrahendis* rests on misconduct in administration.

It need only be added that this list of four has an artificial air, as has been noted. Additions might have been made to the list, without passing beyond the civil law claims. Thus many cases which give rise to *condictiones* might have been stated here, *e.g.*, *condictio ob rem dati*. Many which seem admissible are excluded, though they are certainly within the conception, because the remedy is purely praetorian. Nothing is said for instance of those rights which are protected by interdict, or even of *curatio*, the remedy for which is a praetorian action, the *actio negotiorum gestorum utilis* (*contraria*). It is not obvious why praetorian obligations are excluded here while they are admitted under the quasi-delicts.

134. We pass now to a new type of *obligatio*, that arising from a delict. A delict is essentially a wrongful act involving *dolus* or *culpa*, which renders the wrongdoer liable to an action for a penalty, the action being brought by the person aggrieved, and the penalty being payable to him. Such a general definition covers many wrongs other than those mentioned under this head in the Institutes. As in the foregoing case, the list of four is a very artificial arrangement. It certainly mentions the delicts which far outweigh the others in importance, but it only makes four of them by treating as distinct delicts theft and robbery, the latter being really an aggravated form of theft. It is impossible to enumerate those which might have been added, but *metus* and *servi corruptio* are familiar examples.

It is not easy to say exactly what is a penalty, or what is a penal action; indeed the jurists do not seem altogether clear on the point. It is certain that where a multiple of the damage inflicted was payable, the action was essentially penal. So also was any action in which the amount recovered might exceed the loss to the plaintiff, as in the case of the Aquilian action, though here as in some other cases, for instance, *vi bonorum raptorum*, the damages included a restitutory element, the setting right of the harm done. But an action was not necessarily penal because the amount of the condemnation might exceed any profit the defendant had made: indeed it is plain that this might be the case in almost any action. It has been said that the jurists declare an action penal or not according to the need of the moment without much regard for consistency. In view of our definition of a delict it is not very helpful to say that an action is penal if it aims at repressing a delict, but it is not very far wrong to say that in general such an action is penal if its primary object is the imposing of a loss on a wrongdoer, rather than the adjustment of a property relation. It may be said that some of the blame for any inconsistencies ought probably to fall on the compilers rather than on the classical lawyers.

Although, with an apparent, but hardly real, exception in the case of *damnum*, every delict involves an act, it does not follow that every one who is liable has shared in the act. A master is liable for any delict committed by his slave with his privity[1], certain accomplices are liable in theft, and the *actio metus* is available against persons who have profited by the wrong[2]. In none of these cases need this person liable have done any act forming part of the wrong, and in some he need have done no act at all.

135. In modern systems of law, theft is treated as a crime to be met by punishment, rather than as an actionable wrong, though it is usually also a delict. In Rome too it was a crime as well as a wrong, and though in our sources the delictal element is the most prominent by far, this is at least partly due to the fact that our principal sources are concerned very little with the criminal law. It is made plain that in later law the criminal remedy was in actual fact that most commonly used, and it is likely that this was so in the classical law. Ulpian indeed says that it is more usual to proceed criminally. No doubt the civil proceedings were used only where the thief was in a position to pay the damages, which probably was not often the case.

The conception of *furtum* which is put before us by Justinian was only gradually arrived at. Traces remain which shew that Sabinus, one of the earliest of the great jurists, took a much wider view of it. In particular, he lays much less stress than do his successors on the element of guilt. He makes a man liable for assistance, *ope et consilio*, for acts which in fact helped the thief after the theft, and he and Q. Mucius Scaevola, a still older writer, lay down the rule that any use by a *detentor*

[1] D. 9. 4. 2, 3.

[2] D. 4. 2. 9. 8.

in excess of his rights under the contract is *furtum*[1]. He and others held also that there might be *furtum* of land. The requirement that the act must be with a view to profit, that it must be *lucrifaciendi gratia*, is emphasised in the Digest, but it is not mentioned in the Institutes, and there is little trace of it in the surviving texts of the classical age, independent of the *Corpus iuris civilis*. Its antiquity appears, however, from the fact that Aulus Gellius cites Sabinus as laying it down. But any attempt to apply the rule to all the recorded cases of *furtum* calls for so wide a conception of the notion that the rule is of very little value. The only thing that need be said of it is that, as applied in the texts, it seems sometimes to include almost everything but wanton destruction, in others not to include the desire for advantages other than commercial, and in others to exclude even some cases of commercial advantage. As might be expected, the texts which take the wider view are the older. The *animus furandi* which figures in some texts as an essential does not seem to differ much from the *animus lucrifaciendi*, and is of very little service.

It has also been suggested that the conception of *furtum possessionis* and *furtum usus* as distinct types of theft is due to the compilers, *i.e.* that the acts so called in Justinian's law would have been described by the classical lawyers as *furtum* by wrongfully depriving a holder of the use or of the possession of the thing[2].

The owner is not the only person who can have an *actio furti*. The various *iura in rem* less than *dominium* were all protected, and the unit of damages was the *interesse*. The usufructuary may have the action even against the owner, and there are few special principles applicable to these cases. The only thing that need be said is that the man to whom the usufruct is left has an *actio furti* if it is stolen, though he has not taken possession[3], and indeed the notion that prior possession on the part of the plaintiff is necessary to the action has little support anywhere in the texts. But there are three cases of *interesse*

[1] Aulus Gellius, *Noctes Atticae*, 11. 18; 6. 15.
[2] Monro, De Furtis, 116.
[3] D. 41. 3. 35.

which are of special difficulty, and though we have not space to discuss them in detail, a few words on each seem to be desirable.

The first case to consider is that of the *detentor*, the holder with a *ius in personam*, as to whom we are told that his right to the *actio furti* does not depend on the advantages he has lost, but on the liability he is under to restore the thing to its owner. Two things must here be remarked. We are over and over again told that such a holder has the *actio furti*, by reason of the liability, and this without any suggestion that the liability does not arise unless the theft was in some way due to his *culpa*[1]. In some cases, however, this limitation of his liability, and, as a consequence, of his right of action also, is carefully stated[2]. The suggestion is obvious that the cases in which no such limitation is stated are those in which he was under the special obligation of *custodia*[3], which involves liability for theft, and of which it has been above suggested that the cases were in all probability much more numerous in earlier law than they were under Justinian. The other point is the somewhat remarkable rule that if such a person has acquired the *actio furti* and afterwards becomes insolvent, so that his liability to the owner becomes unreal, the action reverts to the *dominus*, the two rights being mutually exclusive, since the *dominus* is not considered to have any *interesse* so long as he can call on the *detentor* to indemnify him[4]. But it is not in accordance with general principle that such a right of action, once acquired, should be lost because the *interesse* ceases. An owner does not cease to have the *actio furti*, because his *interesse* ceases from any cause. We are told that he has the action not because *res abest*, but because *res afuit*. The test is whether it *interfuit rem non subripi*[5]. Indeed the theory of *interesse* in this case does not seem to be very thoroughly worked out.

It is perfectly clear that a pledge creditor has the *actio furti*, but not very much more is clear. There are differences of

[1] *e.g.*, Gai. 3. 206; D. 47. 2. 14. 2. [2] *e.g.*, D. 47. 2. 14. 12; *h. t.* 54. 3.
[3] So in *h. t.* 12. *pr.* [4] *h. t.* 18. *pr. etc.* [5] *h. t.* 10, 46. *pr.*

opinion as to whether the unit is the whole value or his interest, and as to whether his right of action excludes that of the debtor. The case is too complicated for discussion here, but it may be remarked that there are several bases of *interesse* in this case. It might rest merely on his possession (though it is at least doubtful whether mere possession was indeed enough to base an *interesse*) or upon his *ius retentionis*, or upon his liability for *culpa*, or it may be a mere inheritance from *fiducia*. The texts appear to represent at different times all or at least the last three of these, and it seems likely that the notion of his *interesse* as resting on his liability for *culpa* was the last to develop and tended to supersede the others[1].

The *bona fide possessor* also has the *actio furti*. He is so far treated like the holder of a usufruct that the unit of damages is not the full value, but that of his interest, but what has been paid in respect of his right is not taken into account if the *dominus* sues, so that, here, his treatment differs. His right does not rest on the right to usucapt, for the fact that the *res* is *vitiosa* is immaterial, and we are expressly told that it rests on what is lost, not on what might have been gained. It is not the negative *interesse*, resting on *culpa*, for the *bona fide possessor* has not this liability, and he has *actio furti* against the owner which the *detentor* has not. We are told that he has the action "like a pledgee," but in view of what has been said this is not very helpful. Javolenus rests it on his *possessio*, but other cases of mere *possessio* do not give the *actio furti*. On the whole the most probable view seems to be that it rests on his *ius retentionis*, which we have seen to be one of the factors in the case of pledge[2].

To give the *actio furti*, the *interesse* must be *honestum*. The rule is simple. Thus a *mala fide possessor* cannot have the action though he is liable for *culpa*. A depositee who *dolo fecerit* in respect of the thing has no *actio furti* if it is stolen, for his liability, on which his *interesse* depends, is due to his *dolus*. If a thing is stolen from a thief it is the owner, not the

[1] D. 47. 2. 14. 16, 19. 6, 46. 4, 62. 8, *etc.*
[2] D. 47. 2. 15. 2, 52. 10, 72. 1, 75.

first thief, who has the *actio furti*. But to say that his *interesse* must be *honestum* is not to say that he must not have behaved dishonestly. It is his *interesse* in the *res* which is material, not his general conduct. Thus if I steal a man and he steals from me, I have the *actio furti*, my *interesse* is honest enough, though I am not. If a *fullo* lends the property he is acting dishonestly, but he has the *actio furti* if it is stolen[1].

These propositions as to the nature of the *interesse* which give an *actio furti* have been, and still are, the subject of a good deal of controversy. The view has recently been propounded, with a good deal of textual support, that in classical law, while an owner had the *actio furti* if there was no other person interested, no right less than ownership, of any kind, gave the *actio furti*, except against the owner himself, where he was the thief. In all other cases the right to bring the *actio furti* depends, in this view, on the fact that the holder is liable for *custodia*. This is a rule familiar in the case of persons having only a *ius in personam*, but by those who hold the opinion now stated it is held to cover the case of usufructuary, pledge creditor and others. Where this *interesse* exists that of the owner is excluded. On this view the *interesse* based on liability, instead of being, as is suggested above, an imperfectly developed institution, must be regarded as ancient and fundamental. In Justinian's time, according to this view, the notion of *custodia* has disappeared, though the word is here and there retained, and there has developed an *interesse* based on *iura in rem* less than ownership. The confused state of the texts is said to be due to the imperfect way in which these changes have been registered therein[2].

136. An accomplice is as liable as the principal thief if he has helped by what the texts call *ope et consilio*. The two factors are necessary: actual physical help does not create liability unless it was done with the intention of helping. Conversely, advice or encouragement is not enough unless it

[1] D. 47. 2. 14. 3, 48. 4.

[2] See Schultze, Zeitschr. der Sav. Stiftung, 32. 23.

amounts to actual help. Advice to commit a theft does not create liability: advice how to commit one does. There seems no trace in the Digest of any liability as accomplice for anything done after the theft, though, as we have just seen, the older lawyers had held that assistance after the theft might suffice. So too on the one hand Celsus is quoted in the Digest as laying it down that a man is liable as an accomplice, if he has in fact helped, not in order that the thieves should steal the thing, but merely out of spite[1]. This presumably means no more than that conscious help to the thief is enough whatever ulterior motive may exist. On the other we learn that the *Veteres* had held that a man who summoned a mule driver to court, *dolo malo*, with the result that in his absence the mules were stolen, was liable, though the text says nothing of any intent that they should be stolen[2]. We are told however by Paul that if I break down a door, and goods are stolen in consequence, I am not liable unless I contemplated this result[3]. Paul is late, and we are elsewhere told that the views of the *Veteres* had been abandoned later, and that no one was so liable unless there was actual help and *consilium malignum*[4], a vague epithet which does not really clear up the matter. It may be well to remark that there is no special action for accomplices: a man who is liable in this way is a *fur nec manifestus*: he cannot be a *fur manifestus*, since, as he does not actually do the act, he cannot be caught doing it.

There was much discussion as to the exact meaning of *furtum manifestum*, and many modern commentators have given much time to the reasons for the wide distinction in penalty between this form of theft and *furtum nec manifestum*. One point however, not unimportant, has not received much attention. We are told that the thief must be *deprehensus* in the fact, and while there is much discussion of "in the fact," there is little of *deprehensus*. "Caught" is a convenient translation. But in ordinary English speech this may mean either observed or captured. The general verdict of the texts, *i.e.*, so far as can

[1] D. 47. 2. 50. 1.
[2] D. 47. 2. 67. 2.
[3] D. 47. 2. 54.
[4] D. 50. 16. 53. 2.

be inferred from actual decisions, is that capture is needed. But in one text in the Digest Justinian cites Celsus as holding that detection was enough[1], and in the Institutes he adopts this view. This limitation to capture makes the delict of robbery more important. It imposes a penalty of fourfold on those who steal with violence, a fact which must commonly have involved detection in the act, though not necessarily capture. As the fourfold recovered included the value of the thing, the action was of less value than *furti manifesti*, and it had the further disadvantage of being limited to a year. More correctly it is *in simplum* after the *annus utilis*. Here it merely competes with *vindicatio* or *condictio furtiva*, but it has the advantage that condemnation involves infamy.

We are told that in all these cases the owner has either a *vindicatio* with its ancillary remedies (interdicts, *actio ad exhibendum*), against the holder whoever he may be, or a *condictio furtiva*, against the thief or his heirs whether in possession or not. The former group of remedies has nothing to do specially with theft, but the latter is devised for this particular case. It has the peculiarity that, as Gaius states the *formula*, it alleges a duty in the defendant to transfer the ownership (*dare*), which is impossible, since the plaintiff has not ceased to be owner because the thing has been stolen. Gaius gives the practical explanation that this is to give the injured person every possible way of getting the better of the thief, but as has been said, this is a good reason for requiring difficult things of the thief but not impossibilities. It is supposed by Mommsen[2] that it is a generalisation of the *actio rerum amotarum*, the action for compensation where a theft had been committed by a wife, or other person against whom an infaming action could not be brought. But the latter is, it seems, an *actio in factum*[3], and it is difficult to see how a *stricti iuris* action should have arisen out of that. It is however highly probable that it was at first only applied where the thing had perished, or was out of the hands of the thief. None of these points however justifies the anomaly.

[1] D. 47. 2. 7. 2. [2] Strafrecht, 757. [3] Lenel, Ed. Perp. (2), 298.

The delict of *servi corruptio*, which consists in making a slave physically, mentally or morally worse, has no connexion with *furtum*, but a curious case is discussed which involves them both. *A* tries to induce *B*'s slave to steal from his master. The slave informs the master, who tells him to do what *A* has suggested. Gaius takes the sound logical view that there has been no *furtum* because the master assented, and thus it was not *invito domino*, and no *servi corruptio* because the man was not in fact corrupted. What has happened is in fact an attempt to commit these delicts. But Justinian, feeling that there ought to be some remedy on such facts, lays down the astonishing rule that *B* is liable on both counts. Hard cases make bad law: the tendency to make every rogue a thief, if possible, has not been without influence on our own law.

As we have seen, *Rapina*, or robbery, is in fact theft with an element of violence: it involves bad faith. But in the later law it was provided that violent seizure, even in good faith, should involve a penalty. Sporadic legislation against violence is common in all historically known ages of Rome: this particular provision is no doubt an admission that in the increasing disorder of the fifth century the ancient remedies by the interdicts *unde vi* and *quod vi aut clam*, which had but little penal character, had proved insufficient.

137. The Aquilian action for damage to property gave a right to recover the highest value the thing had had within a certain previous time. As this must in many cases have been no more than that it had at the time of the wrongdoing, the action is not noticeably penal except where the damages are doubled for denial of liability. It is true that the damages will commonly exceed any profit to the wrongdoer, who may have made none, but this is not enough to make the action penal. Yet it is absolutely and always an *actio poenalis*[1], and this as to the whole of the damages, not merely as to the penal element it may contain. The point is that its repressive character is more prominent than its restitutory effect. Singularly

[1] D. 9. 2. 11. 2–4.

little is said as to the measure of damages in cases coming under the third chapter. From the express statements of the law it is not quite clear what is the measure of damages under the third head. The words are "*quanti ea res erit, in diebus triginta proximis*[1]." If this means the whole value, the effect would be to induce a person who had damaged any property to destroy it altogether, unless indeed he could claim it, which also would lead to abuses. There is however some evidence that the amount payable was the difference between the value of the property after the damage and the highest value it had had at any time within one month before the wrong was committed[2].

It is clear that contributory negligence was a defence, where the harm was itself negligent. This must not be considered as one negligence set off against another: the rule seems to be in fact the same as in English law, that to create liability the negligence must be the proximate cause of the damage; there must be a relation of cause and effect between the act and the damage. Among the best illustrations of this is the case of the man who is injured and dies from neglect[3]. The wrongdoer has not killed him. This opens the question whether the same rule is to be applied where the act was wilful, and there is an intervening cause which leads to death. Apparently the same rule is applied, though this has nothing to do with contributory negligence[4].

The slightest negligence creates liability[5]. This raises a question as to what the rule is in the case in which a thing is in the hands of a depositee and he injures it negligently, but not with such extreme negligence as to make him liable to the *actio depositi*. If he is liable *ex* Aquilia the rule in deposit is somewhat illusory, at least so far as the actual depositee is concerned, as opposed to his *heres*, who would not be liable *ex delicto*. The matter is much disputed, but the supporters of the view that even here the liability is for slight negligence are in the majority. The textual authority is scanty and

[1] D. 9. 2. 27. 5.
[2] D. 9. 2. 24, 33, 47; Paul, *Sent.* 1. 15. 1.
[3] D. 9. 2. 9. 4, 52.
[4] D. 9. 2. 11. 3.
[5] D. 9. 2. 44.

obscure, and much of the reasoning is *a priori*. One text is freely used by the supporters of each view. But the matter is too controversial to be considered here[1].

We know that in certain cases an Aquilian action lay and in others an *actio utilis* or an *actio in factum*. The field covered by these two praetorian extensions is that of damage done not to the actual thing or not by the actual person of the wrong-doer, or neither, but how this field was divided between them, or whether it was divided at all, is a most difficult question. The specific statement in the Institutes on the point disagrees with Gaius and with the Digest. Lenel[2] is of opinion that the expression *actio in factum* as used here does not necessarily mean an action with a *formula in factum*, but may mean an action setting out the facts, whether it is *in factum* or *in ius*, and *actio utilis e lege* Aquilia may mean one which is in effect an extension of the Aquilian action whether *in ius* or *in factum*, and that the jurists used the names rather at haphazard. There is a further point. In the cases in which the action was really *in factum concepta*, was the substantial effect as under the *lex* Aquilia, *i.e.* condemnation for the highest value, and double in case of denial, or was it simply an action for compensation? The texts do not tell us: the former solution seems to be most widely, but not universally, accepted.

Aquilian liability depends on an act. There are some cases which look like exceptions, *e.g.*, that of a man who burns his grass and does nothing to check the fire when it threatens to pass beyond his borders, or does not watch a fire, so that it burns his neighbour's house[3]. But though these look like cases of mere omission, it will be seen on careful examination that there is always a previous act, or positive undertaking, which imposes the further obligation to watch: the act may be remote, but it is there. The point is however disputed.

The Aquilian action may concur with an action on contract, where for instance a man borrows a horse and founders him.

[1] See Grueber, Lex Aquilia, 232. [2] Lenel, Ed. Perp. (2), 197.
[3] D. 9. 2. 27. 9, 30. 3.

The texts are in conflict as to whether both actions lay. The most probable view seems to be that the Aquilian action, being purely penal, did not bar the other, technically, but that if the plaintiff did not give security not to bring the other action and did bring it, the defendant would be released, *officio iudicis*. This effect produced by procedural devices ultimately became substantive law, and the Aquilian action came to be regarded for this purpose as *mixta*. It barred any action on the contract on the same facts, while if the action on contract had been brought first, the delictal action lay only for any excess which could not have been recovered under the earlier action. But all this is disputed[1].

The action may concur with another action on delict. Here the law is obscure by reason of the multitude of conflicting texts. It is clear that in classical law the rules were not settled. The possible ways of dealing with such a case are very numerous. So too the degree of connexion between the two delicts may not always be the same. Thus one effect may be two delicts, or the same act may cause two effects. If to these factors is added difference of opinion among the lawyers as to where the lines should be drawn, the confused state of the texts is easily accounted for. Mommsen[2] considers the rule to have been that if the two delicts were of distinct character, morally, either may be sued on after the other, for any excess: if they are different remedies for the same evil, one bars the other. He appears to hold that in later classical law they were never wholly independent if they were one act. He remarks that such a rule is very difficult to apply. Karlowa[3] thinks they were originally independent if based on different statutes, and that if one was edictal, or both were, it was a question of the praetor's intention, but that in classical law the surviving action was always barred by some procedural device or limited to any excess. Pernice[4] holds that Justinian adopted Paul's view, which he states to have been that where one effect

[1] Pernice, Sachbeschädigung, 140 *sqq.*
[2] Strafrecht, 887 *sqq.*
[3] Röm. R. G. 2. 994.
[4] *Op. cit.* 131 *sqq.*

constitutes two delicts the action survives only for any excess, but that if the act has two distinct delictal effects they are quite independent.

The action may concur with a criminal proceeding. Here too the texts are very confusing. Mommsen holds that so long as the old criminal procedure lasted the private action would not lie if criminal proceedings had been or might still be brought, with the exception that they are quite independent if the delict is a wrong to property. In later law he thinks no general rule is possible, but so far as the Aquilian action is concerned, it is clear that neither barred the other (except, in practice, where the criminal punishment had been capital), at least in the later law[1].

138. The delict of *Iniuria* differs from the others mentioned in the Institutes in a noticeable way. It is defined not in terms of the harm done, as they are, but of the motive with which it is done. It is anything unlawful done with the object of insulting. This kind of wrong is clearly the creation of a fairly developed civilisation. Though *iniuria* is mentioned in the XII Tables, it does not there mean insult, but violence to person or property. The *malum carmen* of the XII Tables is not libel or slander, but magic incantations which are likely to injure crops or cause other harm. Considerably later, remedies are given by the praetor for defamatory words, and about the end of the Republic an *actio iniuriarum* appears which aims at repressing insults. Gradually under juristic influence it is extended in its scope, since there are many ways of insulting a man beside calling him names, until in the late classical law any wanton interference with right is regarded as an *iniuria*, if, on the evidence, it appears to have been done with intent to annoy or insult, or to lessen the esteem in which the injured person is held.

Iniuria differs also from the other delicts in the mode of estimation of damages, which were obviously difficult to fix in the case of insult. They vary in each case, not merely with

[1] Strafrecht, 891; see C. 9. 31. 1.

the grossness of the insult, but also according to the position of the person insulted.

The fact that an *iniuria* is *atrox*, either because of the nature of the wrong itself, or of the publicity of it, or of the *status* of the person insulted, led to certain well-known differences in treatment, not such as to call for discussion. It may however be worth while to say that the texts do not really justify the view that the distinction was a clearly defined one: it was for the praetor to decide whether the *iniuria* was *atrox* or not, and to issue the *formula* according to his conclusion: the facts just mentioned are only such indications as would guide him.

The manner in which the whole proceeding is stated in the sources shews that it was essentially intended as a *solatium* for the wounded *amour propre* of the insulted man. Hence it was that unless he had shewed, at the time, that he was stung, the action did not lie, that he must bring the action within one year, and that though he died within the year his heir could not bring the action or continue it[1], unless it had reached *litis contestatio*.

The fact that if insult were intended to a man the action lay, even though the wrongful act or speech had no direct reference to him, led to the possibility that several persons might have an action for the same insult. Thus, for an insult to a *filiusfamilias*, his *paterfamilias*, besides the action which he might bring on behalf of his son, might have one on his own account, and they were quite independent[2]. For an insult to a woman, she, her husband and her father, might all have actions. For an insult to a slave any person interested in him might conceivably have an action if intent to insult him was proved. Where a common slave was insulted each of his masters might have the action, and we are told that the damages would not necessarily be proportionate to the shares in the man, but would be affected by the position of the plaintiff. It must be admitted however that the texts are in apparent conflict on this point[3].

The master's action for an insult to his slave might be

[1] D. 47. 10. 13. *pr*. [2] D. 47. 10. 5. 6, 7. [3] Inst. 4. 4. 4; D. 47. 10. 16.

either *suo nomine* or *servi nomine,* the former if there was intent to insult the master, the latter if there was not. But in both cases the *iniuria* must be *atrox,* a matter as to which the Praetor himself decided. There are however two points to be made. If the insult to the slave not only was intended to insult the master but was actually expressed to be such, this restriction does not apply. It was a direct *iniuria* to the *dominus,* the slave being only the medium through which it was inflicted. On the other hand, if there was no intention to insult the master at all, the Praetor's action *servi nomine* lay in all probability only where the *iniuria* was, so to speak, flagrantly *atrox,* a higher standard of *atrocitas* being taken than in ordinary cases. It is provided for by an edict which gives it in cases of *Verberatio* or unjustified torture, and adds that it will be given in other cases, *causa cognita.* The other cases must have been of something like the same degree of atrocity. The whole rule seems to be a praetorian extension of a provision of the *lex* Cornelia *de iniuriis,* which gave a special remedy for *verberatio* of a freeman or violent entry on his house.

The class of Quasi-Delicts is not found so called before Justinian, though the cases discussed by him under this heading are not new. For Gaius they are grouped together with quasi-contract in a class called *Variae causarum figurae,* which however he does not mention in his Institutes. They are all praetorian, but it is plain that the short list of the usual four is far from exhausting the list of praetorian obligations which have not been dealt with under earlier heads. Justinian's language suggests that they are all cases of vicarious liability, cases in which a man is made responsible for an act which was not, or at any rate need not have been, committed by him or with his privity. This is obviously true in all the cases mentioned except that of the unjust judge, and even here the name given to the wrong, *litem suam facere,* brings in the notion of liability for another's act. In the case of innkeepers and others liable for the malpractices of their servants the case is practically one of insurance, resting on grounds of prudence which have led to the establishment of similar rules in other legislation. It is somewhat odd that the text makes an attempt to explain it on an altogether untenable ground. It is said that there is a certain negligence in the employer for having set the service to unsuitable men. But it is evident that no amount of care in training or selecting them would save him from this liability.

139. The subject of delict may be left with two remarks. The obligation on a delict was in some cases ended by lapse of a very short time, as we have just seen in the case of *iniuria.* This is no doubt due to the fact that these remedies originate as substitutes for revenge, the desire for which ordinarily cools with time. This origin also accounts for another rule of an exactly opposite tendency. Delictal obligation is permanent in a special way. A person who is *capite minutus* is, as we know, a new man, and his old obligations cease to bind him. But this is not true of obligation on delict. We are clearly told that a man did not cease to be liable for his delicts by undergoing *capitis deminutio*[1]. Thus, if a man who had committed a theft chanced to be enslaved, and afterwards regained his freedom, he could still be sued upon his theft, though his obligations on contract would not revive. He might be a new *persona,* but he had the same body on which vengeance could be wreaked.

It may also be pointed out that it seems clear that a mere pact was a defence on an action for delict, not as in other cases merely a praetorian defence *ope exceptionis,* but a complete defence at civil law. This is no doubt due to the fact that the XII Tables expressly so provide in relation to a certain class of delicts[2].

140. The last topic for discussion in connexion with the law of things is the question, how far, and under what circumstances, the act of another person can acquire obligations for us or put us under obligation to a third person.

[1] D. 4. 5. 2. 3.

[2] Bruns, Fontes, 1. 29.

So far as concerns the acquisition of obligations through slaves and *filiifamilias*, the rules are in general those which we considered in connexion with property, but there are some points which need mention.

The acquisition does not rest on any notion of agency or representation, since it occurs even though the transaction were prohibited by the master. As the slave is incapable of any rights, the acquirer is the master at the moment of the contract, even though a condition of the contract is not satisfied till the slave has, for instance, been freed. But though a slave's capacity is entirely derivative (and thus he cannot be an *adstipulator*, whose rights are personal to himself), he can acquire for a lunatic master, being thus gifted, somewhat illogically, with capacities which his master has not[1]. The individuality of the slave is recognised, however, in many ways. Thus if it is he who contracted, any notice necessary must be made in general to him, and his knowledge will bar the master from an action on the ground of *dolus*[2].

Since the slave is incapable of a right there is a rule that if he stipulates for a right to be conveyed to him, *mihi dari*, the stipulation is void as being impossible. But in many cases this is eluded by construing the technical words descriptive of a right in a non-technical way, though the result of this is often that the master acquires a right entirely different from that which was intended. Of course the difficulty does not arise if the slave avoids the word *mihi*[3]. And where the *stipulatio* is for some advantage or privilege to the slave not amounting to a servitude or *ius*, there is no difficulty. But as the Institutes tell us, the master gets only what the slave bargained for. If a slave stipulates for permission for him to cross a field, this is not a servitude: it is a mere contractual right. But the contract is for the slave, not the master, to be allowed to cross it. Hence though the master can enforce it, if necessary, it is only through the slave that it can be enjoyed:

[1] D. 41. 3. 28; D. 45. 3. 40; D. 27. 8. 1. 15 (*arg.*).
[2] D. 21. 2. 39. 1; D. 41. 4. 4. 17.
[3] D. 45. 1. 38. 3–9; D. 45. 1. 130.

it is literally construed: *quae facti sunt non transeunt ad dominum.*

As to rights *ex delicto,* they are acquired in the same way. Theft from a slave is theft from his master, and the remedies for it will remain with the master though the slave passes out of his *familia*[1].

The personal nature of obligation is expressed in the fact that no obligation could be acquired through a third person, outside the *familia.* Nor was this rule ever relaxed so as to allow acquisition by *iure gentium* contracts, as was the same rule in acquisition of property. Even under Justinian, if a friend purchased a thing in my name, and took delivery for me, the thing would vest in me, but I could not sue on the contract except in certain urgent cases[2]. Of course the rule might be more or less evaded by such devices as *procuratio in rem suam,* but this is at best an assignment of contract subject to the defences which might have been available against the original contracting party: it is very far from agency.

141. On the subject of the imposition of liabilities on a man through the act of another person, there is a good deal more to be said. So far as persons outside the *familia* are concerned, the general rule, here also, is that no obligation can be imposed on a man by their contracts or their delicts. In relation to contract we have already seen that there might in certain cases be an *actio ad exemplum institoriae,* on a contract by a third person, the action being itself an extension of the *actio institoria,* to which we shall recur. With regard to delict there are also exceptions, but these are matter of express legislation, on the part of the Praetor. The case of a third party's liability for *metus* is perhaps an instance. The cases of *res deiectae et effusae* and of suspension to the danger of passers are also instances, though the acts of the unknown third party, for which the occupier is liable, are not always delicts. A slave guilty of the *deiectio* can, if identified, be noxally surrendered[3]. And the last quasi-delict mentioned by Justinian is a remainder

[1] D. 29. 2. 79. [2] *Ante,* § 130. [3] D. 9. 3. 1. *pr.*

of a rather elaborate scheme of remedies designed to meet cases in which the danger of wrong was great but the circumstances made it practically impossible to find the actual wrongdoer. It is not possible to go into details, but it may be said that there were two edicts, which have become confused in the Digest[1], one dealing with robbery and damage done by the *publicanus* or his employees in the collection of taxes and the other with theft by them. In one of them, and probably in both, the *publicanus* is made liable for these acts whether the employees are his slaves or not, and with no need for identification of the wrongdoer. Again there was an *actio in factum* against *nautae, caupones* and *stabularii*[2] for theft or damage committed by their employees whether slaves or not, though it seems that here the actual offender must be pointed out. And these *nautae, etc.* were under the obligation to account for what they received, as has already been said. This has no necessary connexion with delict, but it is in point here since, though the facts were shewn to be a delict, there was no question of noxal liability: the *nautae, etc.* are liable personally in full[3].

142. The liabilities of the *paterfamilias* on contracts by slaves and *filiifamilias* are enforced by a well-known group of actions. If he expressly authorised the contract he is liable for the whole debt (*actio quod iussu*), as he is also if the contract was made in connexion with a business to which he had appointed a son or slave, or even an outsider, manager (*actio institoria*), or where such a person had been appointed to command a trading-ship and had contracted for its purposes (*actio exercitoria*). If there had been no sort of authorisation he was liable to the extent of the *peculium* of the contracting son or slave, and to the extent to which he himself had profited (*actio de peculio et in rem verso*), having however the right to deduct what was due from the slave to him, while if the master had been aware of the slave's trading he was liable to the extent of that part of the *peculium* which had to his knowledge been

[1] D. 39. 4. 1. *pr.*, 12; Lenel, Ed. Perp. (2) 324.
[2] D. 47. 5. [3] D. 4. 9.

so employed, without any such right of deduction, but a right to claim with the other creditors (*actio tributoria*). These liabilities are created by the Praetor's Edict and the words in which the rules were laid down are fairly well known to us. As might have been expected, the Edict contents itself with laying down these rules and says nothing of any general principle which may underlie them. The jurists, so far as their observations survive, do little to help us to fix these principles, and it will therefore be well to give some attention to each of these actions.

The *actio de peculio*, with its limited liability, looks at first like a case of carefully guarded agency or representation. Ulpian, indeed, speaks of it as a case in which the third party relies on the *peculium*[1], but a little examination of the rules will shew that the basis of the liability is certainly not any notion of representation. Most modern systems of law (our own is the chief, if not the only, exception) require, as a condition of the principal's liability, that the agent shall have contracted expressly as agent, so that the third party knows that he is not dealing with the principal directly. The *actio de peculio* had no such requirement. The third party need not know that the person with whom he was dealing was not the principal, or that he had a *peculium*[2]. Indeed it is by no means clear that at the time of the contract there need have been a grant of *peculium*: it is certain that there need have been nothing in it provided there was when it was sued on. All systems require actual authorisation, express or tacit, or ratification: authority is the very essence of agency. But the *actio de peculio* lay even though the master had prohibited the contract or forbidden the slave to contract at all, and this to the knowledge of the other party[3]. All this does not look much like a recognition however imperfect of the principle of agency or representation: it looks rather as if the Praetor and those who interpreted the Edict started from quite a different notion, which resembles a limited insurance. The person who provides a man with a *peculium* has to run the risk of its loss by the person to whom he has entrusted it. The rules of the *actio*

[1] D. 15. 1. 32. *pr.* [2] C. 5. 18. 3. [3] D. 15. 1. 29. 1, 47. *pr.*

de peculio are so fully recorded that we can speak with some confidence on this point. The case is different with some of the other actions of this group. Although they are discussed at length, and we have in some cases the means of reconstructing the Edict and the formula, we find on reading the texts that a number of what seem to us the most elementary points are left open, are not indeed so much as mentioned, so that, so far as they are concerned, we are left to make our own interpretation of the Edict. This has of course given rise to a great mass of controversy into which it is impossible for us to enter. It may however be worth while to indicate in regard to some of these actions just what the open questions of principle are, and what are the most widely held opinions as to their solution.

The *actio de in rem verso*, though ordinarily it is only a clause in the *actio de peculio* may be considered, indeed it is considered in the Digest, as an independent action: in fact one of the unsettled questions is the problem whether it could be brought in a case in which the slave never had a *peculium*. But a more interesting question is this: what constitutes a *versio in rem domini*? According to one view anything is a *versum* which has been applied to the master's concerns as opposed to those of the *peculium*, the question always being, was there an increase of the master's wealth, as opposed to the *peculium*[1]? According to another view there is a *versio* only where the slave has applied the property in such a way as would, if he had been a third party, have given him an action *ex negotiis gestis*[2]. According to a third opinion there is a *versio* only if the third person who is suing had handed over the property with a view to its being applied to the master's concerns[3]. None of these opinions is proved by the texts: perhaps none is wholly consistent with them. On the other hand each finds a good deal of support in them. We will not attempt to decide between them: it is enough to say that it is a rather hopeless thing to attempt to decide for Roman law

[1] *e.g.*, D. 15. 3. 1. *pr.*
[2] *e.g.*, D. 15. 3. 3. 2.
[3] *e.g.*, D. 14. 6. 17.

points on which the jurists themselves were in disagreement. We are indeed a long way now from the time when the Digest was supposed to contain an absolutely harmonious set of principles in which there was no contradiction. We are almost as far from the time when it was thought that the "classical law" was a completely developed, logical, but technical set of principles of which Justinian destroyed the symmetry by utilitarian reforms. The truth is that from A.D. 50 to A.D. 150 the law was developing with extreme rapidity, and the surviving texts, so far as they are unaltered, represent clashing opinions on scores of points. Of these conflicts the texts on the actions we are now discussing are a very striking illustration.

The fact that of all these actions the *actio quod iussu*, in which the element of authorisation is most prominent, is that which the texts discuss with most brevity is not insignificant. The most fundamental questions are left undecided. Was it enough that the master had in fact authorised the contract whether this was known to the parties or not, or was it necessary that the authorisation should have been communicated to the slave, or must it have been made known to the third party or to both? Starting from the point of view that the case is one of agency, it is easy to understand that the view most widely held in Germany is that the authorisation must have been actually made to, or at least made known to, the third party. For in modern German law a third party cannot sue the principal on a contract made by an agent, unless he knew when he made the contract that there was in fact a principal behind the actual contracting party. Starting from the same point of view an Englishman would not feel the same difficulty, for English law allows the third party to sue the principal, when he learns that there is such a person, even though he had supposed when he made the contract that the person with whom he was contracting was the principal. If we disregard the principle of agency altogether, as not being in the Roman way, but consider the Praetor as merely making the master responsible for the results of a transaction which he has himself set going (just as he was personally responsible for his slave's delict, if he was privy to it), then there is still less reason for requiring notice to the third party. Here, too, all views are held, but of course all writers are agreed that the authorisation would usually as a matter of fact be known to the third party.

In relation to the *actiones institoria* and *exercitoria* there are questions of the same kind left equally open by the texts and decided by modern commentators, according to their prepossessions, either for or against the application of the conception of agency or any particular form of that conception. Must the third party have known when he contracted that the transaction concerned the business? Must he have known further that the *institor* was in fact an *institor* and not the real principal? It is not necessary to repeat what has been said above in the other cases[1].

An important characteristic of this last group of actions is that the liability applies even though the *institor* is not a member of the *familia*. No doubt the earliest cases were appointments of members of the *familia*, but even the slaves of another man might be appointed, though this does not seem to have been common[2], and in later law free *institores* were general. This looks therefore like a definite case of agency outside the family. But as we have said, we have no right to think of it in terms of representation at all, and it is unlikely that, if it had been so thought of, the rule would have stopped where it did. For the employer became liable under the contract of the *institor*, but did not acquire under it: the right of action vested in the *institor* himself if he was free or in his master if he was another man's slave, and would need to be transferred[3].

The *actio tributoria* differs in character from the others. The picture of it presented in the Institutes is somewhat misleading. It is the last step in a rather elaborate machinery. Without going into details it may be said that the rules are

[1] See on these points Buckland, Slavery, 702 *sqq.*

[2] D. 14. 3. 7. 1. [3] D. 14. 3. 1.

these. Where the creditor knows that the master was aware of the slave's dealings he need not rest content with the *actio de peculio*, which may be futile, if the slave is deeply indebted to his master, but can call upon the master to distribute the *peculium* or the part of it which he knew to be employed in the trading, among the various creditors *pro rata*, he himself having no prior right. It is thus a sort of bankruptcy of the slave, the administrator being the master[1]. If the master fails to distribute the fund properly, then, and then only, is the *actio tributoria* available[2], gaining its name from the previous *vocatio in tributum*. The action does not lie for mere error or negligence, but only for *dolus*[3], and thus it has a certain delictal character which marks it off sharply from the other actions of the group. There is some controversy about the matter, but on the whole the better view seems to be that it was not treated as delictal but as contractual. Thus it is *perpetua*, and lies against the *heres*[4]. It is penal to the extent that the defendant must hand over what he would have handed over apart from *dolus*, and thus may have to give more than the *peculium* now contains, since there may have been diminution by accident.

It will be noticed that Gaius describes this system of remedies as available only for contracts by slaves and *filiifamilias*. For the case of persons in *manus* and civil bondsmen he has a different story to tell, but it is so defective, owing to the state of the manuscript, that what we can read is rather a puzzle. He says that for persons in these positions the rule is that on their contracts the *paterfamilias* may be sued, and, if he does not defend *in solidum*, the goods which would have been the property of the man or woman may be seized and sold. We have seen that this is the law for contracts by an *adrogatus*, made before the adrogation[5]. If this is to be applied in our two cases to the same cases of contract, we have the difficulty that the bondsman must have been, and the wife may have been, *alieni iuris* before, so that there could be no property answering this description. No doubt the result is just: there

[1] D. 14. 4. 1. *pr.* 5, *h. t.* 6. [2] D. 14. 4. 7. 3. [3] D. 14. 4. 12.
[4] D. 14. 4. 7. 5, 9. *pr.* [5] *Ante*, § 57.

is no reason for making the present *paterfamilias* liable, as he has received no benefit, and there were always the *actio de peculio annalis*, and in appropriate cases the other actions, against the former *paterfamilias*. But on this view the allusion to the person in bondage is meaningless, and it has therefore been suggested that the case contemplated is that of a woman *sui iuris* who has passed into bondage in the process of *coemptio fiduciae causa*. In any case we are uninformed as to what seems the practically more important case of contracts made after the entry into the family group. It seems a fair inference from the language of Gaius that the ordinary edictal actions, *de peculio* and the rest, did not apply here, at any rate without restrictions. Yet elsewhere he seems to put these persons and slaves on the same level[1]. It seems to be sometimes held that bondsmen and women *in manu* were absolutely incapable of binding the *paterfamilias* even at praetorian law, but in fact there seems to be no material for forming any opinion on the subject.

143. The liability of the *paterfamilias* for delicts committed by members of the *familia*, noxal liability, as it is called, by reason of the rule that the master may either pay damages or surrender the wrongdoer (*noxae deditio*), is a subject of great practical importance, owing to the prominence of slaves in the law. It is observable that while the civil law rejects any liability of the master on the slave's contract, this limited liability for his delict is recognised so early as the XII Tables. The cause of the difference of treatment is that this is not contemplated as liability on any *obligatio* incurred by the slave. It is the slave himself who is liable and on whom the injured person will claim to wreak his vengeance. The rules date from a time when vengeance was regarded as the legal remedy for delicts, and the master's payment is not thought of as a liability of his, but rather as a right. He may, if he will, save the slave for himself, by paying a ransom for him. In course of time the rules come to be regarded as expressing alternative liabilities of the master: he may pay or surrender the slave,

[1] Gai. 3. 104.

and indeed texts are not wanting in which the payment is stated as the primary liability and surrender as a facultative mode of release from this liability[1]. But this conception, though it may be said to represent roughly the classical law, is a complete reversal of the original conception of the liability.

Noxal liability depends in some cases on a statute, such as the XII Tables or the *lex* Aquilia, in others on the Edict, as in the cases of *Rapina* and *Iniuria*. It follows from this that its principles are not necessarily uniform. Where it is based on a statute, the exact words of that statute have to be interpreted and applied. Thus we know that in *furtum* a *bona fide possessor* is liable for the delict of the slave, and therefore has no action against the *dominus* for any theft committed by the slave against him. Further we are told that an owner is not liable for a theft by a fugitive slave[2]. All this appears to be the result of interpretation by the jurists. They conceived the liability as resulting not so much from ownership of the slave as from control over him, which they call *potestas*, using the word here to mean physical power, irrespective of right. There are however certain texts which lay down a different rule for the case of *damnum*. The *bona fide possessor* is not noxally liable for a *damnum* committed by the slave. On the other hand, he has a noxal action against the *dominus* for a *damnum* by the slave to his property, and a *dominus* is liable for a *damnum* by a fugitive slave[3]. It is also noticeable that no text ever speaks of *potestas* as an element, in the liability for *damnum*: it is always made to rest on *dominium*. It has therefore been suggested by Girard[4], that there is something in the language of the *lex* Aquilia which accounts for the difference, and makes the *dominus* always liable and the *bona fide possessor* never liable. Girard hazards the conjecture, and though it is only a conjecture, it is an extremely plausible one, that the lost clause dealing with noxal liability contained an emphatic reference to the *dominus* as the person liable, just as we know

[1] *Cf.* D. 9. 4. 1; D. 42. 1. 6. 1; *cf.* D. 2. 10. 2; D. 9. 4. 2. *pr.*
[2] D. 9. 4. 11, 21. 3; D. 47. 2. 17. 3.
[3] D. 9. 2. 27. 3.
[4] See Manuel (5), 681.

that the *lex* contained emphatic language limiting the right to bring the ordinary Aquilian action to the *dominus*: *actio e lege Aquilia ero competit, id est domino*[1], words which are a comment presumably on the word *herus* in the *lex*. But this opinion of Girard is by no means universally accepted.

It may be noted that a usufructuary or pledgee is never strictly speaking noxally liable. In practice, however, much the same effect is produced as if he were. For if the slave is surrendered by the *dominus*, the usufructuary or any other holder of a *ius in rem* cannot enforce his right without paying up the damages. There is also a machinery by which if an owner refuses to defend, these holders of lesser rights can be required to undertake the defence or abandon their rights[2].

The rules that there can be no noxal action where the injured party is, or becomes, the *dominus* of the wrongdoer, and that a man cannot have a noxal action for the acts of one for whom he is himself noxally liable, presumably originated in the same notion of vengeance. The injured person has, or has had, an opportunity of himself taking his vengeance. But the rules gave rise to considerable difficulties in the classical law. The typical case of difficulty would be one in which Titius has bought a slave under a mandate from Balbus, or where Balbus has transferred a slave to Titius by *mancipatio cum fiducia* as security for a debt. Here if the slave commits a delict against Titius there can be no noxal action, since Titius is at the moment owner of the wrongdoer. The solution arrived at in the classical law is that Titius can recover an indemnity, but not a penalty, in the contractual action against Balbus, unless the latter prefers to abandon any claim to the slave[3]. This in general might do rough justice, though it is easy to see that in some cases the result would be rather unfair to Titius. The mandate may have been to buy this particular slave, so that Titius is not to blame for a careless purchase, and the damage done may exceed the value of the man. It is odd however to find that the same rule survives into the Digest, in an age when Titius would not be, or ever have been, *dominus* of the man, as

[1] D. 9. 2. 11. 6. [2] D. 9. 4. 17. 1, 27. *pr.* [3] D. 13. 7. 31.

the result of the pledge or mandate, so that there would seem to be nothing to bar the ordinary noxal action. The security would be by way of *pignus*, which left the *dominium* in Balbus, and a purchase under a mandate would vest the ownership at once in the *mandator*. There are texts dealing with similar cases which suggest that this rule is left here by mere oversight, one of the not uncommon cases in which the compilers, working hastily, failed to make a correction rendered necessary by changes in the law[1].

Where a delict is committed by several persons, each is fully liable and payment by one would not release the others. This would lead to difficulty, or at least great severity, where a delict was committed by a number of a man's slaves. The Edict provides for the case in *furtum* by a rule that the *dominus* need pay only what would have been due had one freeman committed the theft[2]. The Edict said nothing about *damnum*, though the rule seems to have been gradually extended to this case. But it never applied to *iniuria*: here each slave was treated as having committed an independent wrong[3].

The death of the *dominus* does not ordinarily affect the liability, since the slave will now belong to some other person and the person noxally liable is the owner at the time the action is brought: *noxa caput sequitur*. But the death of the slave is a different matter. His death before any proceedings are brought of course ends the whole liability. After *condemnatio*, which is, as always, for a sum of money, the surrender has ceased to be an alternative liability, or so near an alternative as it was: it has become no more than a facultative mode of discharge, and it is generally held that, at least in Justinian's law, death at that stage in no way releases the owner. But there is, strangely enough, no real authority on the point. From the text of Gaius, coupled with the Autun commentary, recently discovered, it seems to be clear that, in the classical law, surrender of the body or of a recognisable part of it would discharge, the death being proved either by what

[1] D. 13. 6. 22. [2] D. 9. 4. 31. [3] D. 47. 10. 34.

was surrendered or by other evidence. As to death of the slave between *litis contestatio* and *condemnatio*, it is commonly held that the rule was the same: in classical law the corpse or part of it might be surrendered, and in Justinian's law the death was no discharge.

Upon these rules the question has been raised, which is hinted at above, whether noxal obligation is a case of alternative obligation. The better view seems to be that it is in fact *sui generis*: it is not alternative before *litis contestatio*, since, if it were, death of the man, creating impossibility of one alternative (surrender), would not release from the other. It was very like an alternative obligation after *litis contestatio*, but not quite the same. In a true alternative obligation the *condemnatio* would be for the value of the creditor's right, and thus would not exceed the value of the slave, while here it would be the delictal penalty, whether more or less.

If a slave has committed several wrongs, the master is released by delivering him under the first judgment. But *noxa caput sequitur*, the new holder will be liable to the other injured persons in the same way, so that the last of several plaintiffs will keep the slave, since all the others in turn will be noxally liable.

It may be said in conclusion that the right of surrender depends on non-complicity in the master. Complications too numerous to be considered here result from the facts that different statutes may have different rules, that there are different degrees of complicity, and that a slave is sometimes excused if he obeys his master and sometimes is not.

CHAPTER VIII

THE LAW OF ACTIONS

144. THE law of actions is, at least from a modern point of view, the law of procedure, using that expression however in a wide sense, to include on the one hand, the law of actions, properly so-called, *i.e.*, the law which determines what is in any given circumstances the appropriate action or other remedy, and on the other hand the law of procedure, properly so-called, *i.e.*, the law which states the steps which anyone who has a claim against another person, or who thinks that he has, may take in order that a judicial tribunal may decide upon the merits of his claim, and put him in a position to enforce it. This is a fair account of the matter from the classical and later point of view, but it must not be forgotten that earlier law does not always regard decisions by a public tribunal as essential to the conception of an *actio*, and that there are many traces of regulated self-help even in the pages of Gaius. To this matter we shall recur, but there is another, and for our purpose more important, flaw in our description, regarded as a description of the subject of the Roman law of actions.

Both Gaius and Justinian start evidently from the point of view of procedure, of purely adjective law, but they do not adhere to it at all closely. A very brief study of the *ius quod ad actiones pertinet* will shew that much of what must be called substantive law is discussed therein and not elsewhere in the Institutes. Thus the whole of the law which has been considered in the closing pages of the last chapter, upon the liability of a *paterfamilias* on the contracts and the delicts of subordinate members of the *familia*, is discussed in the law of actions, and what little is said of purely possessory rights, as apart from remedies, is said here, in connexion with these remedies. This last fact is not indeed surprising, for, as we have already seen, the right of *possessio, per se,* consists of nothing but the right to these remedies: it has only a procedural content. The other case does indeed constitute a real difficulty in regarding the *ius rerum* as the law dealing with all rights which have a money value, but in view of the close affinity already pointed out between *obligatio* and *actio* and of the fact that both these sets of rights are marked by a strongly specialised form of procedure, it is not very surprising that they have been attracted to this topic. The Roman lawyers were not in possession of a developed theory of representation or agency, such as exists in our law, and would make such a treatment of the subject hardly possible with us. This way of handling the matter is in fact one more expression of the difficulty the Romans always feel in admitting that an *obligatio* incurred by *A* can by any possibility bind *B,* whatever be the relation between *A* and *B.*

It is also worthy of note that Gaius introduces the rules of these types of *obligatio* not as independent subjects of discussion but as illustrations of certain types of action which he is explaining from the point of view of procedure, so that it may well be that it is only for convenience, and to avoid repetitions, that he discusses them in detail here, instead of handling their substantive characteristics in connexion with the law of *obligationes,* where the matter more properly belongs, and their procedural aspect here. As to Justinian, he merely follows Gaius. But the method adopted is no doubt facilitated by the inveterate habit of confusing the action regarded as a series of procedural steps, with the action regarded as the right to take those steps, a confusion which we find difficult to avoid in ordinary speech, and which is at the bottom of the observed affinity between *obligatio* and *actio.*

145. The coordination of the law of actions with the law of persons and the law of things as a third element in the law is the feature of the institutional arrangement which has met with the most hostile criticism. It may be said to have no friends. Some of the criticism however rests on mere misunderstanding. Thus it is impossible to lay much stress on Austin's somewhat severe criticism[1], because it is perfectly clear that he misconceived the nature of the Roman system. The Roman law of persons bears little resemblance to his, at least as the latter is stated in his text, though in one of the scattered notes[2], which are printed in the current edition of his lectures, he describes shortly a law of persons which is in fact that of the Romans, though he blames them for not adopting it, while, on the other hand, it is very different from that which he supports in his text itself. It is difficult to say what part of the law of actions would be suitably placed as a subhead of the *ius personarum* as it really is. The point however that these rules of adjective law should be subordinated to, not coordinated with, the substantive rules they fortify is in itself clearly sound. But if the view is accepted which has already been set forth in these pages, that the law of persons was not a statement of rights but a descriptive chapter, shewing the different kinds of person known to the law, and the law of substantive rights is really the *ius rerum*, then the actual position of the *ius actionum* as an appendix to it is justified, and the treatment of it as a new *genus* sinks to the level of a logical error without effect on the actual treatment. It has been shewn by modern writers (most comprehensively by Professor Goudy[3]), that in the effort to find a triad, the Romans are constantly led into this error. In any case few will dispute Maine's proposition that the author of this arrangement, whoever he was, achieved a great feat of abstraction[4].

It is of course said, with justice, that the whole institutional scheme is defective, that it would have been far better to base the arrangement absolutely on rights or perhaps duties. But the classical lawyers were only gradually attaining the

[1] Austin, Jurisprudence, 2. 750. [2] *op. cit.* 762.

[3] Goudy, Trichotomy in Roman Law.

[4] Maine, Early Law and Custom, 367.

clear cut conception of a right which we possess, and in the conditions which existed, the arrangement under the heads of the persons who can be affected, the elements of wealth which the law will protect for them and the means by which this is done, seems to merit Gibbon's remark that it is "no contemptible method[1]."

146. The *legis actio* was a topic of almost purely historical interest even in the time of Gaius, and a discussion of the countless historical doubts and difficulties which it suggests is not within the scope of these chapters. Space must however be found for discussion of a few points, mostly of a general character, which are significant for the later law.

We commonly speak of five *legis actiones*, but this does not quite accurately represent the language of Gaius. He tells us that there were five ways of proceeding by *legis actio*. Any *legis actio* had to be cast in one of five modes. Of these five, three were "actions" in the modern sense, *i.e.*, forms in which disputes were submitted to a court for decision, cases of actual litigation. The other two do not, at least at first sight, look much like litigation, but seem rather to be modes of actual enforcement of a claim. The question therefore suggests itself how these two, *manus iniectio* and *pignoris capio*, come to be grouped with the others which are so different in character. A sufficient answer might seem to be that they are all formal statutory processes for the enforcement of a right, involving the use of *certa verba*, *i.e.*, strict forms of words prescribed by law, and that, so far as is known, no other proceedings came within this definition. Another answer is however not uncommonly given to this question. It is said that these two are grouped with the others because, though they do not necessarily involve litigation, yet the proceeding may be, or may lead to, litigation. The *manus iniectio* may be met by a *vindex*. The seizure in *pignoris capio* may well lead to litigation. This however could hardly be, as is sometimes said, an action by the debtor to recover the thing, for in such an action the rôles would be

[1] Gibbon, Decl. and Fall of Roman Emp. ch. 44.

inverted, and the person whose property had been seized would be the *actor*. Moreover the action would presumably be the ordinary action for the recovery of property, the *sacramentum*, which has already appeared in the list. It is of course possible that the supposed action may have been set going by a protest *in iure* after the seizure, so that the debtor would still be the defendant[1]. But there is no evidence for this, and as such a protest would certainly be in *certa verba* it is hardly possible for Gaius to have been absolutely silent about the matter. Accordingly the ingenious suggestion has been made that the action was of another kind: it is said that the person who had seized the thing could bring an action to compel the debtor to redeem the pledge[2]. For this action, the only direct piece of evidence is a passage from Cicero[3] in which the *publicanus* is spoken of as a *petitor*, and a *petitor* is a person who makes a claim. But the passage makes no other reference to any such action, though the discussion is a lengthy one. In fact the passage is written of tax-farmers in the provinces, in many of which there never could have been any *pignoris capio*. It may be that *pignoris capio* or a proceeding modelled on it still existed in certain parts, but the very passage speaks of him as *petitor aut*[4] *pignorator*, implying that he has in some places an action, in other a right to seize. Moreover we shall see shortly that there is some evidence that in *pignoris capio* there was no right of action.

It is worthy of notice that Gaius in discussing *manus iniectio* says hardly anything of the potential litigation, which would be between the *vindex* and the seizer, so that it cannot be the *legis actio*, since the debtor is no party to it, and in relation to *pignoris capio* says absolutely nothing at all about it. This is somewhat difficult to reconcile with the view that it was this possibility of litigation which caused it to be grouped with the other *legis actiones*. Further difficulty is created for any form of this view by the fact that Gaius mentions doubt as to whether it was a *legis actio* or not, as

[1] Sohm, Institutes, § 48.

[2] Ihering, Geist des Röm. R. § 14.

[3] *In Verrem*, Act. 2. 3. 11. 27.

[4] *Ac* has good *Ms.* authority.

having occurred to some lawyers, but does not say anything of its potential litigious character as having any bearing on the question. He discusses the reasons for the doubt, and one would have thought that if this was the decisive point it must have been mentioned. But no great weight can be attached to his speculations as to historical origins.

The known cases of application of *pignoris capio* all give the impression that this remedy is applied precisely where there is no action, but public or religious considerations make some remedy necessary. There is no juristic relation between the soldier and those who have to provide his pay and various allowances. Their duty is to the State: his right is against the State. They are under no direct obligation to him. In the same way the taxes are not due to the *publicanus*: they are due to the State. And even if the proceeding be between the debtor and the State itself, as might in some instances have been the case, litigation with a subject is not the way in which an ancient government enforces its rights[1]. And informal selling and hiring gave no right of action in early law. This way of looking at the matter is strongly confirmed by an examination of the curious form of the *actio fictitia* which Gaius mentions as given to the *publicanus* after the decay of *pignoris capio*. That a fictitious action was needed at all shews that he had no action unless he had seized: its actual form goes far towards shewing that he had none after seizure. If he had had an action at civil law all that would have been necessary would have been an ordinary formula in *dare oportere*, with the fiction in the *intentio, si pignus captum fuisset*. The clumsy way in which it is actually put, together with the avoidance of the word *oportere*, and the use of the unique form *luere debere*, seem to point to the fact that under the old system there had been no actionable *obligatio*.

Though to us and even to Gaius the typical case of *manus iniectio* is that under a judgment, it must not be forgotten that this is not the original case. The process dates from a time when the State neither heard disputes nor enforced decisions.

[1] See Poste, Gaius, 470.

Manus iniectio for that epoch is better described as the machinery by which the State permitted a man to enforce his own rights. Even after judgment has become an ordinary part of the legal machinery, it is still incorrect to look upon *manus iniectio iudicati* as the principal type. As was long ago pointed out, an ancient Roman would hardly have said that a *confessus* was as fully liable as one against whom there was a judgment. That is indeed the way in which the classical lawyers state the matter[1], but since a judgment of the *unus iudex* was after all only the opinion of a private citizen, the ancients would have stated the matter the other way: a *iudicatus* is as fully liable as one who has acknowledged his debt.

The case of *Confessio* is one which creates some difficulty. The XII Tables tell us that *manus iniectio* lies for *aes confessum* and for *res iudicatae*. There has been much discussion as to the exact nature and scope of this *confessio*. The obvious suggestion is that it means a formal acknowledgment of indebtedness, *in iure*. The fact however that, as we have seen, for classical writers at least, a *confessus in iure* is put on the level of a *iudicatus—confessus pro iudicato habetur*—has led commentators to the opinion that it must mean something other than what we hear of later as *confessio in iure*. The view has even been maintained that as the XII Tables do not, so far as we know them, give *manus iniectio* in case of *nexum*, while there are many literary texts which hardly admit of any doubt but that *manus iniectio* was available in this case, the reference is to money borrowed on *nexum*. But the language of Aulus Gellius[2], with which he introduces this text of the XII Tables, leaves no doubt that it is of *confessio* in the ordinary sense of which he is speaking, and we have seen that there is no warrant for carrying back this equiparation of *confessio* and judgment to the XII Tables. It is highly probable that besides the *manus iniectio iudicati*, *pro iudicato* and *pura* which we know, there was also a *m. i. damnati* of which the cases of *nexum* and *sponsio* were no doubt the earliest applications.

Aes confessum refers obviously to cases of obligation and of

[1] Paul, *Sent.* 5. 5 a. 2.

[2] Aulus Gellius, *Noctes Atticae*, xv. 13. 11.

certa pecunia. This fact has recently attracted attention. All the texts which speak of *confessio* deal with it in terms which suggest that the case is one of *obligatio,* in fact a case of money debt. No text speaks of *confessio* and its results in connexion with an *actio in rem.* It may be remembered that, so far at least as is known, a *legis actio in rem* must have been by *sacramentum,* and the fact that there is no hint of *confessio in iure* in such cases has been thought[1] to turn on the notion that the whole conception of *legis actio per sacramentum* implies that each side carries out his part in the ceremonial. If there is no formal defence, no counter *vindicatio,* there is no *legis actio.* This is indeed the impression which would be gathered from the account of the matter given by Gaius. The result would not differ greatly from the effect of a judgment, though there would technically be none. The magistrate would *vindicias dicere* in favour of the claimant, who would thus get possession of the property in dispute, and this would be substantially all that he wanted. It is true that the former defendant could still sue as plaintiff, since there had been no judgment or its equivalent, but it is hardly conceivable that he would voluntarily adopt a course of conduct which would shift the burden of making out a title on to his shoulders, if he actually had a case.

It is clear that the formal statements in the surviving texts do not exhaust the cases to which *manus iniectio* applied, but any attempt to make the list complete soon becomes no more than conjecture. Three notions are found very closely connected in the texts: liability to *manus iniectio,* liability to double damages in case of denial, and the use, in a statute or transaction, of the words *damnas esto.* How close this association is cannot be made out with certainty. It is held very widely but not unanimously that wherever this liability to *condemnatio in duplum* in case of denial exists in early law, the remedy of *manus iniectio* is available, and that this turns on the use of the expression *damnas esto* or the like, either by the parties or in the statute creating the liability. We have

[1] Wlassak, Zeitschrift der Sav. Stiftung, 25. 117 *sqq.*

already mentioned the controversies on this point in connexion with *Nexum*[1].

147. It is unnecessary to transcribe here the form of *Sacramentum* as described by Gaius, and early history is not within our scope. But it may be worth while to point out that this is *Sacramentum* in its latest form. The account given by Cicero[2] shews a transition from an earlier stage in which, at least in the case of land, the *manus consertio* was performed on the land itself, not in court. It is generally held that the name is due to an earlier stage in which there was an actual oath of which the falsity was penalised by a money offering (though there is another view, that the offering is not for falsity, but for removing the matter from the arbitrament of the gods), and it has been suggested that the postponement of the appointment of a *iudex* for thirty days, under the *lex* Pinaria, was associated with this secularisation: it was no longer necessary to settle promptly the question before the gods, and it was desirable to give the parties time to come to terms[3].

The information which we have as to *Iudicis arbitrive postulatio* is so scanty that anything which is said about it has little claim to be considered as more than conjecture. It is probable, but no more, that it was introduced to remove from the field of *sacramentum* complex issues which did not lend themselves to a simple yes or no, and it is possible, but no more, that it was the germ of the later *bonae fidei iudicia*. But some doubt on this point is justified by the fact that Gaius seems to say that a *iure civili* claim for a certain sum of money was recoverable by *iudicis postulatio*.

The last of the modes of *legis actio* to be introduced was *Condictio*, an action for the recovery of certain sums or quantities, evidently introduced as a remedy applicable to the contract of *stipulatio*, which it is probable had at first no wider scope. It appears to have involved, at least in the case of *condictio e lege* Silia, *i.e.*, for *pecunia certa*, a *sponsio* and

[1] *Ante*, § 105. [2] *Pro Murena*, 12. 26. [3] Eisele, Beiträge, 222.

restipulatio for one-third of the amount in dispute, which went to the winner by way of penalty, and according to some writers something of the same kind occurred in *condictio e lege* Calpurnia, *i.e.*, for *certa res*. But for this extension there seems to be no evidence. Even for the original proposition the evidence is not of the best. It rests on the fact that we know from Cicero and Gaius that there was such a *sponsio* in the *actio certae pecuniae creditae* under the formulary system. Gaius appears to treat it as optional. As it is called *Sponsio legitimae partis* it is inferred that it rests on a *lex* and that this is the *lex* Silia. But all this is rather uncertain.

Gaius remarks that in his day there was doubt as to the reason for the introduction of this action and himself offers no solution, observing that the *actio sacramenti* and *iudicis postulatio* would serve the purpose. Various suggestions have been made, though they are no more than guesses. It has indeed the advantage that where there is a penal sum, this goes to the winner and not to the State, and no doubt it is simpler than *sacramentum* though the complications in the *actio sacramenti in personam* do not seem to have been great. It may be that it was the first action in which the plaintiff could offer an oath to the defendant. It may however be no more than the introduction of a new remedy in connexion with a new contract[1].

But *Condictio* is more than the last of the *legis actiones* to appear: it is the beginning of the transition to the *Formula*. The story of the transition is not fully known: the proceedings called *Sponsiones* play an important part, and their effect can be gathered from Gaius. Here it suffices to say that by making a bet on the issue by *stipulatio* and counter-*stipulatio* and suing on the bet, any question of right whatever may be reduced to a claim for a specific sum of money, triable by *condictio*. The decision on the bet did not in point of form decide the main issue, and we know too little about the time at which the change took place to say whether there was any formal validity in this decision, to bar a further real action, or whether it was still

[1] See as to these points, Girard, Manuel (5), 992.

possible for the other party to bring his action. But at any rate in real actions the method was effective. The *actio per sponsionem* survived up to the time of Gaius, though a *formula* raising the real issue directly, *formula petitoria*, had been introduced as an alternative long before, probably at latest by the time of Cicero, and probably not much earlier, not long after the recognition of the formulary system. It does not appear however that these actions played any part in the application of the *formula* to personal actions, indeed so far as we have gone there has been no transition: the development of the *formula* out of the *legis actio per condictionem* is still to be explained. But that consists chiefly in the substitution of written for spoken instructions, an idea which would naturally appear when writing became general, and which is said to have been first used in the recuperatory procedure. Into the question of its remoter origin we need not enter.

148. We are told by Gaius that the *legis actio* was superseded and the *formula* established as the normal procedure by the joint operation of the *lex* Aebutia, and the *leges* Iuliae, but beyond this elementary fact there is very little agreement as to the history of the matter. As to the date of the *lex* Aebutia, opinions have differed to the extent of at least a century, but it is now very generally held that it must be put somewhere about B.C. 140[1]. As to its effect it is most generally held that it authorised the *formula* generally as an alternative to the *legis actio*, and that the *leges* Iuliae, about a century later, made it compulsory in most cases. The *lex* Aebutia did not of course invent the *formula*, and, as in the *legis actio per condictionem* there does not seem to have been any formal statement of the issue *in iure*, it is quite conceivable that the Praetor may have used forms of his own devising and issued them in writing. Moreover, though most of the *legis actiones* are heard of after the *lex* Aebutia, this does not seem to be the case with *condictio*, and it has therefore been supposed that the *lex* Aebutia made the formula compulsory for cases of this

[1] See Girard, Manuel (5), 998.

kind, whether it did or did not permit them as alternatives in the other cases. On this view the last of the modes of *legis actio* to appear would be the first to disappear, and this after a relatively short existence, a consideration which is sometimes treated as excluding this view. It may however be urged that it is just the transitional institution which will be the first to go, when it has served its purpose. The view that the *lex* Aebutia did not authorise the *formula* in other cases is held to be negatived by the statement of Cicero, speaking certainly before the passing of the *leges* Iuliae, that *formulae* were available in all manner of cases, and, though this may be held to leave it uncertain whether there was or was not an express authorisation in the *lex*, it seems to be clear that *formulae* were in general use in his time[1].

149. The name *Condictio* survives into the classical law, but with a changed meaning. The jurists use it to denote an action of which the fundamental notion seems to be the readjustment of relations in cases in which one person has become unjustly enriched at the expense of another. The most obvious instance is the *condictio indebiti*. There is a tendency to regard *condictio* as a term equivalent to *strictum iudicium*, or as Justinian calls it *stricti iuris actio*, but in fact not every such action is a *condictio*: the name is not for example applied to an action on a *stipulatio* for an *incertum*. The proper name here is the *actio ex stipulatu*. It must be remembered that there is only one action called *condictio*: it is a general action with a great number of applications. Its special feature in point of form is that the *intentio* does not set forth the *causa* which gives rise to indebtedness. If, for instance, a plaintiff is suing on a loan of money the *intentio* does not refer to the loan: it runs "*Si paret Numerium Negidium Aulo Agerio decem dare oportere*," while, if the basis of the action had been a *stipulatio* for an *incertum*, the *intentio* would have contained the words *ex stipulatu*. The way in which the *iudex* was informed as to the exact nature of the transaction which had been brought

[1] Wlassak, Prozessgesetze, 1. § 6.

into issue is not certainly known. It can hardly have been by a *praescriptio*, for Cicero's language shews that it was not in the *formula*[1]: it must have been in some way, otherwise the judge would have had a roving commission to try any issue raising such a debt, or rather all issues raising such a debt which might have existed between the parties.

There is little or no doubt that under the formulary system the name *condictio* was first applied to claims of a certain amount of money under a *iure civili* obligation, *i.e.*, in just the field of *condictio e lege* Silia. But the name *condictio* for this type of action cannot be found earlier than the great jurists[2]. Cicero knows nothing of it. In his time the action has, as we shall see, a different name. This rather suggests that, notwithstanding the absence of reference, which has been mentioned, the *legis actio per condictionem* did not finally disappear till the *leges* Iuliae, and the new use then became possible without risk of confusion.

The Sources give us what look like classifications of *condictiones*. These break into two classes. One set of distinctions turns on the nature of the object to be recovered. From this point of view we get *condictio certae pecuniae, condictio certi, incerti, triticaria*. Another set of distinctions turns on the nature of the facts which have given rise to the claim. From this point of view we have *condictio furtiva, indebiti, ob rem dati, ex lege, ex poenitentia* and others. It must however be clearly borne in mind that in neither case is this a list of different actions: it is a list of different applications of the same action. Into the many and acute controversies which have existed, and still do exist, as to these various classifications it is not possible for us to enter, but a few remarks may be useful.

The expression *condictio* is found in several of the classical texts, in the sense of, as Gaius puts it, an action in which the *intentio* is in the form *dare fierive oportere*. And some of the distinctions based on the facts which give rise to the *condictio*

[1] *Pro Q. Roscio* 4. 11; Girard, Manuel (5), 613.

[2] As to the terminology, see Lenel, Ed. Perp. (2) 227 *sqq*.

are also represented in these texts, but of the distinctions involved in the epithets *certi*, *incerti*, *triticaria* and the like the classical texts contain no trace. *Condictio certi*, *incerti*, *triticaria* occur only rarely in the Digest, and it is maintained that every text in which any of these occurs shews clear signs of interpolation[1]. There is thus room for much doubt as to what the classical terminology really was. Some of the texts in the Digest shew a tendency to confine the name *condictio certi* to actions for *certa pecunia*[2], of which the original name was certainly *actio certae pecuniae creditae*. This fact together with the language of Gaius has led to the view that when the name *condictio* began to be applied to these claims for a *certum* there were the two names *condictio certae pecuniae* and *condictio certae rei*, which last has acquired in later law the name *condictio triticaria*. On the other hand it is now generally agreed that the rubric in the Edict "*si certum petetur*" covered both *certa res* and *certa pecunia*, and thus both these actions would be covered by the expression *condictio certi*, of which these two actions would be varieties. It may still be doubted whether any of these names were actually in use in classical times. The *condictio* for *certa res* has two forms, that for a specific thing, and that for a specific quantity, to which last alone the expression *condictio triticaria* can properly belong, though even for this application, it is of late post-classical law. The *formulae* for all these cases were no doubt set forth in the Edict. They would all be in the form, *dare* (*facere*) *oportere*, but there were obvious inevitable differences, so that there was in all probability a model for each. It is this fact which accounts for the acquisition of specific labels for each action, either from the compilers or, as is at least possible, from earlier but post-classical authorities, since there is no reason to suppose that terminology was at a standstill from the time of Ulpian to that of Tribonian.

The notion of the so-called *condictio incerti* presents many difficulties. The action itself is of late introduction, though not post-classical: the name is probably much later still[3]. As a

[1] Lenel, *loc. cit.* [2] D. 46. 2. 12. [3] Lenel, Ed. Perp. (2) 151.

stipulation for an *incertum* or for a service is guaranteed by the *actio ex stipulatu*, which is not a *condictio*, and certainly states, in the *intentio*, the *causa*, the field of *condictio incerti* is somewhat narrowed. Girard cites however several illustrations from the texts. A vendor, transferring a piece of land, has by error omitted to reserve a servitude which has been agreed on: a *condictio incerti* lies to have this servitude created. There is a *condictio incerti* to obtain release from an obligation undertaken under a mistaken belief that there was a legal duty to undertake it. A *condictio incerti* lies to recover what has been given by way of *precarium*. Where by oversight a legacy has been paid without security for the possibility of a Falcidian deduction, a *condictio incerti* lies to have this security given[1]. As to the formulation of this action, Lenel[2] is of opinion that owing to its late introduction no model of it was set forth in the Edict. He considers that, like the *condictio triticaria*, it sets out in the *intentio* the specific render or service which is claimed, and states the duty as "*facere oportere*," but like other *condictiones* does not state the *causa*. Another view is that the nature of the render was stated in a *praescriptio*, and the duty stated as "*dare facere oportere*." The former view is now the most widely held, but it may be noted that there is so far as we know, no other action in which the duty is expressed as "*facere*" without "*dare*."

The other grouping or classification of *condictiones*, according to the facts which have given rise to the claim, presents but little interest. As the *intentio* says nothing about the *causa*, this classification is without importance in the matter of formulation, and the names or labels are mere matter of convenience. Some of them are certainly classical. Gaius mentions *condictio furtiva* and *condictio indebiti*. For others we must go to the Digest. Some of those there mentioned, such as the *condictio ex lege* and that *ex poenitentia*, are almost certainly not classical, and the oddly named *condictio causa data*

[1] Girard, Manuel (5), 616; D. 12. 6. 22. 1; D. 19. 1. 5. 1; D. 12. 7. 3; D. 43. 26. 19. 2; D. 35. 3. 3. 10.

[2] Lenel, *loc. cit.*

causa non secuta is pure compilers' work. This name indeed seems to have little or no utility, in view of the existence of *condictio ob rem dati* or *ob causam datorum*, which are probably classical and of *condictio sine causa*, which may be. While this multiplication of names may have been convenient in practice, it has the great disadvantage that it tends to obscure the important fact that *condictio* is only one *actio* and not several.

A text attributed to Ulpian[1], but in its present form largely due to the compilers, speaks of a certain *condictio certi* which is available wherever a *certum* is due on any kind of obligation. To this *condictio* the name *condictio generalis* has been given. Moreover there is a text in the Institutes which tells us that a *condictio* is available as a substitute for the *actio quod iussu* or *institoria* or *exercitoria* or *de in rem verso, i.e.*, for all those actions *in solidum* on the contract of a subordinate member of the family. This has been supposed to refer to the same *condictio*. But the conception here is even wider, for it is evident that the claim under most of these actions would frequently be for an *incertum*. These conceptions involve a great widening of the notion of *condictio*, for it seems to be immaterial whether the obligation is *stricti iuris* or *bonae fidei*, civil or praetorian. These texts seem to provide a single remedy for nearly all obligations, not delictal, under the name of *condictio*, and the language of the Institutes is hardly that which would suggest an innovation. But the nature and scope of the action, and even its existence, are the subject of a mass of controversy into which we cannot enter. It is hopeless to look for a consistent theory of *condictio* in the Digest.

150. The main difference between the Formulary system and that which it superseded is the familiar one that the proceeding depended on *concepta verba*, as opposed to the old *certa verba*. The issue between the parties is now raised, not in a stereotyped form of words, but in a form chosen by the parties in which it can conveniently be stated. The function of the

[1] D. 12. 1. 9. *pr.*

magistrate is therefore somewhat more active, if not more important, than under the old system. The Praetor states in his Edict a number of *formulae*, models which the parties can vary as they find necessary, not of course at their absolute discretion. They cannot alter the main juridical structure of the *formula*, but as the statements of fact in the model *formula* will not be the same as theirs they can vary the statement accordingly. The *formula* is issued under the authority of the Praetor and is thus, so to speak, settled by conference between the parties and the magistrate. It is not indeed his duty to see that the *formula* states correctly the issue between the parties. That is their affair. All that he has to do, in ordinary cases, is to see that it does state a real issue of law and fact, or in some cases, of fact, satisfying himself in this last case that the facts alleged are such as to justify the delivery of the *formula in factum*. It may however be believed that in dealing with unlearned and insufficiently represented litigants he might on occasion be a good deal more helpful.

The construction of the *formula* is in its general outlines well known, but there are few parts of it which do not give rise to questions which in the present and all probable states of our knowledge are not readily answerable. As has been said by Lenel, our real knowledge of the detailed structure of the *formula* is almost negligible. Thus, to take some illustrations, we do not know the relation of the *praescriptio pro actore* and the *demonstratio*, when they could occur together, or when one was applicable and when the other. We do not know when a *taxatio* was available or when an *arbitrium* clause might be inserted. We do not know with certainty when an *exceptio* was expressed in a *bonae fidei iudicium*. Of course many of these questions can be answered by actual texts for specific cases, but these are not numerous enough to give us a real principle. Accordingly there are very divergent opinions, and as it does not seem possible to judge between them, and the general notion of the *formula* can be made out without answering these questions, it seems best to leave them on one side.

A few remarks however on the more important parts of the *formula* may be useful.

The *Demonstratio* is mentioned by Gaius as one of the principal parts of the *formula*. It is found in the *formula* of, at any rate, nearly all personal actions for an *incertum*, and is in form a short statement of the transaction on which the claim rests, acting as a guide to the *iudex*. It need not necessarily state the wrong, but rather the facts which constitute the legal relation in which it is alleged that the wrong was done. The words "*ob eam rem*" in the *intentio* refer back to it, and the statement of the facts in the *demonstratio*, rather than in the *intentio*, enables the case to be more simply stated, though it is not logically necessary. It also has other advantages. Thus it avoids certain risks involved in *plus* and *minus petitio*. The *demonstratio* is sometimes described as a statement of the admitted facts. No doubt it frequently was no more. But it must not be supposed that the statements in the *demonstratio* were presumed to be true. Though it alleged a sale, the sale had still to be proved unless the defendant admitted it. Though Gaius speaks of it as a principal part, it is not important in the sense of being a critical part. Errors in it could be put right in *iudicio*—*falsa demonstratio non nocet*—a proposition of much wider application, but justified even here where the word is used with a technical meaning. *Plus petitio* or *minus petitio* in the *demonstratio* could be amended. We can learn from Gaius that there were certain limits on this power of amendment, and, in particular, that in actions in which condemnation involved *infamia* an excessive *demonstratio* would, in the opinion of some writers, cause loss of the action. What his own opinion on the matter was we do not know, owing to the fact that the essential passage is illegible. We can see however that if the transaction is completely misdescribed in the *demonstratio*, there is no valid *iudicium*: the whole formula is a nullity, and the action can be brought again. The real *res* has not been brought into issue, since the *intentio* refers expressly to the *res* stated in the *demonstratio*. Thus the importance of the *demonstratio* lies in the frequency of its occurrence, and in its usefulness as a guide to the *iudex.*

151. The *Intentio,* on the other hand, is the most important and critical part of the *formula.* It states the exact issue to the *iudex*, and by it the claim must stand or fall. Any error in it may be fatal, for there is no power of amendment of the *intentio* after the *formula* is issued[1]. Not only may the action be lost on account of error in the claim, on well known principles, but as the *res* has been brought into issue, there can be no further claim. Accordingly the *intentio* is drawn with extreme care and precision. A glance at a properly drawn *intentio* will shew at once whether the action is *in rem* or *in personam*, a *strictum iudicium* or one *bonae fidei*, whether it is for a *certum* or an *incertum*, whether it is *in factum* or *in ius*, each type having its technical words in which to state the hypothesis which is to be submitted to the *iudex.* We can gather in the pages of Gaius a good many models of such forms. In these specimen formulae the plaintiff appears as Aulus Agerius, a name constructed out of the word *actor*, the man who *agit, i.e.* brings the action, and the defendant as Numerius Negidius, the man who *negat, i.e.* who denies the claim.

If the action is *in rem,* the hypothesis stated is of a right in the plaintiff, with no mention of the defendant, the words being in fact adapted from the words of claim in the *legis actio per sacramentum, in rem.* Thus if ownership is claimed, the *intentio* runs somewhat as follows: *si paret fundum Cornelianum, de quo agitur, Auli Agerii ex iure Quiritium esse.* If it is a claim to a right of way it will run: *si paret Aulo Agerio ius esse eundi per fundum Cornelianum.* If it is an action on *obligatio,* it necessarily expresses the relation between the two parties and thus both their names appear in the *intentio.* The legal obligation will be expressed by the word *oportere,* which again is the word used in the *legis actio* to express an actionable obligation. But as there are many varieties and sources

[1] But see *post*, § 159.

of *obligatio*, there are many variations in the form of an *intentio* of an action *in personam* formulated *in ius*. If the case is one of *stricti iuris* obligation for a *certum*, the *intentio* will run "*si paret...dare oportere*." Thus in *condictio certi* it will be "*si paret Numerium Negidium Aulo Agerio decem dare oportere*," or "*hominem Stichum dare oportere*." In the case of *condictio incerti* we are rather in the dark, for the action is not a common one, and, as a class, is not mentioned in the classical texts. There may have been a *praescriptio* stating the transaction concerned, and then an *intentio*: "*quicquid paret ob eam rem Nm. Nm. Ao. Ao. dare facere oportere*," but the different form preferred by Lenel has already been mentioned. In *bonae fidei* actions, which are always for an *incertum*, the words *ex fide bona* appear in the *intentio*, so that it runs "*Quicquid paret ob eam rem Nm. Nm. Ao. Ao. ex fide bona dare facere oportere*," the reference being to the *causa* already stated in the *demonstratio*. In at least some cases of delict, the obligation is stated as being "*damnum decidere oportere*." In what, if in any, *intentiones* it is stated as "*praestare oportere*" is much disputed[1]. There are many cases much more complex, notably where the action is brought against a surety, in the divisory actions, in the *actio ad exhibendum*, and in some others to which we shall have to recur.

152. The *Exceptio* does not figure in the list of ordinary or principal parts of the *formula*, given by Gaius. It is indeed secondary in the sense that there is no type of action which will necessarily have an *exceptio* in its *formula*: the *exceptio* occurs only in special circumstances. But it plays such an important part in actual litigation that no excuse is needed for considering it here. It may be defined as a counter hypothesis, in the event of the truth of which the *iudex* is instructed not to condemn, even though the allegations in the *intentio* are proved as a matter of strict law. It does not deny the *prima facie* claim, but alleges collateral circumstances which make it the duty of

[1] Lenel (Ed. Perp. (2), pp. 202, 205, 260, 287) finds it in the divisory actions and in *pro socio*. Others find it in most of the *actiones adiectitiae qualitatis*.

the *iudex* to absolve the defendant. The contract was made, but it was induced by fraud (*exceptio doli*); the liability was incurred, but the other party had agreed not to sue (*exceptio pacti conventi*); the gift was promised, but it exceeded the amount allowed by law (*exceptio legis* Cinciae); the money had been lent, but the borrower was to the knowledge of the lender a *filiusfamilias* (*exceptio senatusconsulti* Macedoniani), and so forth. The *exceptiones* as stated in the Edict are of course framed by the Praetor, and thus they are sometimes described as praetorian devices for introducing equitable defences which do not contradict the *intentio.* But this description needs limitation in several ways. Though *exceptiones,* like the rest of the *formula* are of praetorian design, the defences to which they give effect are not necessarily praetorian. Many of the most important, *e.g.* the *exceptio doli,* are of course praetorian, but as may be seen from the illustrations given above, some are based on *leges,* and some on *senatusconsulta.* In like manner, the defence raised by *exceptio* is not always equitable. It is clearly so in such cases as the *exceptio doli*, but there is nothing particularly equitable about the *exceptio* based on the fact that a promised gift exceeds the legal maximum. Nor does equitable character coincide with praetorian origin. There is nothing particularly equitable about the *exceptio annalis,* which is praetorian, while the *exceptio legis* Plaetoriae may perhaps be called equitable. This distinction must be borne in mind when dealing with the rule that *exceptiones* need not be expressly pleaded in *bonae fidei* actions. This cannot be shewn to be true except for equitable *exceptiones*: there is no authority for making the proposition absolutely general. It may be supposed that questions would arise as to what *exceptiones* came within this conception, though it must be admitted that the texts shew no sign of this controversy.

The *exceptio* does not deny the allegation of the *intentio,* but is a counter hypothesis, introduced by the words "*si non*" or the like, which compels the *iudex* to absolve if the *exceptio* is proved, though the *intentio* is. It may be remembered that the *exceptio non numeratae pecuniae* in the case of *mutuum* conflicts with this principle[1], since it denies the loan on which the liability depends. But this is a mere result of an express piece of legislation, without any general significance. A more serious infringement of principle is involved in the proposition that there were cases in which an *exceptio* though proved did not necessarily destroy the claim. It has been contended that where the *exceptio* is used as a means of compelling consideration of a counterclaim, it causes no more than reduction of the *condemnatio*. The point will arise in connexion with *compensatio*[2]: here it is enough to say that this view is not now generally accepted. So too, while it is clear that, in the cases in which a defendant could not be condemned beyond his means, failure to allow for this would cause only reduction, we are told in the Digest that the means of raising the point was by an *exceptio* "*quod facere potest*[3]." But the description of this as an *exceptio* dates from an age when the true *exceptio* has disappeared: in classical law it was in effect and probably in name a *taxatio*. The text in the Digest, attributed to Paul[4], which says that *exceptiones* sometimes merely reduce the condemnation, is no doubt due to the compilers, and probably has reference to this very case.

Exceptiones are classified in various ways, but only two of these classifications need be mentioned here. Some *exceptiones* are said to be "*in factum conceptae*." These of course are not set forth in the Edict. They are for the most part allegations of fact such as would justify an *exceptio doli* or *metus*: by specifying the particular facts on which the defence relies, the parties limit the task of the *iudex*. The method has the further advantage of making the defence available in cases in which, owing to the relation between the parties, it would be unseemly to bring an *exceptio doli*: for instance, where a patron is suing his *libertus*. A somewhat similar case arises where an *exceptio* is based on a *lex*. Such an *exceptio* is not expressly set forth in the Edict, but there is a general form, applicable to all such cases. It runs "*si nihil in ea re contra*

[1] *Ante*, § 117.
[2] *Post*, § 161.
[3] D. 44. 1. 7. *pr*.
[4] D. 44. 1. 22.

legem vel senatusconsultum[1] *factum sit.*" The defendant might use this, or he might specify the *lex*, or he might use an *exceptio in factum*, alleging the material facts.

Some *exceptiones* are said to be given only *causa cognita*, *i.e.* after enquiry. These *exceptiones* do not seem to have been set forth in the Edict at all. An *exceptio* stated in the Edict is available to anyone who satisfies its conditions, but these are not promised in general terms to anyone: they are in the discretion of the Praetor. The distinction is not prominent in the texts, and probably the class primarily thought of as "*causa cognita datae*" is that of *exceptiones in factum*, which, of course, would not be inserted in the *formula* until the Praetor had satisfied himself that the facts alleged in them, if proved, would constitute a ground for *exceptio doli*, or *metus* or *legis*, as the case might be. But, as we have seen, the *exceptio iusti dominii* is given only *causa cognita*, and it certainly is not *in factum*. Whether it appeared in any form in the Edict at any time is uncertain, and the same may be said of the *exceptio* given on the ground that a promise made by a freedman to his *patronus* was imposed *libertatis onerandae causa*. Of this *exceptio* too we are told that it was sometimes given only *causa cognita*. But the story of these two is very obscure. Lenel places the latter, but not the former, in the Edict[2].

153. The *Condemnatio* is always for a sum of money, and in itself is a simple matter. The *iudex*, besides deciding that the liability exists, has also to decide, where the claim is for an *incertum*, how much is due. There is no *arbitrium litis aestimandae causa*, as there was, in some cases, in the earlier procedure.

The *condemnatio* might however be associated with other subordinate clauses. Thus there might be a *taxatio*, either a fixed maximum as in the *actio iniuriarum*, or a restriction to the amount of a particular fund, as in the *actio de peculio et in rem*

[1] Lenel, Ed. Perp. (2) 492.
[2] D. 17. 1. 57; D. 44. 5. 1. 6; Lenel, *op. cit.* 492.

verso, or a limitation to the means of the defendant, if, as is most probably the case, the classical means of enforcing the so-called *beneficium competentiae* was a *taxatio*, and not, as is said in the Digest, an *exceptio*. In the three divisory actions there would be an *adiudicatio*, an instruction to the *iudex* to divide up the property in the right proportions between the contending parties: indeed it is conceivable that where the property certainly admitted of such exact division, there might be no *condemnatio* at all. Probably this would not ordinarily be possible, since expenditure of all kinds might have to be allowed for, and, apart from this, equal division might be impossible. Here, it would seem, a *condemnatio* would be needed. The *condemnatio* in these divisory actions is commented on in many texts[1].

More important is the *clausula arbitraria*, the clause by which the *iudex* was instructed, if he thought fit, to order actual restitution instead of money payment. There is much controversy as to what actions contained this clause, and on the closely allied question, as to what varieties of restitution it contemplated. Of the latter of these questions something may be said here. The most obvious case is the actual handing over of property of which the plaintiff claims to be owner, and probably at first the *arbitrium* applied only to the delivery or production of a physical thing. But the texts leave little doubt that it ultimately had a wider scope, and it may well be that it extended to any act or render which could be effected there and then, under the supervision of the *iudex*. One case is recorded in which the Edict gives the *iudex* the power, by means of this clause, to order a certain amount of thrashing to be inflicted on an offending slave, as an alternative to noxal surrender[2]. It does not appear that there was any *clausula arbitraria* in actions claiming praedial servitudes. This at least is the conclusion suggested by the texts (though modern commentators are far from agreed on the point)[3], and it is observable that the interdicts which deal with actual prevention

[1] Lenel, Ed. Perp. (2) 202.
[2] D. 47. 10. 17. 5, 6.
[3] Lenel, Ed. Perp. (2) 188.

of enjoyment of a servitude are all prohibitory, not restitutory[1]. We are told indeed that the idea of restitution is inapplicable to such things[2], and it is easy to see that in some cases it would be hard to say in what it would consist.

But the notion of restitution implies one important limitation. It always means undoing something that has been done, restoration of the *status quo ante*. That raises an interesting question. So far as the clause applied to cases on contract, and it is by no means clear how far it did apply, it only undid what had been done. It placed the parties in the position in which they would have been if the contract had not been made. Did the Roman law go any further? Did it admit the idea of what is nowadays called Specific Performance? Could the *iudex*, instead of ordering payment of damages, compel the defendant actually to carry out his contract, a thing for which damages are not always an exact equivalent? It does not seem that the *clausula arbitraria* could be used for this purpose, nor is any further progress in this direction traceable under the formulary system. It is however clear that in the later procedure, where the claim was the ground of non-delivery of a thing, the judgment need not be for damages, but might be an order for actual performance of the render, the officials of the court being directed to procure the actual obedience to the order if necessary. This is clearly laid down in the Institutes in general terms, and there are texts shewing applications of the rule in the case of legacy[3], but it is not clear how far it extended. It is hardly conceivable in cases of contract for continuous service, though in one text Justinian speaks of actual enforcement of an undertaking to serve[4]. But it is clear that in such cases a money *condemnatio* was usual[5]. There is no trace of specific performance in the texts dealing with sale. It is noticeable that in our own law it seems to have been under wills that the first steps were taken by Equity in this direction.

[1] *e.g.*, D. 43. 19. 1. 1; D. 43. 20. 1. *pr.* [2] D. 5. 3. 19. 3.
[3] C. 6. 43. 1. [4] C. 7. 45. 14. [5] D. 42. 1. 13. 1.

Limited as the *arbitrium* was in its field of application, it was still more tied down as to its mode of enforcement. The *iudex* was directed to condemn to damages if his order of restitution was not obeyed, and that is all he could do. The damages would be on a higher scale than if there had been no such order, since instead of being assessed by the *iudex* they were fixed by the plaintiff, after he had sworn that he would assess them fairly. He would certainly not make the mistake of valuing the property too low, and it is clear from the language of Paul that the obligations of this oath were neither very carefully considered by the plaintiff nor strictly enforced by authority[1]. But direct enforcement of the order does not appear to have been possible. The command is not, it must be noted, an order of the magistrate but of the *iudex*, so that there is no disobedience to the magistrate, which might call for his "*coercitio*." It is hardly indeed a command of the *iudex*, for the words of the *formula* clearly give the defendant the alternative of obeying the decree or submitting to *condemnatio*.

The *formula* lays down explicitly the duty of the *iudex*. He is either to condemn for a certain amount, or not exceeding a certain amount, or at his discretion, or he is to absolve. It may happen that he cannot make up his mind. In this case he must swear that he cannot decide, *rem non liquere*, and there will have to be a rehearing before another *iudex*[2]. If he gives a judgment in excess of his instructions, *e.g.* for more or less than the *certum*, or exceeding the *taxatio*, his decision is valid, but he is liable to the party aggrieved, as a *iudex qui litem suam facit*. But a *condemnatio* not for a specific sum is a nullity[3]. The *iudex* is instructed to absolve if he does not condemn. This seems superfluous since *litis contestatio* has destroyed the old claim, and in any new action there would at any rate be the *exceptio rei in iudicium deductae*. It has however been suggested that in early law there were some types of action in which this *exceptio* was not available, so that there would be no bar to a new action unless there had been an

[1] D. 12. 3. 11. [2] D. 42. 1. 36. [3] D. 42. 1. 59.

actual judgment of *absolutio*[1], so that the *exceptio rei iudicatae* would be available[2].

The various duties of the *iudex* when he has received the *formula* are described by the collective term *Officium Iudicis.* We have seen that he is bound to obey the instructions of the *formula,* but we have also seen incidentally that in the course of time certain relaxations were recognised, and perhaps the expression *officium iudicis* is more familiar in connexion with those rights and duties which are not expressly provided for in the *formula.* Thus, if he cannot make up his mind, he is allowed with the leave of the magistrate to swear "*rem sibi non liquere.*" The power to absolve if satisfaction is given after *litis contestatio* is practically to read "*si paret*" as if it were "*si parebit.*" The various *stipulationes iudiciales* do not appear to have been provided for in the *formula,* though in some cases they may be covered by the *arbitrium.* There are other illustrations, but many of the texts in the Digest which speak of things done *officio iudicis,* refer, not to the *iudex* of the *formula,* but to the later system.

154. Justinian gives us a long series of classifications of actions, having followed, but considerably amplified, the treatment of the matter in Gaius. Most of these cross-classifications from different points of view are simple and straightforward, but some of them present difficulties or points of interest which make it worth while to discuss them shortly.

In dealing with *obligatio* we saw that the expression *obligatio civilis* was somewhat ambiguous: the term means different things according as it is opposed to *obligatio iure civili comprobata,* or to *obligatio honoraria* or to *obligatio naturalis.* No such ambiguity attaches in classical law to the expression *actio civilis,* which is always opposed to *actio honoraria.* An *actio civilis* is essentially one which alleges and claims a right, either a *ius in rem* (it must be remembered that this expression is not Roman), such as ownership, enforceable by *vindicatio,* and servitude, enforceable by *actio confessoria,* or an *obligatio* of some kind. It is

[1] Eisele, Beiträge, 13. [2] See note at end of this chapter.

sometimes said that *actiones civiles* assert a right at civil law, and this, though a more guarded statement, does not differ in effect, since in point of fact, no action, so far as we know, asserts a right at all in the plaintiff, except a civil law right. It may be true that the Praetor could give a *formula*, expressly creating a right not existing at civil law, but it does not appear that any action of this sort exists in the surviving texts. The Praetor never purports to create a right: his actions do not allege one. This will be made clear if we look at the different types of praetorian actions, *actiones honorariae*, as they are called. They are of three types.

I. *Actio Fictitia*, of which the *actio* Publiciana and the *actio de peculio* are well known instances. These direct the *iudex* to condemn as if a state of fact existed, but do not allege it to exist. They state the hypothesis that a right would arise if that state of fact existed, and unless there would be a right if the fact were so the plaintiff cannot recover. The conditions of a civil right must exist in all respects but one, and this the *iudex* is directed to assume. But these actions do not in terms assert a right as the facts are. Thus in the *actio* Publiciana the *iudex* is to decide as if the claimant had held the land for two years. The "fictions" are of various types, but it is not necessary to discuss these, beyond observing that, as has already been pointed out, the fiction in the action of the tax farmer is utterly unlike any other known to us.

II. Actions *in Factum*, *e.g.* the *actio metus*, *actio* Serviana (of the pledge-creditor) and many others. In these actions no question of right is expressly raised. A hypothesis of pure fact is put before the *iudex* and he is directed to condemn if the facts prove to be so. It is clear that these actions place a great power in the hands of the Praetor, since they need contain no analogy with any existing action and thus give him a very free hand. It is also clear that in drawing the formula much care was needed: the Praetor had in each case the responsibility of determining whether these facts were of exactly the kind in respect of which he had designed his remedy.

III. Actions on the Rutilian model, of which a well-known instance is the action available to the *bonorum emptor* against debtors of the insolvent estate. Here a right is indeed alleged, but it is not in the actual plaintiff, and it is or may be a civil right. The direction to the *iudex* is that if he finds that A. owes B. something, he is to condemn him to pay it to C. B.'s name appears in the *intentio*, C.'s in the *condemnatio*. If the right of action in the debtor was itself praetorian, as might be the case, the *intentio* would be complex: it might for instance embody a fiction.

All these types of action are designed by the Praetor, and thus it may be said, speaking generally, that actions of either of these types are *actiones honorariae*. But legislation is not always particular about logic. We have already seen that, while nothing could be more praetorian than *bonorum possessio*, the *lex* Papia Poppaea definitely gives *bonorum possessio* in certain cases of succession to *libertini*[1]. The same phenomenon appears in the present case. There is at least one case in which a statute, *i.e.* the *lex* Rubria, of about 45 B.C. gives an *actio fictitia* in certain events[2]. The statute is adopting the praetorian remedy, and it is impossible to say that an action resting on the authority of a statute is *honoraria*.

Before passing from these types it should be mentioned that it is quite possible for an action to be both *fictitia* and *in factum*. Thus we know that the *bonorum emptor*, the purchaser of the estate of a deceased insolvent, has the actions of the dead man with the fiction, *si heres esset*. If the action which the dead man had was an *actio in factum*, such as the *actio de constituto*, it may well have been both *in factum* and *fictitia* in the hands of the *bonorum emptor*. We cannot say that it must have been so, for the *formula* Rutiliana may have been used in such cases.

It has been hitherto assumed that the expression *actio in factum* means an *actio* with a *formula in factum concepta*, but a few words of warning are necessary here. It has been

[1] *Ante*, § 90. [2] Bruns, Fontes, 1. 98.

contended, though the opinion has not met with wide acceptance, that this is an entire misconception, that the expression *actio in factum* has nothing to do with *formula in factum*, but that it means simply any praetorian action, however formulated. It is not however possible to reconcile this with the language of Gaius[1]. At the same time it cannot be said that the expression *actio in factum* is always used with this technical meaning. We have already seen that it is by the assumption that the name *actio in factum* is used in a loose sense to cover any action, whether formulated *in ius* or *in factum*, which specifies the material facts, that the various texts dealing with the praetorian extensions of the Aquilian action have been harmonised to a certain extent[2]. It will be remembered also that the *actio praescriptis verbis*, which is an action formulated *in ius*, but setting forth the facts in a sort of *praescriptio*, is also called an *actio in factum civilis*.

In connexion with this group of actions, the expression *actio utilis* gives rise to a good deal of difficulty. The name is applied to actions of different sorts, so that it has been found possible to enumerate no less than eight kinds of *actio utilis*, but this minute subdivision seems to serve little purpose. The only proposition which can be safely laid down in the way of definition seems to be that it is an extension, on grounds of utility, of some existing action, and it is probably true that it ordinarily contains in its *formula* some reference to what may be called the parent action. It is usually an *actio honoraria* in the strict sense, *i.e.*, it is praetorian both in form and origin. But it is clear that this is not always the case. The later jurists not unfrequently apply the name to some extended action, created by juristic activity without the help of the Edict and after the Praetor has ceased to be a legislative force[3]. Where it is *honoraria* it may be of any of the three types, so that, conversely, either an *actio in factum* or an *actio fictitia* may be an *actio utilis*. Probably nearly all *actiones fictitiae*, if not all, could have been called *actiones utiles*, though

[1] See Girard, Manuel (5), 1017. [2] *Ante*, § 137.

[3] See *e.g. ante*, § 130.

there are many to which this name is not in fact applied. On the other hand there is nothing *utilis* about many *actiones in factum*: there are indeed cases in which an *actio in factum* is itself extended to new cases by means of an *actio utilis*[1]. It will be seen therefore that the *actio utilis* does not fit into the above scheme of *actiones honorariae*, but cuts across it in nearly all possible ways.

155. The division of actions into those *bonae fidei* and those *stricti iuris* is one of great importance in procedure. It should be observed that the expression *stricti iuris* is not in this connexion classical. The actions so described by Justinian[2] are called *stricta iudicia* in earlier law, and in any case the epithet should be applied to the *iudicium*, the procedure before the *iudex*, rather than to the action as a whole. If we look at the various distinctions of result we shall see that they are for the most part matter for the *iudex* to consider. There is some reason to think that the *stricta iudicia* descend from the *legis actio per sacramentum*, in which it will be remembered that the only question which was tried in the *iudicium* was which party had sworn falsely or rather, in historical times, had made a false declaration *in iure* and backed it by the *sacramentum*. One piece of evidence in support of this view is that some of the distinctions are just what would naturally follow from this origin of *stricta iudicia* as opposed to *bonae fidei iudicia*. This is well illustrated by the rule: *omnia iudicia absolutoria sunt*. This rather cryptic proposition means that in considering whether the defendant is liable or not, the *iudex* is entitled to take into account events which have happened since the *litis contestatio*. For instance, if the defendant has satisfied the claim since the *litis contestatio* he is entitled to *absolutio*. This rational rule developed under the formulary system. It was admitted very early in relation to *bonae fidei iudicia* and to *actiones arbitrariae*, but in relation to *stricta iudicia* the point was disputed between the two schools, and it was not till rather late that there was a general

[1] D. 9. 3. 6. 3.

[2] See Roby, Rom. Pr. Law, 2. 3.

acceptance of the Sabinian view that even in *stricta iudicia* the *iudex* might take into account satisfaction after *litis contestatio*. On the hypothesis under discussion the reason for the hesitation is plain. These *iudicia* descend from *sacramentum*. In that action the notion of release in such a way could have no place. All that the *iudex* had to consider was the question whose sacramental declaration had been true, and whose false. This could not be in the least affected by anything which had happened after the *litis contestatio*. Destruction of the thing in dispute without fault or *mora* of the defendant was on the same level in the later law, but the earlier history of the matter is obscure. It is very probable, though the point does not admit of proof, that the same origin accounts for the fact that, in *stricta iudicia*, no interest and in most cases no fruits could be claimed in respect of any time before *litis contestatio*, while in *bonae fidei iudicia* the rule in general was that they could both be claimed from *mora*[1]. The point may well be that as the claim rested on a solemn declaration that a certain sum was due, it would be impossible to claim that anything more was due at the time when the declaration was made.

We have several lists of *bonae fidei iudicia*, one from Cicero[2], one from Gaius and one from Justinian. They differ in completeness, but there is no real conflict, and the rule is clear that the whole classification has no application to any actions but those on contract and quasi-contract. Among these, the *stricta iudicia* are those on unilateral obligations: all others, whether absolutely or only imperfectly bilateral are *bonae fidei*. Actions *in factum* somewhat resemble *bonae fidei iudicia*, since they direct the *iudex* to decide *ex bono et aequo* or the like (the direction being in the *condemnatio*, not in the *intentio*[3], as in *bonae fidei iudicia*), and probably actions on delict have some affinity to *stricta iudicia*, but, in reality, they are outside the classification altogether. *A fortiori* all real actions are entirely outside the scheme. Justinian, however, after his manner, introduces some confusion by providing that *hereditatis petitio*,

[1] D. 16. 3. 24; D. 22. 1. 38. 7–9.

[2] Cicero, *De Off.* 3. 17. 70.

[3] D. 47. 12. 3. *pr.*

which is a real action, is to be *bonae fidei*. This is only his somewhat misleading way of enacting that set off is to be allowed as it is in such *iudicia*, and of confirming what had become the established practice of not requiring an *exceptio doli* to be expressly pleaded in such an action. In a similarly clumsy way he declares an action on *stipulatio* to be *bonae fidei* in one case, *i.e.*, where it is brought, as he requires it to be, in place of the abolished *actio rei uxoriae*, which had been *bonae fidei*. But these late exceptions do not affect the general principle.

156. The distinction between *iudicia legitima* and *iudicia imperio continentia* is one in relation to which it is important to avoid two mistakes which are rather easily made. *Iudicia legitima*, in the classical law, are those which are brought before a single *iudex*, within a mile of Rome, all parties being *cives*. All others are *imperio continentia*. The distinction has nothing to do with other characteristics of the action. Thus an *actio in factum*, or any other peculiarly praetorian action, will give rise to a *iudicium legitimum* if it satisfies these requirements, while a *vindicatio* or an *actio ex stipulatu* will not, if it is brought away from Rome. The other error is a confusion between two distinct ideas. We are told that *iudicia legitima* were perpetual till a certain *lex* Iulia limited them to eighteen months, while the others failed if they were not ended within the term of office of the magistrate under whom they were begun, and thus could not last longer than a year. This has nothing to do with the distinction between *actiones perpetuae* and *annuae*. Our present rule has to do with the *iudicium* only, not with the action as a whole. It merely limits the time which might elapse between the bringing of the action and the decision of it. It has nothing to do with the lapse of time which will bar an action on a claim. From this last point of view some actions were perpetual, while others were limited to an *annus utilis* from the time when they might first have been brought. This distinction does not in the least turn on the question whether the resulting *iudicium* would be *legitimum* or not, and indeed it is not easy to say exactly on what it does turn. It may be said that all purely civil law actions were *perpetuae*, except in rare cases in which an express piece of legislation had cut them down, for instance the action against *sponsores*, which was limited to two years. Those of praetorian origin were *perpetuae*, whether praetorian in form or *iure civili comprobatae*, if they were for mere restitution. Otherwise, *i.e.*, if they were for a penalty, or for an indemnity, they were *annuae*. But there are so many exceptions that this proposition is not very trustworthy. It is quite possible to doubt whether the above is the right principle of distinction. Gaius and Paul[1] do not agree as to the basis, but neither of their principles will go near to accounting for all the recorded cases. Some of the difficulties are no doubt due to interpolation of the texts.

The foregoing remarks on *iudicia legitima* need some supplementing and defining. The word *iudicium* has been used above as if it meant only the proceeding before the *iudex*, but it has been made clear that, at least in some connexions, the word was used by the earlier classical lawyers to denote the whole proceeding. It is maintained by Wlassak that in strictness, and in the old expression, *iudicium legitimum*, it is used in this sense and that *iudicium* is the technical name for the proceedings in an action under the formulary system, as opposed to the *legis actio*[2]. To the word *legitimum* he gives the natural meaning statutory, and arrives at the conclusions, first, that *iudicia legitima* are those in which the *formula* is issued under the directions of a *lex*, so that the *imperium* of the magistrate plays no part in it, from the Roman point of view, and, secondly, that the whole conception has nothing to do with the *legis actio*. It follows that the *lex* in question, at least for the first introduction of *iudicia legitima*, is the *lex* Aebutia, which on his view authorised the use of the *formula* in all cases, but did not command it in any. The limitation of the conception to actions between *cives* follows, according to

[1] D. 44. 7. 35. But see Girard, Manuel (5), 728.

[2] Prozessgesetze, 1. 72 *sqq.*, 2. 26 *sqq.*

Wlassak, from the principle that a *lex* is essentially a matter between *cives*, and the restriction to cases before *unus iudex* is merely the expression of the fact that the *unus iudex* was the normal trier of cases; the collegiate courts being late and exceptional[1]. The limitation to Rome he considers to be a mere result of the fact that the only tribunal—that of the *Praetor Urbanus*—sat at Rome. The *leges* Iuliae, practically abolishing *legis actio* in favour of *formulae*, coincide in time with the *lex* Iulia *municipalis* by which an uniform system of procedure is laid down for all municipalities, and Wlassak holds that, thereafter, litigation in any such town might be *legitima* if it satisfied the other requirements[2]. This is in direct conflict with Gaius, whose language is, on this view, to be explained by the fact that it was essentially the law of the city of Rome that he was expounding, to the complete disregard of the municipalities, as to which he says nothing. Accordingly Wlassak holds, contrary to the general view, that Gaius wrote at Rome. It may be suggested that his argument proves rather that such cases outside Rome ought to have been *iudicia legitima*, than that they actually were such.

157. The distinction between actions *in rem* and *in personam* corresponds to our distinction between rights *in rem* and *in personam*, and it is significant that while our modern distinction is named by borrowing the Roman division of actions, the Romans had no pair of names by which to express what seems to us the more important and primary distinction, that between the rights themselves. What they classify and distinguish is the remedy.

In the classical law the distinction is expressed in the form of the *intentio*. In actions *in personam* the *intentio* alleges an *obligatio* in the defendant to do or pay something to the benefit of the plaintiff. In actions *in rem* the *intentio* alleges a right in the plaintiff, and does not mention the defendant at all. It is this fact that leads to the description of the *actio metus* as an *actio personalis in rem scripta*. As the defendant is not

[1] *Op. cit.* 2. 93 *sqq.*, 192 *sqq.* [2] *Ib.* 2. 265 *sqq.*

necessarily the person who was guilty of the duress, but may be anyone who has profited by it, the *intentio* merely alleges the duress without saying who committed it. The description is however a curious misnomer, for the *actio metus* is in fact an *actio in factum*, and thus, in point of form, neither *in rem* nor *in personam*. With a somewhat similar looseness of thought, Justinian tells us that the divisory actions are both *in rem* and *in personam*, his point being that they express ownership, and allege a duty in the parties. The truth is that they are personal actions alleging an *obligatio quasi ex contractu*, based on the fact of common ownership.

The simplest type of *actio in rem* is the *Vindicatio*, in which the plaintiff alleges that the property in dispute is his *ex iure Quiritium*, a form closely followed in the *Hereditatis petitio*, in which the *hereditas* is contemplated as one thing. But where the right claimed is less than ownership, such as a rustic servitude, since it is conceived of as incorporeal—a mere *ius*—the form is different, and the plaintiff alleges that he has a *ius* to exercise such and such a form of enjoyment. The only case which seems to need special mention is the *actio negatoria*, in which the right of the defendant to exercise a certain servitude is denied. It may not at first sight be clear what is the need for this action. Will it not suffice to prevent him from enjoying his right, leaving him to bring his action to enforce his right if he thinks fit? The point is that if he were in actual enjoyment an interdict would be at his service, by which he would be restored to the enjoyment without proof of right, so that the owner of the land would be no better off. The same thing might of course be said if the dispute were one of ownership, and yet there is no *actio negatoria* in that case. In the ordinary real action the plaintiff never puts his case in the form of a denial of the other party's right, but simply asserts his own. In fact however the principle is the same in this case. The plaintiff asserts his ownership free from this servitude. But as his ownership is not disputed, a mere assertion of this would be of no use to him. What he is called on to assert is that this alleged restriction on it does not exist. The negative form is a mere appearance: it merely cloaks the fact that the action is an assertion of his right as strictly as in *vindicatio* or in the *actio confessoria*.

158. In Roman law reform, as elsewhere, great changes do not come quite suddenly. Thus the frequent shiftings of legislative power were gradual, and the triumph of one method was not always marked by express enactment. This is equally true of other legal changes, and even where there is such an enactment, this is often a last, not a first, step. In criminal procedure the *quaestiones perpetuae* were created by statute, but there had been a preliminary stage, which may be called experimental, of *quaestiones extraordinariae*. The consensual contracts grew, it is said, out of previous practice in bargains to which the State was a party. In like manner, the supersession of the Formulary system, by that of *Cognitio*, though it may have been achieved by enactment, was only the completion of a process already centuries old. The praetorian *cognitio causae* (*extraordinaria*) was familiar in the time of the Republic in cases of *restitutio in integrum*, *missio in possessionem*, and other cases.

Restitutio in Integrum[1] is a machinery under which the Praetor, on application, sets aside, *e.g.*, transactions impeached on various grounds, such as fraud or duress, damage to a minor, and in a lesser degree mistake. Loss of rights of action or property through lapse of time from absence, might be relieved against in the same way, as might cases in which a right of action was consumed, but equity called for a remedy, *e.g.*, where the *actio de peculio* against the vendor of a slave has not procured complete satisfaction[2]. In all these cases the Praetor holds an enquiry into the facts and if he thinks there is a case for *restitutio* issues a *decretum* to that effect. The impeached transaction is null at praetorian law, but it still exists. The claimant of *restitutio* will have therefore only a praetorian

[1] Girard, Manuel (5), 1049.

[2] D. 15. 1. 30. 5.

action, which will vary in form, but commonly will be an *actio fictitia* under which the *iudex* will be directed to proceed as if the impeached transaction or event had not occurred.

Missio in possessionem is also a proceeding by way of *decretum*, after enquiry. It is used in a wide range of cases. Sometimes it is a means of putting pressure on a recalcitrant defendant, *e.g.*, in *damnum infectum*[1]. Sometimes it is a step for the protection of contingent interests[2]. Sometimes it covers the whole property of the defendant, as in *bonorum venditio*, sometimes only specific property, as in the case of *missio in possessionem* against an alienee of goods left by *fideicommissum*[3]. But this is later. The powers of the *missus* vary greatly, in accordance with the difference of purpose in the different cases.

After the establishment of the Empire progress was rapid. *Fideicommissa* were enforced in this way. So were *honoraria*[4] in mandate. Complaints of ill-treatment, made by slaves, were dealt with by the magistrate, as were allegations of failure in a contractual undertaking to free slaves, *servus suis nummis emptus*[5], and so forth. The enactment of Diocletian[6] that for the future there was to be no duplex procedure, but that all cases were to be tried by the magistrate or his deputy, from beginning to end, promulgated in A.D. 294, did not in terms apply to the capital itself. Yet it seems clear from other evidence, and from the wording of the enactment, that so far as the Provinces were concerned it was only confirming and making obligatory a procedure which had been the usual one for almost a century. In Rome itself it is said that the system of *formulae* had lasted longer, but it was clearly obsolete before this date, and the absence of express reference to the city in the enactment is commonly thought to mean merely that there was no need for it, since there is no sign of the ancient *iudices*, who are essential to the formulary system, for a very long time before[7].

The change was, as has frequently been pointed out, only

[1] D. 39. 2. 7. [2] D. 25. 5. 1. [3] P. *Sent.* 4. 1. 15.
[4] C. 4. 35. 1. [5] D. 40. 1. 5. *pr.* [6] C. 3. 3. 2.
[7] Girard, Manuel (5), 1073.

a further and final step in the absorption of civil function by the administrative officials of the Emperor. It infused a new spirit into procedure and in the long run completely metamorphosed it. But, at first, it does not seem to have involved, necessarily, any change beyond the hearing by the magistrate himself. Thus though the *ordo iudiciorum* is gone, it does not follow that the *formula* is, and it seems clear that, for a long time, the case continued to be stated in the old way. But the new system was intolerant of the rigid logic of the *formula*: in A.D. 342 it was provided that the insidious verbal traps of the *formula* were to be abolished[1], and in course of time there was still further simplification. What the exact effect of the enactment of A.D. 342 may have been is obscure but presumably the claim might now be stated in any form which the plaintiff considered apt. We hear of the plaintiff's *Libellus conventionis*, and of the defendant's *Libellus defensionis* or *contradictionis* or *responsionis*. The details of the procedure are fairly well known for Justinian's time, but there is no need to go into them. There is a steady tendency to methods which are administrative rather than judicial, *e.g.*, hearings in private, written proceedings, execution of decrees by direct order of the magistrate, and so forth. The steps in this development are not fully known, but recent research among the increasing number of known documents of this age has filled up many gaps in our knowledge. But though the old procedure is gone, much of its terminology remains[2]. We still hear of *Exceptiones*, and *Replicationes*, of *Litis Contestatio*, of Interdicts. But all these terms are used with a somewhat changed significance. When Justinian says that in given circumstances an *exceptio doli* is available, he means that *dolus* may be pleaded and will be a bar to the claim, just as it would have been under the old system, but he does not mean that the point will be raised in the old way. When he tells us that a possessory interdict is available, he really means that a possessory action will lie, for the actual issue of the interdict is a thing of the past.

[1] C. 2. 57. 1. [2] Girard, Manuel (5), 1076.

NOTE. The student may find it helpful to study one or two simple *formulae*, of which the structure is fairly well known, set out in full, with its different parts distinguished. There is of course no certainty about the minor details of wording.

A. *Vindicatio*. The defence pleads agreement not to sue, to which fraud is replied.

Nom. Iudicis	Titius iudex esto
Intentio	Si paret fundum Cornelianum quo de agitur Auli Agerii ex iure Quiritium esse
Exceptio	nisi inter Aulum Agerium et Numerium Negidium pactum fuerit ne peteretur
Replicatio	aut si in eo pacto aliquid dolo malo Numerii Negidii factum fuerit
Arbitrium	neque eum fundum arbitratu tuo Aulo Agerio restituetur
Condemnatio	quanti ea res erit tantam pecuniam Numerium Negidium Aulo Agerio condemna si non paret absolve.

B. *Condictio certae pecuniae* on a promise, the defence being that it was a gift in excess of the legal maximum.

Nom. Iudicis	Titius iudex esto
Intentio	Si paret Num. Negidium Ao. Agerio sestertium centum milia dare oportere
Exceptio	si in ea re nihil contra legem Cinciam factum est
Condemnatio	Num. Negidium Ao. Agerio sestertium centum milia iudex condemna si non paret absolve.

(There was presumably some clause prefixed indicating the *causa*, but nothing is known of it.)

C. *Actio de peculio et in rem verso* on deposit with a slave.

Nom. Iudicis	Titius iudex esto
Demonstratio	Quod As. Agerius apud Stichum qui in potestate Ni. Negidii est mensam argenteam deposuit qua de re agitur
Intentio	quidquid ob eam rem Stichum si liber esset ex iure Quiritium Ao. Agerio dare facere oporteret ex fide bona
Taxatio and Condemnatio	eius iudex Num. Negidium Ao. Agerio duntaxat de peculio et si quid dolo malo Ni. Negidii factum est quo minus peculii esset vel si quid in rem Ni. Negidii versum est condemna si non paret absolve.

(This is the *formula* suggested by Lenel, Ed. Perp. (2) 273, but the *intentio* is much disputed.)

CHAPTER IX

THE LAW OF ACTIONS (*concluded*)

159. THE greater part of the last chapter was occupied with an account of the framework of the Formulary system, with such remarks on the system which it replaced, and the system which succeeded it, as seemed necessary to make its essential character clear. We have now to consider some of the details of the procedure.

The stage in the proceedings called *Litis Contestatio* occurred in the formulary system at the moment of the issue of the *formula*, the end of the proceedings *in iure*. *Litis contestatio* is not merely a date: it is an event, and a proper comprehension of the results which flow from it depends on a correct understanding of its nature. Of the views which have been propounded the most probable seems to be that it was essentially of a contractual nature; the parties to the litigation agreeing between themselves to accept the issue as it is framed by, or under the supervision of, the Praetor[1].

The most important effect of *Litis contestatio*, that of Novation, is readily explained on this hypothesis: the parties have made a substituted contract, or have substituted a contract for some previous obligation. But in *actiones in rem*, there can be no question of novation, and the same may be said of *actiones in factum*, and yet, here too, any further action on the old claim was barred. The truth is that this effect has nothing to do with the view which is taken of the nature of *litis*

[1] See Girard, Manuel (5), 1011.

contestatio; it is an application of the principle, *non bis in idem*; a simple enough notion in itself, but giving rise to extraordinary difficulties and subtleties as soon as we try to lay down a rule whereby to determine what is and what is not *eadem res*. Into these we shall not enter.

It will be remembered that the effect of *litis contestatio* on the old liability was not uniform. In the case of an *actio in personam, in ius*, and coming within the class of *iudicia legitima*, the destruction of the old *obligatio* was complete; no new *formula* would be issued on the old claim. But in all other cases the old claim still existed at civil law, and there was need of an *exceptio rei iudicatae vel in iudicium deductae* to give effect to the destruction. The first question which suggests itself in this connexion is that raised by Lenel, whether this is the name of a single *exceptio* which in one or other of its branches would cover all cases, or whether there were really two *exceptiones*, as had hitherto been supposed. The answer to this question is not without importance for certain questions, but for our present purpose it has little significance. The language of Gaius is much in favour of the view that it was one *exceptio* in his time, but is not in the least inconsistent with the supposition that there was an earlier state of things in which they were not yet fused. The view that this was the case and the view that in fact they never were identical are not without strong supporters, who are able to rest their cases on texts[1]. More important for us are the questions: why was the destruction complete *ipso iure* in the one set of cases and not in the other, and why is an *exceptio rei iudicatae* needed, since no *res* can be *iudicata* which has not been *in iudicium deducta*? The answer to the first question appears to be that, as this complete destruction of the right is the result of a civil law principle, it can apply only where the issue raised is based on civil law, not where it rests on the Praetor's *imperium* as it does in the cases of *iudicia imperio continentia*. The other distinction suggests that there was, at some time at any rate, a class of actions in which *litis contestatio* produced no sort of novatory

[1] See Lenel, Ed. Perp. (2) 486.

effect at all, so that the fact of their being *in iudicio* was no bar to a subsequent action, while the fact that they had been decided would be a bar. It has been suggested[1] that in the intervening period between the *lex* Aebutia and the *lex* Iulia, the mere bringing of an action had no effect of a novatory kind, in any *iudicia imperio continentia*, that in these cases only judgment was material. Thus there would be three cases: that last mentioned which needed the *exceptio rei iudicatae*, *iudicia legitima in personam* with a *formula in ius*, in which the *consumptio litis* was *ipso iure*, and other *iudicia legitima*, *e.g.* actions *in rem*, in which the *exceptio rei in iudicium deductae* was available. This gives rise to the question: what was the reason for the distinction between these last two cases, since they express claims which would have been equally liable to *ipso iure consumptio* under the *legis actio* system? It has been suggested that the *lex* Aebutia did not allow the *formula* in real actions, so that these would be on a different footing, but this opinion is not generally accepted. Another opinion is that the rule that action barred further claim had no application at all to real actions under the system of *legis actio*. But this is in direct conflict with an express statement in Gaius. This fact, that in the *legis actio* system both types of action were on the same footing, is a stumbling-block in the way of what would otherwise be much the simplest theory, *i.e.*, that the difference is due to the fact that the notion of novation cannot apply to an *actio in rem*. The difficulty has led to a good deal of discussion of the conception of *litis contestatio*. The name obviously suggests a summoning of witnesses (though it might conceivably mean no more than a joint acceptance of a *iudicium*), and some words of Festus indicate that even in the formulary system there remained a trace of this in the custom that each party said, at the time of the acceptance of the *iudicium*, "*testes estote*[2]." There is however no reason to think that at this time there was a real summoning. No doubt some definite step was taken to indicate the precise moment. It may have consisted in the actual delivery of the *formula* to the parties or the *iudex*, in

[1] Eisele, Abhandlungen, 14 *sqq.*

[2] Bruns, Fontes, 2. 6.

writing[1], possibly sealed. In the *legis actio* system there was no doubt an actual summoning of witnesses, but it is by no means certain when this occurred. It can hardly have been at the time of the appointment of a *iudex*, thirty days after the completion of the *legis actio*. It may perhaps have been at the end of the *legis actio*, but Wlassak has shewn some reason for the opinion that it was at the beginning of the *legis actio*[2]. But acceptance of this hypothesis forces the acceptance of the further conclusion that the bar to future proceedings on the same claim had no relation at all in this system to *litis contestatio*, that in fact it was due to the entirely independent rule, *non bis in idem*, which forbade repetition of a *legis actio*, and on the origin of which it is not necessary to speculate.

As the barring effect was thus in reality due to the mere formal prohibition of repetition of the ritual forms, a fresh basis had to be found for it in the new procedure in which these forms no longer occurred. It is then that the contractual and novatory character of *litis contestatio* becomes material. This can apply in strictness only where the action brings an *obligatio* expressly into play, *i.e.* in actions *in personam in ius*. Hence the rule that the bar exists *ipso iure* only in actions *in ius, in personam*, where the *iudicium* is *legitimum*. In all other cases the *exceptio* is needed.

In the procedure of later law, *litis contestatio* appears to have occurred at the moment when the *libelli*, the statement of claim and the pleadings in defence, were complete. But at this time the occurrence of it is far less significant than in earlier times. It must be remembered that the destructive effect of *litis contestatio* was never, in historic times, quite so complete in practice as it appears. The Edict contained well-known provisions for *restitutio in integrum* where, through some error in procedure, not involving great carelessness, an action had been lost[3]. The rule that where the *actio de peculio* had been brought against the vendor of a slave, and full satisfaction had not been obtained, a new one could be brought against the buyer,

[1] See Girard, Manuel (5), 1011.

[2] See Girard, *op. cit.* 978.

[3] Lenel, Ed. Perp. (2) 119 *sq.*

rescisso superiore iudicio[1], is merely an illustration of the rule, the limits of which it is not possible to state, under which the procedural bar could be set aside in a wide range of cases where justice required a remedy. Where the loss was due to excessive claim (*plus petitio*) there was some remedy in the Edict, and a full measure of relief in later law. There were similar modifications in relation to other of the effects of this bar, most of which turn on the notion of *litis contestatio* as fixing the liability. There could be no change of parties or alienation of the property after this event, but the magistrate had power to relieve against this in appropriate cases[2]. There were exceptions to the rule that the state of things at *litis contestatio* fixes the measure of the liability: the chief of these we have already considered in connexion with the rule, *omnia iudicia absolutoria sunt*[3]. But the most sweeping change was that made by Justinian, who finally swept away the novatory effect of *litis contestatio*, if not altogether, as to which there may be doubt, at least for all practical purposes.

160. The law of *Plus petitio* (for which somewhat ungrammatical name, the only authority is the doubtful one of a rubric in the Code[4]) gives a very good illustration of the logical interpretation of the *formula*. If a plaintiff claims ten, and on the facts only nine are due, the defendant is entitled to absolution. The instruction to the *iudex* is to condemn if ten are due and to absolve on every other hypothesis, which includes that in which something less than ten is shewn to be due. For the same reason there can be no *plus petitio* "*re*" where the claim is for an *incertum*: in this case the *intentio* directs the *iudex* to condemn for whatever may prove to be due. It is obvious that the rule must have caused inconvenience, even with the reliefs we have mentioned, but it is not till the *formula* has disappeared that it is modified. It should be added that while Gaius tells us that there can be no *plus petitio*

[1] D. 15. 1. 47. 3.
[2] Fr. Vat. 341; D. 5. 1. 57.
[3] *Ante*, § 155.
[4] C. 3. 10.

where the claim is for an *incertum*, the case may arise of a claim for an *incertum* before the due day has arrived, or while a condition on the liability is still pending. The texts leave some doubts as to the effect. In the case of the condition, the action is certainly lost, but it seems that a new action could be brought, the obligation being regarded as newly arising at the occurrence of the condition[1], and thus not having been brought into issue. As to the other case we have no direct information at all. The more probable view seems to be that, subject to such possible reliefs as have been mentioned, the claim was definitively barred in classical law, while in later law the case is certainly covered by the language of Zeno's enactment which lays it down that in all cases of claiming too soon, the action may be brought again after double the time. It is however held by some writers that the words *ex fide bona* coupled with the *quidquid paret* entitled the *iudex*, at any rate in *bonae fidei iudicia*, to condemn, subject to a *deductio*, giving in fact the present value of the claim[2].

161. The law of *Compensatio*, or Set-off, also illustrates the logic of the *formula* as well as some other principles. It may be well to give some account of the historical changes undergone by the rules. In the early days of the Empire there were two actions of narrow range, to which special rules applied. Where a banker (*argentarius*) was suing his customer, he was required to allow what was called *compensatio*, in the *intentio* of the action. That is to say, he was to claim only the nett balance due to him after deducting anything which was due from him to the defendant, provided that the debt was of the same kind as that for which he was suing, which would commonly be money. If in his *intentio* he failed to make this allowance, he lost his action: it was in fact a case of *plus petitio*. The two debts were treated as one for the purpose of the action, and he had claimed more than was due. But that was a rule special to this action, and not in accord with the general attitude of the Roman law which usually refused to combine two distinct

[1] D. 21. 1. 43. 9. Girard, Manuel (5), 1037. [2] See Girard, *loc. cit.*

issues in one *formula*. Again, in actions brought by the *bonorum emptor*, the purchaser of the whole property of a bankrupt, against a debtor to the bankrupt, it was necessary to insert a *deductio*, that is to say the plaintiff had to allow for any counterclaim; it need not be of the same kind. But this did not affect the *intentio*, the allowance was made in the *condemnatio*, and if it was omitted, there might always be amendment. The action would not be lost, and there could be no question of *plus petitio*.

There was however a more general rule. In all *bonae fidei iudicia*, the *iudex* might, if he thought fit, allow, on grounds of good faith, any set-off arising out of the same transaction, and condemn only for any balance shewn to be due. This is an application of, or an inference from, the words of the *intentio*, *ex fide bona*. The *formula* would contain no other reference to the set-off, so that there is no question of a *plus petitio*. The *intentio* expressly claims only "whatever may prove to be due." The rule was very different in *stricta iudicia*. In these no set-off was allowed. It will be remembered that these actions arose only on contracts or the like which bound only one side, so that there could be no question of any set-off arising in the same transaction, and as we have said, there is in the classical law a great reluctance to allow the joining of two issues in the same *formula*.

Under Marcus Aurelius a change was made. He provided that even in a *strictum iudicium* any set-off of the same kind must be allowed for in the *intentio*, though in such a case it must necessarily have arisen in a different transaction. If this was not done an *exceptio doli* was allowed. It is supposed, though not on very good authority, that the same principle was now applied to *bonae fidei iudicia*, *i.e.* that these counterclaims had to be expressly allowed for, or the action was lost, though the *exceptio doli* would not of course have to be expressly inserted. It is however at least equally probable that they remained under the old rule. In any case we need consider only the case of *stricta iudicia*. Unfortunately, owing to the fact that Justinian again changed the law, there are difficulties as to the working of the rules. The restriction to debts of the same kind cannot be clearly made out on the texts, but it is commonly, though not universally, accepted, on the ground that it is difficult to regard the non-inclusion of debts of altogether different types as shewing *dolus*[1]. There are other difficulties. It is certain that the ground on which the action is lost is not *plus petitio*. If it were there would be no need of the *exceptio doli*. The mere non-allowance of the counterclaim would of itself have destroyed the action *ipso iure*. Moreover the right to sue later on this counterclaim was not affected by the fact that no account of it had been taken in this action, which could hardly have been the case if it had been *ipso iure* in issue in the earlier action: there would have been *res iudicata*.

Another point of great practical importance is this: if the *exceptio doli* was inserted, and it was proved that there was a counterclaim, was the effect to destroy the action altogether, or merely to cause a reduction of the judgment by the amount of the counterclaim? The former solution is the only one which is consistent with the general theory of the *exceptio* in the formulary system. By the logical structure of the *formula* the *iudex* is bound to absolve, if an *exceptio* is proved, subject of course to any *replicatio*, which is not here in question. He is to condemn if the *intentio* is proved and the *exceptio* is not proved: in all other cases he is to absolve. Thus it is most generally held that, in our case, if the counterclaim is not allowed for, the action is lost, if it is proved, and the precaution has been taken of inserting an *exceptio doli*. There are further procedural difficulties if the other view is taken, for instance where the counterclaim is on a single transaction and exceeds in amount the claim. It will reduce the amount of the *condemnatio* to nothing, but will it go further? Will it result in a *condemnatio* of the plaintiff for the nett debt? If not, and the counterclaim was for instance on a stipulation for *certa pecunia*, how, in any later action on this stipulation, which is a *condictio certae pecuniae*, will the fact be brought into

[1] See Girard, Manuel (5), 710.

issue that some of the money has already come into account in the earlier action?

But modern opinion is not unanimous. Some commentators hold that the effect was a mere reduction of the *condemnatio*[1], basing their opinion on the following points. (1) Since the plaintiff could not ordinarily sue again, it is unfair that his action should be lost by failure to take account of some counter-claim the exact amount of which he need not know. The answer to this is that he need not know the exact amount. Gaius gives the *formula* in the case above dealt with of the *argentarius,* and it would be equally applicable here. The demand of the *exceptio doli* is a warning to the plaintiff to modify his *intentio* before the *litis contestatio.* (2) Justinian does not say that there was any difference in effect between the rules as to *stricti iuris* actions under this rescript and the old rule in *bonae fidei iudicia,* and Theophilus uses language which implies that there was in fact no difference. But the evidence of Theophilus on a matter of history is of very small value, and Justinian says that he is making a change, and that under his system the debts "*ipso iure minuunt,*" which suggests that *minuunt* was not the word applicable to the earlier law. (3) An *exceptio* it is urged does not necessarily upset an action even in classical times. There are texts in the Digest in which this is expressly stated for different actions, and for the *exceptio doli* as well as for other *exceptiones*[2]. But in the time of the Digest the formulary system had long been extinct, and very different rules were applied to the system of *cognitio extra-ordinaria.* Thus the word *exceptio* and the rules stated for the *exceptio* by Justinian are of very little weight for the classical law. Thus one of the cases commonly cited in support of this proposition is that of the actions in which a man could not be condemned beyond his means. This caused only a reduction in classical law, and the means of raising it is repeatedly called, in the Digest, an *exceptio.* But we have already remarked that in the classical law the point was in all probability raised not

[1] *e.g.*, Sohm, Institutes (tr. Ledlie) (2), 459; Accarias, Précis, § 909.

[2] D. 44. 1. 22; D. 16. 1. 17. 2; D. 30. 85.

by *exceptio*, but by *taxatio*[1]. In the Digest Paul is quoted as saying that *exceptiones* sometimes have the effect of reducing the *condemnatio*, but this text bears evident marks of alteration, so that it is rather evidence for the contrary view, for the time of Paul.

Neither view can however be said to be proved, and it has been doubted whether the Rescript of Marcus Aurelius was really as wide in its scope as has been supposed.

Justinian allowed *compensatio* of claims of the same or different kinds in nearly every action, provided that the set-off was clear and easily valued. He provided that failure to make the allowance did not involve loss of the action, but the "*ipso iure*" diminution of the *condemnatio*, and that the rule was not to apply to the *actio depositi*. It is not very clear what he meant by the expression, *ipso iure*. Probably the sense is that the deduction is made automatically, without any mention of the counterclaim in the pleadings. It follows that there can be no question of *plus petitio*, and also that the counterclaim is not brought into issue, since it is not stated: there is nothing to bar subsequent action upon it. Apart from these points there are a good many difficulties in the application of Justinian's rather hasty rule, but we cannot go into them.

Of most of the other details of procedure, up to and including the judgment, nothing need be said. But some space must be given to the subject of Representation in law suits, and the necessary securities.

162. We are told that apart from a few exceptional cases, the *legis actio* did not admit of representation, and the cases which are recorded as exceptions do not, so far as is known, use the same machinery as that with which we meet in the formulary system. Under that system we find a scheme of representation of gradual development. The earliest form of the institution is that of the *Cognitor*, appointed in formal words, probably *in iure*, and certainly in the presence of the other party. He became the actual litigant, and whether

[1] *Ante*, § 152.

he was acting for a plaintiff or a defendant the judgment was, so to speak, in his name. Thus at first it was he who had or was liable to the *actio iudicati*, but as early as Cicero the rule is that a *cognitor* so far represents his principal that the *actio iudicati* lies to or against the principal. The procurator is an informally appointed representative, and may indeed act without appointment (*procurator voluntarius*). Here the representation is far less complete, and throughout the formulary period the *actio iudicati* lies against, and is available to, the *procurator* and not his principal. Early in the post-classical age however the *cognitor* disappears, and the appointment of a *procurator* produces the effect of full representation, so that it is the principal who is affected by the *actio iudicati*, at least in the case of an appointed *procurator*, though not in that of the *procurator voluntarius*.

So far all is fairly clear, but the history of the *Cognitor* has other aspects of interest, and has been the subject of much controversy. Gaius gives us two forms for the appointment of *cognitores* and seems to mean that they may be used indifferently. The first and most formal has an air of antiquity about it and in structure closely follows the ancient forms of declaration used in *nexi solutio* and *manus iniectio*, and some other cases. Gaius says it requires "*certa et quasi solennia verba*," and we are told that it might not be conditional. The first form begins "*Quod ego...a te peto*" and the second "*quod ego...petere volo*." It is therefore supposed, since actual *petitio* does not begin till *litis contestatio*, that the first form was used where the appointment took place at this stage and the second where it was earlier. In the controversies a good deal has turned on the exact meaning which is to be given to the word *peto* in this expression. According to one view, supported by texts, it is equivalent to *litem contestor*, so that the appointment must have been at the exact moment of *litis contestatio*. According to another, supported in the same way, it is applied to any time at or after *litis contestatio*[1].

The formal characteristics noted above have led to an

[1] See Eisele, Beiträge, 99 *sqq*.

opinion, that in its inception the *cognitor* is a civil law idea, and not purely edictal, as we know it. In this view the origin of it is to be looked for in the *legis actio* system, where however there is the difficulty that apart from certain recorded exceptions which do not affect the question, *nemo alieno nomine agere potest*. But it is argued that this applies only to the *legis actio* itself and not to the subsequent procedure *in iudicio*. From this and other considerations the conclusion has been drawn that the first form given by Gaius is the ancient civil form, and that, either generally or in some cases, it was possible to appoint at any time from *litis contestatio* a *cognitor* to act *in iudicio*, and some words in the Auctor *ad* Herennium are cited to suggest that this applied at any rate in cases of old age or sickness[1].

There is however no direct evidence for this civil *cognitor*, and it has been pointed out that there are characteristics of the form which do not look like those of an ancient civil form, that superfluous words did not vitiate it (but this is equally true of the civil form of *stipulatio: spondes-ne, spondeo*[2]), and that it might be in Greek (but the evidence for this is late), and that it is a mistake to suppose that formlessness is an attribute of praetorian institutions. On these and other grounds the civil *cognitor* is dismissed as a mere fancy. On the other hand, as the use of the word *peto* in the first form implies that *litis contestatio* has been reached, it has been maintained that there was in the formulary system a *cognitor* to act only *in iudicio*, and that the first form refers to him, and the second to the better known *cognitor* for the whole action. But for this praetorian *cognitor* to act only *in iudicio* there is the same lack of evidence as for his supposed civil law forerunner.

In these remarks no attempt is made to decide in this controversy, or even to state all the material points, but only to indicate its existence and its main lines. It is probable that the majority of modern writers on Roman law would hesitate to accept either of these undemonstrated *cognitores*[3].

[1] Eisele, Beiträge, 91. [2] D. 45. 1. 65. *pr.*

[3] See Girard, Manuel (5), 1025.

163. The rules as to the security required of a party to litigation varied historically. If the parties appear personally the plaintiff at no time gives any security. In real actions the defendant, under the formulary system, gives security, *iudicatum solvi*, *i.e.*, that he will take the proper steps in defence, that he will satisfy the judgment, and that he will commit no fraud. In personal actions he gives in general no security. In later law a defendant appearing personally gives only his personal undertaking that he will attend the hearing.

The matter is more complex where either party appears by representative, the rules being affected by the differences which exist between these representatives as to the extent to which judgment against them is effective against the principal. As a *cognitor* brings his principal's right into issue, a plaintiff's *cognitor* gives no security, and as in course of time the *exceptio rei iudicatae* became available against the principal in other cases, the rule of later classical law is that no clearly appointed representative for the plaintiff need give security. But other persons appearing for him (and in earlier days all but the *cognitor*) had to give security that the principal would ratify their action: *satisdatio de rato.* Where a representative appears for the defendant *satisdatio iudicatum solvi* has always to be given, since the right of action is exhausted. But there is a distinction. If it is a *cognitor* the principal gives the security: in other cases it is the representative. One might have expected the rule to be the other way, since the *cognitor* more fully represents the principal. But the rule is explained by the very fact that these other representatives do not formally bring the principal and his rights into issue, and, moreover, he is not necessarily present as he is in the case of the *cognitor.*

Under Justinian *satisdatio de rato* is required only from a representative whose appointment is not registered in court or made there in the presence of the principal. On the side of the defendant if the principal is not present, the representative gives security *iudicatum solvi.* In the case of a formally appointed representative, the principal gives security *iudicatum solvi*, acting, Justinian says, as a *fideiussor* for his representative. He has also to agree for a general hypothec over his property, and to give further security that he will be present at the proper time so that the *actio iudicati*, if it is necessary, may be given against him.

164. Some account has already been given of the judgment in the formulary system, which was always for a sum of money, and it is desirable now to speak of the steps which would follow if it was not obeyed. The defendant had a time, usually two months, within which to pay. If he failed to do so, further steps might be taken. The plaintiff's first step is to bring an *actio iudicati*. This is an ordinary formulary action, as to the actual *formula* of which only guesses more or less plausible can be made. This action however would not proceed to an actual hearing unless the legality of the judgment was disputed. If however this was denied and the action proceeded to a *iudicium*, the defendant incurred a liability for double damages and had to find a surety for satisfaction of it. Of course the merits could not be gone into, but only the formal validity of the judgment. If it was not disputed, so that there was no *iudicium*, the liability was for the original damages only. In either case proceedings in actual execution would follow.

This necessary initiation of execution by an *actio iudicati* has given rise to some discussion[1]. It is not expressly stated as a requirement anywhere in the texts, and it has therefore been suggested that it is an error to suppose that it was required in all cases, that it was really needed and employed only where the validity of the judgment was disputed. But though it is not expressly stated, there are many texts from which its generality is a reasonable inference[2], and it is replied that there is no text that throws any real doubt on it. The question has naturally been asked: whence arises the necessity

[1] Eisele, Abhandlungen, 125.

[2] D. 20. 1. 13. 4; D. 42. 1. 6. 1; D. 44. 4. 9, *etc.*

for an *actio iudicati* in all cases? Why could not the judgment creditor proceed at once to such modes of execution as were open, as under the old law? To this it has been replied with much force, that in fact the creditor could not so proceed under the old system: the actual seizure was preceded by a solemn declaration of the judgment, before the magistrate, with an opportunity to the defendant to dispute it by means of a *vindex*. Of this formal act it is contended the *actio iudicati* is a praetorian copy. As under the old system there will be double damages if the validity of the judgment is unsuccessfully attacked, and as under that system, the action of the defendant must be supported by a personal security: the third party, who gives *satisdatio*, being practically in the same position as the *vindex*. Other explanations have been suggested: in particular it has been maintained that it is to guard against execution being begun by an audacious creditor who has never obtained any judgment at all. It would be impossible it is urged for the defendant to prove the negative that there had never been a judgment. This action it is contended compels the creditor to appear as plaintiff and substantiate that fact, leaving to the defendant the burden of shewing that this judgment was in some way invalid. It is a corollary to this view that under the *legis actio* system the creditor claiming *manus iniectio* before the Praetor had himself to prove the *de facto* existence of the judgment, though Gaius says nothing of this.

Actual execution of judgment took two forms—personal seizure and *bonorum venditio*. Personal seizure long survives the disappearance of the old *manus iniectio*. The creditor, authorised by the magistrate (*duci iubere*), carries off the debtor and keeps him in chains or lets him work out the debt. Aulus Gellius speaks of *addictio*, but it is not, as it seems, an *addictio* in the old sense. In any case it puts strong pressure on a solvent debtor to pay, and no doubt it was mainly used in the case of such a debtor. It is clear that it remained in use through the classical age[1].

[1] See Girard, Manuel (5), 1044.

Most judgment debtors who fail to satisfy the judgment are however insolvent, and there is another method, purely praetorian, for use in such cases, *i.e.*, *Bonorum venditio*. This procedure must now be considered. The main outline of it can be very shortly stated. On the demand of the creditor, the Praetor issues a decree of *missio in possessionem*, which entitles him to take possession of the goods. But, so far, this is for security merely and does not entitle him to eject the debtor. The seizure must be publicly advertised. Then after thirty days, if the debtor is alive, fifteen if it is the estate of an insolvent deceased, a new decree issues directing the appointment by the creditors of a *magister*, one of themselves, to conduct the sale. He then publishes the conditions of sale, including apparently the inventory of the estate, and the list of debts to be paid. Then after some further delay the estate is sold to the highest bidder, *i.e.*, to the person who offers the highest dividend on the debts. There are further rules determining which is to be preferred among those who offer the same dividend, a large creditor to a smaller, a creditor to a relative, a relative to an outsider[1].

The buyer becomes a sort of praetorian successor, as we have already seen[2]. He has praetorian ownership of the property, and can sue debtors of the bankrupt, by an action with the fiction, *si heres esset*, or the action with a Rutilian formula, the former probably in the case of a deceased insolvent, the latter in the case we are concerned with. He is also liable for the debts, up to his agreed dividend. Secured creditors preserve their rights, and it appears that he must pay privileged debts, of which there are many kinds, first, and in full, if the assets are sufficient[3]. It is the natural assumption that this liability could be enforced against him by the creditors, by the same types of action, but it is surprising to find that this is nowhere stated, though it is generally accepted and is suggested by an imperfect text of Gaius. It is however sometimes held that in the case of a *iudicatus*, as the creditors have dealt with the *magister* and he with the

[1] D. 42. 5. 16. [2] *Ante*, § 57. [3] Lenel, Ed. Perp. (2) 413.

buyer from whom he has taken security, the creditors' remedy is against the *magister*, who in turn can recover from the *bonorum emptor*.

The debtor becomes *infamis* at the time of the appointment of a *magister bonorum*, and ceases to have any rights in his existing property, or in debts due to him. But he still remains liable for his debts: he has suffered no *capitis deminutio*, and thus if he acquires any property his creditors can proceed against him in respect of any balance still due on their debts, subject to *beneficium competentiae* within one year[1], exactly as if there had been no *venditio*. It is only where he had made a voluntary *cessio* that he is in any way protected, and in that case it is only against personal seizure: he may still be sold up again. It may well be that there were creditors who had never heard of the *bonorum venditio*, or from any cause had refrained from claiming, these being apparently in the same position. We are without information on the point, but it does not seem probable that creditors who had not come forward and whose debts were therefore not scheduled could have had any claim against the *bonorum magister*, in whose appointment they had not shared, or the *emptor*. The purpose of the delays and advertisements is to give everyone an opportunity of coming in. A text which is sometimes understood to give them an *actio in factum* against the creditors who have received too high a dividend appears to refer to a different case[2].

165. We are told nothing of the treatment of debts due *ex die* or *sub condicione* either by or to the estate, but presumably these would become ripe for action if and when they would have done so had there been no bankruptcy, so that no special rule was necessary. Nor is anything said as to the amount of proof which was necessary to allow a debt to figure in the list of liabilities or a creditor to share in the appointment of the *magister*. No doubt, when the debt came to be sued on, its reality would be adjudicated upon, but it seems that unless there was a far more exhaustive preliminary

[1] C. 7. 75. 6. [2] D. 17. 1. 22. 10.

investigation than we know anything of, the bid of the buyer must have been made rather in the dark. Such a state of things cannot have made for good bidding, and cannot have been favourable to the creditors. As the result of legislation the practice arose of following the *missio in possessionem* by a sale of the property in detail (*distractio bonorum*), a plan which avoids the *bonorum venditio* and as it seems the *infamia*, and was introduced probably for this reason rather than on economic grounds, since it seems to have been allowable only in the case of persons of some distinction[1]. The person appointed to manage the sale is not a *magister bonorum*, but a *curator bonorum*. This is not edictal, and the *curator* must be distinguished from an edictal *curator bonorum* of whom we hear. This is an officer appointed by the Praetor with the concurrence of the majority of the creditors in cases in which there has been a seizure without judgment, in certain cases of absence or minority. He has wide powers of administration, even of selling and buying, so far as this is required for the protection of the estate. But he does not proceed to *bonorum venditio*[2].

To complete this matter a word should be said of the proceeding for setting aside transactions in fraud of creditors. Distinct remedies are fused in the Digest, so that the classical law is not easily made out. But there seem to have been two distinct remedies. There was an *Interdictum Fraudatorium*, for restitution, available to any of the creditors. There was also a right of *Restitutio in integrum*, available to the edictal *curator bonorum*, giving rise to the ordinary fictitious actions and other consequential remedies. There was also an *actio* Pauliana, but it is held by Lenel that this is only a special name given to the *actio arbitraria*, which would result on ordinary principles from the issue of the *Interdictum Fraudatorium*. It must be noted that these remedies presuppose an insolvency—there must, at any rate, have been a *missio in possessionem*. The transaction attacked may however have taken place at any time within a year before. It must be

[1] D. 27. 10. 5. [2] Lenel, Ed. Perp. (2) 418.

shewn that the transaction damaged the estate and was made with fraudulent intent. The proceedings lie in general only against one who was conscious of the fraud. But it is clear that the Interdict might be given, *causa cognita*, against one not a party to the fraud, and it seems to have been so given where the acquisition was gratuitous. There are also signs of an action even after the year, to the extent of actual enrichment. It is useless to go further into the detail of a proceeding the nature of which is so much controverted[1].

166. Under the system of *cognitio extraordinaria* the judgment need not be for a sum of money. The magistrate has power to order actual restitution of the property claimed, and even, as it seems, actual performance of a service due, but in this case money damages would usually be awarded[2]. Indeed it is mainly in real actions and actions on deposit and the like that an order for actual delivery is made: there is for instance very little sign of anything like a decree of specific performance in contracts of sale. Where the order is one for delivery or production of a specific thing the officers of the court are authorised to see to its actual render, using any force that is necessary[3]. Where the *condemnatio* is in money, there is no longer any *venditio bonorum*. This institution, with its accompanying *infamia* and loss of all property, disappeared with the formulary system. The new practice was for the officials of the court to seize and sell so much of the property as would suffice to meet the judgment, and costs[4].

The *distractio bonorum* which existed in the later law has no necessary connexion with execution of judgments: it is the procedure in bankruptcy, and is the subject of elaborate legislation. It is a generalisation of the earlier *distractio bonorum* already mentioned.

Appeal in the modern sense was unknown to the earlier classical law. There was no hierarchy of courts. It was

[1] See Lenel, Ed. Perp. (2) 425, 475; Girard, Manuel (5), 424.
[2] C. 7. 45. 14; D. 42. 1. 13. 1.
[3] D. 43. 4. 3. 1.
[4] D. 42. 1. 15.

possible in *manus iniectio* (by a *vindex*) and later, in the *actio iudicati*, to attack the formal validity of the judgment, but this would not raise again the question of the merits. The nearest approach to appeal was the *intercessio* of the magistrate who could veto any steps taken in pursuance of the judgment, though he could not thus set aside the judgment itself. And *restitutio in integrum* was available in many cases, but here too there was usually no question of reversing the decision on the merits. In the comparatively rare case in which the *restitutio* takes the form of *rescissio iudicii*, it is commonly on grounds which would not have affected the action of the *iudex*.

In later law there is a complete organisation of appeals, culminating in the court held by the Emperor—the *auditorium*, in which he was advised by his council, but decided on his own responsibility. There is however little or no reason to think that this system ever had any application to cases tried under the formulary system[1].

The details of procedure we have not discussed, or have discussed only shortly, partly for lack of space, partly because the many difficulties they present are in the main difficulties of detail, the discussion of which would not throw light on anything but the details themselves. But in the case of the Interdicts, the subject is found so perplexing by the student that it seems well to end with a more or less systematic account of their working, at least in the case of possessory interdicts.

167. The Interdict is an order of the magistrate issued on application, and giving rise to further proceedings if it is disregarded. In early times it may have been enforced by the magistrate's authority, but, as we know it, it is the initial step of an ordinary piece of litigation, having special formalities. It is in form praetorian, and is, in most cases, set forth in the Edict. But the right which it protects is not necessarily praetorian. There were many rules of the civil law for breach

[1] Moyle, Institutes, Excursus x.

of which no action was given, but the enforcement of them was left to the *imperium* of the magistrate. This is true of most of the interdicts which relate to public interests, *e.g.*, those for the protection of public ways and places[1]. But it is equally true of many private rights. The Twelve Tables contain a clause entitling a man to enter his neighbour's land to gather fruits which have fallen over the boundary. This was enforced by the interdict *de glande legenda*[2], and there are others of the same type. How the order was at first enforced we do not know, but it is probable that from very early times it was, as in the later law, by way of *sponsiones*. These interdicts, and indeed most of the known interdicts, seem to have existed before the Praetor began to issue general edicts. This is a fact which must be borne in mind, since it helps to the understanding of one at least of the peculiarities of the Interdict.

From the account we have in Gaius, it is natural to assume that the interdict was a provisional remedy, *i.e.*, that it, and its dependent procedure, did not make a final settlement of the questions at issue, but merely determined which of the two parties was to be the plaintiff and which the defendant in some litigation of the ordinary kind which was in contemplation. This no doubt is not very far from the truth in the case of possessory and quasi-possessory interdicts, and in relation to two of these, *Uti possidetis* and *Utrubi*, it is evidently their purpose as they are known to us in the classical law. But it is not in the least true of many other interdicts, of *de glande legenda*, which has just been mentioned, or of the mass of interdicts which have nothing to do with possession or quasi-possession. This has been well illustrated by a contrast. It has been pointed out[3] that if a man was in actual enjoyment of a "right of way" over land, and was interfered with by the owner, *X*, he could get the interdict *de itinere*, forbidding the interference, and practically compelling *X*, if he wished to stop the use of the way, to bring his *actio negatoria*, in which the question whether there really was

[1] D. 43. 7–14. [2] D. 43. 28. 1. [3] Accarias, Précis, 2. 1217.

a right of way would be finally settled[1]. Nothing could be more provisional than the operation of this interdict. If however a man was in enjoyment of a right of way, and wished to repair the path, but was prevented from doing so, he could get an interdict prohibiting the interference. But here he would have to prove that he was really entitled to repair the way[2]. There is nothing in the least provisional about this. The possessory interdicts, being fully described by Gaius, are better known to us than any others, and, as they are all provisional, it is easy to fall into the mistake of thinking that all the interdicts are so, *i.e.*, that their provisional nature is due to something inherent in interdicts. In fact however this is not an essential characteristic of interdicts at all: it has nothing to do with their character, but it is the essential characteristic of possessory rights. So soon as the Praetor had resolved that a peaceable *de facto* enjoyment should not be interfered with except by legal process, he had created what may be called provisional rights, and the protection would have been equally provisional whether it had been by interdict, as it was in the classical law, or, as it was in the later law, by possessory action without the previous issue of the interdict.

168. We are given several classifications of interdicts, resting on their form or their purpose. Thus we are told that they are either Exhibitory, ordering production of something, Restitutory, ordering something done to be undone, or Prohibitory, forbidding some act, ending respectively with the words "*Exhibeas,*" "*Restituas,*" or "*Veto.*" It will be noticed that in form they are very peremptory, and they are carefully framed so that the conditions on which the order will be enforced are expressed on the face of the interdict. But when we consider the actual enforcement, we observe that this peremptory form does not mean any direct coercive process by the Praetor. As we shall see in dealing with the procedure, in possessory interdicts (and it is equally true of the

[1] D. 43. 19. 1. [2] D. 43. 19. 3. 11.

others), the enforcement ultimately resolves itself into an *arbitrium* of a *iudex*, with alternative money damages.

They are also classified as possessory or non-possessory. It is with the former that we shall be mainly concerned, but the different types of non-possessory interdicts may be adverted to. Some are for the protection of private rights not dependent on possession, of which type that *de glande legenda*[1] is a sufficient illustration. Others are so far private that they deal with prevention of the enjoyment by a particular person of a public right. Such, for instance, is the interdict, *Ut via publica ire agere liceat*[2]. Others are simply for the protection of public rights, such as that for preventing interference with or damage to a public way[3]. Of this interdict we are expressly told that it aims at *utilitas publica* and that it is *populare, i.e.*, can be brought by anyone. It must be remembered that, as has been stated, the process of enforcement is the same here as in private interdicts.

Of possessory interdicts we are told that they are either single or double, the nature of which distinction will sufficiently appear in the discussion of the procedure. A further classification is into

i. *Adipiscendae possessionis causa*, to give possession to one who has not had it before. Of these a well-known instance is the interdict *Quorum Bonorum*[4] of the *bonorum possessor*, which has already been considered. Like all others it is provisional, but, as we have seen, it may often be final in practice.

ii. *Retinendae possessionis causa*, by which a person keeps or regains possession by reason of having previously held it. The chief of these are the well-known double interdicts *Uti possidetis* and *Utrubi*[5], the use of which was to determine which should have possession and the position of defendant in a contemplated real action. By the terms of the interdict *uti possidetis* which dealt with land, possession was to be adjudged to the actual possessor at the time the interdict was issued, unless he had obtained it *vi, clam aut precario*, from the other,

[1] D. 43. 28. 1. [2] D. 43. 8. 2. 45. [3] D. 43. 10.
[4] D. 43. 2. [5] D. 43. 17; D. 43. 31.

in which case it went to that other. In *utrubi* for moveables it went in classical law to the one who had held it for the longest time in the past year, with the same proviso if he had obtained it *vi clam aut precario* from the other, but under Justinian the rule of *uti possidetis* was applied in this case also. It will be seen that though in name *retinendae possessionis causa*, these interdicts might operate differently.

iii. *Recuperandae possessionis causa*, for restoring possession to one who has been deprived of it. The only one of these of importance is *unde vi* in its two forms[1], the conditions under which return is ordered varying as the force was armed (*vis armata*) or unarmed (*vis cotidiana*). Here too in Justinian's law no such distinction was drawn between the two cases.

There is mentioned a fourth class—double in a special sense[2] —either for giving in first instance, or restoring, possession, as the case might be. Their use was this. In real actions the party to whom possession was allotted was bound to give security for certain purposes. This is included under the general term *litem defendere*. If he failed to do so this interdict was issued to make him give up possession to the other: it is an order to give up possession *si litem non defendas*. There are several cases, all alike except as to the kind of real right claimed in the action, and called *Quem fundum, Quam hereditatem*[3] and so forth, as the case might be. These interdicts are obsolete in the later law, as the law as to the necessary security has changed.

With these various classifications we shall have little to do in dealing with the procedure under possessory interdicts: the only distinctions which it will be necessary for us to bear in mind are those (1) between Single and Double Interdicts, and (2) between Prohibitory and other Interdicts.

169. The procedure in single interdicts differs considerably from that in double interdicts, so that the cases must be taken singly, and as the single are the simpler they must be first handled.

[1] D. 43. 16. [2] D. 43. 1. 2. 3. [3] *Frag. Vat.* 92.

Confining ourselves for the present to the Prohibitory interdicts, we may assume that *A* alleges that he has been in enjoyment of a certain right, *de facto*, and that *B* has interfered with the enjoyment. *A* applies for an interdict, and one is issued to him, in a form prohibiting any interference, but always containing limiting words to shew that the prohibition has no application unless the *de facto* enjoyment is of the kind the Praetor meant to protect. Thus, in the interdict *de itinere privato* the form was, "I forbid any force to be done by which *A* is prevented from enjoying that right of way which he has been enjoying during the present year, his enjoyment not having been obtained from *N vi clam aut precario*[1]." Here it must be noted that this mention of a year has nothing whatever to do with prescription. The question is not whether he has acquired the right by lapse of time, but whether there has in fact been a peaceable enjoyment so recent and so full as to raise a presumption of rightfulness, such that the Praetor thinks it ought not to be interfered with except by legal process.

If, now, *A* is not interfered with, there will be no further process. But if his right is really disputed, if *N* really intends to deny his right of way, and also thinks that *A*'s enjoyment has not been such as satisfies all the requirements of the interdict, he will now proceed to use some force, in order to raise the question. The point is that, if *N* merely acquiesces in the interdict, the result will be that he will not be able to put a stop to *A*'s enjoyment except by bringing his *actio negatoria*, in which, if he is to win, he will have to disprove the existence of the right of way. If however *N* uses force, and *A* proceeds under the interdict, and *N* succeeds in proving that *A* has not been in enjoyment of the right of way in the past year, or not to the necessary extent, which is defined in the Digest as being on thirty days at least[2], *N* will win in the interdict, and can now disregard *A* altogether, obstructing his way, and leaving him either to abandon it altogether, or to bring an *actio confessoria*, under which he will have to prove that he has a

[1] D. 43. 19. 1. *pr*. [2] D. 43. 19. 1. 2.

legal right to the servitude. The same result will of course follow if he shews that though there had been the necessary enjoyment, it had in fact been *precario* from him, or that in some other way the requirements of the interdict had not been satisfied. If he fails to prove one of these defects in the enjoyment, *A* will win on the interdict, and *N* will be compelled either to abandon his objections or to bring his *actio negatoria* in which he will have to prove an ownership free of this servitude.

Let it be assumed that *N* uses force. It will be a mere formal force, but enough to amount to disregard of the interdict. Then both parties go before the Praetor, and the question is raised: has *N* disobeyed the interdict? This question is to be tried by a *iudex*, but the way in which it is raised is noteworthy. *N* says to *A* "Do you promise to pay me 10 if I have not disobeyed the interdict?" *A* then says "I promise, and do you promise to pay me 10 if you have disobeyed the interdict?" *N* answers "I promise." These two counterstipulations are practically a bet. Each then proceeds to sue for the 10, that is to say, two *formulae* for *condictio certae pecuniae* are issued, one to *A*, and one to *N*. At this stage, three points must be noted.

i. (*a*) *N* has certainly disregarded the interdict, but it does not in the least follow that he has disobeyed it. If *A*'s enjoyment was not of such a nature as to satisfy all the requirements of the interdict, the acts done by *N* are not a contravention of its terms, and *N* will win. He will be absolved in the *condictio* for 10 which was issued against him, while *A* will be condemned to pay 10 in the corresponding action brought by *N* against him.

(*b*) As these are ordinary *condictiones* they may have *exceptiones*. Thus *N* may have been induced to disregard the interdict by *A*'s telling him that he did not intend to maintain his claim. This would plainly give rise to an *exceptio doli*. Other defences of like kind may easily be conceived, but these matters have nothing to do specially with the interdict. The proceedings would merely be abortive.

(*c*) The whole duty being based on the Edict, there is no liability except that which it states. That is why the interdict is drawn up so carefully. Each interdict in the Edict carefully expresses all the conditions on which the right which it protects is to depend, and the *iudex* has no need to look outside its terms to see exactly what has to be proved. The importance of the exact interpretation of a given form of words is characteristic of the whole formulary system, but it is shewn more clearly here than anywhere else. Interdicts were matter of extremely careful drafting, to be reconsidered if necessary, every year. The interdict *unde vi* is a good illustration of this. We have it in two forms, one from the time of Cicero, and one from Justinian[1], and the two forms differ materially. We have also some traces of it as it was in classical law.

If *A* fails in the action on the promise, the matter is at an end. He has not been actually enjoying the servitude to the extent, or in the manner, that the interdict requires, and if he wishes to make good his claim he must bring his *actio confessoria.* If on the other hand he wins, a *formula* is issued for a *Iudicium Secutorium,* for abstention from interference and for damages in default. Whether there were damages for the force done between the issue of the interdict and the judgment on the *condictio* is not quite clear. The form of the action is not known and it is suggested that in such cases as this of a right of way the notion of restitution is inapplicable and that the *formula* is simply one for damages[2], while in those prohibitory interdicts which have to do with really possessory rights, such as those for protection of persons who have been *missi in possessionem,* it would be for restitution and only for damages in default. In any case there were certainly no damages for the time before the issue of the interdict, for till then there was no duty. This view that there was no *arbitrium* for restitution in cases where the interdict was concerned with interference with a right of way is supported by the fact that there seems to have been no *arbitrium* in an

[1] Pro Tullio, 19. 44; Pro Caecina, 19. 55; Gaius, 4. 154; *Frag. Vat.* 93; D. 43. 16.
[2] *Ante,* § 153.

ordinary *actio confessoria* in respect of them. How the damages were assessed in such a case of interdict, where no *restitutio* was ordered, it is difficult to say.

170. If the interdict was not prohibitory, but restitutory or exhibitory, there was an alternative somewhat simpler process. After the formal act of disregard of the interdict, while the parties are in court, the defendant is entitled to refuse the *Sponsiones* and to demand an *arbiter*. The effect will be that a *formula* is issued, requiring him to restore or produce, as the case may be, if the conditions of the interdict are proved to exist, or to pay damages, the *arbitrium* clause being of course inserted for actual performance. In this case too, very careful drafting would be equally necessary. The issues are the same as in the process by *sponsio*, though raised in a different way. If the defendant leaves the court without calling for an *arbiter*, then and there, the *sponsio* system applies. These interdicts to which the *arbitrium* system applied are sometimes called *decreta*, the name interdict being in strictness applied only to those which are prohibitory. It should be observed that the use of the *arbitrium* form did not make very much difference. It merely avoided the risk of loss over the *sponsiones*, for it is clear that even in prohibitory interdicts, if the facts were of such a nature as to admit of it, an *arbitrium* clause would be inserted. Exactly why this alternative method is allowed in restitutory and exhibitory interdicts only is not clear. It may perhaps be allied to the fact that they prescribe a positive act, and direct enforcement such as is contemplated by the *arbitrium* is more easy here. There are some prohibitory interdicts to which, as we have seen, it is at least probable that it could not be applied at all[1]. The answer to the other question that suggests itself, *i.e.*, the reason why the defendant prefers the *arbiter* is obvious; he thereby avoids the risk of the *sponsiones*, which we are told were not merely formal, but were actually penal. The plaintiff runs the same risk, but does not appear to have the same privilege.

[1] Lenel, Ed. Perp. (2) 435.

Two or three further observations must be made about single interdicts.

(*a*) The issue to be tried in the *iudicium secutorium* is already really decided in the actions on the *sponsiones*, and the issue in each of the actions on the *sponsiones* is the same. It is therefore very probable that all these *formulae* were issued together.

(*b*) It has been assumed in the foregoing account that the *sponsio* was on the general question: has the interdict been disobeyed? But as the interdict failed if any one of its conditions was not satisfied, the task of the *iudex* might be made considerably lighter. If, as would probably be often the case, only one of the points was really in dispute, the *sponsio* might be expressed so as to turn on that point. Thus, supposing the only doubt was whether the enjoyment in the past year had been sufficient, the *sponsio* might run "Do you promise to pay me 10 if I have enjoyed this right of way on thirty days during the past year?" with the answer "I promise." Any of the other requirements might of course be embodied in the same way.

(*c*) Nothing has yet been said as to the burden of proof, and as we have seen that there were two stipulations, one on each side, each is plaintiff and might seem to have the burden of proof. It is obvious however that it is the claimant of the interdict who is the real plaintiff, and it is he who offers the *sponsio*. It is he therefore who is the plaintiff in these actions and on whom lies the burden of proof. It is he who is affirming, and it is always the affirmative which has to be proved.

171. We have now to consider the procedure in the Double Interdicts—*interdicta duplicia*, of which there are essentially but two, *Utrubi* for moveables and *Uti possidetis* for land, with certain corresponding derivative forms for usufructs and *Superficies*[1], and in the later law for *Emphyteusis*[2]. These interdicts are of a very special character. As we know them in the classical law, their only purpose is to confirm one of two

[1] D. 43. 17. 4; 43. 18. 1. *pr.*

[2] D. 2. 8. 15. 1.

intending litigants in possession of the property which is in dispute, so as to make him the defendant, and the other the plaintiff, in the impending real action, so that the burden of proof will be on the latter. The interdict is, in terms, addressed to both litigants, and directs whichever of them does not satisfy the conditions upon which it protects the actual enjoyment, not to interfere with the other. Thus there are practically two interdicts, though they are contained in one form of words. Hence their name of Double interdicts, and a number of resulting complications in the procedure. The conditions on which *uti possidetis* is available are not, as we have seen, quite the same as those for *utrubi*, but as there is no resulting difference of procedure, we shall deal only with the first. The terms of the interdict, as it stood in the Edict, are not quite certain, as we have two forms not quite identical, which are probably the interdict as it stood at two different dates[1], but it may be stated sufficiently accurately for our purpose, in English as follows: "I forbid force to be done by either of you, whereby one of you is prevented from possessing the land as he now does, not *vi aut clam aut precario* from the other."

If the parties mean really to dispute the question, they proceed to use force against each other, a purely formal force (*vis ex conventu*), but enough to constitute disregard of the interdict. They then proceed to make *sponsiones* as in the case of single interdicts, with the important difference that, in this case, as either of them may have disobeyed the interdict, there would be two bets, and consequently four stipulations, with four resulting *condictiones certae pecuniae*. But at this point another, rather accidental, complication steps in. The whole interdictal procedure will decide who is to be plaintiff, and who defendant, in a forthcoming real action. This is obviously a very important issue. But the question arises, who is to keep the actual possession during the trial of the interdict, a process which may take some time, since the facts necessary to its decision may not be easily got at. That is not a very important

[1] Festus. Bruns, Fontes, 2. 24; D. 43. 17. 1. *pr.*

matter, since no question of procedural importance is prejudiced by it. Accordingly it was simply dealt with. That litigant got it who offered most for it. The opponents *X* and *Y* bid against each other for it. If *X* bid most, it was given to him, and he then made a promise that if judgment should ultimately go for *Y* in the interdict, he would give *Y* the amount of his bid. This would involve a fifth *condictio certae pecuniae.* Sometimes the stipulation was omitted, and when the possession was handed over to the highest bidder, a formula for a *Iudicium Fructuarium* was given to the lowest bidder, apparently for the amount of the value of the interim possession, *i.e.*, the loss to him from not having had the interim possession, whatever that might amount to, in the event of his winning in the interdict. Apparently the lowest bidder might choose. If he chose the *iudicium fructuarium*, the amount of the actual bid would cease to be of importance. It will be seen that this alternative arrangement is convenient and even necessary in the case, which might present itself, in which the interim possession was of uncertain value to one of the parties. He need not bid at all but will still retain the chance of recovering whatever the value of it might turn out to have been.

In addition to all these *formulae* there would be the *iudicium secutorium* (called in this case the *iudicium* Cascellianum) for the definitive transfer of the possession to the non-possessor if he should win in the interdict. It is to be noted that in this action he would recover not only the possession but also the interim fruits, so that, as Gaius tells us, the money recovered under the *iudicium fructuarium* or the *condictio fructuaria* was in effect a penalty.

Thus to each party were given two *condictiones certae pecuniae,* and to the one who did not get the interim possession, either a *condictio fructuaria* or a *iudicium fructuarium* at his choice, and a final *iudicium secutorium* (Cascellianum). In this case as in single interdicts, the trial of one of the *condictiones certae pecuniae* would determine all the questions material to the decision of all the actions, though certain questions of value in the *iudicium fructuarium* and the *iudicium* Cascellianum would still remain open. All these *formulae* appear to have been issued together.

Here, too, disregard is not necessarily disobedience. Both parties disregard the interdict, but it is clear that only one can have disobeyed it. Since one of the parties must have been in possession, for, if that were not so, all the proceedings would be absurd, it seems as if one must have disobeyed it. But the matter is not without difficulty. On the words of the interdict as they are transmitted to us, it might seem that neither has disobeyed it. If, for instance, *X* held the property *precario* from *Y*, the latter could not possibly disobey it, for the possession by *X* is not within the terms of the interdict. On the other hand it is possible to contend that *X* cannot have disobeyed it, for *Y* was not possessing at all. The matter is disputed among the commentators, but the view most widely held is that in this case, *X* has disobeyed the interdict. As against *X*, *Y* is still regarded as in possession. This view is supported, but hardly proved, by the language of certain texts[1].

The *sponsiones* were penal, *i.e.*, they were actually enforced and were not set off against the damages. Here arises an important question. What determined the amount of the *sponsio*? Could a plaintiff, sure of his case, fix them as high as he liked? The answer to this question seems to be that the Edict contained a clause, now only imperfectly known to us, which limited the *sponsiones* to an amount having some relation to the value of the right concerned, but exactly how we do not know[2].

These double interdicts are prohibitory, and it follows that the alternative method of a *formula arbitraria*, without *sponsiones*, is not available for them. It is clear however both that they are in their nature extremely well suited for an *arbitrium* and also that, as a matter of fact, the *formula* of the *iudicium* Cascellianum did contain such a clause. This case therefore

[1] D. 41. 2. 17. *pr.*; Machelard, Interdits, 192 *sqq.*

[2] Lenel, Ed. Perp. (2) 454.

brings into strong relief the problem of the reason for the refusal of the *arbitraria formula* in prohibitory interdicts.

In the procedure of ordinary actions, there was machinery, by means of judgment in default, *missio in possessionem* and the like, to deal with the case of a defendant who disobeyed the *in ius vocatio*, or who refused to take the various steps involved in the defence of an action. As to what took the place of this in interdictal procedure, our information, owing to the defective state of the manuscript of Gaius, is unfortunately incomplete. In double interdicts we are told by Gaius that when a person against whom an interdict had been obtained refused to make the resulting *sponsiones* or to take any of the other necessary procedural steps, there were *interdicta secundaria* by which he could be compelled to do so. We do not know whether they applied also to single interdicts, nor do we know how they worked. There must presumably have been some direct intervention of the Praetor, and it may be that in these cases there was a right to *missio in possessionem*, on the analogy of ordinary praetorian stipulations.

172. We have seen that the issue of the interdict was followed, after other steps, by the issue of *formulae* in which the question was whether the duty declared in the interdict had been broken. The question may be asked, why, in view of this, the issue of the interdict itself was retained at all. Instead of saying, for instance, "I order you to remove the obstruction which you have put in the way which *A* was peaceably enjoying," to be followed when the order was issued in a particular case, by a number of steps all leading up to a *formula* of which the gist was, "If it appears that *N* has obstructed a way of which *A* was in peaceable enjoyment, condemn him to pay or put it right," it seems that the Edict might well have said simply: "If anyone obstructs a way of which another person is in peaceable enjoyment, I will give a *iudicium*." (Of course the nature of the necessary enjoyment might be specified as exactly as it is in the interdict.) By apt words the same issue as that in the interdict might be raised in a more direct and simple way, without any departure from the provisional character of the proceeding. Why then was the issue of an actual interdict retained? The answer seems to be purely historical. Interdicts existed before the Edict did, before the Praetor had begun to exercise the power of directly creating actions, and they afforded an indirect means of doing so. The interdict is an order binding by virtue of the Praetor's *imperium*. Before the Edict existed the interdict could not exist as a standing order. It had therefore to be issued expressly in each case. After it had come to be set forth in the perpetual Edict this ceased to be really necessary: its preservation is a simple piece of conservatism. It is probable that most of the known interdicts were incorporated as existing things into the Edict, on its development, and although there are interdicts which are plainly later than the origin of the Edict[1], it is in no way surprising that the existing method was followed. Once embodied in the Edict as an integral part of it, and of the formulary system, their endurance was guaranteed so long as the formulary system lasted. With its disappearance, they too were superseded. This does not of course mean that the rights which they had protected were henceforth unprotected. They were still protected, but instead of applying for an interdict the aggrieved person brought an action in which the issue raised was the same as that in the *formula* which in earlier days would have been issued after the disregard of the interdict. This is well exemplified in the Digest in the case of *unde vi*. In the old system the interdict was issued in the form: *Unde tu illum vi dejecisti* (*etc.*)...*vim fieri veto*. In the Digest the rule is similar except that the rule is put in general impersonal form, and for the last three words are substituted the words *iudicium dabo*[2]. The same development took place in all interdicts, though in many of them the words of the old interdictal form, are still used in the Digest[3], and in relation to possessory interdicts, which are much the most important in private law, a system of possessory actions was developed, in

[1] *e.g.*, D. 43. 18. [2] Cicero, pro Tullio, 19. 44; D. 43. 16. 1. *pr.*
[3] *e.g.*, D. 43. 2; D. 43. 6, *etc.*

which the issue was exactly the same as in the old interdict, but the order itself was no longer issued[1].

We have seen that interdicts are not necessarily or essentially provisional: possessory interdicts are, but this is only because the protection of possession as such must be so. If it were not, it would not be mere possession, it would be ownership. The true owner must always be able to recover his goods from one who has no title but possession. Many considerations justify, and have produced in various legal systems, protection to a mere possessor: we need not now consider which of these were operative on the founders of the Roman rules. But there is one point which has led to controversy and is worth mention. We know that in the long run, the mere possessor will have to give up the property to the real owner. The *bonorum possessor sine re* might recover the land from the *heres* in the interdict *quorum bonorum*, but he must ultimately give it up if he is sued by the *hereditatis petitio*. A bare possessor may win against the owner in *uti possidetis*, but the owner can then regain his property by means of a *vindicatio*. Why was he driven to this lengthy process? Why might not his ownership be pleaded in reply, for instance, to *uti possidetis*? An *exceptio iusti dominii* would have served the purpose, and under such a plea he would have had to prove his title just as he would in the *vindicatio*. No doubt the explanation is historical. It may be due to a well-known characteristic of Roman procedure. Possession and *dominium* are distinct things, and the Romans did not like mixing up two distinct issues in one *formula*. It was this, for instance, which made them so reluctant to admit set-off (*compensatio*) and led them, in classical times, to drive the parties to *mutuae petitiones*, even where the claims arose out of the same matter[2]. But the application of this solution to the present problem is no more than conjecture.

[1] *e.g.*, D. 43. 16.

[2] D. 17. 1. 38. *pr*.

ERRATA

p. 31, l. 13, after *utilis* insert *e lege.*

p. 131, ll. 4, 17, read *caelebs*, *caelibes.*

p. 169, l. 4 from end, read *caelebs.*

p. 273, l. 26, after 'be' insert 'in many cases.'

p. 312, note 2, read Schulz.

The 5th edition of M. Girard's Manuel de Droit Romain having appeared while this book was in the press, the earlier references to it are necessarily to the 4th edition.

INDEX